The Dylan Companion

THE MAKING OF JAZZ: A Comprehensive History
JAMES LINCOLN COLLIER

U2: The Early Days
BILL GRAHAM, PATRICK BROCKLEBANK, JAMES MAHON, HUGO MCGUINNESS

BOOK OF THE DEAD: Celebrating 25 Years with the Grateful Dead
HERB GREENE

DESOLATE ANGEL: A Biography: Jack Kerouac, the Beat Generation, and America
DENNIS MCNALLY

EDIE: An American Biography
JEAN STEIN

HELLFIRE: The Jerry Lee Lewis Story
NICK TOSCHES

The Dylan Companion

Edited by

ELIZABETH THOMSON and DAVID GUTMAN

Delta

A Delta Book
Published by
Dell Publishing
a division of
Bantam Doubleday Dell Publishing Group, Inc.
666 Fifth Avenue
New York, New York 10103

Library of Congress Cataloging in Publication Data

The Dylan companion / edited by Elizabeth Thomson and David Gutman.
     p.   cm.
    Includes bibliographical references (p.   ), discography (p.   ),
and index.
    ISBN 0-385-30225-8 (pbk.)
    1. Dylan, Bob, 1941–   —Criticism and interpretation.
I. Thomson, Elizabeth, 1957–   . II. Gutman, David, 1957–
ML420.D98D97   1990
782.42162'0092—dc20   90-38926
                                               CIP
                                             MN

Reprinted by arrangement with Macmillan London Limited

Printed in the United States of America

First U.S.A. printing

May 1991

10 9 8 7 6 5 4 3 2 1

RRH

For Ros and Rob

Contents

Acknowledgements

Every effort has been made to trace copyright holders of the material included in this collection. The Editors extend their apologies to those whom it has not been possible to contact or to anyone who may have been inadvertently slighted. Redress will be made in any future editions.

Song quotations are taken from *Lyrics 1962–1985* (London, Jonathan Cape, 1987) and may differ from those sung by Bob Dylan or reproduced in the album folios. All lyrics are quoted for the purpose of study, review or critical analysis.

Picture research was undertaken by the Editors.

We are grateful for the help and enthusiasm of all those who contributed to *The Dylan Companion*; particular thanks are due to Claude Angèle Boni, Tom Constanten, Fran Landesman, Greil Marcus, Philip Saville, Gerald Scarfe, Robert Shelton, Ed Vulliamy and Simon Winchester.

In addition, we would like to thank a number of others who were prepared to share their ideas: Professor Louis Cantor, Maureen Cleave, Professor R. Serge Denisoff, Professor David Dunaway and Jon Wiener.

We are indebted to the following institutions for their assistance in tracking down an extraordinary range of materials: Cambridge University Library, the British Library of Political and Economic Science and the British Film Institute.

Thanks also to Paul Burnell, Dave Carr, David Harman and Ian Woodward, family, friends and colleagues. And to Roland Philipps and all at Macmillan, past and present.

Copyright Permissions

Allsop, Kenneth, 'Beat and ballad', *Nova* (November 1965). Reprinted by permission of South Bank Publishing Group.

Baez, Joan, 'Renaldo and who?', from *And a Voice to Sing With*, London, Century Hutchinson, 1988. Reprinted by permission.

Bangs, Lester, 'Bob Dylan's dalliance with Mafia chic', *Creem* (April 1976). Reprinted by permission of the Estate of Lester Bangs.

Campbell, Robert D., 'Dylan's new morning', *Christian Century* (25 August 1971), © 1971, Christian Century Foundation. Reprinted by permission.

Capel, Maurice, 'The blessing of the damned'. Reprinted from *Jazz Monthly* (December 1965/January 1966).

Christgau, Robert, 'Tarantula', *New York Times Book Review* (27 June 1971), © 1971 New York Times Company. Reprinted by permission of the author.

Constanten, Tom, 'Dr. Z Agonistes: an appreciation', © 1989 Tom Constanten.

Dyer, Geoff, 'Figured I'd lost you anyway', © 1989 by Geoff Dyer.

Fariña, Richard, 'Baez and Dylan: a generation singing out', *Mademoiselle*, 59, 4 (August 1964). Courtesy *Mademoiselle*, © 1964 by The Condé Nast Publications Inc. Reprinted by permission.

Ginsberg, Allen, 'Three poems', from *First Blues: Rags, Ballads and Harmonium Songs, 1971–74*, New York, Full Court Press, 1975. Reprinted by permission of Aitken and Stone Ltd.

Mieses, Stanley, 'The Dead and Dylan', *New Yorker* (27 July 1987), ©
1987 The New Yorker Magazine, Inc. Reprinted by permission.

Miller, Jim, 'Bob Dylan', *Witness*, 2, 2–3 (Summer/Fall 1988).
Reprinted by permission of the author.

Nicholl, Charles, 'Just like the night', © 1989 by The Macmillan
Press Ltd.

O'Grady, Timothy, 'The Prince', © 1989 by Timothy O'Grady.

Pankake, Jon and Nelson, Paul, 'Bob Dylan'. Reprinted from *Little
Sandy Review*, 22 (c.1962).

Peel, John, 'More music: Dylan at Wembley', *Observer* (18 October
1987), © 1987 The Observer Ltd. Reprinted by permission.

Ricks, Christopher, 'Clichés and American English', from *The Force
of Poetry*, Oxford, Clarendon, 1984, © 1984 Christopher Ricks.
Reprinted by permission of Oxford University Press.

Rolling Stone, 'Dylan at Old Nassau', *Rolling Stone* (9 July 1970), ©
1970 by Straight Arrow Publishers, Inc. Reprinted by permission.

Roos, Michael and O'Meara, Don, 'Is your love in vain – dialectical
dilemmas in Bob Dylan's recent love songs', *Popular Music*, 7, 1
(1987). Reprinted by permission of Cambridge University Press.

Rosenbaum, Ron, 'Born-again Bob: four theories'. Reprinted from
New York Magazine (24 September 1979), © 1979 News Group
Publications, Inc.

Rotolo, Susan, 'Bob Dylan', interview from *Rock Wives* by Victoria
Balfour, New York, William Morrow and Company, Inc., 1986.
Reprinted by permission.

Sarris, Andrew, 'Don't look back', *Village Voice* (21 September
1967). Reprinted by permission of the author and *Village Voice*.

Saville, Philip, 'Dylan in the Madhouse', © 1989 by Elizabeth
Thomson and David Gutman.

Shelton, Robert, 'Trust yourself', © 1989 by The Macmillan Press
Ltd.

Sinyard, Neil, 'Bob Dylan and Billy the Kid', © 1989 by The
Macmillan Press Ltd.

Sloman, Larry, 'Bob Dylan and friends on the bus: like a Rolling
Thunder', *Rolling Stone* (4 December 1975), © 1975 by Straight
Arrow Publishers, Inc. Reprinted by permission.

Introduction

Rock has no definitive history. Nor can it. Its chronicling is a wholly idiosyncratic exercise, undertaken within the shifting parameters of taste and commerce, where each new fad requires a rewrite, a conscious re-evaluation of what has gone before. A few players resist downgrading. But straight biography, even when undertaken with the best of intentions, hardly ever explains their survival. Typically, a more or less compelling account of the formative years degenerates into a who-said-what-to-whom assemblage of press clippings, until 'finally', in retreat from a once carefully cultivated public, the star withdraws: Presley to Graceland, Lennon to the Dakota, Dylan to Woodstock and Malibu. Dylan's life story – like so many others – is reduced to a litany of recording schedules and concert dates. Wilfrid Mellers posed the crucial question way back in 1972: 'The Beatles have disbanded, Gershwin died young, Irving Berlin, Crosby and Sinatra remained permanently adolescent, Cole Porter survived by becoming exclusively deflatory. Can Dylan preserve his folk-like integrity from youth through the middle years and even into a venerable old age?'[1] Some twenty years later, the jury is still out, and Dylan plays on, fighting against the monotony in a genre whose constraints preclude any real escape.

The summer of '89 found him on the road *again*. The hardcore fans, keyed in as always to an international network of like-minded obsessives, were in up-beat mood, swapping news of which songs He'd sung at which gig, whether He'd spoken to the audience, the clothes He'd worn. The British leg of the tour sold out on the strength of a few newspaper advertisements. But as the star and his entourage shot across Europe, press reaction was less ardent:

xvi

there was that inescapable sense of *déjà vu*. In October, the faith
of the zealots was at last rewarded by the release of *Oh Mercy*. A
collection of original material, many thought it Dylan's best since
Blood on the Tracks (1974). Curiously, not one of the new songs
showed up on the UK tour. Here was a man, whose production of
classics had slowed to the merest trickle, continuing to command
the fierce loyalty of an audience he treated with apparent disdain.
For the true fan, that too is part of the mystique. But when the
newly created Commandeur de l'Ordre des Arts et Lettres returned
for a series of intimate live dates in February 1990, the band was
remade – and even Dylan smiled.

No doubt our fascination is in part a nostalgia for a generation's shared past. As John Rockwell has pointed out, 'Anyone
who didn't live through the Sixties simply cannot realise how
important his albums seemed then; they defined a community.'[2]
Sociologist Simon Frith went further: 'The experience of pop
music is an experience of placing: in responding to a song, we
are drawn, haphazardly, into affective emotional alliances with
the performers and with the performers' other fans ... Other
cultural forms – painting, literature, design – can articulate and
show off shared values and pride, but only music can make you
feel them.'[3] Those great Sixties' albums somehow helped define
our perception of self, our sense of 'youthfulness'. Failure to
understand the message *then* put you in a bag with those 'mothers
and fathers' of whom Dylan sang so contemptuously. *Today*, the
continued sharing in such emotional experiences – most striking
at the communal concert event but possible even in the isolation
of one's own headphones – ensures that we can indeed remain
'forever young'.

And yet, for a new generation of Dylan followers, this is
scarcely the whole (or even the relevant bit) of the story. The
Wembley crowd was the usual unlikely mix. There were City types
in pinstripes and bifocals, reluctant wives in tow; Ray-Ban-wearing
former hippies and their ladies in Laura Ashley derivatives. But
there were also yuppies in pressed 501s and teenagers in tattered
denim. Many had been to several concerts. Why? We need something more than the associations of lost youth and its values to
account for the obstinate durability of Dylan's appeal. *The Dylan
Companion* aims to sift through the welter of Dylan commentary
and suggest some answers.

The production line was set in motion by Robert Shelton's
celebrated *New York Times* review of the callow newcomer he

tagged 'a cross between a choir boy and a beatnik . . . bursting at the seams with talent'.[4] After Dylan's appearance at Newport in 1963, newspapers and magazines gushed to judgement. The sheer bulk of material was awesome, beyond logic. Within two years, the highbrows were drawing parallels with Yevtushenko.[5] For John Clellon Holmes writing in 1965, Dylan passed as a poet: '*Of course* – though I think we do him a disservice, as a serious artist, if we separate his words from the music he intended to be their proper setting . . . not since Allen Ginsberg has an American Poet insisted on telling so much truth, so uniquely and with such reckless honesty. More than anyone else, I suppose, Dylan reminds me of an American Brecht – the Brecht whose poems were meant to be sung. There is the same cold humour, the same ironic warmth, the same violent and splintered imagery, the same urgent, idiomatic involvement in the way things actually are. Another Dylan returned song to poetry; Bob Dylan has returned poetry to song. He has the authentic mark of the bard on him and I think it's safe to say that no one, years hence, will be able to understand just what it was like to live in this time without attending to what this astonishingly gifted young man has already achieved.'[6] The poet John Ciardi disagreed: 'My nephew (a drummer and an engaging kid who is only as mad as he has to be) would agree that Bob Dylan is a poet but like all Bob Dylan fans I have met, he knows nothing about poetry. Neither does Bob Dylan.'[7]

In Britain, too, the heavyweight pundits had their say. Take the Marxist historian Eric Hobsbawm, writing as Francis Newton in May 1964: 'it's clear – especially from Dylan's fairly numerous bad verses – that he comes from that *Reader's Digest* mass civilisation which has atrophied not merely men's souls but also their language, confining the ordinary person to a mixture of stammering and cliché. Song, however, has given him the courage of speech; folk song a vocabulary, a sense of form, and at the same time – because of its lucky association with the Left – a moral frame.'[8] Even Philip Larkin was not unaffected: 'I poached Bob Dylan's *Highway 61 Revisited* out of curiosity and found myself well rewarded. Dylan's cawing, derisive voice is probably well suited to his material – I say probably, because much of it was unintelligible to me – and his guitar adapts itself to rock ("Highway 61") and ballad ("Queen Jane") admirably. There is a marathon "Desolation Row" which has an enchanting tune and mysterious, possibly half-baked words.'[9]

Dylan biography *per se* began in 1966 with Sy and Barbara

Ribakove's *Folk-Rock: The Bob Dylan Story*, gathered momentum with *Positively Main Street* (1971), Toby Thompson's genuflection at the feet of the master, and achieved maximum hype with Anthony Scaduto's *Intimate Biography* (1972), a supposedly myth-shattering treatment that created a few of its own. At least Scaduto did his own legwork, which is more than could be said for Chris Rowley, author of the formidably pedestrian *Blood on the Tracks* (1984). Or Barry Miles, whose *Bob Dylan: In His Own Words* (1978) granted us access to an unremarkable clippings file. Located further upmarket, Jonathan Cott's *Dylan* (1984) was similarly anodyne. The Rolling Thunder Revue of the mid-Seventies prompted some respectable journalism and two books which captured something of the tour's spirit and creative energy. Both *On the Road with Bob Dylan* (1978), Larry Sloman's dogged pursuit of a troupe of engaging egomaniacs, and Sam Shepard's more impressionistic memoir, *The Rolling Thunder Logbook* (1978), succeeded in part by sidestepping the drawbacks of conventional biography confronted head-on by Robert Shelton. His *No Direction Home* (1986), a long-awaited study some found merely over-length, came in for much criticism. The author, a contributor to this collection, was the first to admit its flaws. 'Definitive' was publishers' hype, not self-aggrandisement, and the adjective was bound to raise hackles. Certainly, Shelton was not, as some have implied, bought off by Dylan. Rather, he had no wish to dish the dirt on an old friend. His biography is surely as good as any in the field of rock, despite the familiar thinness towards the end. If it is true that a portrait is never finished and can only be abandoned, it is especially true of the living, still-productive subject. In 1989, Bob Spitz brought the Dylan story up to date by resorting to caricature. Attempting to make a virtue of his distance from Dylan's circle, his work was presented as impartial. Yet distance too can distort. Spitz did not have access to such significant fellow travellers as Joan Baez, Judy Collins and Pete Seeger. His *Dylan* is Goldmanesque anti-mythology. It will enjoy a limited shelf life if, as is widely feared (though officially denied), the good Doctor is at work on the real thing.

There is a sense in which Dylan has only himself to blame, setting the trend by recasting his rather ordinary adolescence in terms of the outlaw myth. Not all the friends who heard those early anecdotes about gigging with the greats took him seriously. But once enshrined in print – from Gil Turner in 1962 [10] through to Ralph Gleason in 1966 [11] – such tall tales acquired an authority

that beguiled many a later researcher. Not everyone appreciated
Dylan's penchant for the put-on. Maureen Cleave, a journalist on
friendly terms with John Lennon, found his American colleague
quite insufferable. She interviewed him twice. 'The second time
was when they were making *Don't Look Back*. It was in the Savoy
Hotel and they were all stoned and behaving in the most irritating
manner! I asked Dylan if he minded what people thought of him
to which he replied: "It all depends on what you mean by people."
Totally exasperated, I said: "Surely we all know what people are."
That was rather the tenor of our conversation.'[12]

In addition to the unwitting dupes, there were the willing
collaborators. With the aid of Nat Hentoff, author of a celebrated
Dylan profile in the *New Yorker* of October 1964, Dylan's 1966
Playboy interview was transformed into a surrealistic burlesque of
the star interview genre.

Hentoff: . . . what made you decide to go the rock-'n'-roll route?
Dylan: Carelessness. I lost my one true love. I started drinking.
The first thing I know, I'm in a card game. Then I'm in a crap
game. I wake up in a pool hall. Then this big Mexican lady drags
me off the table, takes me to Philadelphia. She leaves me alone
in her house and it burns down. I wind up in Phoenix. I get a
job as a Chinaman. I start working in a dime store and move in
with a thirteen-year-old girl. Then this big Mexican lady from
Philadelphia comes in and burns the house down. I go to Dallas.
I get a job as a 'before' in a Charles Atlas 'before and after' ad.
I move in with a delivery boy who can cook fantastic chilli and
hot dogs. Then this thirteen-year-old girl from Phoenix comes
and burns the house down. The delivery boy, he ain't so mild:
He gives her the knife, and the next thing I know I'm in Omaha.
It's so cold there, by this time, I'm robbing my own bicycles and
frying my own fish. I stumble on to some luck and get a job as a
carburettor out at the hot-rod races every Thursday night. I move
in with a high-school teacher who also does a little plumbing on
the side, who ain't much to look at, but who's built a special kind
of refrigerator that can turn newspaper into lettuce. Everything's
going good until that delivery boy shows up and tries to knife me.
Needless to say, he burned the house down, and I hit the road. The
first guy that picked me up asked me if I wanted to be a star. What
could I say?
Hentoff: And that's how you became a rock-'n'-roll singer?
Dylan: No, that's how I got tuberculosis.[13]

Rock journalism was fast becoming an integral part of the Counterculture, with Dylan's every utterance relentlessly transcribed as Holy Writ. By the time Craig McGregor came to assemble his *Retrospective* (1972), there was plenty to choose from. What appeared between American hardcovers (the UK edition was considerably abridged) not only enhanced our somewhat parochial view of Dylan the artist but also told us something about the changed times in which we lived and functioned. Times when an A. J. Weberman could scratch a dubious living from Underground journalism and the contents of Dylan's binliners:

> I decided to go thru D's garbage with the class, & so they formed a circle around me. David Peel (Dylan Liberation Front) pointed out that his garbage bags were green, like his money. My 'Garbage article' had already come out so there was nothing of interest to be found, but we did the thing anyway . . . 'Holy shit', I thought . . . I looked up and saw Bob standing directly across the street from me . . . 'Al, why'd ye bring all these people around my house for?' 'It's a field trip for my Dylan class, man . . . but actually it's a demonstration against you and all you've come to represent in rock music . . . ' 'You know, Al, you've been in the city too long, the city does something to your thinking – I know how it is.'[14]

No personal archive is ever complete, and to be as successful as McGregor's such anthologies must deploy a wide range of techniques, resources and contacts. *The Dust of Rumour* (1985), a bran tub of British press stories from the files of Dave Percival, threw up some intriguing analysis and reportage, but these remained chance encounters in a package intended strictly for the fans. Dennis Anderson focused on German critical reaction to the Dylan phenomenon in *The Hollow Horn* (1981). More commonly, the collectors have turned to their own shelves to chronicle Dylan's alternative recording career. Paul Cable, Dominique Roques and Michael Krogsgaard have all produced notable discographies. Clinton Heylin's *Stolen Moments* (1988) was even more ambitious, the first attempt to diarise Dylan's life along the lines of Tom Schultheiss's Beatles chronology, *A Day in the Life* (1980). Unfortunately the result was vitiated by organisational shortcomings and perversely lackadaisical proof-reading. Michael Gray was a pioneer of the more cerebral approach, treating Dylan's song as part of the poetic continuum. His *Song and Dance*

Man (1973) was a brave and much discussed textual examination, infinitely more readable than, say, Stephen Pickering's *Bob Dylan Approximately* (1975). Though released into the mainstream, that book smacked of the Dylan Underground, whose members have continued to sustain several fanzines worldwide, most notably *The Telegraph*. Here, trivia and tour dates are leavened with learned articles. Some of the best material from this source was collected by Michael Gray and John Bauldie in their 1987 'fanthology' *All Across the Telegraph*. A related venture, the short-lived *Bob Dylan Study Series*, preached to an even narrower church through such densely argued treatises as Nick De Somogyi's 'Jokerman and thieves' and Bert Cartwright's 'The Bible in the lyrics of Bob Dylan'.

Of course, the abstract meaning of many Dylan songs, their spirituality, their very power to enchant and transport, also makes them resistant to conclusive analysis. Could it be that 'the way to read the tale is to let the imagination carry one along[?] Not, above all, as a rebus to be decoded. By insisting on decoding *him*, the Kafkologists killed Kafka.'[15] Robert Shelton felt Dylan was ill-advised to turn the spotlight on himself: 'He decided – or he was persuaded – that the only way to avoid spending over a million dollars on promotion [for *Renaldo and Clara*] was to give a series of interviews. None of them was very revealing, but suddenly you had this sphinx who was willing to talk, so long as he could sell the visiting rights. So he started to talk and to break up his mystique ... Suddenly he was hustling.'[16]

Given that the response of the listener to Dylan's music has always been so intensely *subjective*, it makes sense to stand back and adopt a rigorously *objective* approach to the examination of his legacy. With no axe to grind and no lurid hypothesis to sustain, *The Dylan Companion* presents the best of thirty years of comment and commentary engendered by the man and his music. There's no reason not to view Dylan's career in its entirety, nor is there any excuse for recycling endlessly received opinion. In making our selection, our first instinct was to include such celebrated (and much seen) items as Shelton's *New York Times* review or Weberman's infamous field report. However, such was the abundance of first-rate material that we were finally able to give full weight to the early years without overlapping with McGregor's *Retrospective*. A mere handful of the articles have appeared in more general anthologies, but the Dylan fan will find that, for once, he has not been short-changed. That the writing be stimulating on its own account, retaining its vitality and impact, was our second, and sometimes overriding, principle. We have frequently opted for contributors on the periphery of the pop world, coming at the subject from a multiplicity of angles, presenting Dylan as literary, political, religious and cinematic icon, as lover and friend, as manipulator and manipulated. There is inevitably an Anglo-American bias, though Haver and Manakov stand in for Dylan's many admirers in Germany and the Soviet Union. Ten pieces are entirely new and fresh, and in some cases highly personal. A recurring theme here is Dylan's 'place' in our shared past.

We have already seen how rapidly Dylan's work caught the ear of literary commentators. The Yevtushenko parallel in Jerome Agel's *Books* prompted other journals to turn a critical eye to Dylan as *writer*. In the *New York Times*, Thomas Meehan pondered Dylan's role as heir to the Faulkner and Hemingway tradition. By the turn of the decade, Dylan lit. crit. was a growth industry – and one that received an added fillip when Princeton 'legitimised' his work with an honorary doctorate. Writing in *Alphabet*, Frank Davey paired him with Leonard Cohen; David Monaghan examined Dylan and 'The Waste Land tradition' (*English Quarterly*); and Greg Campbell waded in with 'Bob Dylan and the pastoral apocalypse' (*Journal of Popular Culture*). In 1972, the ever-stimulating *Esquire* called upon two literary heavyweights to shine their light on 'The metaphor at the end of the funnel': the arguments of Frank Kermode and Stephen Spender still demand our attention.

In England, meanwhile, a lesser-known writer-critic was disturbed by the fact that analytical procedures – for Dylan in particular and rock in general – were 'damagingly tilted towards the descriptive',[17] failing to discriminate between the disciplined and the undisciplined in Dylan's writing. At best, wrote Clive James – for it was he – such criticism was 'simply the articulation of the silent mass receptivity, which never got further than liking some Dylan songs more than others. The basic critical problem – whether the good songs were really as good as they could be – remained untouched ... the idea that there might be conflicts inside the talent itself simply never gained ground.'[18] Not, at least, until Dylan's post-accident withdrawal. Even at this stage in Dylan's career, James saw him as somehow 'uncaring' of his talent – an attitude that most certainly came to the fore in the post-Christian albums of the mid-Eighties.

His expansiveness was always the undisciplined enemy of his intensity; his inclusiveness was always at war with his grasp of detail; and when he finally discovered that he could suggest the totality of experience without going to the trouble of concentrating on any part of it, the temptation to rest on his oars became irresistible . . . The freedom of his linguistic invention, even at its most marvellous, has always had something to do with a fatal detachment from the discipline of concrete perception: Dylan makes a virtue of not knowing exactly what he means. He can't distinguish, in his own work, between the idea that is resonant and the idea that postures towards significance, the image that is highly charged and the image that is merely portentous. The long receptivity which uncritically appreciated everything Dylan did was admiring the cancer as part of the body, which didn't matter so long as they both expanded together, but which mattered a great deal when the body started to shrink as a result of the cancer's growth.[19]

Looking in some detail at 'Like a rolling stone' and 'Gates of Eden', James argued that – viewed objectively – each song was over-long, the use of words and images becoming more 'slipshod' with each passing verse: 'your critical faculties can't be silenced for more than a single stanza . . . Unless, of course, those same critical faculties have been anaesthetised by the means of descriptive justification, which refers every awkwardness back to the traditions from which Dylan drew influence.'[20] He concluded with the central paradox of Dylan's *oeuvre*, pointing out how much of our enjoyment lay in 'following his clear architectural outline and emotionally solidifying it with an imaginative content it hasn't really got . . . never has so much arbitrary stressing met so much melodic angularity in so many awkward marriages . . . Yet when all is sung and done, it can't be denied that the total effect is on a huge scale: he dreams great buildings, even if the walls remain untimbered and the roofs are open to the sky.'[21]

James, by that time, was bursting the bonds of academia. Betsy Bowden remained, in every sense, reined in. *Performed Literature* (1982) began life as a doctoral dissertation, scrutinising the precise relationship between poetry as written and poetry performed. Bowden argued, in the course of 250 arid pages, that the most vital aspect of Dylan's art is the reinterpretation that occurs with each new performance. In comparison John Herdman, in *Voice Without Restraint* (1982), and Aidan Day, in

Jokerman (1988), are models of clarity, though still not for the uninitiated. Not all the academics took a literary approach. In his thesis of 1983, Charles Wayne Hampton examined the role of 'Working-class heroes: counter-cultural politics and the singing hero in twentieth-century America', with special reference to Joe Hill, Woody Guthrie, Dylan and John Lennon. Yases Kuwahara looked at one aspect of the classic American Dream – 'The Promised Land: images of America in rock music' (1987). Charles Benjamin Hersch studied the phenomenon for which the Sixties are best remembered and revered – the synergy of art and politics – in 'Liberating forms: politics and the arts from the New York intellectuals to the Counterculture'.

While the political dimension of Dylan's career should be self-evident, not enough attention has been devoted to 'synthesising' Dylan's work with the turbulent history of the Sixties. There is no full-length study to compare with Jon Wiener's account of Lennon's political struggles in *Come Together* (1984). Daniel J. Gonczy's 'The folk music of the 1960s: its rise and fall' (from *Popular Music and Society*) was a worthy survey owing much to the pioneering efforts of R. Serge Denisoff. Professor Denisoff not only contributed such seminal studies as *Great Day Coming: Folk Music and the American Left* (1971) and *Solid Gold* (1975) but was also a participant in the heady days of coffee house politicking *circa* 1965. From the very outset of Dylan's career, apolitical folk purists vied with the sectarian Left to claim him for the Cause. For Dylan's early friends and patrons, converted to folk music during the Thirties via Woody Guthrie, trade unionism, Depression and war, folk music was an inextricable part of a clearly defined world view. The value of a Dylan song lay in its ability to propagate a particular social, political or philosophical line. His 'progressive' period excited the interest of the Soviet writer Grigory J. Sneerson, whose detailed description of American folk song traditions appeared in Moscow in 1976.

As it was, each musical advance was seen to have a fresh ideological dimension. Irwin Silber's Open Letter (*Sing Out!*, November 1964) sparked off a long-running debate. For Paul Wolfe, writing in *Broadside*, the Newport Folk Festival of 1964 marked 'the emergence of Phil Ochs as the most important voice in the movement, simultaneous with the renunciation of topical music by its major prophet, Bob Dylan'.[22] Dylan's lack of ideological fortitude, his defection into the higher forms of art, was a gross betrayal by the people's champion. For other commentators, the verbal and musical idiom of folk could not do justice to the facts of the Sixties. No artist should ever be expected to sacrifice his personal vision for the sake of the Movement. Of course, from the standpoint of veteran British balladeer Ewan MacColl, the controversy was neither here nor there. MacColl was famously 'unable to see in him anything other than a youth of mediocre talent'.[23] In 1976, a bitterly resentful postlude from one-time Sixties' guru Timothy Leary once again laid into the inauthenticity of Dylan's protest. 'Once stardom is achieved, the snarling rebel retires as a millionaire and adopts a scornful posture toward those unfortunate enough to have opened their nervous systems to the imprint of his cosmic snivel.'[24] Lester Bangs, too, found a lack of genuine compassion in Dylan's stance. And yet, to the far Right, Bob Dylan had been 'the crimson troll' in league with producer John Hammond, 'an extreme Leftist', to subvert the youth of America.[25] For John Birch Society strategists like Gary Allen, Dylan and the Beatles were to be taken seriously as agents of Communist subversion. There was just the smallest grain of truth in the allegations. For many outside and inside the folk music scene, Dylan more than the Beatles deserved the spokesman-of-a-generation tag. It was widely suggested that Columbia Records and Albert Grossman were intent on suppressing Dylan's radicalism. And Columbia Records had, in fact, cut the controversial songs from his first album. They also recalled the original version of *Freewheelin'* and removed 'Talkin' John Birch paranoid blues' after CBS Television refused Dylan permission to sing the song on *The Ed Sullivan Show*. Subsequently, many of his followers saw Dylan as a pawn in a corporate game and few consumers interpreted the release of the *Great White Wonder* bootleg as anything less than a cultural breakthrough.

Of all Dylan's changes, none caused a greater furore than his Born-Again phase. From the start, religion – more specifically, religious imagery – had been a vital part of Dylan's creative mix. His 'prayers' – 'I shall be released', 'Forever young', 'Knockin' on heaven's door' – had about them a happy universality from which no one could feel excluded. As early as 1965, Stephen C. Rose was considering 'Bob Dylan as theologian' in *Renewal*, while in 1971, Robert D. Campbell was allocated space in *Christian Century* to ponder 'Dylan's New Morning'. That yesterday's Angry Young Man should turn into today's fundamentalist was somehow shocking. Yet it could be argued that Dylan was reflecting the mores of the times as accurately as ever he had. Jann Wenner, for one, saw no inconsistency: 'Faith is the message. Faith is the point. Faith is the key to understanding this record. Faith is finally all we have,' he wrote of *Slow Train Coming*. 'These are parables, more numerous and closely woven than ever before, assembled with the judgmental and righteous morality that has transfixed us on every great album and song Dylan has made.'[26] A few commentators lined up behind Wenner – among them Noel Paul Stookey (of Peter, Paul and Mary). Most, however, like Greil Marcus, were affronted by the seeming complacency of Dylan's new role as Brother Bob. Many saw him as rock's Elmer Gantry. If *Saved* prompted less of an outcry, it was not just because we were more used to Dylan's new stance; he seemed to have found a personal fulfilment in belief, refracting some joy through the noisy exuberance of the Black gospel idiom. By 1984, Dylan had retreated to a more ambiguous Judaeo-Christian stance. Nevertheless, as the Los Angeles Olympics approached, some of his Christian friends were still hoping he might participate in 'an Olympics evangelistic outreach'.[27] Alas, Pastor Paul Esmond must have felt let down when Dylan failed to materialise at the stadium.

The many changes in Dylan's personal and private life made him an attractive subject for a psycho-social approach. At Berkeley, Stephen J. Hobbs analysed 'Male mentor relationships: a study of psychosocial development in early adulthood' (1982), taking Guthrie and Dylan as one of four pairs for scrutiny. Hobbs concluded, not too surprisingly, that 'the mentor's role is more paternal than fraternal'. Especially perceptive was Michael Roos and Don O'Meara's lengthy but compelling analysis of the 'dialectical dilemmas' of Dylan's more recent lovesongs (in *Popular Music and Society*).

Musicologists have also had their say, though they have shown less interest in Dylan than in the Beatles, whose *music*, melodically and harmonically more adventurous, proved better suited to analysis. Wilfrid Mellers, a dogged and intensely personal practitioner of pop musicology, tracked Dylan's career through a series of general articles and album reviews, climaxing in a disappointingly irrelevant book-length study, *A Darker Shade of Pale* (1984). Grappling with the perennial problem of rock music criticism – rock musicians commit their work to tape, not paper, and leave no equivalent of classical music's full score – the Mellers equation of song-as-performance equals song-as-composition cannot allow for new and different versions of a song. Nevertheless, in a genre too often preoccupied with sign and surface, his search for permanent critical values with which to assess this music should command respect.

Writers on Dylan's celluloid legacy have less of a problem. Whereas *A Hard Day's Night* played a key role in establishing the image of the Beatles worldwide, Dylan's films merely trade on the public's established perception of him. Rather than seeking to cover performance-related films like the excellent but rarely seen *Festival* or *The Last Waltz*, we have concentrated on three pertinent cinema pieces: *Don't Look Back, Pat Garrett and Billy the Kid* and *Renaldo and Clara*. The interminable arrogance and superficiality of the latter were brilliantly dissected by Pauline Kael and *Renaldo* also prompted some inspired vitriol from James Wolcott:

> So many reputations are sunk ... it's like watching the defeat of the Spanish Armada. Among the shipwrecked victims: Sara Dylan ... the Dark Lady of the Counterculture: exotic, aloof, a sensuous blur. In the shadows is where she should have stayed. Like Marilyn Monroe in *All About Eve*, Sara is a graduate of the Copacabana School of Dramatic Arts: every word, every gesture, is tinny and coarse. When she runs her hands lovingly through Dylan's celestial curls, you want to look away – it's like watching a hooker stroke her john ... The spitefulness of *Renaldo and Clara* – the revenge of an artist on his groupies – might be tolerable if the film had a hateful energy. But it doesn't. It's droopy and disconnected, like a fuckless porno.[28]

For film director Philip Saville, Dylan does have screen potential. In an interview given specially for this book, Saville reveals how he came to bring a young, unknown Dylan over for his BBC production of *Madhouse on Castle Street*. For reasons as much personal as professional, Saville has fond memories of Dylan. Other acquaintances are more ambivalent in their recollections. Suze Rotolo, for example – intelligent, articulate, committed. She finally wanted out. Joan Baez played a more ambiguous mother–lover role and, unlike Rotolo, she had a public reputation of her own to protect and project. Ultimately, the stage was not big enough for Dylan and Baez. Although a happy professional accommodation was reached during the Rolling Thunder tour, their attempt at a further reunion in 1984 failed miserably. Baez herself has provided a spirited and unsentimental final chapter on a relationship in which two titanic egos jostled for time and attention. All rather different from the sentimental, reverential commentary written some twenty years earlier by her late brother-in-law. Richard Fariña compared an evening with Dylan and Baez to one spent in the company of Dylan Thomas and Edna St Vincent Millay.

Allen Ginsberg is one character with whom Dylan seems never to have fallen out, perhaps because the ageing Beat poet has been unstinting in his support and praise of the younger minstrel–guru with whom he seems not to be in competition.

Of great interest (but sadly unavailable for inclusion) was Sam Shepard's enigmatic but strangely touching piece written in the form of a one-act play for *Esquire* in July 1987. Ten years on from Rolling Thunder, 'True Dylan' appears to draw on conversations both real and imagined. As in their collaboration on 'Brownsville girl', 'Sam' and 'Bob' reminisce about *their* shared past. As does Robert Shelton, here, who recalls those joyous, inebriated days in the Village when he and Bob and Suze and Gil Turner and other folkies would 'swill our wine and talk till 4 a.m. We turned nights into days and swapped dreams, only Bobby dreamed bigger than any of us.' For the first time, he tells us what it was like to write that famous life, of the self-imposed moral constraints within which he worked. Ultimately, writes Shelton, Dylan has told his own story in so many songs. Through them, we each can find our own Bob Dylan, but in so doing we should not live vicariously through him.

For Shelton as for so many of us, 'Bob is a maddeningly private person. He is undoubtedly flattered to have been accepted as a serious poet. But there's no way he's going to drop that primitive stance. He'll deny that he pays any attention to what's written about him, but he'll read the stuff like a hawk. He knows exactly who's written what. He is a very contradictory and ambivalent person. You turn your back and there he is checking out the cuttings.'[29] There are so many of those cuttings that we only have space to include a representative sample, even of those articles cited above. Readers wishing to explore further should refer to the bibliography at the end of the book. Meanwhile, we hope *The Dylan Companion* goes some way towards rescuing Bob Dylan from the weight of tabloid journalism which has tended to swamp perceptive discussion.

Elizabeth Thomson and David Gutman
London, February 1990

Notes

1. Wilfrid Mellers, 'Bob Dylan: freedom and responsibility' in *Bob Dylan: A Retrospective*, ed. Craig McGregor (London, Picador, 1975), p. 281.

2. John Rockwell, 'Bob Dylan sums up a life in music', *New York Times* (24 November 1985), II, p. 28.

3. Simon Frith, 'Towards an aesthetic of popular music' in *Music and Society*, ed. Richard Leppert and Susan McClary (Cambridge, Cambridge University Press, 1987), pp. 139–40.

4. Robert Shelton, 'Bob Dylan: a distinctive folk-song stylist', *New York Times* (29 September 1961), p. 31.

5. See Jerome Agel, 'Music, that's where it's at', *Books* (December 1965), pp. 1, 12.

6. Ibid., p. 12.

7. Ibid., pp. 1, 12.

8. Eric Hobsbawm (as Francis Newton), 'Bob Dylan', *New Statesman* (22 May 1964), p. 819.

9. Philip Larkin *in Jazz Review* (10 November 1965); reprinted in *All What Jazz* (London, Faber, 1985), p. 151.

10. See pp. 62–3.

11. Ralph Gleason, 'The children's crusade', *Ramparts*, 4, 11 (March 1966), pp. 27–34.

12. Maureen Cleave, letter to the editors, 13 November 1988.

13. Nat Hentoff, 'The Playboy interview: Bob Dylan', *Playboy* (March 1966), pp. 41–4, 138–42.

14. A.J. Weberman, 'Dylan meets Weberman', *East Village Other* (19 January 1971); reprinted in *Bob Dylan: a retrospective*, op. cit., pp. 258–70.

15. Milan Kundera, *The Novel* (London, Faber, 1988).

16. Robert Shelton, in 'Bringing it all back home', *The Times* (14 June 1984), p. 10.

17. Clive James, 'Bringing some of it all back home', *Creem*; reprinted in *New Musical Express* (20 April 1974), pp. 10–12.

18. Ibid.

19. Ibid.

20. Ibid.

21. Ibid.

22. Paul Wolfe, 'The new Dylan', *Broadside* 53 (December 1964), p. [10].

23. Ewan MacColl in 'A symposium', *Sing Out!* (September 1965), p. 13.

24. Timothy Leary, 'How our paranoias are hyped for fame and profit', *National Review* 28 (16 April 1976), p. 389.

25. Gary Allen, 'That music – there's more to it than meets the ear', *American Opinion* (February 1969), p. 53.

26. Jann Wenner, 'The slow train is coming', *Rolling Stone* (20 September 1979), pp. 94–5.

27. See 'Has born-again Bob returned to Judaism?', *Christianity Today* (13 January 1984), p. 46.

28. James Wolcott in 'He speaks good English and he invites you up into his room', *Village Voice* (30 January 1978), pp. 25–6.

29. In Alan Franks, 'With Bob on His side', *The Times Higher Education Supplement* (3 July 1981), p. 8.

ONE
North Country Blues

TOM CONSTANTEN
Dr Z. Agonistes: an appreciation

Music and magic differ by only two letters.

In both cases the viewpoints of practitioner and appreciator necessarily diverge, although 'art' aims at a mythical asymptote of congruity.

In both cases the distortion is built in. Pervasive. A part of the Game. It's like that funny sound you hear on the playback that's supposed to be your own voice. Or the veracity quotient (usually low) of a newspaper article on something or someone you know about.

So what's to be said about this bard who is not a bard, this folk singer who is not a folk singer, this rock star who is not a rock star, that's neither stupidly sycophantic nor simply smoke rings? He appears to have struck a vein, like Mozart. An enviable curse. Seemingly without effort he distilled thoughts unexpressed but compelling . . . revealed the unlikely as inevitable. It wasn't so much any political or philosophical stance he took – he was preaching to the choir as far as that was concerned – but those quick takes: a gnome disappearing around the corner as you turn to look, leaving a 'gift' you can't ignore.

And those gems are where, and what, you find them. The idiocy of categories and unquestioned stereotypes was part of his message. It wasn't he who changed so much (other than natural evolution) as the scribes and Pharisees stumbling over their oxymoronic tails, trying to criticise what they can't understand.

Powerful stuff. And no less amazing is the simple fact that he got it out there. Past the troglodytes at the cultural spigots.

3

And ringing clear through all that built-in distortion. The D
train. Housing Project Hill. Flesh-coloured Christs that glow in
the dark. The lingering impression is not at how strange these
images are . . .
But how familiar.
I'd go on . . . but I hear a pay-phone ringing.

DANIEL J. GONCZY

The folk music of the 1960s: its rise and fall

Popular Music and Society, 10, 1 (1985)

In October 1958, three college students from universities in
California recorded for Capitol Records a song entitled 'Tom
Dooley'. The group called itself the Kingston Trio. The song
told, in simple lyrics and solemn melody, of the impending
execution of an unfortunate man who had killed his sweetheart.[1] The song was enormously successful. It rapidly became
the number one best-selling record in the country and remained
among the top 100 recordings for twenty-one weeks.[2] The song
launched the young performers on a career of enviable and long-
lasting success. More importantly, the success of 'Tom Dooley'
began what would soon be called a 'folk revival'.[3] In retrospect,
it is difficult to see the thread that binds the Kingston Trio
to the full-blown protest music of Bob Dylan, Phil Ochs and Pete
Seeger in the mid-1960s. The Trio was 'clean-cut' in both appearance and artistry. They sang a polished number which relied on
traditional sources innocuously delivered and intentionally made
palatable to a contemporary urban audience. By contrast, Dylan
and his contemporaries were unconventional in appearance and

performed songs that were predominantly original and personal and whose subject matter was an assault on tradition in terms of content and delivery. Joan Baez's lyric soprano voice had a distinction and individuality that no Kingston Trio harmonies could equal.

Part of the thread that connects the Kingston Trio and their many imitators to the outlaw music of later folk singers is that 'Tom Dooley' and songs like it developed in audiences, especially young ones, an ear for the topical song. Topical songs, many centuries old and found in all cultures, tell a story or express a personal emotion in direct lyrics. They are individual rather than stylised, unique rather than formulaic.[4] With the growing popularity of topical music,[5] such individual expression became increasingly experimental, ever more daring and overtly reflective of the social and political issues of the day, most notably Civil Rights and the threat of nuclear war. Morris Dickstein, in his book on the culture of the Sixties, says: 'More than at any time in recent decades, both art and politics became instruments of personal fulfilment, avenues to authentic selfhood.'[6] The same may be said of the music of the folk revival as the decade opened.

The popularity (and proliferation) of the Kingston Trio, the Limeliters, the Chad Mitchell Trio, the Brothers Four and Peter, Paul and Mary raised the ire of 'purists' in the folk music field. These groups (and others like them) were castigated for having commercialised what was thought to be properly the product of the 'people'.[7] The argument over the issue of what folk music *is* eventually distilled itself into whether or not one had to have *lived* an experience before one could sing about it. Many took the position of Woody Guthrie, who put the matter this way: 'You can't write a good song about a whore-house unless you been in one.'[8] Others, including old guard folk music activists like Pete Seeger, welcomed the sudden emergence of a 'folkish' consciousness.[9] The battle was one that neither side could win, because, in a very important sense, those who opposed the new democratisation of a previously esoteric musical genre would give in under no circumstances. Folk music, whether an expression of dissent or not, was by definition incorruptible. Therefore, any music tainted by commercialism was insincere, especially that which continued to use the label 'folk'. This position would by 1963 become little more than academic. 'Folk music', historian Jerome Rodnitzky observes, 'was clearly non-exclusive; it was available to all comers'.[10] The supporters of the new spirit among young singers agreed, 'One did not have to die in a nuclear holocaust . . . to be opposed to war.'[11]

While this battle over suitability and definition raged, the country, in complicated and frequently contradictory fashion, lurched forward. Majorities and minorities went facelessly about their business or made headlines with distinction. The Eisenhower era was coming to an end, and the Kennedy whirlwind and rhetoric were infectiously capturing the attention of the nation and the world. On 17 January 1961, the retiring President coined the phrase that would be repeated frequently during the coming decade when, in his farewell address, he spoke to the nation of the dangers inherent in the 'military-industrial complex'. This dire warning was, in Charles Alexander's estimation, 'one of the most prophetic statements ever made by an American public figure'.[12] The television and radio audience that evening was not especially moved by the General's insight. Inspiration rather than homily, particularly a dark one, was what the country craved. And the new President fed the maw with commanding presence. On 20 January, three days after Eisenhower's farewell, John Kennedy delivered his inaugural address in which challenge replaced warning: 'Ask not what your country can do for you – ask what you can do for your country.' In style and content, the nation had changed. Or had it? Whatever problems confronted the ordinary citizen in 1961, one seemed as harassing under the new President as it had under the old. With the resumption of atmospheric testing of nuclear weapons by the Soviet Union, Americans again began to worry about fallout, strontium 90 poisoning and the merits of fallout shelters.[13]

The Ban the Bomb movement, begun in England, was the first of two major glimmerings of what would eventually become a hallmark of the 1960s. In the United States in 1959, organised protest – for whatever purpose – was all but non-existent. But undercurrents were evident, however disconnected. From the anarchistic rebelliousness of urban juvenile delinquents to the anti-intellectual and fundamentally romantic alienation of the Beat Generation, there was a core of disaffection in the land. To many people, this disaffection sometimes seemed annoying and even frightening, as in the case of the street gangs, or merely bizarre, as in the behaviour of the Beats. The majority of young people entering college at the close of the 1950s could be characterised not unfairly by one word – respectable. It was what Norman Podhoretz would label the 'nongeneration'.[14] Even when the British anti-nuclear influences began to be felt in this country, they met not a nascent spirit of radicalism, but a modest and polite interest in what everyone agreed was a major and global concern.

Beneath the surface, the issue was being expressed in song. Pete Seeger, after returning from Great Britain where he had talked with topical songwriters, observed that America had its composers as well, but they were just not being heard.[15] For the most part, the closest college students (and the country at large) were coming to arousal was the 'humorous' cynicism of the Kingston Trio in songs such as 'The merry minuet':

> They're rioting in Africa.
> They're starving in Spain.
> The whole world is festering with unhappy souls.
> But we can be tranquil and thankful and proud.
> For man's been endowed with a mushroom-shaped cloud.
> And we know for certain that some lovely day
> Someone will set the spark off
> And we will all be blown away.
> What nature doesn't do to us
> Will be done by our fellow man.[16]

The second portent of the rise of activism was the Civil Rights movement. More than the anti-Bomb sentiment, which slowly took hold among the nation's young people, the cause of Civil Rights already had a groundwork of organisation. Three groups were fairly well-established by 1960. The National Association for the Advancement of Coloured People (NAACP), the oldest of the three, fought discrimination and segregation in America principally through legal tactics. The Congress of Racial Equality (CORE), formed in 1942, applied techniques of non-violence to call attention to racial inequality. And Martin Luther King's newly organised Southern Christian Leadership Conference (SCLC) espoused more militant action, while continuing to emphasise non-violence. In fact, the movement was dividing along generational lines and the result would be the slow but determined formation of a fourth Civil Rights organisation, the Student Non-Violent Coordinating Committee (SNCC), openly militant, its character predicated on the willingness to confront.

In February 1960, a significant and dramatic event took place in Greensboro, North Carolina. Four Black freshmen at North Carolina Agricultural and Technical College sat in the 'White-only' section of the Woolworth Department Store lunch counter in Greensboro. They were refused service but held their place. More students joined the 'sit-in' in the next several days. Within weeks, the protest spread to other cities throughout the South and involved hundreds of young Blacks supported by many White middle-class students in the North. The true power behind the sit-ins was economic boycott. And the effect was significant. By the end of March, many national chains in the southern states were experiencing a drop in sales of between 9 and 18 per cent. The first victory for the Blacks came in May when lunch counters in Nashville were opened. By October, sit-in demonstrators were being arrested by the score in many cities. The 'Deep South was digging in. . . . The great sit-in blitz of 1960 was over and the Blacks paused to consolidate their gains. . . . However, a Negro nation of 18,871,831 was stirring. American Blacks were becoming visible at last.'[17]

Two movements, then, each with great potential for social arousal, were loose in the land. Each would evolve in unpredictable and dramatic ways. The nuclear disarmament sentiment of the early 1960s would, under the impetus of America's military involvement in South-east Asia, become the anti-war mood of mid-decade and wreak significant havoc with the value systems and traditional responsibilities of many Americans. The Civil Rights movement – honourable, dedicated, confident as it was in the first years of the 1960s – would, nevertheless, have the effect of a Pandora's Box unleashed in the hellish ghettos of an otherwise prosperous nation. In neither instance can we simply say that it was a matter of idealism gone sour or realism gone awry. And to some extent the music that recorded feelings, lent inspiration and urged the scaling of new towers reflects the contradictions beyond a country's control. Some may see in the cataclysm of the Sixties a loss of nerve, others capriciousness or schizophrenia. The pseudo-political stance taken by many citizens divided the issues rather simplistically: either all folk singers were Communists, or the supporters of the Asian war were neo-Nazis. Whatever the label, whatever the shouted epithet or painted slogan, the division was real. Its intensity grew as it touched almost every aspect of the nation's life. Draft cards were burned at student rallies and fire hoses were used against the Black citizens of Montgomery. Congress gave the President almost unlimited powers to conduct the war and passed historic Civil Rights legislation. Young men and women turned in alarming numbers to drugs and respected public figures acquiesced when Chicago was made a police state. The paradox and disillusionment of the age were also broadly evident in the role that folk music played.

Folk music, in its early relationship to the nuclear disarmament cause, was esoteric and somewhat marginal. A magazine called *Broadside* was intimately a part of the scene. It was published in New York and edited by Sis Cunningham, an old guard folk singer and one-time member of the famous Almanac Singers in the 1940s, a group which included Woody Guthrie and Pete Seeger. *Broadside*, among its accomplishments and contributions, was responsible for publishing many of Dylan's early songs, like 'Masters of war' and 'Blowin' in the wind', which have become classics.[19] But most songs published in the early issues of *Broadside* were simple, amateur, and imitative. In issue number seven, for example, a song by little-known Bonnie Dobson was printed, entitled 'Take me for a walk'. Its message was direct and repetitive: there *was* no place to walk. Dobson herself states she wrote it after having seen the nuclear holocaust film, *On the Beach*.[20] . . . It illustrates Seeger's belief that there *were* topical songwriters in the United States, but suggests few of them had the ability to contribute anything distinctive or inspiring. It is to those few that the folk music movement owes much, because it asked much of them.

Pete Seeger had been a name and a force in folk music and in radical causes since the late 1930s. His influence ran deep even if his audience was a restricted one. Yet despite his stature, his experience, his incomparable abilities, his music did not ignite the enthusiasm of young people in the early 1960s. Despite the fact that commercial promoters of the new wave of music remained fearful of the power of Seeger's convictions, he reached relatively few young, aspiring activists. Seeger was 'blacklisted' from a folk music television programme called *Hootenanny* in 1963 and his case became a *cause célèbre*. The ABC Network invited Joan Baez, Tom Paxton, Jack Elliott and others to appear on the show, but they refused after being informed that Seeger would not be allowed on because of his questionable political leanings. The spectre of McCarthyism rose and the shocking and significant impact – for those who cared – was that it reappeared at the crest of the golden, progressive Kennedy administration.[21] Others moved the young malcontents of America. Some didn't have the long-building sense of solidarity characteristic of Seeger, but they did have surprising talents in building an audience and consolidating a following.

Of all the cities in which pockets of fervent young singers were congregating, Boston served as a mecca for aspiring guitarists, banjo pickers and topical lyricists. Boston, extravagantly conservative and historically revolutionary, was a fitting environment for the new breed. Quite early, one individual was rising well above the coffee house crowd – Joan Baez. She had a quality and a self-assurance that marked her for distinction. But if Harvard Square was a gathering place for unknown musicians and idealists, New York's Greenwich Village was the seedy Valhalla for both the revered warriors of folk music's stormy history and its eager vanguard. For one thing, Woody Guthrie lay diseased but god-like in a hospital nearby. Many made pilgrimages to sit at his bedside, to pay homage to the hobo whose life and songs had become the epitome of Americana. One devotee who went to bask in the aura of Woody's presence was 19-year-old Bob Dylan. Dylan's worship seemed so genuine and Guthrie's response to him so positive that Woody's mantle was literally passed on to the young songwriter from Minnesota.[22] When Dylan made his New York debut at Gerde's Folk City, 'Sid Gleason [a long-time admirer and friend of Guthrie] gave him one of Woody's suits to wear for the occasion. It was a symbolic investiture whose meaning was lost on no one.'[23] The folk music 'movement', as we now call it, centres principally on these two individuals, Joan Baez and Bob Dylan. Others contributed as much and, in many cases, prolifically, but none achieved the stature or the mystique of these two. The Kingston Trio made money but touched the generation of the 1960s with nothing more than distraction. Baez and Dylan touched this generation by *leading* it and, in an important respect, by shaping it.

The connection between folk music and what would become the anti-war ferment was demonstrated nowhere better than in Dylan's *Freewheelin'* album of 1963. It included scathing and unequivocal denunciations of the psychology and mechanics of militarism. The songs asked questions that would reverberate long after Dylan himself ceased to be interested in them. 'Blowin' in the wind' asked 'How many times must the cannonballs fly/ Before they're forever banned?' 'Masters of war' dwelt on the accusation, 'Just like Judas of old you lie and deceive/A world war can be won you want me to believe.' The surrealistic song 'A hard rain's a-gonna fall' lamented, 'I saw guns and sharp swords in the hands of young children.' And the 'dream' vividly described in 'Talkin' World War III blues' included the chilling observation,

'Well, the whole thing started at three o'clock fast/It was all over by quarter past.'[24] These were clearly not songs inspired by a movie. With Dylan's emergence, the spirit of activism and protest began to take on some coherence and a sense of unity develop.

The Students for a Democratic Society (SDS), founded in Chicago in 1960, held a convention at Port Huron, Michigan, in June 1962 which resulted, in part, in the publication of the famous 'Port Huron Statement'. This manifesto dealt at length with an analysis of the many social ills rampant in the country: bigotry, the Cold War, poverty, political manipulation. Discussing America's increasing dependence on armaments, it included the statement that 'the American military response has been more effective in deterring the growth of democracy than Communism.' The amorphous sentiments of young activists were beginning to co-alesce. And Dylan was further confirming his involvement. His next album, *The Times they are a-Changin'*, not only reached more people but cut directly through the ideological jargon of the Port Huron Statement to lend immediacy and inspiration to the now full-blown spirit of dissent. A strange message was found in the title song – strange because the album was released after John F. Kennedy had been killed. Dylan's prophecy that the times were changing was ironic . . . and deadly: 'For he that gets hurt/Will be he who has stalled/There's a battle outside/And it's ragin''/It'll soon shake your windows/And rattle your walls.' Few if any knew what 'stalled' meant, but many clearly understood how a battle might rattle walls. The music and the mood were meeting in comfortable, if ill-understood alliance.

Dylan often wrote cryptically, but he was also capable of the most unswerving insight. In the same album was the bitterly satiric 'With God on our side'. No manifesto could put the problem so succinctly, so simply, so emotionally:

> I've learned to hate Russians
> All through my whole life
> If another war starts
> It's them we must fight . . .
> With God on our side.

The dissenters had their poet. Dylan's music had, by 1964, become inseparable from the growing radicalism. And although most Americans still supported government policy in South-east Asia, a significant number took Dylan's words to heart. One month after President Johnson's State of the Union address in

January 1965, in which he announced sweeping programmes for building a 'Great Society', he ordered air strikes in North Vietnam. The contradiction was not lost on a large segment of the nation's young people.

By 1963, the year of Pete Seeger's troubles with ABC, Joan Baez had become, with Dylan, a principal voice in organised resistance among the New Left. Her concerts and recordings helped publicise and popularise the songs of Dylan and of radical songwriters like Phil Ochs, Malvina Reynolds, Richard Fariña and Seeger. While she became inseparably identified with the anti-war movement, one cannot generalise about her selection of material. Often, Baez seemed much more a *presence* in the protest fervour of the Sixties than a polemicist for it. At the age of twenty, following the release of her first album and extremely successful tours of college campuses, she was 'America's premier folk singer'. As with Dylan, it was the emotional force of her music more than the ideology that often made an impact. In an extensive interview for *Playboy* magazine in 1970, Baez (not for the first time) elaborated on both her principles and her tactics. Deep commitment to non-violence and opposition to the oppressiveness of many American institutions dominated the discussion.[29] She was articulate, confident, and copious. Yet, in many of her activities,

> she was never a direct political threat. People were generally unwilling to hear her speak unless she also sang. During her February 1971 tour, for example, she drew 7,000 people to a paid concert, but only 400 showed up for a free political talk.[30]

Sustaining Baez's place in the movement, two forces, discipline and emotion, seemed always to be at work.[31] Frequently her control and self-containment reinforced her ability to move and to persuade listeners. On the 1963 album *Joan Baez in Concert, Part 2*, in a performance of 'Battle hymn of the Republic', she asked the audience to join her in singing it. What is evident in the recording is not simply the inspiration of the words (even if one is aware of the incongruity between them and Baez's pacifism). There is the anomalous juxtaposition of her staid delivery. She is not dispirited while singing the song, merely unobtrusive. And the quality seems to lend an authenticity that reinforces feeling. If anything can be said to define the emotional commitment associated with the folk movement and the protest sentiment of the age it is this infectious combination: the sense of honest feelings being shared in solidarity. Unity, however persuasive its outward appearance, was frequently tested within the New Left and often found less harmonious than the voices proclaiming it. This irony became increasingly evident as the movements of folk music and dissent continued their course.

From the activities of the Free Speech Movement at Berkeley to the hair-splitting debates among the Student Peace Union, the War Resisters' League and the Students for a Democratic Society, an array of possibilities was evident with many variations on a theme.[32] At times, the groups seemed capable of a united front, something close to the sense of common cause celebrated in many of Woody Guthrie's songs during the 1930s.[33] The Spring Mobilisation Against the War in April 1967 drew large numbers of demonstrators to New York, San Francisco and other cities and the cataclysm of the Democratic Convention in Chicago, in August 1968, briefly united many otherwise politically discrete men and women. But a spirit of anarchy was reflected in most organisations. In many respects, the spectrum of disunity to be found in the anti-war campaigns[34] became as pronounced within the Civil Rights movement. However, the music associated with Black activism was more cohesive in the sense that it drew on a century-old tradition of religious fervour and a very specifically focused courage in the face of a clearly evident oppressor. Whereas the relationship between music and the anti-war and draft resistance movements was almost artificial in the sense of its immediacy and its very personal character, the music of the sit-ins, the freedom rides, the voter registration drives and the efforts to overcome the disease of discrimination was that of a community which knew its purpose and marched to one drummer.

Some means of communication were ineffective in uniting a suppressed people. Political ideology, for instance, was lost on large numbers of Blacks, whether rural or ghetto. Poetic imagery, in speech or in song, was of marginal consequence to those whose life was a constant reflection of the photographs of 1930s' documentarists. The music of the Civil Rights movement was, first and foremost, collective; it was congregational. It was the natural outgrowth of a religious bond, a spiritual sharing. It came out of the experience of slavery and the struggle for a release from bondage. A longing for freedom gave the music and the movement an inspiration that had little affinity with the predominantly White character of the 'anti-Establishment' folk singers of Boston, San Francisco or Greenwich Village. And this spirit was based both on the field music of many decades past and on the expressions of hope and jubilation traditionally associated with the central role played by the churches in the lives of many Blacks. . . .

Nevertheless, a great number of Civil Rights songs were being written at this point by White folk singers. Two songs illustrate and perhaps epitomise the connections, fusing the committed White, urban sensibility with the necessity for social action for the principles of human rights. The first, 'Oxford Town', was written by Bob Dylan and performed by him on his *Freewheelin'* album. It is an account of (more properly a quiet question about) the social, cultural and political problems that attended James Meredith's intention to enrol at the University of Mississippi. There is a sense of despair here that cuts through to the heart of frustration, marking less the hope than the reality of the struggle for Black assimilation. The second song, written by Richard Fariña and entitled 'Birmingham Sunday', accurately describes the atrocity of September 1963, in which four young girls were killed by a bomb set off in a Birmingham, Alabama, church. The song was recorded by Baez for her album *Joan Baez/5*, and is described by Langston Hughes in the liner notes as a 'quiet protest song'.[35] Both songs *quietly* protest. And it is this characteristic that, again, differentiates the music of the 'leaders' of the folk music movement – Baez and Dylan being archetypal – from the tradition of Black consciousness which is rooted in an experiential rather than an ideological world. Both songs describe real events in unequivocal language and simple melody. They were written by White songwriters and give an account of an exclusively Black experience. They were not songs to be performed by a group of singers but by an individual. And they were uniquely relevant to their time. In these ways, the songs – and many others like them – are markedly unlike the ones most commonly associated with the Civil Rights movement. They confirm the separation between the folk music of predominantly White anti-war protest and the predominantly Black Civil Rights movement. It is a distinction that suggests a deep division of commitment and purpose in the two cataclysmic affronts to the American social and political system during the 1960s.

Two aspects of the music of the Civil Rights movement must be emphasised. First, music was integral to any activity, be it a small, local gathering of people to discuss the need for further desegregation or a massive demonstration to call attention to the need for unrestricted use of voting rights. On the Selma to Montgomery voter registration march in the spring of 1965, for example, there was not a moment without music or chanting, day or night.[36] The five days of the march were filled with the songs that inspired the marchers. Frequently heard pieces like 'Ain't gonna let nobody turn me round' and 'Do what the spirit say do' clearly communicated the intention and the determination of the 25,000-strong participants. The second aspect to stress must be the fundamental contribution of religious fervour and spirit. Even those indifferent to religion were caught up in the effect and the enthusiasm these songs were capable of producing. Conviction and a sense of community were all-pervasive in the movement. In short, 'History has never known a protest movement so rich in song as the Civil Rights movement. Nor a movement in which songs are as important.'[37]

So far, we have discussed the relationship of the folk music movement[38] first, to the anti-war (or, more broadly, 'anti-Establishment') attitudes on the part of many people during the decade and, second, to the Civil Rights activities of the period. In the case of the former, the music's principal characteristics were that it was polemical, carefully composed, individually performed and directed *at* an audience who would, presumably, agree in a manner that was essentially intellectual or ideological. The latter was a music born of tradition and of common experience. It was emotional, spontaneous, participatory, spirited and relied heavily on Black religious heritage. Freedom songs were ones which *everyone* sang and, in that sense, there was no audience. What remains to be discussed is the fact that the folk music 'movement' did seem to end. The revival metamorphosed and, to some extent, actually disappeared.

In 1965, two things happened which had an enormous impact on the nature and direction of the protest vigour of the era. In July at the folk festival at Newport, Rhode Island, Dylan, the universally acknowledged leader of the folk mystique and protest spirit, came on stage with an electric guitar.[39] It was an act that outraged his followers and shocked a whole community of avowed pacifists. He had 'sold out'. It must have seemed to many that the music itself was disappointingly impermanent and therefore suspect. Although Ochs, Paxton and, especially, Baez continued to publish, record and appear in public throughout the decade, there was no longer a direct connection between the forces of dissent and the voices of dissenters' music. Bob Dylan was not solely responsible for the divorce. The diminishing importance of folk music in the characteristics of protest would, in all probability, have continued whatever Dylan's inclinations. Even though protest songs would continue to exert some influence, they were, as Woodstock attests, no longer a significant part of the consciousness and behaviour of young, anti-Establishment activists, but a form of entertainment. The messages seemed almost to be taken for granted and were absorbed sometimes nonchalantly into rock music. The circle closed. Beginning with the Kingston Trio and ending with Country Joe McDonald doing 'I-feel-like-I'm-fixin'-to-die rag' at Woodstock, the music was mass entertainment. In between, from 1958 to 1969, the folk music revival played an important role in helping to define the country's widespread rebelliousness. It made its mark and was overcome by electronics. Woody Guthrie's heritage briefly flared and then receded into the cacophonous style which Janis Joplin and Jimi Hendrix mastered.

The second important event of 1965 was the devastating August riot in the Watts section of Los Angeles. The Civil Rights movement would not recover from the terrible spectre of looting, arson and murder. Long before the assassination of Martin Luther King in April 1968, bitterness, anger, irrationality and open rivalry were changing the cause significantly. As William Manchester puts it,

> Martin Luther King, touring the smoking ruins of Watts, received a mixed welcome. He was growing accustomed to this. The torch had been passed to the new generation of Black leaders, and it had become a real torch.

Only one of the casualties of Watts, Detroit, Cleveland and Newark was the movement's music. The positive and concerted pride of 'We shall overcome' gave way to the combative philosophies of Black Power. . . .

In the case of Dylan, Seeger, Baez and the others, the relationship between the protest movement and its music suffered to some extent because of the 'star system' which seemed such a natural part of American cultural values.[42] The severance of music from the spirit of Black consciousness did not occur because of the negative influences of a 'system', but because frustration and violence supplanted the earlier sense of solidarity. In each instance, the music had initially reflected much, yet within a short time began to reflect very little. The spirit had receded. The heritage of Guthrie and the traditions of Black spiritual music, like the political and social movements themselves, did not last in recognisable form throughout the decade. With Richard Nixon in the White House, with middle-class values again in the ascendancy, with the phrase 'law and order' being heavily used by the nation's leaders, and with that predictable phenomenon, 'backlash', doing its insidious work, it is impressive that folk music – what it represented and how it held our attention – could last at all. Jerome Rodnitzky sums up the matter quite well:

> there had been a time in the 1960s when folk-protest singers Dylan, Ochs and Baez chilled the blood of conservative leaders and inspired the hearts of thousands who sought social change. The young protest singers had committed themselves to social action, and their songs were both calls to arms and indictments of the status quo. However, by the decade's end all but Baez had become disillusioned with musical agitation.[43]

There just didn't seem to be a taste for it any more. The land was by no means silent; it was simply trying to escape. And of all the things the folk music movement had offered, escape was not one of them.

JIM MILLER
Bob Dylan

Witness, 2, 2–3 (Summer/Fall 1988)

Bob Dylan's eyes darted restlessly. Unshaven and puffy, his face poured sweat. Flanked on stage by Keith Richard and Ron Wood, fellow pop aristocrats from the Rolling Stones, he stumbled through a heartless version of his most famous song, 'Blowin' in the wind'. The audience, responding to the nostalgia of the moment and the predictability of the gesture, cheered as if on cue as the scene was beamed live via satellite around the world. It was the climax of the 1985 Live Aid concert. At forty-six, Dylan was rock's unofficial poet laureate. He looked like a waxen effigy.

Twenty years earlier, on another stage, at the Newport Folk Festival, the scene had been entirely different – Dylan had nearly caused a riot. He had done this by deliberately defying the expectations of his audience. His most famous song he ignored. Rather than accompany himself as usual with an acoustic guitar, he had launched into a loud new blues called 'Maggie's farm' with the help of an amplified band. In 1965, the crowd had jeered: 'Play folk music! . . . Sell-out!' Dylan, as was his wont in those days, kept his own counsel. After singing two more songs, he abruptly left the stage, as did his band. He returned alone for an abbreviated encore, performing acoustic versions of two more songs, 'Mr Tambourine Man' and 'It's all over now, baby blue'. Superficially, both were gentle ballads. But their lyrics were filled with obscure and delirious images as remote from the conventions of folk music as the amplified roar of his band. Whether the crowd fully realised it or not, Bob Dylan had just fired another salvo in his one-man cultural revolution. In the months to come, he would become a self-styled rock-and-roll Zarathustra, dramatising a different way to live.

How could the existential daredevil of 1965 have turned into the lifeless pop icon of the Eighties? How could the man once widely acclaimed as the greatest composer of his generation have become the cadaver of Live Aid? These are among the greatest mysteries of Bob Dylan's strange career.

Some great rock stars – Paul McCartney springs to mind – live, breathe and eat music. They take pleasure not simply in fame and money – these things most of them have in excess – but also in composing melodies, writing lyrics, trying to craft a pleasing song. Their audience may abandon them, their creative skills may atrophy – yet their natural and unfeigned joy in making music allows them to grow old with a certain gracefulness and dignity.

Other great rock stars – David Bowie, for example – are essentially manipulators of cultural signs. Their genius is less a matter of musical talent than of giving form to passing fashions, epitomising a certain lifestyle, defining a cutting edge for their audience. Once they lose their knack for defining that edge – perhaps because they become bored, perhaps because their perceptions of the broader culture become dulled by fame and wealth – such rock stars produce a kind of cultural static. They release new records, tour as living legends and even command the continuing attention of the mass media – they are bona fide celebrities after all. But the *music* they produce – and they are, of course, still in the business of pop *music* – is more often than not an empty shell, an inadvertent self-parody. Out of touch with their times, they have become *irrelevant*.

Ever since his heyday in the mid-Sixties, it has been assumed that Bob Dylan was and is a great musician. Yet the mummy on stage at Live Aid makes that claim seem absurd. Could it be that Dylan, like Bowie, matters less as a musician than as a manipulator of cultural signs?

The appearance on compact disc of classic Dylan albums like *Blonde on Blonde*, coming on the heels of the anthology *Biograph* and Robert Shelton's revealing biography *No Direction Home*, encourages a fresh examination of such questions.... To listen again to his first seven albums is to rediscover a major cultural figure – and a major puzzle.

He was born on 24 May 1941, in Duluth, Minnesota, the oldest son of Abraham and Beatty Zimmerman, both second-generation American Jews of Russian ancestry. After the war, the family moved to Hibbing, a Minnesota mining town where the Zimmermans ran a furniture and appliance store. 'Hibbing was a vacuum,' the singer told Shelton many years later. 'I just wanted to get away.' At first, imagination was the readiest means of escape: his father recalls that the boy loved the tall tales surrounding Paul Bunyan. And his high school sweetheart says that 'he was always making up little fantasies and telling little fibs'. She remembers Bob calling her on the phone one night and playing her 'something he had recorded' – it turned out to be Bobby Freeman's hit recording of 'Do you want to dance'.

The Zimmerman boy developed a passion for music early. He began singing at the age of five, got his first guitar in junior high, formed his first band in 1955. During a visit with Bob's parents, Shelton heard some of the group's practice tapes – 'Rock-and-roll is here to stay' was part of their repertoire. Shelton also examined the record collection that Bob had left behind: a pile of 45s and LPs that included singles by Black rhythm-and-blues stars like Johnny Ace and the Clovers, American Bandstand pop idols like Pat Boone, country-and-western artists like Webb Pierce and Hank Williams, rockabilly singers like Gene Vincent and Buddy Holly – and a stack of hits by Elvis Presley. In the 1959 Hibbing High School yearbook, Bob declared his ambition 'to join the band of Little Richard'.

Besides playing and listening to pop music, the Zimmermans' oldest son was an avid reader – John Steinbeck's *Grapes of Wrath* was a high school favourite. He started writing poetry at the age of 10. He was also a great fan of Matt Dillon, the sheriff of the television series *Gunsmoke*. In 1958, he confided to his high school sweetheart that he planned to devote his life to music, adding that 'I know what I'm going to call myself. I've got this great name – Bob Dillon.' That was how he told new friends to spell his (assumed) last name. He also told them that Dillon was his mother's maiden name (it wasn't), and that Dillon was a town in Oklahoma (it isn't).

When he arrived in Minneapolis to attend the University of Minnesota, Dillon was also a confirmed folk fan, hungry to learn more. The scene he discovered in Minneapolis was in many ways typical of what was happening at other large Midwestern universities in the late 1950s. Thanks to their rapid expansion in the previous decade, these institutions were attracting an increasingly diverse population of students, including a large number of East Coast Jews from Old Left families travelling west of the Catskills for the first time. By definition outcasts in the Midwest's predominantly Protestant mainstream culture, these young urban migrants often found themselves frequenting the few bookstores, coffee houses and folk societies that welcomed alienated eggheads and local beatniks. At the University of Minnesota, the folk music society, as one old-timer told Shelton, was '80 per cent Jewish, mostly university people' and 'very much underground. The older people came from the Old Left.'

Dillon fitted in. He quickly became a fixture in Dinkytown, as the city's off-campus Bohemian district was called. 'The whole scene was an unforgettable one,' Dylan recalled in a 1985 interview. 'It was outside, there was no formula, never was "mainstream" or "the thing to do" in any sense. America was still very "straight", "post-war" and sort of into a grey-flannel suit thing, McCarthy, Commies, puritanical, very claustrophobic and whatever was happening of any real value was happening away from that and sort of hidden from view and it would be years before the media would be able to recognise it and choke-hold it and reduce to to silliness. Anyway, I got in at the tail-end of that and it was magic.'

In Dinkytown, he met other young fans of folk music like 'Spider John' Koerner and began to tap their knowledge, poring over their record collections. He discovered the jazz of Monk and Coltrane. He began to read the poetry of Pound and Eliot, Ferlinghetti and Ginsberg; the novels of Jack Kerouac, John Rechy and William Burroughs, and the works of Dylan Thomas, rebaptising himself Bob Dylan. It was here, above all, that Dylan first discovered the music of Woody Guthrie.

. . . What drove Dylan East was his passion for Guthrie. 'Bob almost fell in love with Woody Guthrie,' one old friend told Shelton. 'When he learned Guthrie was in a hospital in New Jersey, he decided he had to go out and see him.' For the next two years, Dylan almost obsessively identified with Guthrie. He would listen to Guthrie's famous Dust Bowl ballads endlessly, mastering his Oklahoma twang, mimicking his vocal style, admitting to one Minneapolis friend that 'he was building a character'.

In the 1940s, Guthrie had been the archetypal 'working-class minstrel,' an Okie who seemed drawn straight from the pages of Steinbeck's *Grapes of Wrath*, a hobo and migrant labourer who embodied the romance of the road, of the West, of the uncorrupted proletarian. When Mike Quin, a writer for a West Coast Communist newspaper, first heard Guthrie sing, he alerted friends. In 1939, Guthrie travelled east; he recorded for the Library of Congress and then joined Pete Seeger's Almanac Singers, briefly living with the other members in a commune in Greenwich Village. A singer of artless simplicity, he was an honest, almost ingenuous craftsman with a vast repertoire of mythic lore, tall tales and traditional melodies. He wrote and sang of hard times with humour and hope. But his own career proved short. He suffered from Huntington's chorea, a crippling degenerative disease; by the early Fifties, he was no longer able to play music . . .

Although his health continued to deteriorate, Guthrie still received visitors on Sundays, at a house near the hospital in New Jersey where he was staying. These Sunday afternoon visits became one of Dylan's entrées into the New York folk scene. Among other people, he got to know 'Ramblin' Jack' Elliott, a folk singer who, like Dylan, ardently admired Guthrie. More than a decade earlier, Elliott had invented a new alter ego for himself by donning a cowboy hat, affecting a Western drawl and mastering Guthrie's musical style. In fact, Elliott was a native of Brooklyn and the son of a Jewish doctor. His 'Ramblin' Jack' character belies the myth that folk music is somehow more honest than pop. At the same time, to an understudy like Dylan, 'Ramblin' Jack' offered living proof that fictive masks and folk music could perfectly well coexist.

Dylan was an eager student, devouring every bit of wisdom he could glean from older friends like Elliott and Dave Van Ronk, another Brooklyn-born folk enthusiast whose speciality was blues. As an outsider new to town, Dylan could freely reinvent the character he was working on. He told people he had come from Gallup, New Mexico. He claimed to have travelled with blues singer Mance Lipscomb. He reported that he had learned songs during some time he had spent on the Brazos River in Texas. He kept on polishing his Oklahoma twang and assumed the seedy look of a heartlands hobo, picking as his trademark a black corduroy cap. 'His concern about image started then,' recalls one New York acquaintance. 'He would ask if he looked right, jiggling with his dungarees.'

It had become a very compelling act. Shelton, for one, was bowled over the first time he reviewed Dylan on stage, in the fall of 1961. 'Mr Dylan's voice is anything but pretty,' he explained in the *New York Times* [29 September 1961]. 'He is consciously trying to recapture the rude beauty of a Southern field hand musing in melody on his back porch.' When Shelton interviewed him afterwards, Dylan cheerfully retailed an elaborate series of lies and half-truths, climaxed by the claim that he had played guitar with Gene Vincent.

When he wasn't on stage or in the streets, Dylan spent endless hours listening to records: Ewan MacColl, Blind Willie McTell and – above all – the three boxed volumes of the Folkways *Anthology of American Folk Music*. First released in 1951, this anthology is an extraordinary collection of eighty-four vintage recordings; as the critic Greil Marcus has pointed out, it is also an important clue to Dylan's sensibility. Most of the material dates from the late 1920s, when the commercial labels, spurred on by the fantastic sales enjoyed by country star Jimmie Rodgers and blues singer Bessie Smith, had feverishly recorded a host of Black and Appalachian singers, often on location. The most striking thing about the Folkways anthology is the air of utter *strangeness* that saturates almost every cut. Listen, for example, to 'James Alley blues', recorded by Victor in New Orleans (1927), by the Black singer Richard 'Rabbit' Brown, whose sandpapery singing is full of disturbing unfathomable mannerisms. Or listen to the equally weird 'I wish I was a mole in the ground', recorded by Brunswick in North Carolina (1928), by 'The Minstrel of the Appalachians' Bascom Lamar Lunsford, an Asheville folklorist (and lawyer). The song describes a topsy-turvy world where the insignificant are mighty. 'I wish I was a mole in the ground,' drones Lunsford. 'Like a mole in the ground I would root that mountain down.' In a 1965 interview, Dylan suggested that the putative 'authenticity' of such music fascinated him far less than its ineffable peculiarity: 'Folk music,' he said, 'is the only music where it *isn't* simple. It's weird, man, full of legend, myth, Bible and ghosts . . . chaos, watermelons, clocks, everything . . . '

It was this sense of strangeness and out-of-time otherness that Dylan now began to reach for in his music. On *Bob Dylan*, his debut album released in March 1962, most of the material is second-hand. The album contains several boisterous imitations of Guthrie. But what jumped out at the time and stands out today are several songs about death. The music is compelling because Dylan's *voice* is compelling – here is the key to his musical greatness. Consider 'In my time of dyin'', a song that the blues singer Josh White frequently sang. White's version on the album *Josh at Midnight* is urbane, atmospheric, reserved – perfect café society fare. Dylan, by contrast, lashes into the song with a crudely played bottleneck guitar. His voice is raw, histrionic, utterly unnatural and perfectly unsettling. He actually *sounds* like he's just about to meet Jesus in the middle of the air so that he can 'die easy'. You hear the lyrics for the first time – they feel real. And then you look at Dylan's picture on the cover, and blink: he's a baby-faced kid of twenty-one.

In retrospect, it seems clear that Dylan knew perfectly well what he was after. 'I hate to say this,' he told Shelton in 1966, 'because I don't want it to be taken the wrong way, but I latched on when

I got to New York because I saw a huge audience was there.' By all reports, he pursued this audience with single-minded diligence. He stalked the streets of the Village with a spiral notebook in his hand, jotting down ideas and observations about everything from the poetry he was reading to animals in the street or a newspaper headline, beginning to work up new songs of his own. At the same time, he became actively involved in a little mimeographed magazine called *Broadside*, which Pete Seeger and some friends, inspired by the resurgent student left and Civil Rights movement, had started up to publish new (left-wing) topical songs.

The folk music craze had by now become a phenomenon certified by the mass media. In the spring of 1963, ABC Television began to broadcast its *Hootenanny* show, an upbeat musical jamboree that enforced the old blacklist against Seeger, was scrupulously boycotted by artists like Dylan – and nevertheless exposed the music to an audience of millions. At the same time, the Civil Rights movement was entering an exuberant new phase of protest. Accurately reading these cultural trends, Dylan sensed that a 'huge audience was there' – and that topical songs were one way to reach it.

He had begun work on his second album in the fall of 1962. It was planned to showcase the songs that he had been publishing in *Broadside*: 'Masters of war', 'A hard rain's a-gonna fall' and, of course, 'Blowin' in the wind'. Meanwhile, Albert Grossman, his new manager, was peddling Dylan's songs to other artists, including the Chad Mitchell Trio and Peter, Paul and Mary, two of the more frankly commercial folk acts that had sprung up in the wake of the Kingston Trio. At one point, Grossman even coaxed Peter, Paul and Mary into investing in Dylan; they then recorded a pretty version of Dylan's 'Blowin' in the wind'. When it was released as a single in the summer of 1963, the record took off, selling over one million copies. Shortly afterwards, when *The Freewheelin' Bob Dylan*, his second album, was belatedly released, it too soared into the upper reaches of the album charts. In late August, Dylan joined Peter, Paul and Mary at the great Civil Rights March on Washington led by Dr Martin Luther King, Jr. By then, 'Blowin' in the wind' had joined 'We shall overcome' as the political anthem of the hour.

But what different anthems! 'We shall overcome' is a song of resolute faith, imbued with confidence in the certainty of final victory. Cast in the mould of an old Afro-American hymn, 'I will overcome', it had originally been given new lyrics in the 1940s to serve as a union song. Pete Seeger and some friends then rewrote the lyrics again, this time to create a Civil Rights anthem, teaching the new song to Civil Rights militants at the 1960 founding convention of the Student Non-Violent Coordinating Committee (SNCC). Passed along orally – and inconspicuously – in this political context, 'We shall overcome' acquired the aura of a 'real' folk song. Even today, most people are unaware that it was almost as much of a self-conscious creation as 'Blowin' in the wind'.

Dylan's anthem, by contrast, was identified from the start with Dylan himself. Grossman shrewdly marketed it using time-tested Tin Pan Alley techniques. Most people first heard the song on the radio, as a hit single. And what they heard, if they were listening to the lyrics and not lulled by the bland melody, was no uplifting affirmation of faith but a series of questions, with no answers offered.

The song's rhetoric of restless searching faithfully echoed the sentiments of the fledgeling New Left, an affinity that Dylan himself recognised and went out of his way to underline. In December 1963, he put in a brief appearance at a national meeting of the Students for a Democratic Society (SDS), where (as one witness later recalled) he mumbled a vague benediction: 'Ah don't know what yew all are talkin' about, but it sounds like yew want somethin' to happen, and if that's what *yew* want, that's what *Ah* want.' A few weeks later, Dylan performed in Mississippi at the invitation of SDS leader Tom Hayden and Bob Moses of SNCC. When *The Times they are a-Changin'*, Dylan's third album, was released in February 1964, young activists were elated – it was Dylan's most topical recording to date, and it reflected the temper and tone of their own politics with almost uncanny accuracy. (This is not entirely surprising: they were members of Dylan's generation, and many of them had first developed a passion for politics and folk music in the same kind of off-campus Bohemian environment that Dylan had discovered in Dinkytown.)

Throughout 1963, Dylan consolidated his reputation as the most promising young folk singer in America. He embarked on a series of concert appearances with Joan Baez, then at the peak of her popularity. He had won the esteem of the first audience he cared about, the folk musicians, Beat poets, and young radicals of the burgeoning avant-garde college-student youth culture. But friends recall that he was already itching to move on to something else. 'He is a complicated, problematic, difficult person,' Baez told Shelton in 1966, 'more fragile than the average person' – and, she added, far more ambitious than the average folk singer. 'At one point in our little scene,' she says, 'although I was enjoying the concerts, I froze up and said to him: "Bobby, you'd be doing it as a rock-'n'-roll king, but I'd be doing it as peace queen."' Later, Dylan himself agreed: 'This is what made me different. I played all the folk songs with a rock-'n'-roll attitude.'

That attitude came across in Dylan's cockiness, in his tacit ambition to touch as large an audience as possible, and in the chip-on-the-shoulder sullenness conveyed by his stock photographic pose. But it also was conveyed in subtler ways. As early as 1962, Dylan had expressed a desire to start writing more songs about himself and fewer songs about other people. Some of his most touching early songs in fact were not topical at all. Singing ballads like 'Girl from the north country' and 'One too many mornings', he evoked a bleak yearning at odds with the hardboiled worldliness he normally affected – and strangely redolent of the keening adolescent ballads that rock singers like Ricky Nelson had made popular in the late Fifties. (Nelson later recorded a number of Dylan's songs – and on his 1986 tour, Dylan in turn sang Nelson's 1958 hit, 'Lonesome town'.) Here was one lost and desolate – and very young – soul, his voice on these ballads seemed to say; and this, too, was part of his 'rock-'n'-roll attitude'.

In February 1964, Dylan set off from New York on a cross-country car trip with three buddies, heading for Mardi Gras in New Orleans, the Rockies, the San Francisco Bay – the heart and soul of America, approached in the spirit of Guthrie and Kerouac. But as the car rolled west, America's airwaves were filled with foreign sounds. The 'British Invasion' had just begun – and suddenly, with the music of the Beatles everywhere, rock-'n'-roll, and not folk music or politics or Beat poetry, was the most exciting and fashionable thing happening on the cutting edge of pop culture.

Within a matter of months, Dylan had begun to turn his own music inside out. In June 1964, shortly after returning from a tour of England, Dylan recorded a number of new songs in a marathon session that would be his last as a solo artist. Love songs like 'It ain't me, babe' were vitriolic and barbed; political songs like 'Chimes of freedom' were a whorl of fantastic imagery; none of the songs was narrowly polemical. On the back cover of *Another Side of Bob Dylan*, he underlined the change. 'You tell me about politics,' he wrote, 'an' i tell you there are no politics . . . i know no answers an' no truth/for absolutely no soul alive/i will listen t' no one/who tells me morals/there are no morals/an' i dream alot.'

The style was clumsy, the sentiments an almost embarrassing mélange of modernist clichés and pulp existentialism. But once the sentiments, set to a howling beat, were groomed for the top ten, the clumsiness of the style scarcely seemed to matter. Dylan had reinvented himself first as a hobo minstrel, then as a troubadour of dissent. Reaching out to a wider audience still, he was about to become a rock-'n'-roll Rimbaud.

When it came, the metamorphosis was abrupt, surrounded by controversy and greeted in some quarters as a shameful artistic scandal. In April 1965, Dylan released a raucously bluesy rock single called 'Subterranean homesick blues', which became his first top forty hit. In the fifteen months that followed, Dylan released three albums with electric band accompaniment (*Bringing It All Back Home* in May 1965, *Highway 61 Revisited* in October, and *Blonde on Blonde* in July 1966). He also released six singles, three of them top ten hits, starting with 'Like a rolling stone' in July 1965. In these months, as he barnstormed across America and England, Dylan became one of the most celebrated figures in rock history, completely transforming the music and its expressive possibilities in the minds of those who played it and those who listened to it.

Dylan's demeanour in those days had just as much impact as his music. A tangled aureole of hair crowned a pale and wraith-like figure. Dylan's face seemed frozen in a scowl. The growing unpredictability of his performances – and his glazed, impassive gaze – fuelled speculation about drugs. At the time, Dylan did nothing to dispel the speculation. 'Being a musician', he said, 'means getting to the depths of where you are at. And most any musician would try anything to get to those depths.' Try *anything* – that was the message. And once again, a huge audience was waiting, ready to listen.

What they heard was, in many ways, singularly odd. Dylan, it should be obvious by now, was no musical virtuoso. Technically, he has always been a singer of severely limited range, with a voice that verges on a whine. His concerts have often been sloppy. Even on recordings like *Highway 61 Revisited*, instruments are out of tune, arrangements a clutter. And some of his most memorable songs and lyrics seem helter-skelter. '"Like a rolling stone" was really vomitific in its structure,' Dylan tells Shelton at one point. 'It seemed like it was twenty pages, but it was really six. . . . You know how you get sometimes.' The voluble lyrics to a song like 'Rolling stone' lie dead on the printed page. What matters, as always, is Dylan's *voice*: the poetry of the song depends on the incendiary energy of his singing. Consider, for example, the way he pounces on a phrase like 'How does it FEEEL?' – turning the question into an insult. The song cannot be separated from the performance – in that sense, 'Like a rolling stone' is rock-'n'-roll through and through, closer in spirit to 'Tutti frutti' than to 'We shall overcome'.

By now, Dylan's distinctive approach was fully formed. Many lyrics he shouted out helplessly, like a sailor at the helm of a storm-pitched ship. His performances often had an exalted, almost ecstatic quality, as if Dylan's songs were singing him. A Long Island reporter who saw Dylan perform in early 1966 described 'a sad marionette . . . he looked half asleep or half dead'. An Australian journalist a couple of months later was reminded of 'Harpo Marx . . . walking like a marionette'. The critic Langdon Winner, who saw him in California that year, remembers 'a puppet with most of his strings missing – he wobbled on stage like he was *unstrung*'. An unnatural apparition giving voice to pell-mell rhymes, Dylan could seem eerily like the medium for somebody else's messages. 'I am just a voice speaking,' Dylan told Shelton in 1966. 'And anytime I'm singing about people and if the songs are dreamed, it's like my voice is coming out of their dream.'

When they weren't simply filled with tumult, Dylan concerts came to resemble a kind of seance. This was something radically new in the world of pop music. In the past people had gone to rock concerts to see somebody famous, to hear a familiar hit, perhaps to dance or to jump up and down and scream – that is what happened when the Beatles and the Rolling Stones first toured the United States, because that is what rock concerts were all about. Folk music concerts of course were different – reverent students thoughtfully hung on every word. What Dylan in 1965 and 1966 managed to do was to blast himself free from the insular complacency of the folk scene while daring the pop crowd to *listen*. His music was full of surprise – and the disembodied, sometimes vehement way in which it was sung made it seem like a revelation.

The best evidence of Dylan's peculiar gifts in this period is *Live at Royal Albert Hall*, a bootleg album recorded in the spring of 1966 during a tour of the British Isles with the Hawks, the group later known simply as the Band. As the group's guitarist, Robbie Robertson, has recalled in an interview, 'That tour was a very strange process. You can hear the violence and the dynamics in the music.' Indeed. From start to finish, the music on the bootleg surges with reckless power, threatening to fly apart at the seams, held together by the relentlessness of the beat, driven furiously forward by Robertson's guitar solos – anything but flashy, they are rough and hard and spiked with rhythmic tension. Dylan's singing is demonic. He barrels through 'Tell me, mama' and 'I don't believe you' and 'Baby, let me follow you down' and 'Just like Tom Thumb's blues', his voice rising and falling, almost without pitch, before homing in on a note with a dive-bomb drone. On the climactic 'Like a rolling stone', he taunts. He yells. Words come hurling out. The atmosphere is thick. Anything could happen, you think – even listening twenty years later.

Of course, Dylan once more was acting out a role – but this time, the role was also devouring him. He sounded on edge because he *was* on edge: the unpredictability and volatility in his voice was real – more real, because far less controlled, than the Woody Guthrie imitations and protest songs of his previous incarnation. Dylan throughout this period was a key cultural bellwether, but he was also, for those few months in 1965 and 1966, something more, and something far more disturbing: an artist flirting with death.

The most revealing pages in Shelton's book describe an interview that he conducted with Dylan on an overnight flight from Lincoln, Nebraska, to Denver, Colorado, in March 1966. For several months, Dylan had been on the road with the Hawks. He had become adept at putting on – and fending off – the press with non-sequiturs, sarcasm, and humiliating jokes. On this occasion, though, talking through the night with his would-be Boswell, he simply flew, riffing on ideas and images, breathlessly leaping from topic to topic.

On his music: 'My thing is with colours. It's not black and white. It's always been with colours, whether with clothes or anything. Colour. Now, with something like that driving you, sometimes it gets very fiery red, you understand? And at times, it gets very jet black.'

On Woody Guthrie: 'What drew me to him was that hearing his voice I could tell he was very lonesome, very alone, and very lost out in his time. That's why I dug him.'

On folk music: 'Folk music was such a shuck. I never recorded a folk song. My idea of a folk song is Jeannie Robertson or Dock Boggs. Call it historical–traditional music.'

On drugs: 'It takes a lot of medicine to keep up this pace. . . . I got very strung out for a while. I mean, really, very strung out. . . . I can do anything, knowing in front that it's not going to catch me and pull me . . . 'cause I've been through it once already. A lot of times you get strung out with people. They are just like junk. . . . The same thing, no more, no less. They kill you the same way.'

On death: 'I have a death thing, I know. I have a suicidal thing, I know. . . . I was actually afraid of death in those first years around New York. When I started writing all those songs and everyone started calling me a genius . . . I knew it was bull, because I still hadn't written what I wanted to. . . . I've really got a sickness, man. I don't write when I'm feeling groovy, you understand. I play when I'm feeling groovy, I write when I'm sick. . . . Man, nobody knows what is the matter with me, and I'm not going to tell anybody. . . . I can't decay. I would not let myself decay. I'm against decay. That's nature's will – decay. I am against nature. . . . I think nature is very unnatural. I think the only truly natural things are in dreams, which nature can't touch with decay. . . . I don't want to see myself die. . . . All this talk about equality. The only thing people really have in common is that they are all going to die.'

On 29 July 1966, while joy-riding on his motorcycle, Dylan was thrown from the bike, suffering concussion and several broken vertebrae in his neck. For more than a year, he disappeared from public view.

It was the seedtime of Dylan's myth. In his absence, *Don't Look Back*, D.A. Pennebaker's documentary film about Dylan's British tour of 1965, made the rounds of college campuses, offering a behind-closed-doors glimpse of Dylan's cruel and deliberately mystifying manner. Meanwhile, fans played Dylan's old albums over and over and over again, giving the music fresh weight and more importance than it had ever had before.

For some, the music largely served as a backdrop – mood music for acid trips and anti-war rallies. For others, the lyrics acquired a mysterious new resonance: keys to experience were waiting to be discovered in the epic dreamscapes of 'Desolation Row' and 'Sad-eyed lady of the lowlands'. And as the country's political culture progressively unravelled in 1967 and 1968, the barely contained chaos and violence of Dylan's rock came to seem more and more *right*, inevitable, a prophetic mirror of the disorder and uncertainty of the times.

In one of his earliest essays, the rock critic Greil Marcus described how, after watching the police riot at the Chicago Democratic Convention of 1968, he put on *Blonde on Blonde* and let the record track through 'Memphis blues again'. 'I've heard that song hundreds of times before,' Marcus wrote, 'but this time it was different. It became a journey, a rite of passage, a struggling effort to pass out of an inexplicable contradiction, only to find another, with no escape, only a change to a new chord, a new movement of the guitar or organ, intensifying the desire that it all be over . . . ' For Marcus, and for many others, Dylan's music became a paradigm of what pop culture can mean: a song like 'Memphis blues again' was not a stereotyped entertainment but a work of phantasmagorical creativity, something that could seduce a listener, capture the imagination, challenge the understanding, move a person to *think*.

The period of Dylan's greatest popularity was still to come. In the 1970s, he enjoyed three number one albums, sang to sell-out crowds in cavernous arenas, even belatedly made the cover of *Newsweek* magazine. But in the twenty years since his motorcycle accident, the palaver of many critics to the contrary, Dylan has never come close to making music of the power and freedom and apocalyptic intensity of *Blonde on Blonde* or the *Live at Royal Albert Hall* bootleg.

Perhaps that is because Dylan's greatest music was, just as he told Shelton in 1966, in part the product of 'sickness' – a suicidal will to live in an unnatural and chemically sustained state of feverish free association. It was also the product of a fleeting moment – the tumultuous few months in which Dylan furiously fed off the hostility and adulation of the pop music process at its most frenzied and least predictable. For a time, he seemed a spectral whirling dervish, a musical magician smashing and recombining images with manic energy and blinding brilliance.

After the crash, all this changed. 'Until the accident,' he told Shelton in 1971, 'I was living music twenty-four hours a day' – but now, he confided, writing songs had become a labour. In pastoral retreat in Woodstock, isolated from his audience, glad to be healthy and apparently wary of the vertiginous nihilism and wild cultural myths hatched in his own delirious imagination, Dylan cut himself off from the wellsprings of his greatest work.

You could hear the change in his voice: after 1966, he never again sang with the same authority and abandon. Instead, he sounded like a chastened and sadly weary pilgrim (perhaps his most appealing post-accident voice, heard on *The Basement Tapes* and *John Wesley Harding*), or like a trumped-up smoothie (as on *Nashville Skyline*), or like a mean-spirited caricature of his former self (as on his widely hailed 1985 'comeback' album, *Empire Burlesque*).

Since many members of his audience by the end of the Sixties felt chastened and weary too, an album like *John Wesley Harding* had a real resonance. But with the old spark gone, and his personal demons in retreat, what Dylan did have honestly to say – for example, about the need for faith in God – most of the fans didn't want to hear. Out of touch with his times, the once brilliant manipulator of cultural signs was fated to produce cultural static.

For better or worse, Dylan's claim to greatness rests on the music of his early years – the soundtrack of his singular quest to reinvent himself as something irreducibly *other* than the Robert Zimmerman who grew up in Hibbing, Minnesota, listening to 'Hound dog', watching *Gunsmoke* and wishing he were Elvis, or Matt Dillon, or Leadbelly, or almost *anybody* else. In pursuing this quest with relentless energy and a vaulting ambition to touch the heart of a mass audience just as Elvis, Matt Dillon and Leadbelly had touched him, Dylan helped to make the modernist themes of exuberant negation and romantic reaffirmation into the shared obsessions of a generation. In his day, he was a genius at such cultural alchemy. At the same time, he was a great and unusual singer, passionate in his disembodied mannerisms and able to convey, in the chaotic ecstasy of his most memorable performances, an unsettling and unforgettable sense of death-haunted yearning. Just listen, again, to his first seven albums. The music is protean, but with each passing album, the voice rings truer. It is the sound of someone 'very lonesome, very alone, and very lost out in his time'. Which is one reason why that voice, more than twenty years later, still defines that time.

MICHAEL ROOS and DON O'MEARA

Is your love in vain – dialectical dilemmas in Bob Dylan's recent love-songs

Popular Music, 7, 1 (1987)

In a recent interview, Bob Dylan said that he has learned never to 'give 100 per cent' – a person, particularly a public artist, should always hold something in reserve. Somewhat taken aback, the interviewer pressed for a follow-up to this puzzling statement. Wasn't Dylan giving 100 per cent on those great albums of the 1960s, *Highway 61 Revisited* and *Blonde on Blonde*? All right, Dylan finally admitted, maybe he was. The reporter dropped the question and went on to other subjects, leaving the readers, like Mr Jones, wondering just what is going on here. Most people who have followed Dylan's work throughout his career would agree that, in his work of the 1980s, he seems to be holding something back. There are flashes of brilliance, of the old verbal acuity, the ability to come up with the startlingly perfect phrase to fit his needs in a song. There have been truly great songs, like 'Jokerman', 'Dark eyes' and 'Brownsville girl'. But there have also been embarrassingly awful songs, like 'Never gonna be the same again', lacklustre singing and woefully inconsistent production values on his records. We know what he is capable of – he knows what he is capable of – yet he doesn't give us his best. Why? In our view the answer, like most aspects of Bob Dylan, is not simple but may well involve a complex combination of factors all pertaining to the attempt to balance the dialectical forces pulling upon him from both the public and private areas of his life. One thing is certain: the Bob Dylan revealed in his songs of the 1980s has not been a happy man. Indeed, he has been a bitter, cynical, paranoid, lonely, self-pitying man, searching in vain for love yet ironically unable to give himself in trust to another person. It is possible, however, to trace through his songs the emotional path he has taken since 1970. Our approach, therefore, is an exercise in an 'autobiographical' interpretation of Dylan's lyrics. This, clearly, does not exclude the possibility of other types of reading, but it is our contention that, if Dylan's art of the past seventeen years is to be remembered in the future, it will be primarily because of the way it focuses intensely on the enormous difficulties that a public artist has in finding a harmonious balance between public and private forces in his life. That has been the major theme of his music during that period, and it is the only way to understand at all the unhappiness of his recent years and the inconsistent quality of his work.

In this article we will combine elements of biography and literary analysis with emerging social science perspectives on personal relationships to examine Dylan's work since 1970. Specifically, we will focus upon a dominant theme woven throughout this work – the inherent dialectical strain expressed between the public world of the performing artist and the private world of close personal relationships such as marriage and family. These worlds both lure and repel Dylan, offering him opportunities for personal well-being yet also threatening him. The influence of these two sets of opposing forces manifests itself in a continuing dilemma reflected in Dylan's songs. He is constantly attempting to balance these sets of bi-polar forces as he seeks a meaningful life synthesis.

This challenge of synthesising opposing life forces has recently been emphasised by social scientists interested in the phenomena of inherent strains within all social relationships. W.K. Rawlins identifies the basic tenets of this dialectical perspective. First, contradiction or conflict between opposing factors is a basic structural characteristic of relationships, not an aberrant property. Second, the social domain is seen as a set of interconnected relationships. Thus, as described above for Dylan, the public and private domains are not distinct separate worlds. Instead, the properties of each intrude and impact upon the other in Dylan's everyday reality. Third, 'change is viewed as constant, ubiquitous, and rooted in the contradictions of social life'.[44] This ever-present state of change results from the individuals' constant attempts at resolving contradictory social forces to reach a new life synthesis.[45] Social scientists have applied this perspective to primary relationships such as marriage and friendships.[46] Here, we develop a model based upon this perspective which emphasises the inherent contradictions within both the private and the public worlds of Dylan's life.

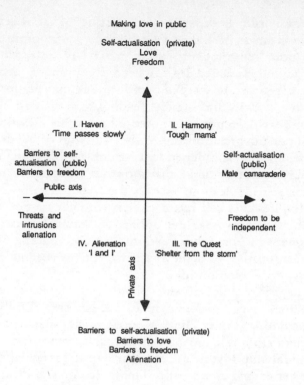

Making love in public

Self-actualisation (private)
Love
Freedom

+

I. Haven
'Time passes slowly'

II. Harmony
'Tough mama'

Barriers to self-
actualisation (public)
Barriers to freedom

Self-actualisation
(public)
Male camaraderie

Public axis

−   +

Threats and
intrusions
alienation

Freedom to be
independent

IV. Alienation
'I and I'

III. The Quest
'Shelter from the storm'

Private axis

−

Barriers to self-actualisation (private)
Barriers to love
Barriers to freedom
Alienation

The model consists of two axes representing the private and public worlds, with intersecting poles defining the positive and negative forces of these worlds. Understanding the polar properties of each axis is essential before we can fully explain the actions of these forces in Dylan's songs.

According to Dylan's songs, the positive pole of the private world includes a series of attractive dimensions of personal relationships. These include the potential for self-actualisation. E. Erikson describes this higher-order human motive as 'the desire to become more and more what one idiosyncratically is, to become everything that one is capable of becoming'.[47] The potential for self-actualisation in the private realm of personal relationships is represented in Dylan's songs by the opportunities for solitude, for security and a sense of belonging, for stability, acceptance, authenticity in relationships, and for affirmation of personal identity through interaction with significant others. In addition, there is the potential to experience human love. As R. J. Sternberg and S. Grajen have recently emphasised,[48] love is

a multi-dimensional experience consisting of an affective component – intimacy; a cognitive component – commitment; and
a motivational component – passion. Dylan's attraction to love
appears to be generated by his need for intimacy and passion,
while he appears to be wary of commitment (except, possibly, that
it offers the security and stability leading to actualisation). Finally,
the private world represents potential freedom. Rawlins emphasises that personal relationships offer two types of freedom. There
is the freedom to be independent, which 'involves self's decision
to act autonomously and other's option to concede or impede
this privilege'. In addition, there is the freedom to be dependent,
which 'implies that self has a choice whether or not to rely on
other and that other has the option of granting or withholding
his prerogative'. These two freedoms require ongoing negotiation
within relationships to achieve a compromise acceptable to both
members of the relationship.

The negative pole of the private axis consists of several
basic factors. First, intimate relationships can also be barriers
to self-actualisation. As Dylan's music makes clear, he too often
experiences close relationships as intrusive, temporary, betraying,
imposing false or 'mythical' definitions upon his actual self, superficial, rejecting and inauthentic. There are also significant barriers,
in close relationships, to experiencing love. This is particularly
true for Dylan with regard to the component of commitment.
He periodically experiences commitment's dialectical opposites
– the sense of being personally overwhelmed by another in a
relationship, the stultifying sense of losing his sense of identity to
another, and the requirement that he must come face to face with
his own personal deficiencies as reflected back to him from other
human beings – his private looking-glass (*c.f.* C. H. Cooley's 1902
concept of looking-glass self as a process of self-definition).[49] The
private world also presents obstacles to personal freedom, just as
it offers potential. The freedom to be independent is limited by
the other's freedom to be dependent. There is the potential for
expectations for future behaviour to become part of the socially
defined rules of the relationship – expectations which may limit
future options. Similarly, as relationship obligations of all types
(behavioural, emotional, financial, etc.) increase, these begin to
take on the property of burdensome restrictions. In addition, the
freedom to be dependent presents the risk that the other person
will reject that need due to his or her own need for independence;
curiously, the alternative risk is the potential to lose one's sense

of self in a relationship with a person who accepts one's freedom to be dependent to the point of one's identity loss. Finally, this pole represents the potential for personal alienation from the private everyday world. Following M. Seeman's disaggregation of this global concept,[50] it has four basic dimensions – a sense of meaninglessness in the world around one, a parallel feeling of powerlessness, a sense of being isolated from significant relationships, and a loss of sense of personal identity (self-estrangement). Dylan's songs repeatedly deal with this subterranean sense of alienation within the private world.

The public axis, as reflected in Dylan's songs, has a positive pole with compelling attributes which beckon the performing artist and even seem to impel Dylan to follow the public road. First, there is, once again as in the private world, the potential for actualising the artistic dimension of self. As Erikson himself stated, 'A musician must make music, an artist must paint, a poet must write, if he is to be ultimately at peace with himself.'[51] The attraction of artistic achievement, resolution of social problems, fame, glory, and enhanced opportunity for self-expression, all contribute to the public world's potential for adding to Dylan's sense of self-actualisation. In addition, Dylan appears to be drawn to this realm by the opportunity to forge bonds of male camaraderie. This represents a shared sense of doing and achieving with persons who identify with and who affirm Dylan's definition of an artist and of the function of artists. Finally, the public world offers the freedom to be independent, to be on the road and responsible to no one who would significantly limit the boundaries of this freedom – to choose without relational restrictions.

However, the same public world offers Dylan negative dimensions dialectically opposed to these positive components. First, there are significant barriers to public self-actualisation and freedom. These include the overwhelming demands and expectations expressed by the numerous groups attached to the role of artist (the artist's 'role set'), and the inauthentic, immoral and manipulative character of relationships in this world. Second, the public artist's life is continually threatened by intrusions into one's time of solitude, by criticism from the audience, the fans and the critics, by impersonal manipulation, and even potential physical harm, such as that represented by the assassination of John Lennon by a fan. The result of these threats is an emergent self-definition of artist as martyr which permeates Dylan's songs. In addition the public world which defines the artist can be potentially responsible for creating a core sense of alienation in that artist. Just as in the private realm, a parallel sense of alienation from the public includes a sense of meaninglessness regarding the world (the world of the 'Idiot wind'), a sense of powerlessness over events, a feeling of isolation from significant relationships and a deep feeling of distance from one's own artistic self or self-estrangement. Finally, the search for satisfaction in male camaraderie has its negative dimension in the sheer superficiality which males offer to one another in tentative friendship bonds. Lacking role models for sensitivity, lacking early socialisation into the art of sharing, self-expression and sensitivity, taught to be competitive and not co-operative, and being generally homophobic, most men are incapable of experiencing deep, lasting friendships. Rather, males tend to 'do things' and share only a breadth of activities rather than a depth of self-disclosure'.[52]

The opposing forces of these four poles create what we will term four 'life structures'. D. J. Levinson defines a life structure as the 'underlying pattern or design of a person's life at a given time'.[53] It includes a person's socio-cultural world (e.g. social class, religion, occupation, family status), social relationships and roles (e.g. father, husband, artist), and one's self (including the segments of self that are lived out in that life structure and those that are neglected by that life structure). For Dylan we have identified four life structures based upon the balance of forces of the public and private worlds.

The first structure is labelled 'The Haven' and represents the state wherein the positive aspects of the private world compensate for the negative dimension experienced in the public world. Dylan's songs in this life structure focus upon the positive aspects of the private world (e.g. 'Time passes slowly'). The second cell represents 'Harmony', where the positive aspects of both worlds are experienced as mutually reinforcing, creating a balanced life. Here, Dylan's songs emphasise the negotiation and co-operation required to balance the positive aspects of both worlds (e.g. 'Tough mama'). The third cell is 'The Quest', a term which captures the life structure in which the positive aspects of the public world compensate for the negative dimension experienced in private life. Here, Dylan's songs deal with the compelling need to create as a performing artist and with the personal forces which push him away from the private world (e.g. 'Shelter from the storm'). Finally, the fourth cell represents the life structure of 'Alienation'. Here, the negative aspects of both worlds are mutually reinforced to create a deep sense of alienation from relationships within both worlds. This structure is exemplified by Dylan's song 'I and I'.

Each life structure represented by these four cells is inherently unstable and temporary, since they represent opposing dialectical forces resulting in some degree of ambivalence for the person living each life structure. As Levinson pointedly emphasised, no single life structure (be it Harmony, Quest or Haven) fully satisfies an individual, since there are always aspects of the social domain which are deleted from that structure and which, at some future time, may re-orient the individual toward a new life structure. For instance, Dylan appears to miss the positive aspects of 'The Quest' which are deleted from the experience of 'The Haven' and vice versa.

Dylan's music since 1970 has, at one time or another, reflected the experience of these four life structures. Indeed, his music and personal biography reflect a distinct pattern with regard to these structures, continually experiencing the crossing of borders as he has moved from one to the other in sometimes ambiguous and other times quite clear statements of being. His songs during this period thus reflect the continual interpretation of the meaning of his private and public worlds, and continual attempts at synthesising the dialectical forces of these worlds. The results of these syntheses are the formation of life structures for limited periods of time, and the crossing of borders (axes) into new life structures which themselves do not fully satisfy the total person known as Bob Dylan.

It can be readily established that Dylan began the 1970s in the life structure of the Haven. He retreated there in the late 1960s following his motorcycle accident and the chaotic period of alienation evident in the songs of *Blonde on Blonde* from 1966. Dylan married Sara Lowndes in late 1965, but only settled into true domestic life after the forced recuperation from the accident in the summer and fall of 1966. By 1970, Dylan's reclusiveness and image as a moderate family man were well documented. His public felt betrayed and accused him of turning his back on the atrocities of Vietnam and the Nixon years. But there were few indications that Dylan had any real desire to return to the public arena. All signs seemed to indicate that he was comfortably enjoying a life of domestic bliss. The release of *Self Portrait* early in 1970 was met by howls of rage (the infamous *Rolling Stone* 'What is this shit?' review, for example) or complete bafflement. Dylan seemed to be going to great pains over four sides of music to deny everything his 1960s fans wanted him to be. *Self Portrait* seemed then, and still seems today, an elaborate joke (especially the goofy rendition of 'Like a rolling stone', which was, after all, *the* anthem of the 1960s). *Self Portrait* is a light-hearted, completely self-satisfied rejection of Dylan's public, possible because of the comforting domestic haven in which he found himself. It was quite reasonable at the time to wonder if Dylan would ever return. There was no hint of any desire to do so.

When *New Morning* was released a few months later, the worst fears of 1960s' diehards seemed at first glance to be confirmed. Dylan was singing joyfully of love – love of wife and love of God – in ways which were unprecedented in his music. 'If not for you', 'Winterlude', 'New morning', 'One more weekend', and 'The man in me' are all unabashed hymns to his woman and in each song there is a strong sense of home and family, a simplicity that can't be found in the public arena. In 'Day of the locusts', apparently written about Dylan's experience when receiving an honorary doctorate from Princeton University in June 1970, public life is strongly rejected. In contrast to the stifling formal public atmosphere of the graduation ceremony, the locusts sing to him of the joy and freedom of the natural life. At the end of the ceremony, he quickly takes his diploma, seizes his sweetheart and heads for the Black Hills of Dakota, leaving the public far behind, glad to 'get out of there alive'. The only song on the album that deals with a broken love affair is 'Sign on the window', but even there the sorrowful, jilted lover curiously claims in the end that the answer lies in building a domestic paradise: 'That must be what it's all about.'

But the rejection of public life is not quite complete on this album. There are the tiniest hints of something else going on. One such example is 'Time passes slowly'. Like several songs on the album, this one seems to be set some time in the last century in a rural, secluded locale. The sleepy life is captured perfectly by Dylan's lazy piano playing, the waltz rhythm and the yawning sound of David Bromberg's electric guitar. The lyrics appear simple on first hearing but on closer study are deceptively complex. They hinge upon the irony inherent in the tendency of a pleasurable experience to speed up time, as it does in the song 'New morning', where Dylan sings, 'The night passed away so quickly,/It always does when you're with me.' But in a true haven experience, one untainted by demands to return to a public life, it is possible to approach a quality of timelessness. Time itself seems to be a creation of the public world and, when we turn our backs on that world, it is only natural that time should seem to stop or at least slow down. Again, as in 'Sign on the window', fishing in mountain streams is used as a metaphor for the slow life-style, as are the domestic scenes of the second stanza, where the singer is courting his lover in her mama's kitchen. The bridge of the song seems to crystallise the singer's rejection of the public realm. But as we listen to the way Dylan sings the lines, it becomes evident that the emotions expressed in this song are much more complex than they might appear on the written page. Dylan's voice takes on a curiously plaintive quality, particularly the last line, 'Ain't no reason to go anywhere', and this makes the song much more than a simple celebration of timelessness. His performance adds a measure of uneasiness which the printed version only partly conveys. There seems to be an undercurrent of distress, which is also reflected in the closing lines of each stanza. In the first stanza Dylan sings, 'Time passes slowly when you're lost in a dream.' Dreaming may have both good and bad connotations, but being 'lost' in a dream would seem to be a primarily negative condition. The second stanza too takes some of the shine off the lovely scene in the sweetheart's kitchen. Dylan sings, 'Time passes slowly when you're searchin' for love', not when love is solid and secure as in a good marriage but during that yearning period of youth when we haven't yet found a peaceful love. So we have to reconsider any facile interpretation of this song as a paean to reclusiveness. This is all reaffirmed in the sadness of the final verse:

> Time passes slowly up here in the daylight,
> We stare straight ahead and try so hard to stay right,
> Like the red rose of summer that blooms in the day,
> Time passes slowly and fades away.

These words, while evocative of pastoral beauty, hint at restlessness and sorrow. In such a timeless environment, why must the singer 'try so hard to stay right'? If he is surrounded by beauty, why must he 'stare straight ahead' and miss seeing much of it? And finally, the fading rose of the last two lines is a clear foreshadowing of death, a most curious concept in a truly timeless world. Ultimately, this song isn't a celebration at all; it's a pastoral elegy – a song written about life in the Haven, certainly, but one which clearly anticipates the need to escape and return to the fair and the town and the Quest. Even in the heart of domestic bliss, Dylan was sending out subtle signals of dissatisfaction, and though it would be three years before he would record another full-fledged album of new songs, the longest such hiatus in his career, there was reason to believe that such a return would be impossible for him to avoid for ever.

The few songs Dylan wrote in 1971–2 clearly reveal the ambivalence he was feeling about returning to public life. In the spring of 1971, Dylan recorded with Leon Russell two especially interesting songs: 'Watching the river flow' and 'When I paint my masterpiece'. In the first he chides himself for his lack of public involvement: 'What's the matter with me?/I don't have much to say.' Though clearly troubled by the problems of the world, and wishing he were back in the city, the singer is content for the time being to sit contentedly on 'this bank of sand and watch the river flow'. He lacks the motivation for a full-fledged return to public life. 'When I paint my masterpiece' goes a bit further. Here the singer is travelling the world, considering his own place among the established great artists of world culture and reconsidering his commitment to his art. But he doesn't seem ready to put up with the demands placed upon a public artist; he wants to do it on his own terms. As in 'Watching the river flow', there is also a woman involved. Here she is represented as 'Botticelli's niece' who has promised to be 'right by [his] side when [he paints his] masterpiece'. Is she his inspiration or his security blanket if, as it appears, he needs her by his side as he creates? Such a need may explain why it took Dylan so long to decide to return fully to public life. He was still waiting for that 'Someday [when] everything is gonna be diff'rent'.

By 1973, however, though there were still powerfully ambivalent feelings involved, the urge to reclaim his position on the world stage was too great to deny. Having moved with his family the previous year to Malibu, California, a move which in itself would help facilitate a return to public life, Dylan and members of The Band made plans for recording an album of new songs and following it with an ambitious North American tour. The album, *Planet Waves*, was recorded in Los Angeles over a mere three days in November. The performances by all involved are stirring and the writing, while tentative in places, shows flashes of the old brilliance, as if Dylan were flexing his muscles after the long lay-off. Most importantly, the predominant theme of the album is the ambivalence about a return to the arena. The subject clearly accounts for the ambiguity which underlies many of the songs. Is he singing to his wife or to his audience? Is he celebrating the domestic life or rejecting it? Is he enthusiastically embracing a renewed life on the road or restating what he hates about it? The answer in each case is probably 'both'. Apparently, though, Dylan is trying to achieve the life structure of Harmony, where the positive forces of both the public and private poles are supporting, not contradicting, each other. Renewing the quest for Truth and Beauty with vigour and intensity while trying to maintain the home and family that had sustained him throughout the hiatus period is a difficult, maybe impossible goal, a delicate balancing act in the attempt to achieve harmony between the opposing public and private poles.

Not surprisingly, this situation produced sharply contrasting images in different songs, sometimes in the same song. 'On a night like this', which opens the album, celebrates a passionate reunion with an old lover, someone other than his wife, someone he hasn't seen in a while. Since the song is the first one we hear on *Planet Waves* we can easily interpret it as a song to his audience, a warm expression of renewed love, couched in sexy language that conveys the passion of his commitment to his music. A touch of ambivalence does appear on the bridge, however, a plea for elbow room which turns up again later in 'Tough mama'. Dylan seems eager to take his place in public, but he's laying down conditions, unwilling as always to sacrifice his identity and personal freedom. As already explained, the negative ends of both public and private poles can deny personal freedom. This song, like several others on the album, cuts both ways.

Throughout the album, Dylan seems to vacillate between strong positive and negative emotions as he attempts to walk the tightrope of harmony. Is he saying goodbye to his wife and the stultifying life of domesticity in 'Going, going, gone'? Perhaps, but he clearly pledges his eternal love to her in 'Wedding song', which ends the album. And what are we to make of 'Dirge', that frighteningly ominous expression of sheer hatred? Is it a song to his audience? Are we the ones he hates himself for loving? Very unlikely, but the song could also be interpreted as being addressed to a woman. And then, how can he contradict himself so blatantly as in 'Something there is about you'? Is this love or not? Is he committed to the woman or not? If he doesn't have to look any further, why can't he be faithful? We can imagine the confusion of the woman, who can only assume that he is talking about two different kinds of fidelity: spiritual fidelity (which he seems to be pledging) and sexual fidelity (which he can't pledge). As he is going back out on the road, with his hand 'on the sabre', he seems to be proposing an open marriage, open at least for him, as the only realistic kind of relationship under the circumstances.

The song on the album which seems best to capture both sides of these swinging emotions is 'Tough mama', a largely overlooked song in the Dylan catalogue. The lyrics constitute the strongest, most sustained piece on the album, and the music showcases some of the finest driving rock of Dylan's career. The song presents the singer at a crossroads, a moment to reflect on the past and the changes that have occurred and to gather his creative energies for a renewed push forward. It's also a time to reaffirm his love to his wife, who will be making sacrifices as he returns to the road:

> Tough mama,
> Meat shakin' on your bones
> I'm gonna go down to the river and get some stones.

Throughout the album, and at other times in his career, Dylan implies that he is doing his work for his woman. Going to the river and getting some stones would seem to be a metaphor for the return to the life of the public artist, to do the work that he is called to do. In the second stanza, he restates the concept:

> Dark beauty,
> Won't you move it on over and make some room?
> It's my duty to bring you down to the field where
>   the flowers bloom.

Again there is the need for elbow room, so that he can get about his work, to find beauty and share it with her. Through most of the first three stanzas he sings her praises, alternating between physical and spiritual qualities. She's a 'tough mama' and 'dark beauty', a sensual lover and mother, but she's also a 'sweet goddess' and 'silver angel', a soul mate and image of spiritual perfection. She is also a survivor, a woman with the strength to make it through severe struggles:

> You came through it all the way, flyin' through the skies.
> Dark beauty
> With that long night's journey in your eyes.

The images from the past are mostly negative, a trail of death or imprisonment for Sister, Papa, Jack the Cowboy and Lone Wolf. But, the woman he is singing to has outlasted them all.

By the fourth stanza, Dylan is ready to talk about what the future holds in store for them, re-pledging his love to her by offering her a 'golden ring'. But for all he says she wears the 'badge of the lonesome road' on her sleeve, he seems to be the one who is about to hit the road:

> Today on the countryside it was a-hotter than a crotch.
> I stood alone upon the ridge and all I did was watch.
> Sweet goddess,
> It must be time to carve another notch.

The powerful sexual imagery is curious again, similar to the language in 'Something there is about you'. But sex here seems to be used more as a metaphor for the creative urge, the intense desire, akin to lust, that drives him to his art. The fifth and final stanza is unique in that it doesn't open with an epithet to the woman. The focal point is now upon the singer: 'I'm crestfallen./ The world of illusion is at my door.' Now that he is ready to return to the road and 'carve another notch', the old ambivalence seems to be returning. He reminds himself of everything he hates about the public life and seems quite aware of the difficulty in achieving the kind of harmony he is seeking between the public and private realms. Is he reassuring himself or his woman when he declares: 'I ain't a-haulin' any of my lambs to the marketplace any more'? As in 'When I paint my masterpiece', he clearly intends to return to the road on his own terms, not compromising with the demands of fans and record companies, but unlike 'Masterpiece', 'Tough mama' asserts that the 'someday' when everything will be different is now. He is stepping into the road, with trepidation, yes, but he is definitely taking the step. Significantly, his closing words are addressed to his woman again: 'Dark beauty/Meet me at the border late tonight.' The lonesome roader is pursuing his art, but wants to maintain the life-sustaining relationship with his wife, balancing the forces of public and private, perfectly symbolised in the border image.

Dylan and The Band went on the road in January 1974, touring through mid-February and playing to sell-out audiences in the large arenas of major cities of the USA. By any standards, the tour was a success, acclaimed by critics and fans alike, but if Dylan's next batch of songs, written in the spring of 1974, are any indication, life on the road was not what he seemed to be striving for on *Planet Waves*. By September, when Dylan entered a recording studio in New York to make his next album, there

were reports that he and Sara were separated and the marriage
was on the rocks. The title of the new album, *Blood on the Tracks*,
clearly reflects the fact that Dylan, though pursuing life on the
road, did not find it a life of harmony. Yet the album is not as
bleakly negative as one might expect. Dylan was not yet into the
life structure of Alienation. For though he had clearly moved to
the negative side of the private axis – his marriage had failed and
his children were out of reach – there is plenty of evidence in the
songs themselves that he still remained energised by the pursuit of
his art. Blood has been spilled, there has been sorrow and suffering, but the overall tone of the album is of regret, tenderness and
compassion, overlaid with a drive to 'keep on keeping on'. There
is surprisingly little anger. Only on 'Idiot wind' does Dylan give
full vent to a feeling of rage over what he and his loved one have
gone through; only there does he seem to drift into alienation.
By and large, it is a curiously upbeat album, a truly great album,
perhaps Dylan's most mature album, in its understanding of pain
and sorrow and its compassion for those with whom it is shared.
These qualities set it apart from Dylan's other work, which, at its
worst, tends towards self-righteous anger and self-pity. Dylan was
in the life structure of the Quest, purposeful and driven towards
Truth and Beauty, separated from his loved ones but able to look
back on them with love and regret. There is an awareness that
relationships are temporal, that suffering is shared by us all, as
illustrated in 'Tangled up in blue' and 'You're gonna make me
lonesome when you go'. Here as in few other Dylan albums
we hear him admitting fault. 'I can change, I swear,' he sings
in 'You're a big girl now', where he also says, 'I know where
I can find you, oh,/In somebody's room./It's a price I have to
pay/You're a big girl all the way.' He has found that there can
be no double standard in the sexual freedom he was asking for
in *Planet Waves*.

But the song which best represents the mood of the album as a
whole is 'Shelter from the storm', one among a set of classics that
deal in one way or another with a man's separation from home.
The song is carefully structured in ten eight-line verses in ballad
form, the first five verses looking backward to the time in which the
singer sought refuge in the Haven and the last five verses detailing
the painful present, before looking ahead to the future. The ballad
form itself places the song in a classical folk-song tradition, giving
it a sense of formality and dignity that heightens the song's seri-
ousness. Beginning with the archaic-sounding ''Twas in another

lifetime', the singer looks back to a prior period of alienation, a period of formlessness and chaos, when 'blackness was a virtue' and he was 'burned out from exhaustion'. In autobiographical terms, Dylan may well be singing about the mid-1960s, the *Blonde on Blonde* period. The language here reflects clearly the negative aspects of the public axis which he needed to escape at the time. The public life was destroying him, making him an outlaw, a wanted man, a martyr. In this state of desperation, he is saved by the woman, who, like some angel from heaven, walks up to him 'so gracefully' and takes his 'crown of thorns'. This is one of several instances on the album where Dylan uses Christian imagery to symbolise his own predicament. In 'Idiot wind', there is a 'lone soldier on the cross', and in 'Tangled up in blue' a stripper in a topless joint bends down to tie the shoe-laces of the hero, echoing Mary Magdalene bathing the feet of Christ. And later in the ninth verse of 'Shelter from the storm' Dylan sings, 'In a little hilltop village, they gambled for my clothes'. This obsessive identification with Christ can be seen as a product of Dylan's intense awareness of the negative end of the public axis. The crushing demands of his audience and their rapid betrayal of him when he doesn't satisfy those demands can only produce the sense of martyrdom apparent in these songs. So, in the first half of the song, he is demonstrating to us, justifying to us why he took refuge in the shelter. To some extent, he is almost apologetic about it: 'Try imagining a place,' he says, 'where it's always safe and warm.' If we could have been in his place, he seems to be suggesting, we would have sought shelter also.

But there were problems. He can see that now as he looks back in retrospect: 'Not a word was spoke between us, there was little risk involved./Everything up to that point had been left unresolved.' That might have seemed like the best approach at the time, but it's not likely to lay the foundation for a strong long-term relationship. The unresolved issues remain and fester: ultimately they will force themselves upon us again, throw us back out into the wilderness. And the singer is more than willing to accept the blame for the failure of the relationship. He 'took too much for granted', he tells us, and got his 'signals crossed'. So he has left the Haven in the aftermath of the ruined relationship and has returned to the road, not in the life structure of Harmony, but not really in Alienation either. For one thing, he still has tender feelings for the woman who saved his life: 'And if I pass this way again, you can rest assured/I'll always do my best for her, on that I give my word.' For another, there is still the Quest, a sense of purpose to drive him onward in search of beauty.

Still, there are elements of despair in the song's closing stanzas, particularly in the seventh, where the singer seems haunted by images of death and of those who might be on his trail again, the deputy and the preacher. 'It's doom alone that counts,' he says, and even the 'one-eyed undertaker' can't escape it. But he isn't so far gone that he can't extend his hand in sympathy, in the eighth verse, to others without love, 'the old men with broken teeth' and 'newborn babies'. He is fully aware that his plight is shared by many. However, the ninth verse brings him perilously close to Alienation. It is the angriest verse on the album apart from 'Idiot wind' and seems to be a full venting of Dylan's anger at the audience who have made him their martyr; but the words as printed differ, at least as we hear them, from what he sings on the *Blood on the Tracks* version of the song. We hear him sing the third and fourth lines as 'I bargained for salvation./And *she* [not *they*] gave me a lethal dose' (our italics). The difference is critical and affects the way we should interpret his attitude toward the shelter she offered him. If *she* is the one who gave him a lethal dose of salvation, then he is singing about the negative aspects of the *private* axis, not the *public* axis as appears on the printed page, and he is emphasising why he has had to leave it. If in fact it is his audience who gave him a lethal dose then he is only re-emphasising why he needed the shelter. The contradiction has to remain unresolved, especially since we don't know how much Dylan was involved in editing the textual presentation of his songs. But we lean toward the interpretation that the last two stanzas reflect the singer's ambivalence toward the shelter, which could very well become too much of a good thing – could in fact become lethal. Our case rests primarily upon the tenth and final stanza, in which Dylan affirms the fact that he is in quest of Beauty: 'someday I'll make it mine,' he says. Though living in a foreign country he is not completely in Alienation. He regretfully wishes he could 'turn back the clock to when God and her were born', but there is the present purpose of walking the 'razor's edge' in pursuit of Beauty that keeps him moving forward.

By 1977, Dylan was divorced. There had been periods of reconciliation and separation since 1974, but the end was, by all accounts, bitter and sometimes violent. From all appearances Dylan was devastated. A glance at *Street Legal*, his album released in 1978, immediately reveals the fact that his mental state was bleak. It is easily Dylan's darkest and most pessimistic album, much more so than its 1960s counterpart *Blonde on Blonde*. Clearly Dylan was now in the life structure of Alienation, paranoid and distrustful of everyone. We would contend that, for the most part, he has remained there ever since. His turning to fundamentalist Christianity in 1979 is best explained as one more attempt to find shelter from the storm and a kind of Haven. But the negative, defensive characteristics of his brand of Christianity were bitterly attacked by many critics and this has seemed only to reinforce his general paranoia and martyr complex. As a result the Bob Dylan of the 1980s has seemed a very bitter man, trapped in his own myth, unable to form meaningful intimate relationships. While his writing has occasionally shown flashes of the old brilliance, its quality is tainted by cynicism, by the absence of warmth, compassion and humour. 'Shot of love', the title song from the 1981 album of the same name that Dylan has several times in recent interviews called the most indicative of his current mental state, is as bleak a piece of paranoia as has ever been put on record. Never has he seemed so angry at his public. The implication seems to be that his life is in ruins, and the public is at fault. The tone of cynicism makes much of his writing during the past ten years difficult to take, but he *has* been able to provide us with some powerful studies of the struggle for the public artist to find true love in intimate relationships. And some of these songs must rank artistically among his best work.

Among these, 'I and I', from the 1983 album *Infidels*, is the most revealing and complex. A stark and frightening trip into the alienated self of the public icon, 'I and I' clearly shows that Dylan still has enormous creative powers and the ability to explore psychological regions within himself that go well beyond most artists. The song opens with a startling confession: 'Been so long since a strange woman has slept in my bed.' Why is Dylan, this very guarded and private man, revealing this to us? Is he playing with our voyeuristic desires to see behind his closed doors? As the song drifts onward, we come to realise that its subject is not only Dylan's private life or lack of one, but also his relationship to us, his audience. The first line helps to suck us right into the trap he is setting. We show our hands, and he plays his trump, setting us up for the amazingly bitter closing lines of the song: 'I've made shoes for everyone, even *you*, while I still go barefoot.' But if the opening and closing lines seem to be cynically directed at his audience, the heart of the song is an interior monologue, a haunting and gut-wrenching exploration of the nether reaches of the soul. And it shows Dylan to be a lonely, isolated figure, divided against himself, unable to make human contact.

The barriers to intimacy are apparent in the opening stanza but at this point it isn't clear why they are there. The situation is obvious. Dylan has just had a sexual encounter with a woman he doesn't know, and in the aftermath he studies her as she sleeps in his room. He gropes for some emotional response to the situation:

> Look how sweet she sleeps, how free must be her dreams.
> In another lifetime she must have owned the world, or
>   been faithfully wed
> To some righteous king who wrote psalms beside
>   moonlit streams.

He feels tenderness for the woman, but hardly intimacy. They are lifetimes apart. He can imagine her married to someone like himself, a righteous songwriter, a King David – but in another lifetime, not in this one. There is no connection between them. The barriers are insurmountable. So, feeling empty and unsatisfied, he goes out for a walk. 'Not much happenin' here,' he says sarcastically. 'Nothing ever does.' We see now that she is just another woman who likely has come to him *because* he is Bob Dylan. Like the others, she wants the myth, not the person behind it: 'Besides, if she wakes up now, she'll just want me to talk./I got nothin' to say, 'specially about whatever was.' Another empty-headed fan, one of us. In fact, she *is* us. The despair in Dylan's voice is deeply disturbing. We come face to face with the hopelessness of his predicament, his entrapment within the myth of Bob Dylan – his ultimate and final alienation from us.

As he continues his walk in the third stanza his thoughts wander to other paths he has taken and the verse becomes a meditation on disillusionment. He thinks of an 'untrodden path' that he once took, like Frost's 'Road not taken'. Here, as in the Frost poem, it can be seen as a symbol of the path of the artist, a lonely path, but one untainted by crass commercialism and competitiveness, where the race is won by those who can 'divide the word of truth'. The next two lines of the song remind us of the strange woman again: 'Took a stranger to teach me, to look into justice's beautiful face/And to see an eye for an eye and a tooth for a tooth.' Here the stranger is the agent of disillusionment, who teaches him to see the true nature of justice and the world at large, where justice more often equals revenge. The use of 'an eye for an eye' is poetically brilliant because it reminds us of the title of the song and the terrifying chorus which immediately follows each verse:

I and I,
In creation where one's nature neither honours nor forgives.
I and I,
One says to the other, no man sees my face and lives.

After each stanza, as Dylan's despair seems to grow ever deeper, we are reminded that he is a house divided against itself. Even the self is no haven here; one side is alienated from the other, until he cannot relate to anyone and reacts to others only with paranoia and threats of violence.

The remaining two stanzas of the song only heighten the sense of loneliness and gloom. 'The world could come to an end tonight,' he laughs sardonically, 'but that's all right./She should still be there sleepin' when I get back.' Again the remark can be taken as a backhanded slap at his audience's lack of awareness toward the world's problems. Like the groupie, we might find that we have slept through the end of the world. The final stanza finds Dylan still walking, at noon-time, still alone, treading through the 'narrow lanes' of life, 'the darkest part', where he can't 'stumble or stay put'. Always on his guard, in a world filled with vipers (as he says in another song on this album) he must keep moving in order to survive. But the division of the self remains: 'Someone else is speaking with my mouth, but I'm listening only to my heart.' And he turns on us with his final attack about making shoes for us, yes, even *us*, while he, forced to walk these perilous and dark narrow lanes, must still go barefoot. It is difficult to imagine any artist so nakedly exposing himself to the public as Dylan does in this sad, sad song, but in exposing himself, he also brilliantly exposes us as the empty, voyeuristic exploiters of the lives of our heroes. There isn't much more to be said on the subject. This is the top of the end.

Where can Dylan go from here? Will his public ever let him step down from the realm of myth? Can he ever let himself step down? Ten years after his divorce, he has not remarried, although he has often said that he believes in marriage. His songs of the Eighties, however, reveal a scrapheap of broken relationships, of grooms still waiting at the altar. Fundamentalist Christianity proved only a temporary relief from a world without love, a world where a hero, like John Lennon, can be killed by someone who loves him. And therein lies the ultimate irony for Dylan. For while he desperately needs a shot of love, probably both the private love of a woman and the public love an artist gets from his fans, that relief, that drug, that shot can also be a gunshot, literally or figuratively, that kills, literally and figuratively. And so the Dylan of the Eighties remains a tragically lonely figure, entrapped by who he is, unable to escape the profound alienation he feels from his public and those with whom he might be intimate.

Notes

1. The song was an arrangement of a nineteenth-century ballad which told of a hanging in North Carolina in 1868.

2. Joel Whitburn, *Top Pop Records 1955–1972*, Menomonee Falls, Wis., Record Research, 1973, p. 138.

3. 'If any one event touched off the present folk boom in popular music, [Tom Dooley] was it'. *Time* (23 November 1962), p. 59.

4. While it's true that the Kingston Trio and many groups like them relied on stylistic formulae, the subject matter derived from the folk music tradition rather than from Tin Pan Alley.

5. Relatively speaking. Top forty teenage music and entrenched rock-'n'-roll continued, throughout the period 1958–65, to dominate sales and listening habits. For a chart of top-selling albums of 1960–71, see Charles Hamm, *Yesterdays: Popular Song in America*, New York, Norton, 1979, p. 464.

6. Morris Dickstein, *Gates of Eden: American Culture in the Sixties*, New York, Basic Books, 1977, p. 137. The discussion of Dylan, pp. 187–94, relates this analysis to music.

7. R. Serge Denisoff, *Great Day Coming: Folk Music and the American Left*, Urbana, University of Illinois Press, 1971, pp. 167–71. For a summary of the controversy see also Stephen N. Gottesman, 'Tom Dooley's children: an overview of the folk music revival 1958 – 1965' in *Popular Music and Society*, 5 (1977), pp. 67–9, 'Folk

songs and the Top 40' in *Sing Out!* (February/March 1966), pp. 12–21 gives a concrete example of the contention which pre-occupied critics whenever the spectre of commercialism was raised.

8. Gordon Friesen, 'Introduction', *Broadside*, 1 (1964), p. 6, quoted in Denisoff, p. 170.

9. Jerome L. Rodnitzky, *Minstrels of the Dawn: The Folk-Protest Singer as Cultural Hero*, Chicago,Nelson-Hall, 1976, p. xvi; and Denisoff, p. 170.

10. Rodnitzky, p. xvi.

11. Denisoff, p. 170.

12. Charles C. Alexander, *Holding the Line: The Eisenhower Era 1952–1961*, Bloomington, Indiana University Press, 1976, p. 290.

13. Calvin D. Linton (ed.), *The American Almanac: A Diary of America*, Nashville, Thomas Nelson, 1977, p. 394.

14. Norman Podhoretz, 'The young generations' in his *Doings and Undoings: The Fifties and After in American Writing*, New York, Noonday Press, 1964, p. 105.

15. Denisoff, p. 170.

16. The Kingston Trio . . . *from the Hungry i.*

17. William Manchester, *The Glory and the Dream: A Narrative History of America 1932–1972*, Boston, Little, Brown, 1974, p. 1038.

18. Seeger was himself advisory editor of *Broadside*.

19. See *Broadside*, 6 (May 1962), p. 1; and *Broadside*, 20 (February 1963), pp. 1–2. Issue 1 in fact printed a Dylan song, 'Talkin' John Birch' (February 1962), p. 4.

20. *Broadside*, 7 (June 1962), p. 1.

21. The *Hootenanny* affair is discussed from the impassioned perspective of the folk enthusiast in the following: Nat Hentoff, 'Hootenanny on TV – McCarthy style', *Sing Out!*, 13 (April/May 1963), pp. 32–3; Irwin Silber, 'A report to the readers: Hootenanny on TV', *Sing Out!*, 13 (April/May 1963), p. 2; *Broadside*, 21 (February 1963), p. 10; Gordon Friesen, 'There's no blacklist in Heaven', *Broadside*, 24 (April 1963), pp. 8–10.

22. Joe Klein, *Woody Guthrie: A Life*, New York, Knopf, 1980, p. 427.

23. Ibid.

24. All quotes from *The Freewheelin' Bob Dylan*.

25. For a slightly abridged version of the Port Huron Statement see Massimo Teodori (ed.), *The New Left: A Documentary History*, Indianapolis, Bobbs-Merrill, 1969, pp. 163–72.

26. Bob Dylan, *The Times they are a-Changin'*.

27. Ibid.

28. Rodnitzky, p. 85.

29. *Playboy* (July 1970), pp. 53–64, 136, 152–7.

30. Rodnitzky, p. 89.

31. John Cohen, 'Joan Baez', *Sing Out!*, 13 (April/May 1963), p. 6.

32. See Teodori, pp. 55–63.

33. Jerome L. Rodnitzky, 'The mythology of Woody Guthrie', *Popular Music and Society*, 2 (Spring 1973), pp. 239–40.

34. For a discussion of the 'militaristic' aspects of the counterculture, see Lawrence J. Dessner, 'Woodstock, a nation at war', *Journal of Popular Culture*, 4 (Winter 1971), pp. 769–76.

35. Liner notes to *Joan Baez/5*.

36. Personal recollection, but see WNEW's *Story of Selma: Songs of the Selma–Montgomery March*.

37. 'Without these songs', *Newsweek* (31 August 1964), p. 74.

38. The term 'movement' has been loosely applied throughout this paper without any attempt to describe its ambiguities.

39. Described in Sy and Barbara Ribakove, *Folk-Rock: The Bob Dylan Story*, New York, Dell, 1966, pp. 60–70.

40. *Woodstock*.

41. Manchester, pp. 1304–5.

42. Rodnitzky puts it well: 'Activist entertainers were caught in a double bind. Not only were they expected to be super performers, but also extraordinary public leaders. As social reformers they were encouraged to pose as experts on social problems. There are some obvious dangers when artists assume public leadership. Not the least is that they may be corrupted by power or its illusion.' *Minstrels of the Dawn*, pp. 147–8.

43. Ibid, pp. 143–4.

44. W. K. Rawlins, 'Negotiating close friendship: the dialectic of conjunctive freedoms', *Human Communication Research*, 9 (1983), p. 256.

45. J. J. La Gaipa, 'A systems approach to social relationships' in *Personal Relationships*, 1, ed. S. Duck and R. Gilmour, London, Academic Press, 1981, p. 69.

46. For example, J. Askham, 'Identity and stability within the marriage relationship', *Journal of Marriage and the Family*, 4 (1976), pp. 535–47; La Gaipa and Rawlins.

47. E. Erikson, *Motivation and Personality*, New York, 1970, p. 46.

48. R. J. Sternberg and S. Grajen, 'The nature of love', *Journal of Personality and Social Psychology*, 47 (1984), pp. 312–19.

49. C. H. Cooley, *Human Nature and the Social Order*, New York, Scribners, 1912.

50. M. Seeman, 'On the meaning of alienation', *American Sociological Review*, 24 (1959), pp. 783–9.

51. Erikson, p. 46.

52. See R. A. Lewis, 'Emotional intimacy among men', *Journal of Social Issues*, 34 (1981), pp. 108–20, and L.C. Pogrebin, *Among Friends*, New York, McGraw-Hill, 1986.

53. D.J. Levinson, *The Seasons of a Man's Life*, New York, Knopf, 1978.

TWO
Tears of Rage

JON PANKAKE and PAUL NELSON
Bob Dylan

Little Sandy Review, c. 1962

In the entire tidal wave of fan enthusiasm that has welled up
to welcome Bob Dylan to folk music circles, there are perhaps
none more appreciative of the truly remarkable nature of the
entertaining, marketable and expressive image Bob has created
for himself than those Minneapolitans who knew him in the days
before he hoisted himself up by his bootstraps to singlehandedly
conquer the folk song big time. Your *LSR (Little Sandy Review)*
editors, who generally love to bask their mossy bones in the sun of
reflected glory, first met Bob in the summer of 1960, while he was
still a student at the University of Minnesota. Bob, who is listed in
official university enrolment records as Robert Zimmerman, was
then a promising member of a group of singers who performed
at a local coffee house called the Ten O'Clock Scholar. We recall
Bob as a soft-spoken, rather unprepossessing youngster: he lived
then at the Epsilon Alpha Mu fraternity house near campus, was
well-groomed and neat in the standard campus costume of slacks,
sweater, white Oxford sneakers, poplin raincoat and dark glasses,
and sang the standard coffee-house songs (two of his best numbers
were Josh White's 'Jerry' and Odetta's 'Another man done gone') in
a skilful but not noteworthy manner. Bob did become acquainted
with Woody Guthrie recordings that summer, listening to all
he could, and first heard Jack Elliott on *LSR*'s copies of the
British albums that preceded Jack back to the United States.
He fell, obviously, quite hard. Dylan left both the university

59

and Minnesota that autumn, hitting the road for New Jersey and a fateful rendezvous with his idol and soon-to-be mentor Woody Guthrie. That was the last we saw of Bob until May 1961, when he returned for a brief, but extremely telling, appearance at a university hootenanny. The change in Bob was, to say the least, incredible. In a mere half-year, he had learned to churn up exciting, bluesy, hard-driving harmonica and guitar music, and had absorbed from Guthrie not only the Great Okie musician's unpredictable syntax but his very colour, diction, and inflection. Dylan's performance that spring evening of a selection of Guthrie and Gary Davis songs was hectic and shaky, but it contained all the elements of the now perfected performing style that has made him the most original newcomer to folk music. Yes, folks, a star was born that night. Bob Dylan was on his way.

Indeed, Dylan's possibilities as both songwriter and performer are so vast that *LSR* doesn't hesitate to say that, in time, with a lot of good luck, continued and sure progress and hard work, he has a chance (although the way is full of dangers) to be our next big-name folk singer and/or folk legend. In time, he may join such vaunted company as Woody Guthrie, Pete Seeger, and Cisco Houston as one of the gods of post-1940 'professional' folk song. No performer that we know has the excitement and the magic that Dylan has with a song, either singing it or writing it. Throughout the city folk music scene, Dylan is absolutely unique.

There seem to be two major reasons for this: first, his Guthriesque cowboy-Texas blues style – the most advanced step yet on records to attempt a universal city style of folk singing which will remain true to the folk, yet also true to the city singer; and second, his great ability to write songs. His efforts here are easily the best we've had since Woody Guthrie sheathed his pen: right now, he is certainly our finest contemporary folk song writer. Nobody else even comes close.

Dylan's style seems to come directly from Woody, with liberal detours along the way through any number of people in both city folk music and White and Negro traditional music. Jack Elliott is certainly a big influence; so is Jesse Fuller. But Woody is clearly the biggest. From him, Dylan seems to have taken not only his style but his whole philosophy of folk singing and songwriting and, quite possibly, of life itself. Dylan is a more excitable, mercurial, less laconic singer than either Elliott or Guthrie. His guitar and harmonica playing, much superior to Elliott's and much closer to Guthrie's, clearly indicates a debt to Woody's old 78s (where the playing and singing is about twice as fast as most of the would-be Guthries drone it today), and the singing on the Guthrie-type songs is almost straight inflection-for-inflection imitation. Yet Dylan is no boring imitator: he has made this style his own, lived with it, breathed it, mixed it with outside influences and personal idio-syncrasies, and moulded it into something that sounds both like Woody's and his own. He has a natural free and easy way with it and is capable of both brilliant good-time humour and great emotional depth. Yet there are some shortcomings: the style is not yet perfected and sometimes goes wrong and/or gets out of control, sometimes becoming painfully over-mannered and pretentious, full of tricks and quirks which don't always come off. Dylan is treading a very thin line and a difficult one: he has taken a city style out beyond limits anyone else has dared to try; he is not afraid to take a chance – when he gets it right, the final results are dazzling, unique and truthful; when he gets it wrong (which is not often), the results are mere self-parody.

Just a note about Dylan's songwriting ability: Barry Hansen, our blues reviewer and an excellent judge of folk songs and folk singers, heard Dylan singing 'Talking New York' in concert recently and described it to us as a new Guthrie song he hadn't before heard. The fact that Dylan's songs ring absolutely true, without a false note, as being nearly the equal to those of one of the greatest folk song writers our country ever knew attests to Dylan's terrific skill.

All in all, *Bob Dylan* is a magnificent debut LP and we sincerely hope that Dylan will steer clear of the protesty people, continue to write songs near the traditional manner and continue to develop his mastery of his difficult, delicate, highly personal style. We'll close with Woody Guthrie's words upon hearing this album: 'It's a good 'un, Bob!'

GIL TURNER

Bob Dylan – a new voice singing new songs

Sing Out! October/November 1962

> Let me drink from the waters where the mountain
>   streams flood,
> Let the smell of wild flowers flow free through my
>   blood,
> Let me sleep in your meadows with the green grassy
>   leaves,
> Let me walk down the highway with my brothers in
>   peace.

These are the words of the most prolific young songwriter in America today. Bob Dylan has sung them, along with scores of songs he 'put together', in coffee-houses, night-clubs, taverns, 'strip joints', living rooms and the stage of Carnegie Recital Hall. At the age of twenty-one he has won critical acclaim, a Columbia recording contract and a clear place as a significant figure in American folk music.

In February 1961, Bob Dylan landed on the New York Island at the end of a zig-zaggy thumb ride across the country from South Dakota. He was wearing a pair of dusty dungarees, holey shoes, a corduroy Huck Finn cap and he had a beat-up Gibson guitar and two squeaky harmonicas. He wanted a try at singing his 'folky' songs for the people in the big city and to meet the man whose life and music had had a great influence on his own – Woody Guthrie. He had first seen Woody in Burbank, California, a number of years before but had only the opportunity to watch and listen from a distance and say a brief hello after the programme. The second meeting bridged the gap of several generations and began a friendship based on the love of good songs and a common view of life.

Born in Duluth, Minnesota, in 1941, Bob Dylan began his 'rambling' at the age of a few months. For the next nineteen years he made his home in Gallup, New Mexico; Cheyenne,

South Dakota; Sioux Falls, South Dakota; Phillipsburg, Kansas; Hibbing, Minnesota; Fargo, North Dakota; and Minneapolis. He dates his interest in music and his own singing 'as far back as I can remember'. Everywhere he went his ears were wide open for music around him. He listened to blues singers, cowboy singers, pop singers and others, soaking up music and styles with an uncanny memory and facility for assimilation. Gradually, his own preferences developed and became more clear, the strongest areas being Negro blues and country music. Among the musicians and singers who influenced him were Hank Williams, Muddy Waters, Jelly Roll Morton, Leadbelly, Mance Lipscomb and Big Joe Williams.

Dylan's first appearances in New York were at hootenannies held in the afternoon hours in Greenwich Village coffee-houses. It was at one of these that I first heard him, blowing blues harmonica with singer-guitarist Mark Spoelstra. There was apparent in his singing, playing and lyric improvisation an expressive freedom seldom encountered among White blues singers. Bob Dylan in performance, however, is more than a blues singer. His flair for the comic gesture and the spontaneous quip, the ability to relate his thoughts on practically any subject from hitchhiking to the phoniness of Tin Pan Alley, and make it entertaining, mark Bob's stage personality. It is not a contrived, play-acted personality. One gets the impression that his talk and storytelling on stage are things that just came into his head that he thought you might be interested in.

Part of Dylan's magnetism lies in the fact that he is not the slightest bit afraid of falling flat on his face. If he gets an idea for a song or a story, he does it on the spot without worrying about whether it will come out exactly polished and right. There's a sense of 'what's he going to do next?' Whatever comes, it is often as much a surprise to the performer as to the audience. Harry Jackson, cowboy singer, painter and sculptor, summed up a Dylan performance rather graphically one night: 'He's so goddamned real, it's unbelievable!'

Reality and truth are words that Bob Dylan will use often if you get him into a serious discussion about anything. They are his criteria for evaluating the world around him, the people in it (especially other folk singers), songs to sing and songs to write. If the reality is harsh, tragic, funny or meaningless, it should be thought about, looked at and described. Says Dylan, 'I don't have to be anybody like those guys up on Broadway that're always writin' about "I'm hot for you and you're hot for me – ooka

dooka dicka dee." There's other things in the world besides love
and sex that're important too. People shouldn't turn their backs on
'em just because they ain't pretty to look at. How is the world ever
gonna get any better if we're afraid to look at these things?' Some
of 'these things' are lynching, fallout shelters and peace. ('The best
fallout shelter I ever saw is the Grand Canyon. They oughta put a
roof on it and let all the generals and big-shot politicians go and
live in it. They seem to like these fallout things pretty much so
let 'em live in 'em.')

Although he can execute some intricate blues runs, do fancy
three-finger picking and play in a variety of open tunings, Dylan
sticks mostly to simple three-chord patterns and a rhythmic, driving, flat-picking style. For him, the words are the important thing
and don't need a lot of show-offy instrumental ballast to help them
out. 'I could sing *Porgy and Bess* with two chords, G and D, and still
get the story across.'

His vocal style is rough and unpolished, reflecting a conscious
effort to recapture the earthy realism of the rural country blues. It
is a distinctive, highly personalised style combining many musical
influences and innovations.

His first Columbia album, titled simply *Bob Dylan*, while
capturing some really superb performances, does not show the
breadth of his talent. It contains only one humorous selection –
a talking blues about some of his New York experiences – and
one other song of his own composition, 'Song to Woody'. With
this relatively minor reservation, the record can be wholeheartedly
endorsed as an excellent first album and also, incidentally, as
a reflection of the growing maturity of the Columbia A & R
department. According to advance reports, the second Bob Dylan
album will contain a good deal more of his original songs, which
usually reveal him at his interpretive best.

Dylan's reception from the critics has been mixed and promises
to stir up controversy as his audience grows. Robert Shelton of
the *New York Times* finds him to be 'bursting at the seams with
talent' and is appreciative of his 'originality and inspiration', while
McCall's magazine regards him as 'a young man with the style and
voice of an outraged bear'. Dylan's reaction to the latter: 'Hah,
they don't even know what a bear sounds like. Probably never saw
one. Anyway, I don't even know if it's so bad to sound like a bear.
When a bear growls, he's really sayin' somethin'.' *Newsweek* says
he 'looks and acts like the square's version of a folk singer' (whatever that might be). A prominent critic privately dubs him the 'Elvis

Presley of folk music'. The latter designation is not meant to be derogatory, but merely reflects his wide appeal to young audiences.

His night-club appearances at Gerde's Folk City in New York have attracted predominantly youthful and enthusiastic audiences while the elders in the crowd seemed puzzled at his style of singing. Several teenage imitations of Dylan, harmonica, Huck Finn cap and repertoire, have already made their appearance in the Greenwich Village folk song scene. Although he maintains his performance is not consciously tailored for the young, the largest portion of his growing following is made up of persons near his own age.

While Bob is a noteworthy folk performer with a bright future, I believe his most significant and lasting contribution will be in the songs he writes. Dylan avoids the terms 'write' or 'compose' in connection with his songs. 'The songs are there. They exist all by themselves, just waiting for someone to write them down. I just put them down on paper. If I didn't do it, somebody else would.' His method of writing places the emphasis on the words, the tune almost always being borrowed or adapted from one he has heard somewhere, usually a traditional one. I remember the first night he heard the tune he used for the 'Ballad of Donald White'. It was in Bonnie Dobson's version of the 'Ballad of Peter Amberly'. He heard the tune, liked it, made a mental record of it and a few days later 'Donald White' was complete. About this song Dylan says: 'I'd seen Donald White's name in a Seattle paper in about 1959. It said he was a killer. The next time I saw him was on a television set. My gal Sue said I'd be interested in him so we went and watched . . . Donald White was sent home from prisons and institutions 'cause they had no room. He asked to be sent back 'cause he couldn't find no room in life. He murdered someone 'cause he couldn't find no room in life. Now they killed him 'cause he couldn't find no room in life. They killed him and when they did I lost some of *my* room in life. When are some people gonna wake up and see that sometimes people aren't really their enemies but their victims?'

One night, two months ago, Bob came flying into Folk City where I was singing. 'Gil, I got a new song I just finished. Wanna hear it?' The song was 'Blowin' in the wind', one of his best efforts to date in my opinion. I didn't recognise the tune at the time and neither did Bob, but Pete Seeger heard it and pegged the first part of it as an imaginative reworking of 'No more auction block'. . . .

Dylan is adamant that his songs remain as he has written them without being watered down. There is at least one major record company A & R man bemoaning Dylan's stubbornness in refusing to alter one of his songs. He wanted to use 'Rambling, gambling Willie' for one of his popular recording stars, but wanted a verse changed so that the cause of Willie's gambling became an unfortunate love affair. Dylan refused on the grounds that Willie was a real person whom he knew and the change would not conform to the truth as he knew it.

Dylan's plans are simply to keep on singing wherever people want to hear him (but preferably not in night-clubs) and putting down songs as fast as they come into his head. The present record is five songs in one night. The latest is a song about blacklisting, inspired by the case of John Henry Faulk. The chorus of it goes:

> Go down, go down, you gates of hate,
> You gates that keep men in chains.
> Go down and die the lowest death,
> And never rise again.

PHILIP SAVILLE
Bob Dylan in the Madhouse *

Personally, I loved New York – and England too – in that period. It was wonderful to see young people truly arrogant. Their ideas were spilling out in design, graphics, architecture, clothes . . . I was involved with film, television and theatre even then. It all started in the late Fifties.

In 1960, I was in New York, doing a television production with Alan Lomax, who was the person principally responsible for my interest in folk music. He was such a brilliant man, so very well-connected. We were working on *Dark of the Moon*, an American play [by Howard Richardson and William Berney], and I asked Alan if he would organise some folk songs for the soundtrack. I was

* From an interview with the editors, London, 10 May 1989.

very into that whole area. We got together a marvellous collection, including 'Hang down your head, Tom Dooley' and 'By the rivers of Babylon'. No one knew about that stuff then. We found field recordings and Lomax brought all these wonderful musicians into the studio: they just came in their caravans and drifted back. It was difficult – you're technically ordered on the one hand and on the other you've got to give people space for their feelings without encroaching too much on studio time.

I'd seen Dylan playing down in Pastor's Place in Greenwich Village, a very well-known jazz club and place for avant-garde musicians on Fourth Street. Back in London, I was preparing a theatrical piece, Evan Jones's *Madhouse on Castle Street*, and I suddenly had the idea that it would be exciting to cast this young American poet in the role of an anarchistic young man. I approached him and discovered that there was this bogeyman, Al Grossman, to deal with. He also had under his belt Peter, Paul and Mary, then the biggest folk singers in America. And now there was this young buck coming up! We struck a deal. Al Grossman said Dylan was coming to Hamburg to do his first European concert. Al liked the script very much, didn't understand it, couldn't understand why I wanted Dylan to be in it, but he'd heard a lot about me. He said he'd pay for the trip back if I'd organise the outward fare.

It was an extraordinary move for the BBC at that time: *I* was there as an independent, working on contract; *they* literally didn't know who Bob Dylan was. I'd brought him over, at enormous cost relatively speaking. I rang up the people from *Monitor* and asked whether they'd like to do an interview. And they all said, 'Bob Dylan? You say he's a poet. You mean the Welsh poet? Well, we'll call you back.' As far as the BBC were concerned Bob Dylan was just an unknown. He could have been someone off the Liverpool docks. At the Mayfair Hotel, where I went to see him, it was obvious he was very excited about the 'new' England. I said to my assistant, 'You've got to keep tabs on him: tomorrow is the first reading of the play.' Dylan said, 'Don't worry, I'll be there.' He wasn't, so we went to get him and eventually he arrived half an hour late.

We had a very difficult time on the days of the camera rehearsal because he would go missing. He liked his smoke and he usually had a fair amount on him. One time, I literally found him under a car two streets away from where I lived. He wasn't irresponsible, just very involved with the present. He had this wonderful way of living in the now, so very appealing to young people constantly being restrained by society, by their parents. A lot of his things were about the immediacy of experience, about life *now*. It was very unnerving to a lot of people.

You saw the arrogance in him because he was quite outspoken and he had strong beliefs which were not easily shaken, even though he wasn't particularly articulate. He *did* like girls. Al Grossman, whatever people say about him, handled his career very well. Whenever he spoke to me, he took whatever I said into real consideration, never gave me the run-around, was always direct.

Anyway, we began to realise that Dylan wasn't able to deal with the dialogue at all. He was quite honest with me – he did find learning the lines genuinely difficult. Being a poet, he felt he could distil a whole mass of prose in one or two stanzas. He asked whether he couldn't write his own part. I think he felt that what he had to say was quite important and he was uncomfortable, as any American speaking 'English' would be. More important was his complete inability at that time to act someone else's dialogue: 'Do I have to act – why can't I just be a singer?' He was supposed to be playing a young anarchist student living in a boarding house. So we began talking about various songs that he could add to the production. I talked to Evan Jones and I asked what would happen if we made his character two characters – if we were to have two students sharing the room, one a rather uncommunicative American who's very articulate in song, the other English, perhaps North Country, red-brick university, the original young anarchist.

Luckily, I'd just met David Warner who was playing Henry VI in Stratford. David was very interested. He'd have yards and yards of words but of course he was very good at words. I introduced him to Dylan and we had two parts. Every now and again the character Bob was playing would chip in with a scat-type song. This would work all right.

One day, as I got to know Bob quite well, I asked if he'd like to stay at my home – I had a house in Hampstead. He was complaining about the Mayfair Hotel being so worried about his appearance, his not wearing a tie, his playing a guitar in the foyer, staying up all night and dragging in groupie girls off the streets. So he came to my place for two days. At about 5 a.m. on the morning of the first night he stayed, I could hear this song – 'How many roads . . . Blowin' in the wind . . . the wind . . . the wind . . .' (*mimes adjustment of chords*). I got up – I had two young boys then and their nanny was up in the top of the house – so we all got up, made a cup of coffee and sat round listening to him sing. I said, 'That's a wonderful song' – this was before 'Blowin' in the wind' really hit – 'I'd love you to play that over the opening credits. Shot on the staircase with light and everything.' He'd written the song in New York, planned it in his mind, but he still seemed to be working it out in my house. Its first recorded performance was on *Madhouse on Castle Street* [broadcast 13 January 1963] and it's an absolute tragedy that the production was wiped – because those bureaucrats at the BBC didn't understand anything about it. The play was very controversial and the blue-suited gentlemen upstairs didn't like that. But it was staggering that he wrote this piece, played this piece. I've still got a bit of tape somewhere off the original soundtrack.

He was making notes on other songs, even including material that became *Highway 61 Revisited*. I remember he left stuff on the table – he wrote in bits of notebooks and he'd put them all in his hat. He was an avid collector of ideas and lyrics and graffiti, a great guy for graffiti. He liked my books, but I remember he'd say, 'All those books. Throw 'em away. You wanna stop reading. Come on the road with me!'

At that time, Carnaby Street was beginning to happen – it wasn't a whole street, there were just three or four shops – and Bob, I remember, tried on a whole load of hats. I think I actually filmed him. That's where he got his image from. He loved London. It was his first visit. I took him around the various parties. He had an interesting relationship with me – and with my first wife, the playwright Jane Arden. They had something of a love–hate relationship. He liked her poetic-anarchic views but couldn't come to terms with her radical feminism. It was a bit too much for him to handle. She was an articulate woman. And he got on very well with my young son, Sebastian. Somewhere I've got pictures of Bob with Sebastian on his knee.

At the end of filming, we went off to a Greek restaurant – they were something different in those days – and we had a wonderful time. I saw him a lot over the next few years. In fact I went to his wedding in London. Al was there and we all had lunch the next day at Rules Restaurant in Maiden Lane. Bob went back to his hotel, the Savoy, and I remember him saying that he was going to go back to Bear Mountain. I kept seeing him; then I lost touch.

Apart from the actual musical qualities of his songs, which were highly individual, there was the influence of Woody Guthrie. When I met him I knew I was looking at a singular American in the Carl Sandburg tradition. Dylan was *going out on the road*. That was the main reason, I think, why he had such an impact on the England of the Sixties. Sort of 'Wake up! You're young and therefore you're *somebody*!' People like Donovan were carbon copies. You saw hundreds of kids hitting the road with their guitars and their mouth organs and their little leather hats and they'd be sleeping rough. It's very rare for that to happen except in places like Ireland or Scotland where there's more of a surviving minstrel tradition. You had this whole new generation of middle-class young people who used Dylan as a role model of rebellion against parental restraint. This is where he was a really major influence all over the world. When I met him he was so very unspoiled. Creating his own world, influenced by very ordinary things. That's what I found so wonderful about him.

Much later, Sam Peckinpah called me when he was casting *Pat Garrett*. He asked me whether I thought Dylan would be 'difficult'. By that time, Dylan had learned a lot, 'sophisticated' himself, *could* perhaps project his own iconic value. I think he is a good actor, not a natural actor, but it's difficult to judge when you're watching somebody who has a kind of legendary status. Richard Marquand had a very difficult time with *Hearts of Fire*. I'm sure the strain must have killed him off. I'd love to work with Bob again, though I don't have anything in mind. I'd love to cast him as a rabbi. He'd make the most marvellous-looking rabbi.

For my part, I've always liked trouble and if it doesn't exist I tend to *create* chaos. I find it a stimulating atmosphere: it can bring out the best in people. Bob Dylan was always ready and willing to confound you.

SUSAN ROTOLO
Bob Dylan *

from *Rock Wives*

The cover photo of Bob Dylan's second album, *The Freewheelin'
Bob Dylan*, the 1963 release that would finally establish him as
a songwriter, shows a very youthful Dylan strolling down West
Fourth Street arm-in-arm with a smiling woman. The woman is
lovely-looking, but she is not, as some might think, just a hired
model. Her name is Susan Rotolo and, at the time that picture was
taken, she was Bob Dylan's nineteen-year-old real-life girlfriend.

When Susan met Dylan in 1961 in New York, he was certainly no
star: he was just a scruffy new kid in town who was not even being
paid for his appearances at Gerde's Folk City Monday night hootenannies. Yet, as a performer, he stood out even then, remembers
Susan. 'He was charismatic. Even though he was one of the imitators of Woody Guthrie, he had something of his own.'

Susan witnessed the phenomenon of Dylan's growing fame first
hand: she was there when Dylan was singled out in a review in
1961 by *New York Times* folk music critic Robert Shelton and was
with Dylan when his car was mobbed by hundreds of fans after his
triumphant Carnegie Hall concert in 1963. Susan Rotolo was the
inspiration for many of Dylan's early songs, including 'Boots of
Spanish leather', 'Don't think twice, it's all right' and 'Tomorrow
is a long time'.

As Dylan grew more famous, Susan discovered that the fame
was affecting their relationship in negative ways and they parted
in 1964. Susan spent the first few years after the break-up trying to
hide from fanatic Dylan fans. Fortunately, enough years have gone
by for Susan to feel comfortable with talking about what life was
like with Dylan in those days: 'It's history now,' she says. Today,
Susan lives in New York with her husband, a film editor, and
their five-year-old son. She works as a freelance illustrator. It's
amazing how little she's changed in appearance in the twenty-one
years since she appeared on the cover of *The Freewheelin' Bob*

---

* Part of a longer interview with Victoria Balfour.

Dylan. When this observation is presented to her, she says shyly that she and her son were walking through Tower Records the other day and that she had seen the album out on display. 'Just for fun I said, "Do you know who that is in that picture?" And he looks real carefully and he looks at me and he said, "That's you, Mommy." It was cute.'

Luckily for Susan's son, Susan is teaching him all the folk songs that her Italian-American music-loving parents taught her when she was a little girl: 'Pete Seeger and Woody Guthrie and Leadbelly – they were all part of the music in our home while we were growing up,' says Susan.

As well as getting a solid education in music (and not only folk, but classical, opera, jazz and blues), Susan and her older sister, Carla, were taught by their parents to be politically aware. 'This was the fifties, the McCarthy era. Teachers, especially, were losing their jobs if they did anything out of the ordinary, so it took courage to do any kind of speaking out at all. I was involved with an organisation called SANE – for a Sane Nuclear Policy. I got into trouble in high school because I tried to collect signatures on a petition to ban the bomb. Those were the days of the loyalty oaths. Even students had to sign in order to graduate. I remember agreeing to sign, since I really had no choice, but I wrote "under protest" under my signature. I was taught the value of our Bill of Rights and the Constitution. To have to sign an oath of loyalty to God and country was against one's civil rights.'

Because of her political activities and interest in folk music, Susan always felt like a bit of an outsider in high school. 'I didn't have too many friends. I was considered too weird. My idols were Edna St Vincent Millay and Lord Byron, poets instead of movie stars.' So she began to hang out with kids from other high schools 'who were like me, who were not part of the mainstream, who were socially conscious the way I was. We picketed Woolworth stores here in New York City in conjunction with those in the South who were fighting to integrate the lunch counters at the Woolworth stores there. We were a bunch of young idealistic kids. It was black and white and everything. We were under no danger in New York, but the people in the South were putting their lives on the line.'

On Sundays, Susan and her friends would congregate in Washington Square Park to listen to the likes of Woody Guthrie, Jack Elliott, and Pete Seeger play – 'a lovely atmosphere for a fourteen-year-old kid,' Susan says. Then, when Susan and her friends got to be a little older, they started going to the hootenannies at Gerde's Folk City. Her friends' activities were pretty tame by today's standards. 'There were no drugs. Nobody really drank. So it was easier for a mother then to let the kid go out than it is now, when there are drugs and all kinds of things.' . . .

In the summer after she graduated from high school, Susan worked at odd jobs, waitressing, working at the five-and-dime, and in the evenings going as often as she could to hootenannies and folk concerts at Carnegie Hall and other places to hear people like Pete Seeger, Ewan MacColl, Odetta, Tom Lehrer and others. A friend took her to Gerde's Folk City where Judy Collins, Dave Van Ronk, Carolyn Hester, Peter Yarrow (before he became part of Peter, Paul and Mary) and many, many others sang. One of the most popular events at Gerde's there in that summer of '61 was the Monday night hootenanny – 'Anyone could get up and play,' remembers Susan. It was at one of these hootenannies that Susan first laid eyes on Bob Dylan. 'He would play with some guy called Mark Spoelstra. And Mark Spoelstra had lovely shoulders. I thought, "God, who's that guy with the nice set of shoulders?"' But it was Dylan's harmonica-playing that ultimately proved to be more of a magnet than Spoelstra's shoulders. 'I'm a sucker for anyone who plays a good harp,' she says – and has been ever since as a child she heard and loved the recordings of a Black blues harmonica player named Sonny Terry. 'So that was the jump. When I met Dylan, what I loved about him was the way he played the harmonica, I loved the sound. He played with an earthiness that was wonderful.'

In Dylan's performances in those early days, Susan also remembers that there was 'a clowniness, a funniness about him. He used to clown around on stage tuning his guitar. He didn't cut the strings, so he would say, "This guitar needs a haircut." He was funny. He had an impish kind of personality, like Harpo Marx.'

After his performances, Dylan would mingle with the audience ('He was just folks then,' says Susan) and sometimes he and Susan would talk. Right from the start, she noticed that there was 'an enormous ambition in him, 'cause he had even said he was going to be very big. I took it seriously at the moment, but I had no idea what it meant. *He* didn't know what it meant, he couldn't know then what fame of that magnitude could do to his life.'

From time to time, Susan and Dylan would run into each other at parties. At a get-together after a day-long hootenanny at

Riverside Church in July, at which Dylan had performed, Susan remembers, 'I really got to know Dylan more. We were kind of flirting with each other.' She blushes, as if it had all happened yesterday. Then, it seems, all of a sudden they were a couple. 'We were working our way into what was to become a serious romance. We were young and vulnerable. A lot of crazy things happened. It is strange to think that so much is made of us together in those years. It could have run its course naturally, but it was shaded and formed by all these outside influences because of his growing fame.'

Susan and Dylan had been going together only a few months when *New York Times* folk music critic Robert Shelton wrote his now-famous glowing review of Dylan in September 1961. From that point on, Susan remembers, Dylan looked at himself differently. 'He was touched by the Establishment. He got a review.' His friends looked at him differently too. 'A lot of people were glad for him. But there was a lot of envy, I'm sure. Everything began to change.'

By the time Dylan had signed his first record deal with Columbia a few months later, Susan could see that he was becoming more and more wrapped up in his career. 'Then he began snubbing his old friends. But it was all so understandable in an odd way. He could see these things happening to him and he wanted to make sure they would happen, so at the same time he didn't have time to just hang out any more. He was working on his image and his career.'

And Dylan was working *very* hard at creating just the right image. This involved manufacturing a mythical background for himself about being an orphan from New Mexico who had lived on the road for a long time and going to great lengths to hide the fact that he was really Robert Allen Zimmerman from a middle-class Jewish family in Hibbing, Minnesota. In Susan's opinion, all this hiding from his real background made Dylan 'paranoid'. 'I guess he was paranoid of anybody saying, "I know who you really are."'

If some people, at least for a while, believed Dylan's invented stories about himself, right from the beginning Susan's mother did not. 'She was smart. I think she knew right away that his name wasn't really Dylan or she could sense, "Oh, this is some kid from somewhere putting on a whole story." And by the time I was going out with Dylan, neither she nor Carla really approved of him at all.' In fact, Susan's mother's nickname for Dylan was 'Twerp'.

Eventually, Susan and Dylan took an apartment together on

West Fourth Street. As a couple, Susan remembers that they could be very exclusive. 'We'd always be huddled together or holding hands or arm-in-arm. In *many* ways, we kept to ourselves. He would never want anybody to come over, he would never want anybody to be around. I don't think I really liked it that much, 'cause I'm the kind who is very trustful of people usually, but I would acquiesce to all of that.' As a result of his paranoia, she says, 'He made *me* more paranoid and distrustful. You take on somebody you're with, their traits, you live the man's life. What a shame,' she says, shaking her head.

While Dylan was working on his career and becoming more famous by the hour, Susan, in addition to her odd jobs, was doing the scenery for a series of off-Broadway plays. One production was *Brecht on Brecht* at the Circle in the Square, then located on Sheridan Square in the Village. She loved the work. 'Bertolt Brecht was someone who influenced me enormously at that time, so naturally I shared that with Bob,' she says. 'Brecht was a Communist and he chose to live in East Germany, knowing full well how difficult it would be to survive as an artist in such a rigid society. This man was in terrible conflict. He couldn't live in the East or the West. In those years I was fascinated by that and through Brecht's works I tried to understand how he resolved that dilemma.'

As she got older, Susan still maintained her sense of idealism. 'I had a strong sense of the injustice of the world and a need to rectify that injustice.' These beliefs prompted her to take a job with CORE (Congress of Racial Equality). 'It was essentially a minimally paid, envelope-stuffing clerical job, but the atmosphere was dramatic, to say the least. There was a man named Jim Peck, a White man who believed in integration. He was on the first freedom rides in Birmingham. He was at many demonstrations and continually getting beaten up very badly. The phone calls would come in from Alabama and elsewhere saying Jim was in the hospital or in jail. All the real danger getting transmitted to the CORE office in New York City. And there were a lot of marches and I probably went on every one.

'The March on Washington in 1963 when Martin Luther King made his "I have a dream" speech was significant in a personal way. I remember listening to King and looking around me. It was wall-to-wall people, no longer were we a small group of protesters. A lot had happened to the Civil Rights movement and to me since the days of picketing Woolworths. It felt like an eternity but it hadn't been that long ago. And those words coming over the loudspeakers, "I have a dream . . . " I remember thinking about idealism and reality. This was definitely a turning point, a special time.'

By that time Dylan had written his first political songs, 'Masters of war', 'Blowin' in the wind', 'A hard rain's a-gonna fall', and 'The lonesome death of Hattie Carroll'. But in spite of her political activism in that period, Susan tends to play down her own part in influencing Dylan. 'It was the climate of the times,' she says. 'People were interested in what was going on, because it was a carry-through from Woody Guthrie and Pete Seeger.'

As time went by, Dylan got more and more possessive of Susan. 'There was a period when I was part of his possessions,' says Susan. 'I don't think he wanted me to do anything separate from him. He wanted me to be completely one hundred per cent a part of what he was. He was tied up with his own development, and it was just his world, his music. The assumption is that the female doesn't really do anything, and he didn't enjoy the idea of me being separate from him.'

As a result, Susan was 'letting go of my other interests. And I was very much insecure and not self-confident. But', she adds, 'somewhere deep down I must have had an instinct to survive, to have an identity of my own, not just as "Dylan's girl". I took classes at the School of Visual Arts, worked in the theatre and also had a waitressing job during the day. I made new friends who knew nothing about my life with Dylan. I tried to keep both lives separate but it was difficult and I was under a lot of pressure.

'It's funny,' she continues. 'Dylan did say to me once, "Never let anybody take up your space." Which I always thought was the most profound thing he ever gave me, one of the best things he ever gave me. Because in spite of what I appear to be, then or now, every woman has the tendency to be sucked in by the life of the man she is with and, in spite of everything that was going on, I believe he was aware of that. With that statement I felt he was acknowledging the conflict I was in; he saw my vulnerability and my strength. It meant a lot to me then and after all these years I still think it's a goodie.'

In 1962, Susan had the opportunity to sail to Italy with her mother and new stepfather, a college professor who 'couldn't believe that this woman he was marrying had two vagabond daughters'. She agonised over whether to go. 'I remember asking

everybody, "What do you think? Should I go or shouldn't I go?"'
In the end she went. Once she was in sunny Italy, Susan knew
she'd made the right decision. She began to think of New York as
'this dark tunnel – dark clubs and bars, and sombre'. Here, she was
also able to get a fresh perspective on her relationship with Dylan.
She began to see that it had become 'too heavy-duty 'cause we
were too serious – too much too soon. He was too young for
that kind of thing and he was pursuing his career, which he was
so single-minded about.' At that point in her life, Susan knew that
she could not be exclusive. 'Something was wrong with the whole
environment. It was fun, we had good times, but it became too
exclusive. That's when I felt that I didn't want to be a string on
his guitar, because I wasn't ready to retire. I hadn't even started
out yet. And I saw that period in Italy as . . . let loose to be young
again. It was in a town called Perugia. It was relaxing and the sun
was shining and I was discovering life again. It was wonderful to
be thrown into this, once I got over the terrible sadness of leaving
my love at home.'

Dylan, on the other hand, couldn't seem to stop missing
her. 'He would call me every day. He called and wrote, and
I remember there was a turning point when he called and I
didn't want to go to the phone. 'Cause I was enjoying life, which
I should have been doing at eighteen.'

In Italy, Susan met lots of new people, including the man
who would become her husband some years later. But at the
time, Susan stopped herself from getting totally involved with
him because 'I did want to resolve that relationship with Dylan.'

So she returned to New York nearly a year later, feeling that
she had grown up and matured in Italy and was ready to handle
anything that came her way. Dylan was still on tour in England
when she got back, but his friends gave Susan quite a reception –
although not the one she would have expected. 'I was hit by all this
gossipy stuff, with people saying, "How could you leave him? How
could you do that?" Apparently he had gotten even more famous.
Certainly he didn't write to me about his fame and fortune and all
the bullshit that was going on. He was public property by then.
When I came back from Italy, I was surrounded by these people
I didn't even know intruding into my personal life. There were
people who were actually angry that I had abandoned him at the
"most important time of his life". I was "the woman who deserted
him".'

One of the people, it seems, who was angry about Susan

'deserting' Dylan was Johnny Cash. Susan, who had always been a fan of his, spotted him one night at the Gaslight and told the owner of the club that she would like to meet him. 'And I remember the guy said, "He'll probably want to meet you but not the way you want to meet him." And I said, "What do you mean?" He explained that Johnny Cash had been with some woman who destroyed his life and he had a growing friendship with Dylan and would probably feel, "Who's this bitch?" I thought, "I'm someone Johnny Cash doesn't like. Oh, shit."' When Susan was introduced to him, he 'just kind of stonily looked at me. And I just said, "You know, I really like your music", and I said who I was, and he just nodded. But he didn't say, "Sit down."'

At another time, at another club, Susan remembers, 'Somebody got up and sang "Don't think twice, it's all right" with such vehemence, turning the song inside out, trying to tell me something and then somebody else, to make me feel real weepy, sang "Tomorrow is a long time". *Everybody* was trying to be his spokesperson.'

But someone must have spread the stories about Susan in the first place – and obviously, it was Dylan. 'It's all his fault!' laughs Susan. 'He mooned in public. He created the image of himself as the abandoned, wounded lover. I'm sure he was having a fine time also. Classic.'

Even though Susan felt the attacks on her were unjustified ('I was not his wife or his property'), nevertheless she was shaken by people's responses to her. And by the time Dylan got back from London, Susan 'was totally confused again. All my confidence had blown out the window.'

Reunited with Dylan, Susan began to notice that there were some definite changes – and not for the better – in her boyfriend and his life-style. 'There were a lot of people around him that I didn't like at all. It wasn't the old folksy crowd. He had bodyguards and managers. Just as Dylan got more and more famous, things got more and more oppressive and there were more and more people around him – bloodsuckers. I was more aware of ambition and infighting than I had been before.'

All this depressed Susan. 'It was all looking very bleak,' she says. 'It was a whole bad time, and I really crumbled. I had a kind of nervous breakdown. I began to see everyone as wanting my friendship and companionship just to get close to Bob. And that means everybody. . . . I was losing Bob to his fame and realising that this was something beyond anything that

I could conceive of being part of any more. I didn't see myself as Bob Dylan's wife. Suddenly I saw it was something far away, knowing that I didn't belong there for some reason, the way his life was.'

So Susan began to wean herself away from Dylan, although they still kept in touch over the phone and occasionally saw each other. 'I went to his concert in Forest Hills [in 1965] when the first part of the concert was acoustic and the second part was electric.' Although Dylan was booed by some diehard folk fans during the second half, Susan, for her part, loved it. 'I guess they felt he was the spokesman for these things and he betrayed them. But the music goes on. You can't stay in one spot. I don't know whether I told him that,' Susan says softly, 'because at that time I was trying to be separate. But I liked what he did. I remember talking to him afterward and I wonder if I was as complimentary as I felt. But I hope so in retrospect, 'cause I really did feel that I did know him then, that I did know what his music was.'

How does Susan feel now about being the inspiration for so many of Dylan's songs? She replies, 'I got a really touching phone call from Pete Seeger once, asking the same question. It's just me and it was part of my life and I had no idea it was this big, important influence. So to think that I had an influence on him for songs, well, he had an influence on me in my life. It's very nice to know if I'm in the songs that are lovely that I was an inspiration for them. People have asked how I felt about those songs that were bitter, like "Ballad in plain D", since I inspired some of those too; yet I never felt hurt by them. I understood what he was doing. It was the end of something and we both were hurt and bitter. (If I could have written a song . . .) His art was his outlet, his exorcism. It was healthy. That was the way he wrote out his life . . . the loving songs, the cynical songs, the political songs . . . they are all part of the way he saw his world and lived his life, period. It was a synthesis of feeling and vision and he made poetry from it. He was like a sponge, he drove in very deep, absorbed all he could, and then let it all out in his own unique way.'

How did Susan feel when Dylan married Sara Lowndes in 1965? 'Well, I knew Sara,' she answers. 'She was a friend of Albert Grossman's wife, Sally, so we were friendly, all of us. I just knew she was a Scorpio and she was in for it. I'm a Scorpio and he's a Gemini, and they don't mix.'

A few years after the break-up with Dylan, Susan married the man she had met when she was in Italy. They lived in Italy for a while where, as is the custom there, Susan kept her own maiden name. 'But as soon as we moved to New York in 1970, I was right away going to cancel Rotolo off everything, because if my name was listed in the phone book, people were going to call, because they used to call all the time. They'd call to find out where he was. There were a lot of weirdos. He attracts weird fans. Poor guy. I don't know how he survived. I just didn't want any more. I wanted to live my own life. I didn't want to be this thing that was looked upon as something that was one step closer to God. "Can you tell me what God is like?" and "How did you like living with God?" It was Woodstock and people were still praying to the great Allah, Dylan. I hated it. I felt pushed into a Bob Dylan identity that I didn't want. My identity for those years was no longer mine.'

Susan and Dylan did not keep in touch. Then sometime in the mid-Seventies, out of the blue he called. 'He was with Lillian and Mel Bailey, old friends of both Bob and me. As I remember it, Mel was annoyed with Bob for calling me up again. "Leave her alone, she's married." I felt nervous, he wanted to see me and I would have liked to see him, but I was uncomfortable for my husband's sake. And I am sorry in a way. Screw it! Why didn't I see the guy? After all those years it would have been interesting. I shouldn't have gotten myself in the bind of protecting my husband's feelings over my own. That is why I value the statement, "Never let anyone take up your space."'

RICHARD FARIÑA

Baez and Dylan: a generation singing out

Mademoiselle, August 1964

When Bob Dylan drove across the Berkeley campus with his songs in a hip pocket and a station wagon full of friends, it was as if the undergraduates had been whispering of his imminent arrival for months. They seemed, occasionally, to believe he might not actually come, that some malevolent force or organisation would get in the way. From north into Oregon and as far south as Fort Ord, near Monterey, college-age listeners had found time to make the trip, secure tickets and locate seats in the mammoth Berkeley Community Theatre. They had come with a sense of collective expectancy, some attracted by already implausible legend, some critical of an idiom that seemed too maverick to be substantial, but most with an eye to taking part in a passing event that promised more than usual significance for their generation.

Each of Dylan's concerts this past year had had a way of arousing the same feeling. There was no sensation of his having performed somewhere the previous night or of a schedule that would take him away once the inevitable post-concert party was over. There was, instead, the familiar comparison with James Dean, at times explicit, at times unspoken, an impulsive awareness of his physical perishability. Catch him now, was the idea. Next week he might be mangled on a motorcycle.

The Berkeley performance did little to set anyone at ease. It often looked as if it were calculated to do the opposite, as a result both of its haphazard form and the provocative nature of its content. There were songs about the shooting of Medgar Evers, the Mississippi drowning of Emmett Till, the corporate tactics of munitions executives, even a fiercely cynical review of American war history called 'With God on our side'. Dylan appeared as usual in well-worn clothes, said whatever occurred to him at the time and sang his songs in no particular order. When he surprised everyone by introducing

Joan Baez from the wings, the students were electrified. Their applause was potent, overwhelming, unmitigated. Had a literary audience been confronted by Dylan Thomas and Edna St Vincent Millay the mood of aesthetic anxiety might have been the same.

To professional observers – and I talked to a good many – this mood threatened to overreach the abilities of the unassisted performers. They spoke of the fragility of the two people on stage, the lack of props and dramatic lighting, the absence of accompanying musicians, the banality of costume. A writer from one of the new folk magazines told me, 'They can't be *that* confident, man; sooner or later they're going to play a wrong chord.' But he was talking in terms of show-business proficiency, while the performers themselves were concerned with more durable values. They never doubted their capacity to equal the ovation and, if anything, they felt applause was a dubious reward for their efforts.

They claimed to be there not as virtuosos in the field of concertised folk music but as purveyors of an enjoined social consciousness and responsibility. They felt the intolerability of bigoted opposition to Civil Rights, the absurdity of life under a polluted atmosphere, and they were confident that a majority of their listeners felt the same way. 'I don't know how they do it,' said a San Francisco columnist, 'but they certainly do it.' When they left the stage to a whirlwind of enthusiastic cheers, it seemed that the previously unspoken word of protest, like the torch of President Kennedy's inaugural address, had most certainly been passed.

Significantly, when Joan and Dylan are together and away from the crush of admirers and hangers-on, the protest is seldom discussed. They are far more likely to putter with the harmonies of a rock-'n'-roll tune or run through the vital scenes of a recent movie than consider the tactics of civil disobedience. Like many another person in his early twenties, they derive a sense of political indignation from the totality of everyday conversation and the media that surround them – a process more akin to osmosis than ratiocination. And because of this subjective approach to the problems at hand, metaphor is better suited than directness to their respective dispositions.

'I don't like the word "bomb" in a song,' Joan said one evening, watching a fire in her sister's small Carmel cabin. The flames were the kind that hissed and crackled, causing small coals to pop and sometimes explode with surprising violence. They seemed to reinforce her feeling that simple, explicit reference to heat and radiation was too easy to slough off, that it never evoked anything more than superficial interest and sympathy. Speaking or singing with regard to megatons, fallout, strontium 90, nuclear deterrents, overkill ratios, genetic mutation, all in so many facile phrases, might have been necessary for raising the initial indignation of the populace, but it was certainly not sufficient. 'People don't listen to words like those,' she said. 'They hear them, sure, but they don't listen.'

Certainly, popular American reaction to these bald concepts had been little short of apathetic. A more meaningful vocabulary was needed to loosen fundamental feelings. Students across the country were helplessly aware of this fact whenever their civil or political protests were met by blatantly bureaucratic responses from public officials, elders and even fellow students. Posters scrawled with 'Ban the Bomb' or 'No More Jim Crow' were invariably treated with a disdain that belied any awareness of the gravity of the causal situation. The students, seeking a more profound language and finding such language in folk music, looked to folk musicians as their spokesmen; and the musicians said and sang what they could. Last year, however, the vivid and topical imagery of a self-styled Midwestern folk-poet finally lent their arguments more vigorous meaning. And even from the point of view of the bureaucrats, this meaning was difficult to evade.

'It ain't nothin' just to walk around and sing,' Dylan said: 'You have to step out a little, right?' We were strolling in the pre-dawn London fog a year and a half ago, six months before he made the now historic appearance at the Newport Folk Festival. 'Take Joanie, man, she's still singin' about Mary Hamilton. I mean where's that at? She's walked around on picket lines, she's got all kinds of feeling, so why ain't she steppin' out?'

Joan quite possibly had asked herself the same question. As much as any of the young people who looked to her for guidance, she was, at the time, bewildered and confused by the lack of official response to the protesting college voices. She had very little material to help her. At one point she was concerned enough about the content of her repertoire to consider abandoning public appearances until she had something more substantial to offer. Traditional ballads, ethnic music from one culture or another were not satisfactory for someone whose conception of folk singing extended so far beyond an adequate rendering. Her most emphatic song was 'What have they done to the rain?' and she was, one felt, more personally moved by the image of a small boy standing alone in a tainted shower than by the implication of the remaining lyrical content.

By May 1963, however, she'd had a first-hand opportunity to hear Dylan perform at the Monterey Folk Festival in California. His strong-willed, untempered, but nonetheless poetic approach to the problem filled the gap and left her awed and impressed. Moreover, by the time she had finished going over the songs he left behind, it seemed his lyrics would finally provide the substance for her continuing, campaigning role. . . . By living the life many university students would like to live, were it not for the daily concerns of textbooks and money from home, and by spending most of her public time in and around the nation's campuses, she has had no trouble keeping a half-conscious finger on an eager college pulse. Young people are very much aware that she drives an XKE and that it has been in the repair pits an inordinate number of times. . . . To most students it comes as no surprise that she is refusing to pay 60 per cent of her income tax, a figure that corresponds to the government's allocation for defence. Occasionally one gets the feeling that people try too hard to relegate her to a premature immortality and the subsequent rumours are in kind: she has come down with a mysterious paralysis and will never sing again; she has been arrested at the Mexican border with a Jaguar full of narcotics; she is living with Marlon Brando on a Choctaw Indian reservation. In what many would call the alarming calm of her California surroundings, the exoticism of these stories seems absurd.

It was to her home in Carmel that Dylan came last spring just after the Berkeley concert. He was on his way to Los Angeles in the station wagon, travelling with Paul Clayton, once the most recorded professional in the folk revival; Bobby Neuwirth, one of the half-dozen surviving hipster nomads who shuttle back and forth between Berkeley and Harvard Square; and a lazy-lidded, black-booted friend called Victor, who seemed to be his road manager. They arrived bearing gifts of French-fried almonds, glazed walnuts, bleached cashews, dried figs, oranges, and prunes. Here again the legions of image-makers might well have been disappointed by the progress of the evening. How could so volatile a company get itself together without some sort of apocalyptic scene dominating the action? Instead, Joan's mother, visiting from Paris, cooked a beef stew. We talked about old friends, listened to the Everly Brothers, and finally got Clayton to do a number of songs that few others can sing with such understated composure. The only overt references to Dylan's music came when Joan said she might want to record an entire album of his songs and he told her, 'Sure thing.'

The college students' reaction to Dylan has been somewhat more complex than their acceptance of Joan. It was clear from his initial entry on the folk scene that he was neither as musically gifted and delicate, nor as consistent in performance as she. Yet Robert Shelton, now the editor of *Hootenanny* magazine, predicted that these very qualities would contribute to his popularity. 'He's a moving target,' Shelton said in New York, 'and he'll fascinate the people who try to shoot him down.' In the beginning, when he was better known for his Huck Finn corduroy cap than his abilities as a composer, he jumped back and forth between Boston and New York, developing a style and manner that brought the manifestation of the pregnant pause to uncanny perfection. Some still found a discomforting similarity to Jack Elliott, or too much affectation in his droll delivery; but everyone agreed his smirk implied a certain something left unsaid and that, whatever it was, if he got around to letting you in on the secret, it would be worthwhile.

It developed that this something was his writing. In no time at all, Dylan virtually abandoned established material for songs of his own composition. The transition from one to the other was nearly imperceptible since he had the good sense to keep his overall cadence within the framework of familiar traditional music. He begged and borrowed from the established ballad styles of the past (in some cases quite freely), from the prolific works of Woody Guthrie, from the contemporary production of friends like Clayton. But the stories he told in his songs had nothing to do with unrequited Appalachian love affairs or idealised whorehouses in New Orleans. They told about the cane murder of Negro servant Hattie Carroll, the death of boxer Davey Moore, the unbroken chains of injustice waiting for the hammers of a crusading era. They went right to the heart of his decade's most recurring preoccupation: that in a time of irreversible technological progress, moral civilisation has pathetically faltered; that no matter how much international attention is focused on macrocosmic affairs, the plight of the individual must be considered, or we are for ever lost.

Such a theme has often been associated with the output of folk poets; in fact, since the time John Henry laid down his hammer and died from the competition of the industrial revolution, they have celebrated little else. But even including the dynamic figures of Guthrie and Leadbelly in this century, no creator of the idiom has ever received such a wide cross-section of public attention. It is quite possible that already, within the astonishing space of a single year, Dylan has out-distanced the notoriety of still another spiritual forebear, Robert Burns. And like Burns he has the romantic's eye for trading bouts of hard writing with hard living. He often runs the two together, courting all the available kinds and degrees of disaster, sleeping little, partying late, and taking full-time advantage of the musician's scene in New York's Greenwich Village where he keeps a small apartment. Using a blowtorch on the middle of the candle is less aesthetic than burning it at both ends, but more people see the flame. He can dip in and out of traditional forms at will, shift temperament from cynical humour to objective tragedy and never lose sight of what people his age want to hear.

This wanting is in no way a passive or camouflaged matter. It is part and parcel of a generation's active desire to confront the very sources of hypocrisy, which in early years deceived them into thinking that God was perforce on their side, that good guys were always United States Marines, that if they didn't watch the skies day and night the Russians, Vietnamese, North Koreans, tribal Africans and Lord knows who else would swoop down in the darkness and force them all into salt mines. Dylan feels a very critical trust was betrayed in these exaggerations. He feels further, in what amounts to a militant attitude, that it is up to him to speak out for the millions around him who lack the fortitude to do so for themselves.

Because he speaks for them, undergraduates in many ways seek to identify with his public image, just as they have with Joan's. They search for the same breed of rough Wellingtons and scuff them up with charcoal before wearing. They spend weekends hitchhiking, not so much to get somewhere as to log hours on the road. I've even come across an otherwise excellent guitarist and harmonica player from Fort Ord who tried a crash diet with Army food in order to achieve the necessary gaunt look. The image, of course, has shifted with Dylan's increasing maturity. Some fans are reluctant to accept his early attempts at playing with his past. Last winter, an article in *Newsweek* went to great pains recalling his middle-class upbringing in Hibbing, Minnesota, and alluding to a prior, less attractive surname which had been removed in the courts. After the Berkeley concert a nineteen-year-old girl in a shawl told me, 'He has a knack for saying what younger people want to hear. It's only too bad he had to change his name and not be able to accept himself.' I reminded her that she liked his music, but she went on: 'People want an image. They carry it around to make their scene look more important. There're so many guys wanting to be something they're not, that Bobby makes a nice alternative. At least he has integrity.'

The seeming paradox between name-changing and integrity is significant. His admirers enjoy possessing a certain amount of private information and using it against him as insidiously as they try to hasten Joan's premature immortality. But he has done something they will never do: stepped so cleanly away from his antecedents and into the exhilarating world of creative action as to make the precise nature of an early history look insignificant. Behind the college students of America today, no matter what their protest against segregation, injustice, and thermonuclear war, are the realities of their parents, the monthly cheque and their home town. *The Freewheelin' Bob Dylan*, as the title of his second album sets him up, lives in a world that is the realm of their alter ego.

But in the meantime the word still has to be passed and both Joan and Dylan go to the campuses to make sure that it gets there. After the evening of the French-fried almonds and beef stew, both of them journeyed into Southern California – Dylan with his friends in the station wagon, Joan in the XKE. There was some anticipatory talk of getting together at one or more of the concerts, but circumstances were not propitious and they went their separate ways. Dylan stayed at the Thunderbird Motel in Hollywood, drifting out to parties and local folk night-clubs between engagements; Joan stayed with friends of the family in Redlands, lying in the sun, going to bed early. She sang at her old high school one afternoon and was moved to tears by the standing ovation. When she did an encore, her mention of Dylan's name brought cheers. That same night, he returned the compliment to a devoted audience in Riverside.

It was during these performances, as with each of their concerts before predominantly young crowds, that their specific relationship to their generation is most unhindered and best understood. They utter a statement of unmistakably mortal grievance against what they stand to inherit as a result of the blunders of their immediate forebears. In the one case this statement is from the source, in the other through interpretation, but in neither is there any distance between expression and experience. To the young men and women who listen, the message is as meaningful as if it were uttered in the intimacy of their own secluded thought.

ANDREW SARRIS
Don't look back

Village Voice, 21 September 1967

I heard Bob Dylan sing 'The lonesome death of Hattie Carroll' in a movie called *Don't Look Back*. I remember being moved by the last stanza without understanding what it really meant. Somewhere in the song I had lost all the connections. All that moved me was the strange intensity of Bob Dylan's climbing up the metre of his song–poem as if he were on all fours, wailing at the world he never made but understood too well. When I got home I consulted a transcript thoughtfully provided by D.A. Pennebaker to assist reviews of his movie, but not for publication. I was startled to discover that I remembered the case from a few years back. It had really happened and I had been outraged, as any self-respecting liberal should be outraged, and then I had completely forgotten the incident. Bob Dylan's song is the only memorial Hattie Carroll is ever likely to have. Her misadventure is too morally one-sided to interest our more stylish moralists. Art Buchwald would find her caning too lacking in parody potential. Murray Kempton would be frustrated by the absence of irony and paradox. The civilised intellect finds it difficult to render a simple cry of pain. Or to respond to the more obvious outrages. Dylan is made of sterner stuff. He made me remember something I never should have forgotten. I am grateful to him. I dig Dylan. I don't even mind the accusatory tone of the refrain. And I am far past thirty.

Why didn't I understand the song fully when I heard it? It

wasn't the fault of the audience. Though the house was packed with Dylan devotees, they were very quiet and attentive during the songs. They obviously were listening to the words. But they probably knew most of the words from listening to Dylan's records. They were educated in Dylan, as I was not. Dylan is not the easiest singer to understand at first hearing, but there is something electric in his performance that justifies a second and third effort. However, some anti-Dylan critics assume that Dylan's fans listen to him in mindless incomprehension simply because the critics themselves are unsophisticated in pop-rock-folk-jazz recordings. It is as if the cultivated playgoer went to a performance of *Hamlet* without any prior acquaintance with the play. (Did he say 'What a ruddy peasant slave am I,' or what? The actor doesn't enunciate properly.) Of course, there is less cultural pressure and pretence with Shakespeare than with Dylan, but ignorance of either is not the best qualification to evaluate either. Dylan's fans are probably more qualified to discuss Dylan than are his detractors, but since the former are usually younger than the latter, it is easy to put down scholarship and expertise as the whims of youth.

Some of Dylan's critics seem to think that the singer is taking impressionable young people away from the poems of John Donne. Bob Dylan should be compared to Bobby Darin rather than to John Donne. Indeed, young people who dig Dylan will probably be more responsive to Donne and all poets as a consequence of their devotion. When I think of Dylan and the Beatles and compare them to Perry Como and the Andrews Sisters and Bing Crosby and Al Jolson and the pop singers of the past, I hold my head in collective shame for all of us over thirty. Kids today have so much better taste in pop singers than their elders did that the human race may still be saved.

Many reviewers of *Don't Look Back* indicated a preference for the personality of Joan Baez. (She smiles more than Dylan does.) I disagree. Joan Baez is a relatively conventional folk singer. She takes the sting out of everything she sings with her very professional charm to the point that she could make 'La Marseillaise' sound like 'My love is like a cherry'. Dylan projects a unified personality as a performer. He is what he sings – warts, obscurities and all. He is certainly not a great musician and it can be argued that he is not a great performer. The value of his lyrics as literature is still debatable, as are the facile shock effects of electronic noise for its own sake. What makes Dylan electrifying is that his art is connected to the wholeness of his personality.

What makes Dylan modern or even ahead of his time is the lack of coquettishness in his despair. What makes him truly admirable is the absence of self-ridicule in his arrogance.

Don't Look Back does Dylan's fans a service by giving them a closer look at their hero. What of Dylan's enemies? It is unlikely they will be converted in the numbers credited to the Beatles after *A Hard Day's Night*. Richard Lester gave the Beatles a showcase for their talents and, although they played themselves, we never imagined for a moment that we were getting the inside story. *A Hard Day's Night* was a self-enclosed movie. *Don't Look Back* seems to be a contrived documentary, but most of the time the audience is not let in on the joke. Even with the transcript, I can't figure out what some of the scenes signify. The Leacock-Pennebaker school of documentary holds that a film-maker should not impose his point of view on his material *a priori*. As the material emerges, its truth emerges with it. This entails a passive, voyeuristic role for the camera. The truth exists; the camera must capture it. Roberto Rossellini attacked Jean Rouch at a film festival for abdicating his (Rouch's) moral responsibility toward the material recorded by the camera.

Florence Fletcher of *Cue* claims that Pennebaker wants *Don't Look Back* treated virtually as a fictional movie, starring Bob Dylan as Bob Dylan. Joe Morgenstern of *Newsweek* and most of his colleagues have treated *Don't Look Back* as an authentic record of Dylan's tour through England in 1965. Nothing in the film led me to suspect that it was being staged for my benefit. I am certainly not going to call up Pennebaker to find out what is truth and what is jest in *Don't Look Back*. The work of art should speak for itself. I didn't have to call up Richard Lester to review *A Hard Day's Night*.

Besides, I don't trust the Leacock-Pennebaker school of documentary. Ugliness and awkwardness are subtly transformed from technical necessities to truth-seeming mannerisms. When Leacock came up to Montreal in 1963 with *Jane* and *The Chair*, the National Film Board people were sceptical about the crudities in the films. It wasn't the usual underground problem of money, but something more insidious, an attempt to con an audience into thinking that something is more real when it is awkward, or rather that awkwardness is truth. The fact that you can't hear conversations clearly in *Don't Look Back* makes you strain to listen to something that presumably you are not supposed to listen to and that makes you 'in' if you listen to it. Even when you can make out the words, you can't figure out the context. What is Joan Baez laughing at? You don't know, man? Well, you're just not where it's at, man. Just sit in your seat and listen and don't make any noise and don't expect any exposition or heavenly-Father narration. All right, I abase myself for the sake of Bob Dylan's very real talent and then I am told all this ear strain and eye strain is contrived to make me suffer for a spurious realism. Am I angry? Hell, no. It doesn't really matter.

What comes through *Don't Look Back* is beyond dissembling. Jean-Luc Godard put it well when he said that Leacock was interesting when he dealt with Kennedy in *Primary* and boring when he dealt with Crump in *The Chair*. In this kind of cinema the subject is everything and the style nothing. *Don't Look Back* makes me want to fill in on Dylan's recordings, but not Pennebaker's movies.

The camera can capture only that truth that chooses to exhibit itself. If there were nothing of the exhibitionist in Dylan, the camera would register a blank. Many truths are hidden from the camera and this is a fact that too many makers of documentary refuse to face. The great ideal of the documentary movement was to tell the truth about everything, but the truth was often lost in a collection of external details. The highest art of the cinema consists of relating what is shown to what is not shown and of defining essences in terms of surfaces. Pennebaker's mock passivity before his plastic material does not alter the fact that Dylan is performing in front of a camera. What Pennebaker records is not Bob Dylan as he really is – whatever that means – but rather how Bob Dylan responds to the role imposed upon him by the camera. Compared to most of the public figures of his time, Dylan responds very well indeed.

THREE

Most Likely You Go Your Way (and I'll Go Mine)

KENNETH ALLSOP
Beat and ballad

Nova, November 1965

Ira Gershwin, who wrote the lyrics for the music of Jerome Kern, Kurt Weill and Harold Arlen, as well as for brother George, once listed several dozen phrases ('eat humble pie', 'upset the apple cart', etc.) stigmatised by Partridge's *Dictionary of Clichés* as those which 'careful speakers and scrupulous writers shrink from'.

The unshrinkable Mr Gershwin then explained that he'd used every last son-of-a-gun one. He owned up to this, he said, not flauntingly but because 'the literary cliché is an integral part of lyric-writing' and continued: 'If I were doing an editorial I might never write, say, "Things have come to a pretty pass", but I like it when it is sung to start the verse of "Let's call the whole thing off". The phrase that is trite and worn out when appearing in print usually becomes, when heard fitted to an appropriate musical turn, revitalised.'

Of course Mr Gershwin, as have just a few of his peers such as Lorenz Hart and Cole Porter, made the basic moon–June crudities look like drawing in mud with a stick. They introduced elegance and abrasiveness, a language of genuine emotional contact, into this fleeting idiom of disposable minstrelsy. When clichés were used, they were used deliberately, with a literate, mocking awareness that pointed up their puerility.

Even so, lyric-writers – finks and fine masters alike – have always steered carefully along the simple lowlands, skirting the dangerous escarpments of the most mildly unfamiliar word. It might strain ear and mind both. Most lyrics are ready-boned, rhymes and sentiments pre-digested for easy assimilation, musical TV tray dinners prepared for warming up and serving on turntable or bandstand.

So what might Mr Gershwin think of such pop song lines as: 'Yonder stands your orphan with his gun/Crying like a fire in the sun' and 'Statues made of match sticks/Crumble into one another,/My love winks, she does not bother,/She knows too much to argue or to judge'? An astonishing change has come upon the pop song – and, most amazingly, at the mass-marketing, chart-contest basement level, where the range of expression has always been rudimentary, not to say protoplasmic.

Those lines are, of course, from a couple of compositions of Bob Dylan, that young American who looks like Dame Edith Sitwell in a Davy Crockett cap and whose ambivalent woodenness gives him the air of having dragged his feet purposefully into the hit parade. Some cutting things have been written about Dylan, the self-made hobo who pads barefoot around his Savoy suite when in London, the folknik philosopher disowned by the stern ethnics for having embellished himself with organ, strings [sic] and – fie! – *amplified* guitar for his 'Like a rolling stone', the pop star who mooches off out of the promotional orbit and, if trapped, signs autograph albums with any old name.

As Dylan demonstrates repeatedly with great hauteur, he is no compromiser. He shuffles his own peripheral and peripatetic way – very cool, very throw-away, very hunch-shouldered and shrugging, not putting anyone else down, but not making a big folk song and dance about publicising *anything* – just writing and doing it his way. And the curious and fascinating outcome has been that he is the leader, down this outlandish trail, of an entire new breed of performers, the individualistic and radical New Wave.

They are different from the rather high-minded and wholesome folk singers who trill bawdy old shanties with antiseptic jolliness. They are different from the Group Era popsters, very showbiz-conscious with their melodramatic rebel uniforms of rags and lions' manes. They are also utterly different from the period Beats, with their excitable whoops and sensational literature. Main Street America hasn't really caught on much to its native-bred Dylan – in San Francisco this summer I heard a disc jockey, clearly baffled by the six-minute, chanting strangeness of 'Like a rolling stone', say: 'That was Bobby Die-lan.' But everywhere the Dylan sound (part country-and-western, part talking blues of the Woody Guthrie

Thirties, part free-form surrealism, a kind of vocal 'happening') is colouring and transforming pop music.

The contemptuous anti-Establishment intensity of Joan Baez is part of it. The Civil Rights marches and student peace corps are part of it. The affectionate comradeship of Sonny and Cher's 'I got you, babe' is part of it. It has even thrust a passionate anti-Vietnam, anti-nuclear weapons ballad called 'The eve of destruction' by Barry McGuire (a sort of one-man teach-in from the other side) on to the public airwaves in America.

Here it is reflected in the gentle, dungareed Donovan (one of our band of raggle-taggle Ramblers who live an impoverished life with sleeping-bags and guitars around our coasts and city coffee bars) with his 'Colours', which so sweetly celebrated life and living, and his 'Universal soldier' [actually written by Buffy Sainte-Marie] protest. And the Dylan style and sound has certainly soaked through into the Beatles' music and composing.

Dylan has originated a movement that is not a breakaway from pop patterns, but an entirely independent growth now transfiguring pop patterns – because at the centre is a brave individualism that strikes chords in the young. The chemical force is Dylan's writing. He has given the lie to the assumption that pop songs can support only the most moronic abstractions about love and the loss of love. His imagery is beautiful and bizarre, an exalted poetry from an outsider's vision, wonderfully wild metaphor piled on metaphor wilder yet.

'In the dime stores and bus stations/People talk of situations/Read books, repeat quotations,/Draw conclusions on the wall.' Dylan sings at a far sardonic remove from the clock-controlled, wage-earning populace. Elsewhere: 'Money doesn't talk, it swears.' And the lovely: 'She's got everything she needs,/She's an artist, she doesn't look back ... She never stumbles,/She's got no place to fall.' He sees pictures in the mind: of 'the beach where hound dogs bay/At ships with tattooed sails'; of 'Utopian hermit monks/Side-saddle on the Golden Calf'; of 'The motorcycle black madonna/Two-wheeled gypsy queen'. His early songs were applied pretty directly to issues and outrages. His 'Oxford Town' was about the tear gas bombs, guns and clubs down in that Mississippi community where 'Ev'rybody's got their heads bowed down/The sun don't shine above the ground'. His 'Masters of war' was directed against those who have 'thrown the worst fear/That can ever be hurled/Fear to bring children/Into the world.' He wrote 'Blowin' in the wind' and 'Chimes of freedom', implicit now wherever voices are raised for human rights and underdogs. In 'Motorpsycho nightmare' he describes, slapstick fashion, the dreadful clash with a Kiwanis Club Midwest farmer. Dylan hoboes in looking for a job, swearing he's a doctor and a 'clean-cut kid/And I been to college, too'. But when, with a desperate shout, he blurts out that he likes 'Fidel Castro and his beard', the farmer throws a *Reader's Digest* at his head and chases him out with a gun, for being an 'unpatriotic,/Rotten doctor Commie rat'.

But recently his lyrics have become obscurer – if you find them obscurer – stacks of marvellous images. In that nasal yell, amid the clangour of guitar and mouth organ: 'She wears an Egyptian ring/ That sparkles before she speaks . . . She's a hypnotist collector,/ You are a walking antique.' What does it mean? What does it matter? It arrows, as poetry should, beyond the compartments of literal meaning and impales; he is himself 'The empty-handed painter from your streets,/ . . . drawing crazy patterns on your sheets'.

Dylan, in 'I shall be free', wisecracks: 'I'm a poet, and I know it./Hope I don't blow it.' He is, I think, the most remarkable poet of the Sixties, who has, incredibly, cropped up in the area where poetry – still a little magazine and Network Three alien to the majority – can become a significant enrichment of the *Ready Steady Go* diet. I hope, too, that he doesn't blow it.

ED VULLIAMY
Highway 61 revisited

Guardian, 10 September 1988

Highway 61 is almost certainly the most celebrated stretch of American asphalt ribbon – at least it is on the European side of the Atlantic. This is, of course, on account of the Bob Dylan song 'Highway 61 revisited'. It was a good enough song: 'Oh God said to Abraham, "Kill me a son"/Abe says, "Man, you must be puttin' me on."'

Bob Dylan spent his youth in or around Duluth, Minnesota, which sits on Highway 61. Last year, the city authorities initiated moves to rename a street Bob Dylan Boulevard; and even to christen a flyover on Highway 61 as it passes the docks Bob Dylan Underpass. The state highway authorities were OK on the boulevard over which they had no authority, but said they could not authorise a sign for the underpass. In any event, the proposals were dropped after Dylan caused people to take umbrage by failing to turn up to a Duluth High School reunion to which he had been invited as guest of honour.

The bard remains more of a local legend in the other town of his youth, Hibbing, which is a few miles to the west of Highway 61. All you need to do there is to show signs of a camera at the gas station before people start asking 'Say, have you seen *the House* yet?' and the pump attendant even takes time out to escort you to the little grey suburban inter-war construction on the corner of 7th and 27th.

In the Main Street Bar, a Vietnam vet called Bennie, who says he has been 'waked up three days drinkin' and stuff' and who rides a motorbike, informs you that Dylan can still be seen shopping in Hibbing while up at his lakeside cabin nearby. 'People think he's just another kid in leathers,' says Bennie, adding respectfully: 'He was the first guy in this town to get a motorcycle and the jacket.'

Bennie assures me that he had heard Dylan – in those days he was Bob Zimmerman – being booed at high school concerts and that 'my sister went with Bobby'. 'Like a rolling stone' was on the bar juke-box – a track from *Highway 61*; so back to the highway.

Duluth is known locally as the 'air-conditioned city' because of its mild winters and cool summers. This summer, however, has been drought summer and Duluth and its section of the famed highway have been thrown topsy-turvy as temperatures reached record highs.

Business in the Great Lakes port of Duluth has boomed unexpectedly, capturing much of the Mississippi's export traffic for Lake Superior as the river dropped perilously low and barges were stranded on the sandbanks. But some of the most threatened farmers in the Midwest are those who work the small dairy farm-steads along Highway 61.

When Bob Dylan wrote his song back in 1965, Highway 61 was still one of the great North–South arteries, the early routes that stretched from Canada to the Gulf of Mexico. Highway 61 still has its genesis north of Duluth, within Canada itself – it threads its way southwards through Minnesota, Wisconsin, and Illinois; it bobs up in St Louis, Missouri, and Memphis, Tennessee, and finally it breaks out across the great Mississippi Delta, navigating through the deep green cotton fields and the heavy, damp, hot air, down to Louisiana and New Orleans, where the land of a continent dapples away into the ocean. It was a proud and mighty highway then, running well over 1,000 miles.

But then came the age of the freeways, the Interstates – the American equivalent of the motorways to our A roads. The result is that Highway 61 now twists and drifts, undignified and uncomfortable, around the Interstate. Sometimes along the way it is swallowed up completely, only to re-emerge some miles later as a tributary. In Bob Dylan's Minnesota, Highway 61 has now been demoted to County Highway 61, although it is also known by the sad name of Old Highway 61.

There is a saying in Minnesota: the year has two seasons – winter and road repair. This was the height of road repair season; you circumnavigate plenty of orange plastic tape to enter the country town of Carlton ('Friendly, Progressive and Home of the Northern Pacific' – the railroad was begun there in 1871). There, at the Cozy Cafe, between the railroad and Main Street, waitress Maria Wenesson and her nine-year-old son Wayne reflected proudly on a state law that had taken effect that very day. Through the efforts of eighteen children, including Wayne, the blueberry muffin had become Minnesota's official state muffin. The State Governor – like Dylan a son of Hibbing – had come up to Carlton to sign the Muffin Bill into law.

The summer of '88 on Highway 61 has been hard for the farmers. Dan Paulson and his family have kept a dairy herd on their land beside the highway at Mahtowa over three generations. Usually, he grows enough hay to feed his herd and sell $8,000-worth on the open market. This year, he had nothing to sell and would have to spend as much as $25,000 to feed his cattle. 'If I was fifteen years older, maybe I'd sell out,' says Dan. 'But I'm still only thirty-five.'

Highway 61 weaves away from Paulson's land through gently undulating pasture and birch woods that should look silver and brilliant, but are now tired and bleached in the late afternoon sun. Despite the current drought, the favourite pastime, fishing, apparently proceeds unchecked. Shops on the highway advertise 'Night Crawlers, Worms, Giant Leeches' on the same unappetising boards as '6-Pak Coke, Breakfast'. But apart from the leeches and breakfast, Highway 61 has now given up most of its commerce to the Interstate which rages alongside it, some five miles away. Thus have the fortunes of the harmonious and genial town of Hinckley been put to the test in recent years.

Hinckley wears all the medals of history. Its wood-frame houses are peeling just a little. The old railroad station is now a museum to commemorate a great fire of 1894. The white timber Lutheran and Presbyterian churches stand elegantly side by side, and teenagers chatter around their parked motorcycles. Railroad tracks criss-cross the little streets.

But on one street corner, Vern Volk recalls the buses and businesses that have either disappeared or taken residence 'up on the freeway there', and left old Hinckley behind when the Interstate came through. 'I guess if the bank and the grocery store had moved up there, which they were going to do, then this place'd be finished,' Volk says.

Before the freeway was built in the 1970s, Tobie's bar and restaurant, on the corner of 61 and Main Street, was a focal point in town and also an important staging post on the Greyhound Bus route from Minneapolis to points north. 'Tobie's', says Vern, 'was it.' On the old site of Tobie's, Jon's Auto Parts now stands. Across the road, the Farmer's Inn is closed.

Tobie's has moved up 'on to the freeway', which is to say it has joined the sprawling development that is effectively 'New Hinckley'. Now there is a new Tobie's, where the hordes of tourists and travellers can gorge themselves on 'a sumptuous 36-ounce sirloin smothered in mushrooms for the discerning gourmet'. Not to mention the Theme Park, the Holiday Express Breakfast Drive-Thru, and the rest.

Interpreting Bob Dylan's songs is a dangerous and often fruitless exercise, particularly the more overtly esoteric (or deliberately obscure) ones like 'Highway 61'. But it seems reasonably safe to say that Highway 61 was chosen in the song for the sacrifice of Isaac, the dumping of 'a thousand telephones that don't ring', and eventually the 'promotion' of World War III by a 'rovin' gambler', because it was such a quintessential slice of the American Midwest along which life was stable and looked unlikely to change much – even as recently as 1965–66. Twenty-three years later, driving off the old Highway at Hinckley and up to the thundering clamour of the Interstate, it felt as though that slice of America had been –

perhaps mercifully – left behind. And it is the same all over Middle America – the deserted town centres with their gracious, quirky wooden buildings on Main Street; and then the bright lights on the four-lane strips, never asleep, and always looking exactly the same – the motels, new Tobie's and the rest . . .

'Yep,' mused Vern Volk, 'if you want to go to have a beer on a Friday or a Saturday, it's hard to get a seat at the bar up there – so many folks coming through. It's funny, I go to Minneapolis and I say I'm from Hinckley, and people just say, "Hey, that's where Tobie's is on the freeway, right?"'

MAURICE CAPEL
The blessing of the damned ★

Jazz Monthly, December 1965/January 1966

The old-time blues were the product of a way of life and expressed a specific American attitude. The way of life – that of the poor Negroes of the United States – was transcended by an attitude of secret but ineradicable rebellion against that society.

Today, the American Negro is saying openly what the interracial code of the blues was 'whispering' yesterday: God's country is the Black man's hell. Sociologically, the medium has thus outlived its usefulness, but aesthetically we are witnessing a genuine transfusion of the blues in various and unexpected directions: from the blues-inflected pop songs of the British scene to the contemporary White blues à la Dylan. In the United States, young city dwellers, radical students, intellectual dissenters are enthusiastically taking part in the Civil Rights movement, the source and impetus of the folk revival. In Great Britain, working-class youths and

---

★The second half of this article originally appeared separately under the title 'The man in the middle'.

home-grown hipsters are immersing themselves anew in the blues, the self-emancipating Negro's parting gift and, in a very real and historical sense, the blessing of the damned.

The adoption of such a rich language by a community of 'absolute beginners' (as Colin MacInnes 'baptises' the under-twenties) has far-reaching implications. John Lennon, Mick Jagger and Bob Dylan have caught the imagination of a wide public for reasons deeper than the ever-present commercial exploitation (empty mines cannot be exploited for long): they are offering to their contemporaries their own version of the blues. Contributing their individual brand of humour and non-conformity to the music's basic form or rhythm, they have brought a fresh approach to the old city blues, transforming them from within into a new, urgent, completely modern idiom. 'The valid if different setting' the Editor refers to in June's *Jazz Monthly* is with us now: it has already been shaped. But this White blues revival is not fully appreciated by the critics, for its initiators are young pop or folk singers and their 'image' is anything but middle class. A just assessment of the Beatles' own brand of blues, of the Rolling Stones' distinctive and aggressively English sound, is clouded by the middle class's mindless revulsion at this sudden vigorous upheaval in its current and fixed notion of 'what is jazz'. What appears to be, at the same time, a 'lower' and more classless social group has the disturbing audacity to remind one that jazz and blues are meant to be enjoyed by entertainers and audience alike, that their function is precisely to make people feel like dancing and free them from their inhibitions. The paradox of jazz, as a cult, is that every time its original popular function is successfully rediscovered and renewed, middle-class 'taste' runs for cover: the spectacle of a happy working class making its own music, against and in spite of the surrounding restrictions, is too uncomfortable a reminder of the actual birth of jazz! The self-appointed guardians of the music's 'purity' take over and the vital breakthrough becomes one more kind of background music: the post-war traditional jazz expires into 'trad' and skiffle into rock-'n'-roll.

The unprecedented vitality of British pop music and of the new American folk movement is due to the momentous transmutation of the blues from one culture into another. The gates of the Negro ghetto are opening: the blues are at last being heard and understood by the young. More receptive than other groups because of their comparative freedom from social and racial cant, their lack of sense of guilt for the ills of their time, they have acquired an insight into the way of life of the American Negro which enables them to use the blues unselfconsciously and in complete sympathy. They have grasped that the idiom expresses a specific way of looking at society – a rejection and a total commitment of the individual to his own style – a defiance. The musical language becomes personal consciousness. With this key, they enter the Afro-American universe, which in turn illuminates and explains their own.

For the blues are simple and they are now clear. Their meaning has been spelled out not only by Bessie Smith and Robert Johnson but also by James Baldwin and Malcolm X. Their spirit is too strong and elemental to be corrupted: the stark, daily fight for remaining alive in a society organised to destroy one is the material and subject of the blues. They can be fused with various other idioms or obscured for a while under labels such as rock or soul: they cannot be overlooked and they survive as truth and creative imagination survive lies and synthetic by-products. They will not become overnight another middle-class fad like Third Stream or bossa-nova: classical or Brazilian exercises in artificial breathing. This recurring cycle which ironically transforms jazz into a meaningless and effete background music for the middle class is the fatal outcome of the 'jazz fan's' refusal to hear what the jazzman is saying: namely, that he, as an individual, will not be anybody's background.

The American Negro is today achieving his freedom. How? By which means? How did the poorest become the richest source of genuine national unity? Sustained by his example, the non-Protestant Anglo-Saxon elements of the country are looking to the Negro for an answer. It is no accident if two of the best exponents of the American folk movement – Bob Dylan and Joan Baez – are respectively of Jewish and Mexican origin. The preservation of the Afro-American identity through the blues and jazz idiom in a hostile, philistine and puritanical environment may well be the bedrock of the American psyche. The Protestant's schizoid dichotomy between White and Black, rich and poor, good and evil, repression and sex, has been overcome by at least one particular group of people. The African genius for sympathy, communion and synthesis has triumphed over the Protestant spirit of exclusion, division and analysis.

The young White who takes part in the sit-ins, marches and freedom rides of the Civil Rights campaign is given a fresh insight into his society. Like the Negro slave in Congo Square, trapped between the auction block and the White preacher, he discovers that the American way of life means selling or being sold, consuming and being consumed by the economic machine; and that the Church contains no Saviour but only a fiery Cross. No wonder he finds it easier to sing the blues; after a few months of insults, bashings and near-lynchings, he acquires the language.

Bob Dylan belongs to this generation of new Americans. Anyone who sings the blues expresses not only himself but also the group he belongs to and to which he speaks of the common past and of the problems of the day. This is, after all, the meaning of the word 'folk': a specific group of people sharing memories and engaged in a collective endeavour. Dylan is the spokesman of a group that is not easy to define, for it is obviously not an old, tightly knit country community but a larger, new and emerging young audience: the White supporters of the Civil Rights movement and the post-Hiroshima generation. These young men are not the victors of the last war but the inheritors of the 'peace'. They are the 'owners' of the void. Faced with this crumbling 'heritage', the individual is forced to choose and decide alone. After all, the fathers have tried literally everything and nothing as yet has come off: final solution, semi-final or apartheid, and Nagasaki.

The new generation knows that the nuclear stalemate has stopped history as a fight to be won and has restored the age-old conflict in the heart of the individual. The ever-present threat of cosmic catastrophe makes his effort more pathetic but more precious than ever. The function of the blues being to describe disaster from an individual standpoint, the medium suits the modern predicament remarkably well. A sad tale has to be told, an unbearable situation has to be borne: man's ghetto is now the earth and there is no heaven into which he can escape. The blues are specifically meant to produce a mood of controlled emotional aggression, so that the shouter is left with a cooler, calmer and more exact appreciation of his true problems. This very modern feeling of helplessness and yet rebellion has found in Bob Dylan, its interpreter.

The strength of the blues is preserved and renewed by Dylan's completely natural attitude. The emotional necessity of his songs' content determines and shapes the style: Dylan's voice sounds angry and genuinely frustrated in, for instance, 'Masters of war'. Certain key words ('children' in the line 'Fear to bring children/ Into the world' and 'I know' in the line 'There's one thing I know') are uttered with a note of furious and passionate conviction. Dylan's remarkable vocal flexibility and his power to load a single word with drama simply through intonation belongs completely to the blues idiom. We are not yet used to such mastery by a White man, which may explain why the uniquely expressive timbre of Dylan's voice – often blurred by the very intensity of the emotion – is jeered at or ridiculed by many critics: this reaction is a kind of unconscious protection against the newcomer's disturbing originality.

The expression of a single emotional mood in one song is akin to an act of instant if temporary salvation; a musically violent effort to protect one's reason by relieving the nervous tension through words set to a rhythmic shout. This pattern, largely unconscious for the old-time blues singer, is deliberate and conscious for Dylan. His situation and targets are not those of a Big Joe Williams but, in the present context of American society, a city intellectual can also be moved to depths of rage and master the emotional wryness and irony of the blues.

The purpose of such songs as 'With God on our side' and 'The times they are a-changin'' is to define a newly revealed strength, to create a mood of defiant readiness. Under the pressure of one overwhelming feeling – such as his anger against the Southern politicians in 'Only a pawn in their game' – Dylan gives the impression of making the effort to decide and then, making up his mind during the course of the song, he resolves the tension by pointing clearly to the guilty men. In 'With God on our side', the emotional involvement of the man in his story ends by the discovery of the inescapable intellectual conclusion: 'If God's on our side/He'll stop the next war.' Most of Dylan's blues end with the necessity of a precisely stated decision: 'Masters of war' concludes with the determination to go to the enemy's funeral and 'to stand o'er' his grave ''Til I'm sure that you're dead'.

The desperately urgent need to invent some kind of human stand in an inhuman predicament is again at the heart of 'A hard rain's a-gonna fall'. Time is not running out: time has *run* out. Directly triggered by the 1962 Cuban Crisis, the song is an attempt to describe atomic death from the standpoint of the living. Yet, even then, an ultimate decision must be taken and a choice made, the only possible one left: the manner, the style of one's own death. In this blues, Dylan sings as if it were indeed for the very last time. It is an effort to gather together what he loves and cares for in front of the approaching disaster. 'Let me die in my footsteps' was the title of the first song Dylan wrote on the same theme, and it conveys the mood of inner resolution: the will to understand exactly what is in store and die with his eyes open. So that his death will have some kind of style and therefore a meaning conveyed by that style. He cannot avoid the ultimate disaster: what he *can* avoid is accepting it, with its futility and arbitrariness. He cannot win but he can fight; the certitude of victory is no longer a contemporary feeling or a relevant attitude. What matters is to be oneself to the last; accept the struggle as it comes, under whatever form or guise, and die in one's own footsteps. This urge to cast the most anonymous event – death – into a profoundly personal choice and individual pattern is also in evidence in Dylan's first LP, *Bob Dylan*, where he vehemently recreates such blues classics as 'In my time of dyin'', 'Fixin' to die' and 'See that my grave is kept clean'. Strangely, this very violence of expression gives Dylan a fresh courage, the strength that is found as an unexpected bonus on the other side of despair: the strength of the blues, which is the power of a truth being faced, accepted and conquered.

Like all blues singers, Dylan is committed. This commitment is a conscious and wilful act of freedom. (The Negro blues singer had no choice: the commitment was imposed upon him from outside and he had to fight every day for his life, his bread, his sanity.) To be committed is to refuse to abandon to others decisions that affect the individual's existence. In a world where so many pressures, machines and systems seem specifically designed to ensure that nobody understands anything that could remotely affect him, it is the individual's determination to take part without prompting in the major battles of his time. These are his only chance to be himself for, if he does not become involved, he will still be used, whether he knows it or not, as a tool, an accomplice or a 'neutral'.

The modern poet, as all writers, is separated from the mainstream of popular culture by a social and emotional abyss. Today, this intellectual segregation is tighter and more complete than only fifty years ago. The progress of mass communications, together with the purely mercantile nature of what is being conveyed, has left the under-twenties with no other means of expression and personal reference than the music of the Stones, the Things, the Beatles, the Animals and the Yardbirds. This awareness of having to start from scratch (so that they do not express anything they haven't experienced for themselves) is plainly and wilfully suggested by the names they have chosen.

In this context, how did a poet like Dylan manage to make himself heard and acquire his audience? By immersing his poetry in the living culture of the blues – a people's music *par excellence*. The abandonment of the idiom by the present-day Negro does not mean that the blues themselves – as a form – have lost their power, but, to the contrary – that the music's meaning is so emotionally shattering to the Civil Rights fighter that he can no longer stand its implications. The combination of poetical directness of the Negro idiom with the personal poetry of a blues singer in his own right could not help but produce a powerful, even intoxicating new form. Dylan has taken the solemnity out of poetry. The poet is restored to his original function of direct story-teller, reporter of events *that matter* such as the death of Hattie Carroll or the legal killing of Davey Moore. In his article of 6 April in the *Guardian* ['Homer in blue jeans'], Mr Jeremy Rundall shows his cultural broadmindedness by comparing Dylan to Homer. But it would be more to the point to compare Homer to Dylan. After all, Homer was the first of the great reporters, his aim also was topical: to ensure that what was precious, brave and worth celebrating would not disappear without being registered, sung and propagated by the human voice.

By approaching his poetry from the humblest level – that of the blues – Dylan has created a new audience to which he chants, talks or shouts in an immediacy and authenticity of rapport that only the blues can provide. For the blues have no existence outside their own performance: one has to commit oneself to open one's mouth and strum a guitar at the very least to become a blues singer. And this private, initial communion between the voice and the guitar is echoed and amplified by the public performance, the communion of the singer with his audience.

Because of the use of the newspaper as a source of inspiration, Dylan has been described by Francis Newton [*New Statesman*, 22 May 1964] as a spokesman of the *Reader's Digest* generation. I cannot imagine a more necessary function. The *Digest* is, of course, one more medium of non-communication that even the word reactionary would not describe adequately. But can one not imagine a good *Reader's Digest* commentator, a kind of Brechtian 'newscaster', with the emphasis on feeding rather than digesting? Is this not in fact the function fulfilled with such complete conviction by Bob Dylan? The vital books, the original sources of information, are not always easy to obtain. Often, they appear to be concealed under the shroud of academic pursuit, and time and money limit drastically the reading capacity of the young. In this context, a singing encyclopedia of modern ignominies is of crucial importance: for the songs help one to remember what our apathy would prefer forgotten.

The conscious use of the blues by Dylan is paralleled today by the deliberate transformation of old spirituals and gospel tunes into what the Civil Rights movement pointedly calls 'freedom songs'. Traditional melodies such as 'Get on board, children' or 'I'm so glad' have been given words with a completely secular meaning and are sung during the demonstrations. We are witnessing an ironical twist of history, a truly poetical justice of the natural folk process. Just as jazz was the result of the cultural taming of the African's heritage through such Western safety devices as church or martial music, the new spirituals are a fusion of the Negro's musical past and of his present-day spirit of militant self-consciousness. This time, the cultural transformation is wilfully initiated by the Afro-American himself and not imposed from outside and unconsciously absorbed. By becoming at last aware of the shape and content of his past, the Negro is beginning to see the direction, the purpose and the ultimate culmination of his present struggle. The various stages of the long repression – New Orleans, Chicago, Kansas City, Harlem and Bop – can now be looked upon as the necessary moments of one single dialectical process. The past has been transcended, for its meaning has been grasped once and for all, and this new awareness of a whole people has changed the function of their own music. Blues, spirituals and gospel songs produced a strictly individual emotional release. The new freedom songs are used as a collective weapon, a means of gathering the community together emotionally and making it aware of its own strength. The aim is now to remember the past, not to forget it. The new function of the freedom songs is thus diametrically opposed to that of the blues. The intoxicating but temporary cathartic power of the latter has been succeeded by an aggressive and tenacious self-consciousness. The group is aware that the revolutionary momentum must be maintained, that the urgent task is to heighten each man's sense of participation and individual alertness. The social revolution's strength is in the new version each militant has of himself. This existential commitment of the free man, choosing and creating his new self by an act of will, must be constantly activated and organised by the movement so that no one will go back to his old apathy: the rejection of the blues and the use of the modern gospel song as a functional stimulus expresses an irreversible historical decision. As Dylan sings in 'The times they are a-changin': 'The line it is drawn/The curse it is cast . . . ' and 'don't speak too soon/For the wheel's still in spin . . . ' The whole song is a description of an irreversible historical momentum and of the necessity for each individual to stimulate this momentum. This feeling of being part of a community on the move, while at the same time expressing his own personal freedom, is Dylan's relevance and fascination: his freedom does not exclude other freedoms but includes and mirrors them.

* * *

The blues record events in the singer's personal history, relating him to his social conditions and giving a direct picture of an individual attempting to retain his humanity against 'a sea of troubles'.

Dylan does not depart from this tradition. His blues are about love, cruelty and courage. In a first group of songs he celebrates the pleasures of the instant or recalls past friendships and love affairs, nostalgically but without bitterness: 'All I really want to do', 'Spanish Harlem incident', 'Love minus zero/no limit', 'Tomorrow is a long time', 'One too many mornings', 'Girl from the north country', 'Bob Dylan's dream' and 'Ballad in plain D'. (This last song is a remarkably complex modern blues, with a delicately expressive vocal tone and an extraordinary precision of autobiographical detail.)

A second group of blues deals with the social and political problems of today. Dylan knows that history is made by individuals who refuse to be objects – from the Jewish carpenter who decided to teach ('Long ago, far away') to the Negro student who decided to learn ('Oxford Town'). In a society where human beings are treated as tools ('The lonesome death of Hattie Carroll', 'Who killed Davey Moore?', 'Only a pawn in their game', 'Masters of war', 'With God on our side'), the individual's unique chance is to sense the changing climate, seize his opportunity, and commit himself to the struggle ('Blowin' in the wind', 'The times they are a-changin'').

Dylan has understood that in this 'torn . . tired . . hungry . . . funny ol' world that's a-comin' along . . . ' (as he sings in his 'Song to Woody'), youth is, in itself, a value. Life is holy to him because he is young and cannot conceive without a pang of revolt that one can feel otherwise. Hence his appeal to a generation that has broken away from the victors of Nagasaki: the Freedom Riders do not look up to their elders any more. The demographic explosion now ensures that the young will progressively outnumber the old the world over for coming decades. Not so long ago, to be young meant a purely potential state; one had to grow older in order to be listened to. The middle-aged is beginning to experience himself as the negative, the lesser; and his example is ignored not only because he does not give one but also because he has lost his audience. He cannot tell anyone how to live for he is in love with death; and Dylan's great satirical blues paint the 'adult's' society as obsessed with profit, murder and self-destruction.

The first group of songs define what is precious: love, however temporary or eventually disastrous, and freedom, the need to move from one landscape to another. The second group points to the dangers that threaten the individual and the very possibility of love. The former cycle celebrates a very humble, almost primitive and unambitious human achievement – the preservation of a small degree of warmth in a universe of hatred. The latter cycle describes a world in which crime has become the accepted 'morality', a way of life and the quickest path to social promotion, under the guise of jingoism, racial exploitation, or free enterprise ('The ballad of Hollis Brown' and 'North country blues' are two superb indictments of the American social system.)

An effort to gather himself together is thus followed by Dylan's horrified vision of the world surrounding a fragile and threatened individual. No longer precious, he becomes expendable, no longer contained in 'love's false security', he is instead included in large, anonymous and murderous syntheses: race hatred, war, nuclear threat, economic exploitation. Dylan is the poet of our modern contradiction and his tension lies in this constant denial of the private treasures of freedom by the public, accepted hypocrisies of the social Leviathan. But it is also the intuition that he cannot win alone and that his own life is, to others, as cheap as that of Hollis Brown: hence the necessity of commitment, of 'sharing the walk' (as Dylan suggests in 'Paths of victory').

There is a third movement in Dylan's approach: the autobiographical attempt at describing his own identity and the painting of the collective and historical context are brought together in songs of decision-making, of choice and resolve. This last movement inspired 'It ain't me, babe', 'It's all over now, baby blue', 'Restless farewell', 'To Ramona', 'My back pages' and 'Don't think twice, it's all right'. The third group is probably the most powerful of Dylan's many-sided output. For, within these songs, the individual faces head-on the tragic ambiguity of human relationships, the

existential knot to be cut if freedom is to be saved. 'It ain't me,
babe' casts away an over-possessive woman; 'It's all over now,
baby blue' rejects another with a ferociously revengeful and
almost exultant feeling of violent liberation; 'Restless farewell'
and 'To Ramona' are imperative statements of individual choice
beyond any self-imposed or social limitations. Dylan is always on
the look-out for the alienating powers of society. To behave as
he is expected to, even in the privacy of an affair, is for him the
beginning of bourgeois enslavement and the germ of all potential
crimes. The supreme betrayal is the betrayal against the individual,
who must never be taken for granted. 'Neither slave nor master'
could be Dylan's motto: better one's own chaos than anyone else's
order. Fear of becoming a square is at the heart of 'It ain't me,
babe' and 'Don't think twice, it's all right'. Torn between sensual
raptures and his passion to be free, Dylan's impact in these songs
is made by the necessity of choosing the next step. Freedom has
to win, to ensure the possibility of the next rapture.

This constant fight for freedom springs from an intuition that
indifference to other people's lives is the reflex of self-hatred and
the product of the individual's incapacity to love. For Dylan the
dialectical resolution of the conflict between authentic private life
and bourgeois entanglements is on the highway, in an unceasing
movement from private to social commitment, and again from
the public battlefield to personal involvement. In 'Baby, I'm in
the mood for you', this constantly repeated and wilful double
movement is described very clearly. The individual's private
experiences are needed to understand more fully the nature and
aim of the political fight which, in turn, make him more aware of
the value and precariousness of happiness. Dylan realises that his
public commitment can only be worth what he is worth; it cannot
be a refuge or an excuse for his own failures.

In 'It's alright, ma', Dylan sings: 'I got nothing, ma, to live up
to . . . ', and in 'She belongs to me', he describes with admiration
an independent woman: ' . . . She never stumbles/She's got no
place to fall'. This conscious tightrope act, this poise between
the impossibility 'to fall' and equally 'to live up to' any given
'ideal', defines Dylan's special tension, his swing – in all senses of
the word – between the two ever-present temptations: to rest or
to obey, to forget the world's tumult in the privacy of one's 'own
parade' (as he puts it in his great song of escape, 'Mr Tambourine
Man') or to abdicate one's own responsibility by being led from
outside.

Pace and rhythmic suspension characterise Dylan's technique – the spare, drawn-out voice (the instrumental melodic line an extension rather than an elaboration of the vocal line) is strongly reminiscent of the Texan school of blues, from Lightnin' Hopkins to Mance Lipscomb. Dylan's way is to take his time, to hold the attention throughout the exploration of one particular subject, from the experimental and light-hearted approach of 'Motorpsycho nightmare' to the complex poetry of 'Gates of Eden'. He has the capacity to make one share his own tension, while he strives to produce the mood that will meet and reflect each predicament. His aim is to remain an individual against the twin pressures of conformism and of a purely abstract revolt, to define and to hold a middle ground between social lies and self-deception, acquiring thus a permanently questioned and constantly renewed concrete identity. The dialectics of change and movement – from the private to the outside world and back again – enrich and resolve his individuality. In 'My back pages', Dylan describes ageing as the need to see the world in black and white (with the old on the side of the angels), and to believe one has ' . . . something to protect' – segregating oneself from the unprotected. And in 'To Ramona', two lines repeat Dylan's conviction: 'you're better 'n no one/And no one is better 'n you', there is 'nothing to win' or lose. To arrive, to succeed, to rest, are synonymous with personal destruction, the triumph of an anonymous and freedom-hating society. Authentic liberation can only be found in movement, in a determined wrench from the 'Leviathan's' encroachments. Some of Dylan's best songs have the exhilarating quality of a ferocious struggle – a fight to the end between forces of nature. In 'When the ship comes in', for instance, a marvellously happy song, the bouncing hymn of victory describes the rare and precious communion of the individual within the revolutionary group, thanks to the impetus of the common struggle.

In 'It's all over now, baby blue', Dylan seems to be forcing the words out of his throat, in the painful and violent effort so characteristic of old-time blues: the shouting, anguished vocal tone builds up into a passionate resolve and rejection. Dylan hits back and frees himself from disaster by *inventing* his own stand. He faces emotional onslaught by *producing with his own words a different, stronger emotion*: a controlled, creative anger replaces the icy rage of defeat. The feeling of betrayal and outrage gives way to the rewards of revenge and self-assertion. The technique of the blues is to change oneself from within by the immediate, improvised and necessary invention of a fresh emotional mood. This technique Dylan uses masterfully. Each one of his blues is an answer: *his* answer.

If one accepts the terms of the existential view of consciousness – consciousness is consciousness *of the world* and has no 'inside' apart from its object – the unavoidable conclusion is that, from his own standpoint, *the blues singer changes the world by the strength of his emotional reaction*: he keeps himself alive and sane by refusing degradation, by rejecting the horror of the world that surrounds him and keeping himself aggressively independent. A self-impelled exuberance replaces the joyless obedience that is required of him.

The world becomes unexpectedly inhabited by havens of grace ('She belongs to me') and love ('Tomorrow is a long time'). At worst it is a battlefield ('It's alright, ma'), which is an improvement on a penitentiary or work camp. Always it is a human challenge, not a God-given fate to be accepted and endured. The effectiveness of the blues is that of a self-made weapon – of a secret reserve of power the individual is able to draw on at moments of stress and crisis.

The critics of Dylan and of what has been termed 'the blues approach' fail to understand that the capacity to experience and describe the American reality is the precondition of any revolutionary change. If the individual is not able to change himself *here and now*, no revolution will ever do it for him. The Negro had to survive physically and mentally in order to begin to think in terms of Civil Rights: Martin Luther King owes not a little to the Big Bill Broonzys and the Big Joe Williamses. To enjoy freedom one has to be in some way already free or prepared by the judicious use of one's own energies for further and more organised struggles. The blues singer's supreme concern is the preservation and renewal of his energy and courage. He knows that if he gives up, his life will be literally stolen from him and he will become an expendable pawn. The blues are nothing less than the constant re-affirmation and self-creation of the individual in the abyss of extreme and total oppression. Where others are content to be led by 'supermen', or to abdicate their freedom in return for a promise of heaven or the millennium, the blues singer knows that the real victory is the one he can feel in the beat of his own pulse.

Dylan responds to threats and challenges at the level of his emotions before reason or habit blunt the edge of his anger or the thrust of his sympathetic imagination. His voice's weary irony manages to catch and to project this emotional conviction in a manner hitherto unknown in a White man. Above all, his reactions are not only quick and spontaneous, they are also effective and relevant. There is a time to dodge ('Subterranean homesick blues'), a time for awe and admiration ('She belongs to me', 'Love minus zero/no limit'), a time for escape ('Mr Tambourine Man'), a time to stand up ('Masters of war'), a time to decide ('Restless farewell'). And there is, always, a time to move, to change, to go away, to refuse to be imprisoned in the terms of somebody else's dilemma and to invent instead and conquer one's own individuality.

Dylan's songs are an attempt to explore a middle road between the blind obedience demanded by the state and the refuge into private dreams or 'pure' poetry. The trick that absorbs Dylan's attention – his vigilance – is the way society manages not only to convince one that 'God is on your side', but also that God is within oneself – as an investment to be protected. This fear to be found worthless is the lever society pulls each time the individual is needed to keep jingoism alive and to feed racial or social competition. Dylan refuses to reject one term in favour of the other. For him there is no existential difference between private and public commitments. The individual is flattered by the State when he is needed (the Beatles get the MBE) and the world around him gets correspondingly unworthy (nobody works hard enough, not enough exports, etc.). But if the existing order has to be preserved, the private man is quickly turned into a potential scapegoat and the basic human mainsprings – fear, love, hatred – become buttons for our 'masters' to manipulate unfailingly. The individual can no longer experience anything on his own terms, for his own ends. In 'Chimes of freedom' or 'When the ship comes in', Dylan refuses the dichotomy between himself and the world. By the all-embracing movement of his imagination, he makes himself the mouthpiece of universal suffering in 'Chimes of freedom', and of universal liberation in 'When the ship comes in'. In 'A hard rain's a-gonna fall', he identifies himself with universal destruction. In his song, the imminence of death suppresses in Dylan the sense of his own future: he can no longer look forward, so he looks outwards in a last effort to embrace what he is going to lose. In this moment where his own fear reflects so many others, the cosmos invades his consciousness: the dying world feels his emptiness to the brink. 'A hard rain's a-gonna fall' is the song of a man who intoxicates himself with a proliferation of cares – in which he loses himself to forget the unbearable actuality of the threat.

Dylan has been referred to as an 'anti-artist' by Ewan MacColl [*Melody Maker*, 18 September 1965]. I do not think that Dylan would regard the expression as a slur: self-betrayal can be the price the artist has to pay to achieve formal perfection. A blues singer does not want to be mistaken for one of ' . . . the guardians and protectors of the mind . . . ' so scornfully dismissed in 'Chimes of freedom'. Authority and living culture cannot mix, however skilful the attempt; and today the artist has inherited something of the priest's failing powers. All that matters to Dylan is the transformation of images and rhythm into life-energy for himself – so that he can remain 'his own man'. Art does not achieve salvation and beauty is a lie fed on lives and unpaid labour. Effective salvation has to be fought for daily: there is the lesson of the blues. Their aim is to keep the individual's instincts alive and aware in the unceasing fight that is his condition: a purely secular and physical endeavour compared to which any 'spiritual', religious or even artistic project would be an escape and a mockery. The blues are not an art form. They are a cunning emotional device, instant analysis, a way to create, save and store energy, the violent rejection of damaging emotions and their replacement by creative ones.

If there appears to be a mythical element in Dylan's personality, it springs solely from his American context, where any deviation from conformity requires rare courage and gives heroic proportions to the simplest act of defiance. The dissenter's stature and style are, in themselves, a comment on the strength of the order he opposes.

Each society has the rebels it deserves.

FRITZ WERNER HAVER

All these people that you mention . . .

Allen Ginsberg calls them 'chains of flashing images'. They pile up in Bob Dylan's surrealist songs of this period – colourful, bewildering figures tripping through fantastical landscapes. Anarchistic poetry replaces appeals to senators and congressmen as Dylan ceases to be a singer of newspaper headlines. But his surrealism must be viewed against the social upheavals of the mid-Sixties. Without the hippie and anti-war movements, songs like 'Desolation Row' or 'Ballad of a thin man' would not have been possible – and vice versa. Side-stepping a detailed examination of those years, it's possible to find some order in those people that he mentions. To analyse, categorise, classify and simplify. To rearrange their faces and give them all another name . . .

All the authorities they just stand around and boast

The early 'Song to Woody' divides Dylan's society into 'paupers and peasants' on the one hand and 'princes and kings' on the other. These members of the aristocracy symbolise the political establishment, the people in power. Some years later, Dylan tells us about 'The kings of Tyrus with their convict list' in 'Sad-eyed lady of the lowlands' or that 'king of the Philistines' in 'Tombstone blues'. But already 'Gates of Eden' had shown quite a different picture: 'paupers change possessions/Each one wishing for what the other has got/And the princess and the prince/Discuss what's real and what is not . . . ' They are no longer the people in power, but belong to a social class that has lost contact with real life. Just like that 'princess on the steeple' in her fairy-tale world of 'Like a rolling stone' who has never learned 'how to live on the street' and now has 'to get used to it'. Does Dylan feel sorry for her? Just listen to some of his versions and find out – just as Betsy Bowden did [in *Performed Literature*].

It was not until the late Seventies that Dylan, in 'Slow Train', condemned those 'men stealers talkin' in the name of religion'. The clerical establishment was not that important to him in the mid-Sixties – although in 'It's alright, ma (I'm only bleeding)' 'preachers preach of evil fates' and in 'Stuck inside of Mobile (with the Memphis blues again)' we meet the baffled clergyman with 'twenty pounds of headlines/Stapled to his chest'. We had to wait some time until hearing about 'The ballad of Frankie Lee and Judas Priest' or – in 'Idiot wind' – about the priest who 'wore black on the seventh day and sat stone-faced while the building burned'. That was all he could do!

In the Sixties, it was the 'Masters of war' that Dylan cared about and fought against, the 'fallout shelter sellers' in 'Playboys and playgirls', the holders of economic power. It is not so much the 'farmers and the businessmen' ('Sad-eyed lady of the lowlands') or even the businessmen that drink his wine ('All along the watchtower') who are criticised by Dylan. Rather, the tycoons from the war industry – like the 'roving gambler' and his 'promoter' that want to start a Third World War out on Highway 61. There are greasy, gloomy figures like the 'pawnbroker' and the 'landlord' in 'She's your lover now' and a Dylan character who embraces them all: the 'guilty undertaker' of 'I want you', who in 1978 became a 'gypsy undertaker'. In 'Shelter from the storm' – after Dylan's country-and-western period – there's 'the one-eyed undertaker, he blows a futile horn'. And even in 'Blind Willie McTell' from 1983, 'the undertaker's bell' can still be heard. In this symbolic figure, different associations are melded together – economic power, capitalism, darkness, death, cheating. Just think of that scene in the funeral parlour in 'Bob Dylan's 115th dream'.

Another powerful Dylan character is the doctor, be it the rambling 'country doctor' of 'Love minus zero/no limit' or good old 'Dr Filth' treating his 'sexless patients' in 'Desolation Row'. Can we expect any help from a doctor who, in 'Tombstone blues', tells 'the hysterical bride' (who says, 'I've just been made'), 'My advice is to not let the boys in'? Dylan's doctors are cynical traitors – like the one in 'Just like Tom Thumb's blues': 'And my best friend, my doctor/Won't even say what it is I've got'. This line is taken up again in 'Sitting on a barbed-wire fence': 'Well, this Arabian doctor came in, gave me a shot/But wouldn't tell me if what I had would last . . . ' And in 'Leopard-skin pill-box hat' the narrator tells his girl: 'Well, I asked the doctor if I could see you/It's bad for your health, he said/Yes, I disobeyed his orders/I came to see you/But I found him there instead . . . ' Powerful, treacherous doctors who have secret knowledge and who keep their hands on the drugs.

There's no use talking about the Establishment if you leave out the State and its agents. Dylan did not. From his earliest years Dylan mistrusted judges – in 'The death of Emmett Till' or 'The lonesome death of Hattie Carroll', the 'old lady judges' in 'It's alright, ma (I'm only bleeding)'. And in 'Most likely you go your way (and I'll go mine)', a Salvador Dali kind of judge is 'badly built/And he walks on stilts/Watch out he don't fall on you!'

So, by the mid-Sixties, Dylan had stopped his moral appeals to the State and started making fun, anarchistic fun, especially of the police: 'the heat' and 'the plain clothes' in 'Subterranean homesick blues', 'the cops' in 'Just like Tom Thumb's blues', 'the blind commissioner' with his 'riot squad' and 'all the agents/And the superhuman crew' who 'Come out and round up everyone/That knows more than they do' in 'Desolation Row'. They are often shown as silly – 'crazy as a loon' in 'Bob Dylan's 115th dream'. And the holders of political power who give orders to those agents seem to be no more intelligent. Certainly not the 'city fathers' who elected Jack the Ripper 'head of the chamber of commerce' in 'Tombstone blues' and surely not the 'drunken politician' who 'lcaps/Upon the street where mothers weep' in 'I want you'. 'Now the senator came down here,' Dylan tells us in 'Stuck inside of Mobile (with the Memphis blues again)', 'Showing ev'ryone his gun,/Handing out free tickets/To the wedding of his son . . . ' Many of those characters and institutions are definitely American: the 'Welfare Department' in 'Highway 61 revisited', the 'National Bank' in 'Tombstone blues', the 'National Guard' in 'Maggie's farm'. Dylan famously summed up his position in 'It's alright, ma': ' . . . even the president of the United States/Sometimes must have/To stand naked.'

Last but not least – Dylan busily undermined another fundamental of society: the family. 'Grandpa died last week/And now he's buried in the rocks,' he sings in 'Stuck inside of Mobile'. 'Mama's in the fact'ry/She ain't got no shoes/Daddy's in the alley/He's lookin' for the fuse,' he tells us in 'Tombstone blues'. 'Your mama she's a-hidin'/Inside the icebox' while 'daddy walks in wearin'/A Napoleon Bonaparte mask' – you'd better be 'On the road again', he suggests.

'Now all the authorities/They just stand around and boast,'

Dylan sings in 'Just like Tom Thumb's blues'. These authorities, these people in power in mid-Sixties' society are wearing masks. The king and queen, prince and princess, clergymen, doctors, professors and judges – all turn into mysterious, cynical caricatures. No use having any faith in *them*. Brutal, hungry for power and really rather silly – that is how the representatives of State and society are characterised and caricatured. It's a dark and gloomy picture that Dylan paints. But in the Sixties there was also a movement against the so-called Establishment, and that movement is also reflected in Dylan's lyrics of those years.

The circus is in town

Mr Jones is in trouble. Just who is this character in 'Ballad of a thin man' – a journalist, a homosexual intellectual, or simply that 'fella that came into a truck stop once'? I think he's just a 'man on the street', a well-educated member of the bourgeoisie who finds himself the victim of a burlesque show. The whole story seems to be a dream – or a nightmare. Mr Jones has lost his way – 'Is this where it is?' – and he has also lost the security of apperception and of property – 'What's mine?' Sexual events confuse him – a naked man with his 'pencil' in his hand. But who are these people who are getting poor Mr Jones in trouble? The key is in the third stanza: 'How does it feel/To be such a freak?' The freaks and geeks, the 'one-eyed midget', the 'sword-swallower' – they represent the puzzling people of the Counterculture. Colourful, radical figures who do not accept the values of bourgeois life – property, prudery and good behaviour – they symbolise something Mr Jones is deeply afraid of: freedom.

Such 'freaks' appear in many of Dylan's mid-Sixties songs. In 'It's all over now, baby blue' we meet the 'empty-handed painter', the 'orphan', the 'gamblers' and the 'vagabond who's rapping at your door'. Each represents a new way of life that is free but has about it a bitter taste of loneliness as well. The outward appearance of such Counterculture figures was supposed to be new and meaningful, a protest against industrial fashion and the demands of the 'authorities': long hair, picturesque beards, colourful, worn-out hippie clothes. Dylan's freaks prefer ragged clothes – like that 'vagabond' in the 'clothes that you once wore', 'Napoleon in rags' or a combination of two Dylan elements – the 'ragged clown behind'.

'Mr Tambourine Man' suggests also the importance of music as an element uniting all those freewheeling freaks. In addition to the eponymous 'Tambourine Man' lots of other musicians appear – the 'pied piper', 'Gypsy Davey', the 'fiddler'. But the most important character in that whole group is the clown. 'Fifteen jugglers' in 'Obviously five believers', the 'jugglers and the clowns' in 'Like a rolling stone', 'all the clowns that you have commissioned' in 'Queen Jane approximately'. Dylan's clowns dance to the music and are 'circled by the circus sands'. They believe in fortune-telling gypsies and 'the rainman' with his 'magic wand' who, just like 'Mr Tambourine Man', could be the provider of some mysterious and illegal substance.

'An' I walked my road an' sung my song/Like a saddened clown/In the circus a my own world,' Dylan wrote in the jacket notes to the album *Joan Baez In Concert, Part 2*. The clown is certainly one of his favourite characters, a mask he often likes to wear himself. Anybody who saw his concerts in 1978 or even 1984 can remember his clown-like appearance and behaviour on stage: clothes, masks, the way he moved and played – just like that comedian Robert Shelton described in the early Sixties.

The pretty people in Dylan's surrealist songs – like some of the protagonists in his early protest songs or those from the Seventies and Eighties – cannot really be classed as characters. Most of these figures appear in a short line, sometimes a stanza, and most of the time they just act as a signal, a cipher. They stand for something else – a group, a movement, but also for danger, loneliness, threat, fantasy, other feelings or values. Many of these figures combine different elements – just like the 'undertaker' – and suddenly we're into an ambiguous picture puzzle, a distorting mirror where everything flows and changes. It all depends on the context and, of course, how Dylan performs the line. Only a few female characters are finely worked out – those in 'She belongs to me', 'Love minus zero/no limit' or 'Sad-eyed lady of the lowlands'.

One of the few real characters appearing from time to time is Dylan himself. It's a bit like an Alfred Hitchcock movie – you *think* you saw him, but the song goes on and you really can't remember. Dylan loves wearing a mask. The central image of the mask in 'On the road again' and even 'Desolation Row' anticipates a thought Dylan expressed ten years later in 'Abandoned love': 'Everybody's wearing a disguise/To hide what they've got left behind their eyes.' In the mid-Sixties there was just this clown, a freak or a 'Mr Tambourine Man' dancing in front of us. It wasn't until *New Morning* that the writer himself stepped visibly through his songs – as he'd done in his early love-songs like 'It ain't me, babe' or 'Don't think twice, it's all right'. But, by the Seventies, Dylan had found new heroes – and that's another story.

CHARLES NICHOLL
Just like the night

The early summer of 1966: our last year at school. We lived for the music, lived in the beautiful landscape of pop. We were playing *Aftermath* and *Otis Blue* and *Revolver*. We were ear-plugging through the static into Radio Lux. We were poring over *Rave* and *Record Mirror*.

Dylan was different, we knew that, but also he was part of the landscape. Exclusive colour pics brought us the latest look: Cuban heels, black shades, high-tab collar, the wild halo of hair. These were important matters, indices to a mystery.

It was the time of the great Dylan controversy: the folkies and the rockers. In May he wound up his European tour at the Albert Hall. People heckled and booed when he played his electric set. Some of them walked out. Years later there was a bootleg. The folkies yell 'Judas', and Dylan says 'I don't be*leeve* you', and then this great rip-tide of music comes sweeping in behind him as the band moves into the intro of 'Like a rolling stone'.

At the time this controversy didn't mean much to us. This was 1966. *Of course* Dylan was playing electric.

We expected Dylan to surprise us, but *Blonde on Blonde* bewildered us. Almost it scared us. We had heard the beauty and anger of his previous albums: now he hardly had time for either. *Blonde on Blonde* came from somewhere else, somewhere we didn't really want to be. Musically it couldn't be labelled: not folk, not pop, not country. The up-tempo songs like 'Leopard-skin pill-box hat' and

'Obviously five believers' were rough and spiky, but it wasn't the roughness we loved in the Stones and the Pretty Things. The slow songs carried you off like soul music.

The sweep and size of the album took our breath away. Four sides, fourteen songs, one song lasting *a whole side*, a song full of questions you had no answer to:

> And with the child of the hoodlum wrapped up in your arms,
> How could they ever, ever persuade you?

We know more about it now – that the 'Sad-eyed lady' was Sara, that he stayed up for days in the Chelsea Hotel writing the song, that it was recorded in one take, down in Nashville in February 1966, with a bunch of musicians who had hardly even heard of him until that evening – but we still don't have the answers.

The songs took us into weird subterranean stories: amphetamines and pearls, guilty undertakers and riverboat captains, Honky Tonk Ruthie dancing beneath a Panamanian moon. We were schoolboys. We had never tasted railroad gin, never been anywhere like that, but Dylan spoke to us from there. That was what was scary: if you kept on changing and questioning and pushing on through, like Dylan did, these were the places you ended up.

Even more than *Highway 61*, I think of *Blonde on Blonde* as opening up for us a whole new imaginative world. These places he sang from were inside his head, somewhere else to be, separate realities. Later we took drugs, but perhaps it was Dylan's poetry that first kicked us out of ourselves. The poetry and the music, coming out of its special twilight: the voice, the band, the harmonica blowing it all away at the end.

The song I always come back to is 'Visions of Johanna'. It's an hour-of-the-wolf song. It comes up out of some back-room of the soul. Dylan's smoky voice wraps around those long, long lines: 'But Mona Lisa musta had the highway blues/You can tell by the way she smiles.' Behind him there's his night-owl band: Al Kooper's bluesy keyboards, Robbie Robertson's caged guitar, Kenny Buttrey's drums, soft and feathery and somehow furtive, pacing quietly like footsteps in the hall.

In my mind this song is the anthem of my first all-nighters at school: sometimes solitary, sometimes with a few good friends, down in the gun-rooms with the lights on low and a towel under the door: Terence, Eddy, Nick and me, and our unspoken leader Charlie Pilkerton.

Pilk had already *been there*: his parents were divorced, he had written a novel, he had read *The Waste Land*, above all he had gone all the way with a girl called Rhona. Maybe we never quite believed him, but on the matter of the music there could be no doubt. Pilk had some kind of hotline: he heard a new sound almost before it happened. He slips a new single out of its coloured envelope, feeds it on to the trusty Dynatron, flicks back his greasy fringe. 'This one's called "Hey Joe". This guy plays guitar with his *teeth*. . . . '

It was Pilk who first had a copy of *Blonde on Blonde*, Pilk who plumbed its mysteries for us, Pilk who told us, puffing on a Perfectos at three in the morning, that ' "I want you" isn't about a woman at all, it's about heroin.'

In the night you were free. It was like hearing the sound of a train in the darkness, and suddenly you weren't under the bedclothes any more, you were on the train, gunning down the track through all those extra, secret hours. And then the dawn: putting out the lights, turning back to the communal day, heading off down the school's underground corridors known as Plug Street, carrying the untouchable secrets of your existence in a song.

Blonde on Blonde still holds its charge. It's still there to accompany you through whatever it might be that keeps you up past the dawn. Now that the controversies are over, now that you're older, you perhaps care less about the gesture of it, or the surreal extremities of the poetry. You see it now as a more human thing: a collection of love-songs, texts of betrayal and despair and supreme gallows-humour.

You also see it now as just a chapter of Dylan's story. Ahead lay the burn-out: even in our innocence we knew that burning out was what *Blonde on Blonde* was all about. Ahead lay the motorcycle crash, *The Basement Tapes*, *John Wesley Harding*. And then the Isle of Wight concert. That was the first time I saw Dylan. He wore a white suit and a scrubby beard. His hair was short, his voice was in its country comic-opera guise: 'Lay, lady, lay' time.

It was 1969. We were massed in this field, thousands of people, a shanty-town of polythene and blankets. We were there because of what he'd given us, but Dylan himself was hardly there at all.

FOUR

Time Passes Slowly

POLLY TOYNBEE
Pop festival blast-off

Observer, 31 August 1969

As crowds gather in their thousands for the Isle of Wight Festival, the great arena set up on a hill at Woodside Bay is crammed almost to capacity. More are still arriving to hear Bob Dylan sing tomorrow. It seems doubtful whether everyone will fit into the vast enclosure built to hold 150,000.

Fans sat on their sleeping-bags all day so as not to lose their places in the tents. Others slept in the open. At night the encampment that slopes down from the arena glitters with thousands of fires. People curl up to sleep by them, some playing quietly on guitars and harmonicas. A sharp wind blows round the site.

Thousand of fans cheered as a naked girl danced today in front of the stage, wearing only a red bandanna and with red paint on her arms and nose.

The cheers grew louder as the girl, who was very attractive, bounded into the press enclosure and turned cartwheels and somersaults. She was circled by photographers as she danced for ten minutes, writhing on the ground at times, while the Edgar Broughton Band played. The dance was stopped by a security guard. As she was taken away she said: 'Why can't they let me be what I am? I just wanted to be free.'

By night, as the lights on the stage dazzled in the dark, the crowds still surged in. Ryde was packed to bursting. The whole island was full of strange scenes – groups with guitars resting by the road, clumps of people sleeping in bushes. Cold winds swept the island. The vast, huddled audience faced another icy night in the open.

Until a few years ago, perhaps only religious feeling could have gathered together a crowd like this. To get here many, like pilgrims, have tramped for miles. The average age seems about eighteen.

What brings them? It seems like the gathering of a clan: people who feel set apart from society who have come together to draw support from one another. 'It's a question of alienation,' said a seventeen-year-old girl. 'In the town where I come from there are only a few of us and we're laughed at in the streets for the way we look. It's comforting here, with so many of us.' And of course there is Dylan.

But there is no hysteria. As at the concert in Hyde Park earlier this summer, the crowd is quiet. They are not the mindless screamers of Elvis and Adam Faith days: they are almost as excited by poetry and multimedia events as by music.

The organisers, Ron and Ray Foulk, are young local promoters. As they wander around backstage they look frightened and distracted, amazed at what they have created. But the efficiency of this huge operation is staggering. The tents, the catering, the tickets: everything runs smoothly. British Rail has cooperated by putting every boat it has got into ferrying passengers across the Solent. Buses on the island run all night.

The problem that is worrying the Foulk brothers is how to get the crowd away after Sunday. It has been suggested that staging another concert on Monday would help to keep some people longer and stagger the rush for the boats. British Rail estimates that at the most it can ferry only 8,000 passengers an hour away from the island.

The Environmental Playground today has been a tremendous success, with jousting between beautifully painted, bizarre-shaped cars. The other spectacle has been the slow inflation of enormous plastic phallic-shaped balloons called Swizprix: when the Who play, the balloons are expected to ejaculate foam and tinsel into the air, burst into flames, and burn themselves out.

A huge area of soapsud foam was blown out of a machine. As it undulated in the wind people hurled themselves into it, rolling around, looking like strange snowmen.

CHRISTOPHER LOGUE
A feir feld ful of folk

The Times, 13 September 1969

Imagine a seventy-acre field bounded on three sides by lanes. Under normal circumstances a dell sheltering a polite holiday-camp forms its fourth, eastern side: for the time being this retreat has been separated from the field by a line of pavilions centred on a long, fifteen-foot-high stage whose wings support triple banks of loudspeakers, clearly labelled: Do not approach without ear muffs.

The stage is topped with cut-out gods nailed to a hardboard pediment; golden dogs lie on its acroteria; across its entablature the words ISLE OF WIGHT FESTIVAL OF MUSIC. On stage, Mr Rikki Farr, every bit his father's son, announces the musicians to an audience of 100,000.

I would not have gone uninvited. Apart from the groups whose work aids my own, whose songs I know, I am not an enthusiast. I have to be told: Led Zeppelin are good, buy their record. I suffer greatly from vanity, though, and when a letter came offering me the chance to read my work to what I guessed would be a crowd of many thousands, yes, I said. Yes, yes.

Even so, I intended to leave as soon as my bit was done. Middle age will not sanction an allegedly first-class hotel crammed with star toadies, a boarding house with nits, or a tent. The event sent such thoughts to the wall.

I last visited the Isle of Wight as an evacuee, eating spam fritters in British Restaurants and crossing the Solent on blacked-out paddle-steamers. On this occasion a seven-minute hovercraft trip landed me beside a car that drove straight to the festival site.

Mr Robert Cotton, a young man brimming with good nature (and just as well for that, seeing as he was in charge of press relations) introduced me to Mr Farr (black sombrero, big shoulders, confident lope) and Mr Ronald Foulk ('The Boss', twenty-two, blond, delicate), who, as the weekend blossomed, retired into a harassed gloom reminding me of nothing so much as my friend Michael White after a successful opening.

Mr Cotton: This is Chris.
Mr Foulk: Oh.
Mr Logue: Hello.
Mr Foulk: Oh.
Pause.
An enormous man smothered with tattoos escorts an old lady holding a carrier bag full of pound notes between us.
The man: Bloody ridiculous.
Mr Farr: Stuff it in the boot, ma.
Mr Foulk: Poetry?
Mr Logue: Yes.
Mr Foulk: Oh.
The back of the stage was faced with huge plywood sheets, topslung at both ends (like hangar doors) towards whose openings a pair of ramps broad enough to take a large van had been built.

The performers arrived, drove into the rear-stage compound and backed up the 'on' ramp. This arrangement allowed the Third Ear Band, say, to off-load their numerous violins, tambours, harpes et luthes, on one side, while the Bonzo Dog Doo-Dah Band loaded their cymbals, exploding clavichords and amplified sackbuts on the other.

At such a moment Mr Cotton took me backstage. The noise was terrific.

'You want to go next?' Mr Farr roared in my ear.

'Who's on now?'

'Nobody. We're playing records to cover the change.'

'Isn't it distorting?'

'Quarter volume. Turn this lot up and you'd hear it thirty miles away. Come on – I've got some messages to read.'

I followed him on stage.

Seventy acres of people is no mean sight; unified by authority they would make me leave without delay; but these were multi-coloured, casually disposed, moving across each other, resettling themselves without hindrance, and, whenever the loudspeakers died, emanating a confident hum.

Their undulating surface reminded me of floral silk. When a famous group completed a set the applauding hands gathered light, and reflections as bright as those from Seurat's Honfleur seascapes came up towards the stage.

How slim my book is! I thought. If I dare read at all it must be Blake – at least.

'Will Judy and Pam who've got Henry's asthma inhaler please meet him at the Winky Hot Dog Stand stage left, he needs it.'

I came off and waited until Mr Farr had got the next group settled. My knees were trembling.

'Can I wait until dark?' I said.

'Sure. Go on whenever you like. What did you say your name was?'

I wrote my name into his running order and edged away from the stage mouth.

'If it's poems you'd better do it today or Sunday – tomorrow we've got the really heavy electronic stuff.'

'Tonight then.'

'Fine. Be here about eight. I'll stick you on between the Pretty Things and the Family.'

In the press tent, the atmosphere was less tense and less friendly. Numerous informants of the people squatted amid heaps of de luxe photographic accessories; portly men, determined to be out of it ('objective'), and convinced of their own importance. 'Whatdayah mean – you never heard of the *Daily Express*?' 'I *must* have eighty, eight-o, very special seats for NBC – and I must have them *now*.' 'You realise Clive Barnes is *flying in* to see Dylan – but *only* Dylan' [see: *New York Times*, 2 September 1969]. 'Typical bunch of sex-crazed layabouts if you ask me,' said the man from the *Sketch*. But nobody was asking him.

Richard Neville's long, sad Australian face was the only one I knew. We crossed the press-enclosure (a semi-circular pen in front of the stage), went through the pass gate, into the crowd.

Although it took us the best part of an hour to pick our way across the field, the audience was not so dense as it looked from the stage. When the festival was over those who had missed it surmised that a ticket to the enclosure would have been essential to their comfort. I think they meant status. I had such a ticket. There was no great comfort margin. Indeed, by Sunday evening, when the enclosure was choked with free-loaders, spongeing aristos, and all the velveteen parasites star groups carry in their rucks, the field was a better place to be.

The thousands were grouped in knots, sharing food, daydreaming, playing chess, patience, knitting and reading. Teams of BBC cameramen paced stately by, their cameras aloft like eucharists, lights like canopies, and after them the interviewers, microphones held as if they were for sale, questions struggling towards the heart of the matter, but for the most part discovering only assumptions present in the asker's mind.

Out here the triple-banked speakers made sense; a mile from the stage you could hear everything perfectly.

One of my worries about going on was audibility. When I did, my reading copy of *New Numbers* shaking in my hands, I was heard all over the field in silence and with modest applause. If I didn't bring the field down, at least I made the *Guinness Book of Records*.

A lot of the music I found monotonous, confused and many of the lyrics trivial and repetitive. There are those who assert that crowds like this are bound by a self-deceptive, religious fervour; they will take anything, it is said, provided the noise is loud; very often I have found that these assertions express their author's view of most things produced after 1945 or even, alas, 1956.

As far as the music was concerned – for the poetry played so small a part there was no way of judging – I did not think the crowd was self-deceived. Everyone performing was heard in silence; everyone received applause; a few were acclaimed – Tom Paxton, for example.

Paxton is a short, cherubic West-Coaster [*sic*] who dresses like a German submariner from the First World War. He holds his guitar at right angles to his body and, save for his hands and lips, hardly moves while he sings funny, philosophical ballads about our current wars and those who profit from them.

There is a passage in James Jones's *Thin Red Line* where an American soldier encounters and kills an enemy while both of them are taking a quiet shit. The writing is good. Paxton sings about a similar incident in which an enemy soldier gives an American a cigarette rolled with finer cannabis leaf than that available to the US Army.

Sentimental? Especially for those so conditioned to enmity that their early romance has turned to querulous cynicism. In any case, it is all in the words: Hotspur moaning about prisoners could be sentimental.

At lunchtime on Saturday a sixty-foot sausage-shaped balloon was inflated and rolled on to the crowd. Easily it skated across thousands of palms, now disappearing, now bounding out of reach; an image from Tenniel or Magritte.

How discouraging to read so little about these games in the

news reports. The best of the newspapers ran somewhat bewildered, well-at-least-there-has-been-no-bloodshed stories, while the worse went looking for scented pus.

The question arises: why mention their troublemaking at all? Easier to write about devils than angels. Why share their trap? Easier to please resentful minds with devils than angels.

Somehow, but how I am not sure, popular newspapers reflect the attitudes of those who buy them and have special contact with those whose worst side they deepen and confirm. Pinning their influence exactly, by example or image, is difficult: they use common words cleverly; certain public figures nourish their vocabulary; in a few years we have seen 'permissive' and 'immigrant' gain new meanings.

In this way the good, essentially naive conventionalists of the Isle of Wight, the police who undertake the dirty work, and the Spokesmen for British Railways found themselves confused: the crowd actually behaved *well*. They were really *very* orderly. We had almost nothing to *complain* about.

Why not the other way round? That a large, migrant crowd should not attack each other, not ruin the locality they visit and not destroy their means of transport is the very *least* we can expect.

If those of us who went to the Isle of Wight are so disliked and resented by the majority of us who did not, surely the source of distrust has to do with something more than age, apparel, taste in music and length of hair?

Maybe the amiability of the crowd who went springs from a rejection of the values to which the larger crowd find themselves hopelessly committed.

Dylan was the star only in name. A marvellous songwriter and a great recording artist he may be. What I saw was a good-looking boy in a nice shiny-white suit, accompanied by skilled but uninspired musicians, singing a Bob Dylan melody à la Sinatra. A couple of choruses of 'Mr Tambourine Man', two more of 'To Ramona', a quick look at 'It ain't me, babe', followed by a country-and-western round-up, then off. No presence. No message. No soul. But a nice smile.

Still, eleven hours of music is a lot. I wouldn't care to go on at the end of it. A great moment is needed to fulfil the hope generated by such a weekend. We got that moment.

For three days the weather had been autumnal. Skies overcast, cool winds, a touch of rain. At about eight on Sunday evening

Mr Farr, his voice almost gone, announced Ritchie Havens. On he came with his bass guitarist and his bongo drummer and straight off we knew we were on to a good thing.

Havens is big, gentle, commanding; his image fills the stage. Wearing a white robe decorated with paths of blue and yellow beads, he set a clear, strong rhythm going and sang plain, almost single-word riff-lyrics to it.

While he sang the sun came out and made a sunset glorious enough to delight Turner. One of those long, endless skies streaked with lines of pink cloud, emerald light behind them, the on-coming darkness pouring through it, changing the upper greens to blue, to cobalt, to indigo, and the helicopters fluttering their red and amber guide lights overhead.

By the time he was allowed to finish it was dark, and the crowd were on their feet calling out for more. It was as if Apollo had noticed us and, in passing, given the show a nod.

Dylan at Old Nassau

Rolling Stone, 9 July 1970

Princeton, New Jersey – Yes, it's true, Bob Dylan accepted an honorary degree from Princeton University, but first-hand observers say he was very nervous and hesitant about the whole thing and seemed 'appropriately out of place' during the ceremonies.

Dylan checked in at the Princeton Inn the night before graduation with his wife Sara, David Crosby and an aide, Ben Saltzman. The next day, 9 June, he appeared in Nassau Hall's exquisitely appointed Faculty Room at 10 a.m., an hour before graduation ceremonies were to begin.

'He came romping in in his shades and he was very nervous,' reported Meir Ribilow, Class Day Chairman and one of a committee that chose the honorary degree recipients.

Ribilow, who spoke with Dylan briefly, said he found him 'extremely uncommunicative', tending to mumble and speak through either Crosby or Saltzman. Another student, Brent Ogden, said Dylan would ask either Saltzman or Crosby if he wanted to know something, or 'even if he wanted a glass of water', and then the message would be relayed.

Because Mrs Coretta King, another of the nine persons honoured with special degrees by Princeton that day, was late arriving, the ceremonies were delayed slightly and Dylan seemed to grow more uncomfortable. At one point a number of photographers and reporters began asking questions and taking photos, and he stomped out of the Faculty Room. 'I don't like it. They're asking questions,' he told his wife in the hall.

Among other persons receiving degrees were Mrs King and Walter Lippmann, eighty-one, nationally known liberal commentator and columnist. Mrs King's honorary degree was a doctorate in Humanity; Lippmann's was an honorary Doctor of Law degree. Dylan chatted briefly with Mrs King, but eyewitnesses say neither Dylan nor Lippmann seemed aware of the other's presence.

Because of the heat and presumably in sympathy with the majority of the day's 1,200 graduating seniors, Dylan at first refused to wear a black robe. (All but twenty-five of the graduates refused to wear the traditional robes. Instead, they donated the money they would have spent on caps and gowns to the Princeton Community Fund, an organisation which supports anti-war and anti-draft activities.) According to Ogden, Dylan seemed to be so upset just before the ceremony that he started for the door, but 'saw so many people outside' he changed his mind.

When the ceremonies did begin, Dylan put on an academic gown over his dark blue, pin-striped suit, but refused the 'mortarboard' cap. He also tied a white arm-band on, like the majority of the graduating seniors. The band was engraved with the peace symbol and the insignia of the graduating class, a number '70'.

Honorary degree recipients are not required to make speeches, so Dylan was silent during the reading of citations. Ribilow, however, who was near Dylan on the outdoor stage, said he was 'ostentatiously listening to what was being said, which was more than the other recipients'. He smiled slightly when mention was made of his 'approaching the perilous age of thirty'.

Dylan was presented with an honorary doctorate of Music by University President Robert F. Goheen. It was inscribed in Latin on a parchment scroll, and said: 'Since it is fitting that to those who have conferred the greatest benefits either upon their country or upon mankind as a whole the greatest honour should be given and awarded, and since Bob Dylan not only has so brilliantly distinguished himself in good works and *Carminibus Canendis* [his forte] that he is deservedly worthy of the highest public honours. Therefore we the President and Trustees of Princeton University to this same person do give the title and degree of Doctor of Music, and confer the power of enjoying the individual rights and privileges wherever they may pertain to this degree.'

A less formal citation was also read. It said in part: 'Paradoxically, though he is known to millions, he shuns publicity and organisations, preferring the solidarity of his family and isolation from the world. Although he is approaching the perilous age of thirty his music remains the authentic expression of the disturbed and concerned conscience of Young America.'

All during the ceremony, Dave Crosby was licking a half-orange and looking greatly amused. When asked what he was doing with Dylan, Crosby laughed: 'I was standing by the New Jersey Turnpike, looking for America, and Bob saw a freak and stopped to pick me up.'

Saltzman said he felt Dylan had decided to accept the degree as a gesture to the student movement and to what has been happening on campuses across the country. A source at Princeton said Dylan had called after he'd been notified that he was to receive the honour, 'to find out just what kind of a degree it was'.

After the ceremony, Dylan left the stage, took off his robe and, with his party, got into a waiting car and drove on down the road.

ROBERT D. CAMPBELL
Dylan's new morning

Christian Century, 25 August 1971

A society that too often glorifies fools while ignoring prophets can still occasionally surprise one and surprised I was to find an essay on Bob Dylan's work in one of the nation's leading intellectual magazines recently. Although the essay was primarily a comparison of Dylan's poetry with that of William Blake – I question whether Dylan has ever read a word of Blake – its publication was nonetheless a notable step forward in the cultural establishment's acceptance of Bob Dylan as a legitimate poet. Perhaps the day will come when the clergy, too, open themselves up to Dylan's work. For his music, even apart from its many references to Christ, God and the Bible, has a general spirituality about it. This spirituality has endured in Dylan's music because of his determination to maintain his integrity, to continue to make an honest personal statement about his life.

From his earliest recordings, Bob Dylan has been trying to develop independently, to discover his own reality; this resolve has been evident from the first. In 'Restless farewell', one of his early songs, he says: 'So I'll make my stand/And remain as I am/And bid farewell and not give a damn.' Probably the chief obstacles to this effort have been Dylan's followers among the youth culture who appointed him their most important leader and attempted to translate his words into a mass consciousness. Ironically, Dylan himself does not see his music as an attempt to convert the masses, but rather as a defence behind which he can maintain his integrity and preserve his sanity.

'My songs don't take any responsibility,' Dylan recently remarked. 'They don't care what people do with them. How can I? You write a song to do one thing and it does another, and so you write a song about what happened and you don't know what that's going to do.' *New Morning* is squarely within that tradition. It is a straightforward personal statement of Bob Dylan's present stance in his spiritual life.

The LP leads off with 'If not for you', a love-song probably written for Dylan's wife. But it is common for Dylan's lyrics to carry double or even triple meanings. This song could as easily be written to God who is, after all, the Spirit of Love.

'Time passes slowly' is a song about Dylan's life in the mountains. Long before a return to the countryside became popular, Dylan periodically retreated to the mountains for writing and meditation. Secluded from what he once termed the 'rat race choir' of the city, Dylan establishes a balance with nature. Here, he accepts life so openly that he experiences a sense of timelessness which is like the discovery of eternity: 'Like the red rose of summer that blooms in the day,/Time passes slowly and fades away.'

On the surface the album's title song, 'New morning', describes Dylan's joyful response to the beginning of a new day. But the song might also be interpreted as a declaration of a spiritual rebirth. Again, the second person referred to in this song may be Dylan's wife, or God, or both:

> This must be the day that all of my dreams come true
> So happy just to be alive
> Underneath the sky of blue
> On this new morning with you.

'Three angels' is one of the songs that shows the broad change of emphasis that has taken place in Dylan's work. In the early years his songs spoke of war, poverty, race relations. Now the poet's concern has shifted to the individual's denial (or acceptance) of his own spirituality. The lyrics focus on three angels – Christmas decorations placed on poles over a city street. The representatives of mankind pass by during the day, all of them too wrapped up in the concerns of their everyday life to see the divine nature of existence: 'The angels play on their horns all day/The whole earth in progression seems to pass by/But does anyone hear the music the play,/Does anyone even try?'

The final cut on the LP, 'Father of night', is a simple song in praise of God, the creator of all things:

> Father of night, Father of day,
> Father, who taketh the darkness away,
> Father, who teacheth the bird to fly,
> Builder of rainbows up in the sky,
> Father of loneliness and pain,
> Father of love and Father of rain.

Now that I think about it, one *might* perceive strains of William Blake in Dylan's poetry. But, I would quickly add, there are also elements of Whitman and Thoreau. And Woody Guthrie. Perhaps there is some Leadbelly, too, and a bit of Jesus Christ. Put these elements all together and you only get confusion. Best not to make comparisons. Bob Dylan is Bob Dylan, thank God.

ROBERT CHRISTGAU
Tarantula

New York Times Book Review, 27 June 1971

The official appearance of Bob Dylan's *Tarantula* is not a literary event because Dylan is not a literary figure. Literature comes in books and Dylan does not intend his most important work to be read. If he ever did, his withdrawal of *Tarantula* from publication five years ago indicates that he changed his mind. Of course, it's possible that he's changed his mind again – with Dylan, you never know. Most likely, however, his well-known quest for privacy, his personal elusiveness, lies behind the unexpected availability of this book. The pursuit of the artist by his audience has been a pervasive theme of his career, and the bootleg versions of *Tarantula*, hawked on the street and under the counter over the past few years by self-appointed Dylanologists and hip rip-off artists, were simply a variation on that theme. For Dylan to permit the release of the book now (at a non-rip-off price, it should be noted) is to acknowledge the loss of a battle in his never-ending war for privacy. Quite simply, his hand has been forced by his fans. He is a book-writer now, like it or not.

To assert that Dylan doesn't belong to the history of literature is not to dismiss him from the history of artistic communication, of language. Quite the contrary. A songwriter does not use language as a poet or novelist does because he chooses his words to fit into some larger, more sensual effect; an artist who elects to work in a mass medium communicates in a different way from one who doesn't and must be judged according to his own means, purposes and referents. That much ought to be obvious. I would also argue, however, that Dylan's choices not only merit their own critical canons but must be recognised as incisive responses to modernism's cul-de-sac, in which all the arts, especially literature, suffer from self-perpetuating intellectual elitism.

What makes this all so confusing is that Dylan's fame and influence are based on his literary talents and pretensions. Just for fun, I might suggest that Dylan is no greater an artist than Chuck Berry or Hank Williams, but only Dylan could have become the culture hero of a decade of matriculating college classes. Even at first, when Dylan's best songs were mostly acute folk music genre pieces, he was thought to embody transcendent artistic virtues. The standard example was 'Blowin' in the wind', which interspersed straightforward political questions with metaphorical ones, always concluding: 'The answer, my friend, is blowin' in the wind,/The answer is blowin' in the wind.' The song's 'poetic' language, effective in its musical and emotive context even though it appears hackneyed on the page, captured listeners sympathetic to its apparent assumptions and inspired much unfortunate image-mongering. But in retrospect we notice the ambivalence of the title – can the answer be plucked from the air or does it flutter out of reach?

Dylan may not have been aware he was equivocating when he wrote the song, but that doesn't matter. Equivocation was inherent in his choice of method. Like most of his confrères in the folk movement, Dylan got his world-view from the listless Civil Rights and Ban the Bomb radicalism of the late Fifties but was forced to find his heroes elsewhere, among the avant-garde artists who helped young post-conformists define for themselves their separation from their fellow citizens. Once Dylan conceived the ambition to use those artists as his own exemplars, he had to come to terms with their characteristic perspective – namely, irony. Sure enough, in 'My back pages' (1964) he was renouncing politics with a nice ironic flourish – 'I was so much older then,/I'm younger than that now.' Moreover, the same song signalled his debut as a poetaster with a portentously clumsy opening line: 'Crimson flames tied through my ears/Rolling high and mighty traps.'

Between early 1964 and mid-1966 – a period that includes

the four albums from *Another Side of Bob Dylan* to *Blonde on Blonde* and the switch from acoustic to electric music – Dylan became a superstar. Pioneers of youth bohemia seized upon his grotesque, sardonic descriptions of America as experienced by a native alien and elevated Dylan into their poet laureate. In response, professional defenders of poetry declared themselves appalled by his barbaric verbosity. Many of us, his admirers, even while we were astonished, enlightened and amused by Dylan's sporadic eloquence, knew why John Ciardi wasn't [in Jerome Agel: 'Music, that's where it's at', *Books*, December 1965]. But we didn't care, not just because Dylan's songs existed in an aural and cultural context that escaped the Ciardis, but because we sensed that the awkwardness and overstatement that marred his verse were appropriate to a populist medium. No one was explicit about this at the time, however, least of all Dylan, whose ambitions were literary as well as musical and whose relationship to his ever-expanding audience was qualified by the fascination with an arcane elite to which his songs testified.

Tarantula is a product of this period; in fact, Dylan fans who want a precise sense of what the book is about need only refer to the liner notes of *Highway 61 Revisited*. The basic technique is right there: the vague story, peopled with historical (Paul Sargent), fabulous or pseudonymous (the Cream Judge, Savage Rose) characters, punctuated with dots and dashes and seasoned with striking but enigmatic asides, all capped off with a fictitious letter having no obvious connection to what has preceded. That's all, folks.

Tarantula is a concatenation of such pieces. Most of them seem unconnected, although a few characters, notably someone named 'aretha', do recur. The only literary precedent that comes to mind is *The Naked Lunch*, but in a more general way *Tarantula* is reminiscent of a lot of literature because it takes an effort to read it. Unless you happen to believe in Dylan, I question whether it's worth the effort, and don't call me a philistine – it was Bob Dylan who got me asking such questions in the first place.

For the strangest aspect of Dylan's middle period is that although it was unquestionably his literary pretensions that fanaticised his admirers and transformed the craft (or art) of songwriting, Dylan's relationship to literature as a discipline was always ambivalent. In fact, to call it ambivalent is to compound the confusion – it was actually downright hostile. From *Tarantula*:

'wally replies that he is on his way down a pole & asks the man if he sees any relationship between doris day & tarzan? the man says "no, but i have some james baldwin and hemingway books"."not good enough" says wally.' From the notes to *Bringing It All Back Home*: 'my poems are written in a rhythm of unpoetic distortion'.

Dylan borrowed techniques from literature – most prominently allusion, ambiguity, symbolism and fantasy – and he obviously loved language, but he despised the gentility with which it was supposed to be tailored. His songs do seem derivative, but (like *Tarantula*) they aren't derived from anyone in particular. Obvious parallels, or 'influences' – Blake, Whitman, Rimbaud, Céline – share only his approach and identity: the Great Vulgarian, the Magnificent Phonus Balonus. Dylan wrote like a word-drunk undergraduate who had berserked himself into genius, his only tradition the jumbled culture of the war baby – from Da Vinci to comic strips, from T. S. Eliot to Charlie Rich. His famous surrealism owes as much to Chuck Berry as to Breton or even Corso, and, even though his imagery broadened the horizons of songwriting, it was only a background for the endless stream of epigrams – which songwriters call good lines – flowing into our language, some already clichés ('The times they are a-changin'', 'Something is happening here/But you don't know what it is'), others still the property of an extensive, self-informed subculture ('Stuck inside of Mobile/With the Memphis blues again', 'Don't follow leaders/Watch the parkin' meters'). Dylan may be a poor poet, but he is a first-class wit.

But such talk accedes to the temptation of placing Dylan's work in a page context, always a mistake. Literature may have engendered the Dylan mystique, but rock-'n'-roll nurtured it. We remember those lines because we've heard them over and over again, often not really listening, but absorbing the rhythm of unpoetic distortion just the same. *Tarantula* may contain similar gems, but we'll never know they're there, because *Tarantula* will never be an album. The wonderful letters, the funny bits, as well as the dreary, vaguely interesting stuff and the failed doomsday rhetoric – all will go. Aretha Franklin's continuing presence through the book is a portent, for shortly after *Tarantula* and *Blonde on Blonde* Dylan made another switch by abandoning the verbal play (and excess) of his long songs for brief, specifically pop works. For a while, it appeared that this meant a total abandonment of the complexity of his vision, but his latest album, *New Morning*, makes clear that it is only a condensation. More and more, Dylan affirms the value of the popular and the sensual over the verbal. This book will find its way into A.J. Weberman's Dylan concordance and doubtless become a cult item, but it is a throwback. Buy his records.

KEN KESEY

Summing up the '60s, sizing up the '70s *

from *Crawdaddy*, 19 December 1972

'I saw very early that Dylan was doing something with our consciousnesses, the extent of which will only be known hundreds of years from now. Dylan's not only a poet, he's as well a prophet, a prophet like happens once every five hundred years or so. When you heard Dylan in those first songs he was really talking to you in some way that was not customary linear communication. There'd be a phrase that would strike like a Rorschach, setting off a personal image that would start a whole crystallisation of thinking and leave your head in a place it had never been before. It's as if, inside of us, there's always been the proper solution and Dylan tossed in the proper crystals. But the crystals weren't connected. One thought running and connecting with the next, and that one connecting with the next to present an inductive argument. This was imagery leading out and connecting lyrically to form brand new thought crystals in people's heads. And that's as subversive an act as you can possibly imagine.

'This all reminds me of a dream I had a while ago. This was a dream that happened after waking up, not getting up and going back to sleep. Faye had enrolled us in a new class. She had sent

* Part of a longer interview with Linda Gaboriah.

away and gotten in the mail a class key with the name of a hall
that we were to go to, with the number of the room – it was
125A. So we took this bus, driven by a Mexican bus driver, to
this old European-looking college. We got there and went along
the corridor to 124, 125 – and 125A turned out to be in the ceiling.
The key unlocked this door in the ceiling. It opened, and out of it
fell sand, all over us. Then a ladder came down and we climbed up
the ladder and went inside. It was a long room, as long as this barn,
dimly lit with benches along both sides. There was no teacher that
you could see and there was about forty or fifty people in there.
People of various ages, doing a lot of strange things that had no
meaning that we could interpret. When we went in, there was no
traditional opening made for us, like a professor might have made
by saying "Attention, class, these are the new students", etc. This
opening wasn't made, so we just had to go sit on the bench. People
were reciting strange things and as they would stop somebody
would start tapping on the wall with pieces of bamboo. Other
people were just moving and making noises. We began to feel very
uptight sitting there, the way you might feel if you went into the
market-place in a strange town, all dressed up like American
tourists. All the people are doing the market-place thing, talking
in a language you can't understand, dealing with each other, and
you're not part of it. That's a Dylan feeling. That's the feeling he
talked about in "something is happening here/But you don't know
what it is/Do you, Mister Jones?" (It finally even came around and
got Bobby himself.)

'Anyway, in this dream, Faye had to get up and go to the
bathroom or someplace; and I was sitting there by myself. I was
watching and seeing – finally I see, "There's something important
going on here, something really important. They can't stop and
bring us in in the traditional way, because then there's no way
of doing what they're doing. To forge this new communication
that's going on, they have to continue what they're doing, even
when it seems rude and heartless. It's up to us to discover our
own expression, our own way to enter into it!" There's a lot
of the dream that I've forgotten, but I can remember waking
up and feeling inspired the rest of the day by that kind of
communication that I think now is the answer to all our global
problems. A total communication of dance, song, of word-salad
Dylanesque expression, where conversation doesn't restrict itself
to the way we're used to conversing, but goes to the true core of
humanity.'

ALLEN GINSBERG
Three poems

from *First Blues: Rags, Ballads and Harmonium Songs, 1971–74*

Postcard to D

Chuggling along in an old open bus
       past the green sugarfields
            down a dusty dirt road
                    overlooking the ocean in Fiji,
thinking of your big Macdougal street house
       & the old orange peels
             in your mail-garbage load,
                    smoggy windows you clean with a squeejee

                         3 March 1972

Blue Gossip

I guess he got sick of having to get up and get
           scared of being shot down
Also probably he got sick of
           being a methedrine clown;
Also he wanted to go back explore
           Macdougal Street New York town

I guess he got sick of a Cosmic
           consciousness too abstract
I guess he wanted to go back
           t'his own babies' baby shit fact
Change his own children's diapers not get lost
           in a transcendental Rock & Roll act.

I guess he thought maybe he had
           enough gold for the world
Saw red white & blue big enough now
           needn't be further unfurled
I guess he felt prophet show good example,
           bring himself down in the world.

I guess he took Zen Chinese vows
                and became an anonymous lout
I guess he figured he better step down off stage
                before he got kicked out
I guess he felt lonesome and blue
                and he wanted out.

I guess he did what anyone
                sens'ble would do
Otherwise like Mick Jagger go out on stage
                wearing curtains of blue
And fly around the world with great big
                diamonds and pearls made of glue.

I guess he felt he'd used up
                'nuff of the 'lectric supply
I guess he knew that the Angel
                of Death was nigh –
I guess he sighed his
                next mortal sigh.

I guess he guessed he could
                find out his own mortal face
I guess he desired to examine
                his own family place
I guess he decided to act with
                more modest *silent* grace

I guess he decided to learn
                from ancient tongue
So he studied Hebrew
                as before he blabbed from his lung
I guess he required to learn new
                tender kind songs to be sung.

I guess he thought he was not guru
                for Everyone's eyes
He must have seen Vajra Hells
                in old visions he'd devised
He must've seen infernal assassins
                stealing his garbage supplies.

I guess he decided to die
                while still alive
In that way, ancient death-in-life,
                saints always thrive

Above all remember his children
        he already picked a good wife.

I guess he decided to Be
        as well as sing the blues
I guess he decided like Prospero
        to throw his white magic wand into the Ocean blue –
Burn up all his magic books,
        go back to Manhattan, think something new.

I guess he decided like Prospero
        World was a dream
Every third thought is grave
        or so Samsara would seem –
Took Hebrew Boddhisatva's vow
        and saw golden light death agleam.

I guess he decided he
        did not need to be More Big
I guess he decided he was not the
        Great Cosmic Thingamajig
I guess he decided to end that sweet song
        and such is his Suchness I dig.

                23 October 1972, Davidson College

On reading Dylan's writings

Now that it's dust and ashes
now that it's human skin
Here's to you Bob Dylan
a poem for the laurels you win

Sincerest form of flattery
is imitation they say
I've broke my long line down
to write a song your way

Those 'chains of flashing images'
that came to you at night
were highest farm boys' day dreams
that glimpse the Angels' light

And tho the dross of wisdom's come
and left you lone on earth
remember when the Angels call
your soul for a new birth

It wasn't dope that gave you truth
no money that you stole
– was God himself that entered in
shining your heavenly soul.

27 July 1973, London

NEIL SINYARD

Bob Dylan and Billy the Kid

'How does it feel?' asks Billy the Kid (Kris Kristofferson) of sheriff Pat Garrett (James Coburn), who has sold out and is now siding with the cattle barons and politicians who were formerly his enemies. 'It feels like times have changed,' replies Garrett sardonically, to which Billy retorts: 'Times maybe – not me.'

Scripted by Rudolph Wurlitzer, this sharply etched pre-credit verbal exchange in Sam Peckinpah's *Pat Garrett and Billy the Kid* (1973) serves a dual function. On the thematic level, it is an admirably concise exposition of character and theme. It contrasts the pragmatic opportunism of Garrett, whose main desire now is to live to be 'rich, old and grey', with the independent adventurism of Billy, who knows he is running out of time and territory but who would play out his destiny to the finish rather than accommodate himself to new and corrupt social forces. Stage by stage, this conflict of values will lead the two friends inexorably towards a violent confrontation. On a secondary level, however, the dialogue seems consciously and humorously to foreshadow the imminent appearance of Bob Dylan for an expectant audience. For the Dylan connoisseur, who has come to the movie primarily because of his contribution to it, a line like 'How does it feel?', delivered in a tone of quizzical contempt, would instantly summon up the identical refrain in one of Dylan's most vengeful and sarcastic songs, 'Like a rolling stone'. Similarly, in a film featuring and scored by Dylan, a discussion of changing times could not help but evoke the lyric and world of that most famous song. Specifically, in the film, those times are the early 1880s, but allegorically they are undoubtedly to be understood as referring also to modern times. The point is that the film is signalling from the beginning that Dylan's presence on screen and soundtrack will amount to something considerably more significant than a commercial guest slot. His persona, as personality and musician, will be deployed to underline and amplify some of the film's main concerns.

'Who are you?' enquires Garrett of a strange, owlish character who looks quite at odds with his environment, sporting a hat with a feather and occasionally wearing spectacles but never a gun. 'That's a good question,' says the man (Bob Dylan), who then studiously neglects to answer it. He has first been seen emerging from a newspaper office wearing a printer's apron and obviously drawn into the street by the commotion that has accompanied Billy the Kid's bloody escape from prison. In this scene with Garrett, who is trying to round up a posse to recapture Billy, the man takes off his apron, as if shedding a former identity and possibly preparing to offer his services to the posse. Yet on his next appearance he is not with Garrett but eyeing up Billy and his gang with wary admiration. 'What's your name, boy?' he is asked again, to which he replies 'Alias . . . anything you please.'

Thereafter Alias is often glimpsed on the fringes of the action. He is trusted by Billy, joining him on a turkey shoot, sharpening the knife of one of Billy's *compadres*. By contrast, Garrett treats him contemptuously as comic counterpoint, standing him in a corner to recite the labels on provisions ('Beans . . . fine quality tomatoes . . . plums . . . ') whilst in the foreground of the frame, the sheriff sadistically dispatches two of Billy's gang. Inevitably, Alias will also be on hand to witness the final showdown between Billy and Garrett, where the lawman's murder of the outlaw is an attempt at exorcising his own outlaw past that becomes instead an act of moral suicide.

Alias plays a curious role and it's difficult to decide if that's *because* of Dylan or whether the original conception demanded someone like Dylan to play it. He seems half inside and half outside the movie, both in terms of the action (on which he has no impact whatever) and in terms of style, for, in comparison with the hardened reality of Peckinpah's other cowboys, Alias's frail sensitivity seems quite out of time. This is perhaps partly the effect of Dylan's limited acting ability which, rather as Richard Lester had done with the Beatles, Peckinpah attempts to overcome by giving him only one line at a time to negotiate. Yet it also seems a deliberate strategy: the presence of Alias in a scene provides not so much an additional character as a different *ambience*. The man views this passing of an age and the build-up to this anachronistic confrontation from a safe remove and with a decidedly modern squint – rather like Peckinpah himself. As befits his name, Alias is given no real identity and is more observer than participant, except for one occasion when he indulges in a spot of knife-throwing to help an outnumbered Billy. Although it is clear where his sympathies lie, he keeps himself out of trouble through a mixture of stealth and cunning: he might not like the new establishment but he knows how to survive. At times he plays the Fool to Billy's Lear, being watchful, offering advice and support, but always deferring to the other's charisma. At other times he seems a sort of Fate figure who materialises mysteriously as events build to a momentous climax.

Insofar as he can be categorised in terms of the contemporary Western, Alias is a variation on the kind of figure memorably portrayed by Hurd Hatfield in Arthur Penn's Billy the Kid film, *The Left Handed Gun* (1958) and exuberantly sent up by Stubby Kaye and Nat 'King' Cole in *Cat Ballou* (1965): namely, the hero-worshipper-cum-troubadour who follows like a devoted disciple and will take it upon himself to spread the legend. In this sense the songs can be read not simply as Dylan's score but as a representation of Alias's reflections on his encounters with Billy and Garrett. (This might have been clearer if Peckinpah had been allowed by the studio to keep to his original intention of structuring the film as an extended flashback, beginning with Garrett's death at the hands of the people who had hired him to kill Billy.)

Dylan's score for *Pat Garrett and Billy the Kid* can be seen in the context of several different movie conventions. MGM were certainly alert to the profit potential of a Dylan soundtrack album, so much so that Peckinpah's regular film composer, Jerry Fielding,

felt obliged to leave the picture when Dylan's music gained pre-
cedence over his own. At the same time, one would not reduce
the score to the level of Burt Bacharach's blatantly commercial
and excruciatingly incongruous music for *Butch Cassidy and the
Sundance Kid* (1969): Dylan's is musically far superior to that and
dramatically more appropriate to the film in hand. Indeed, one
could see the score as a continuation of an honourable film
music tradition for Westerns, a tradition personified by Dimitri
Tiomkin in the 1950s with such classics as *High Noon* (1952) and
Gunfight at the OK Corral (1957), where the score serves a choric
rather than a strictly background function and is part narrative,
part characterisation, part atmosphere, part prophecy. Frankie
Laine's saddle-sore leathery vocal chords fulfilled this purpose
for the traditional Western: Dylan's vocalising brings a new kind
of Western sound – one that has been described as that of a prairie
dog caught on a barbed-wire fence.

Yet the score is remarkably effective. When Slim Pickens's
Sheriff Baker is mortally wounded while helping Garrett and
rushes to a stream like a stricken animal before setting himself
down and readying himself for death, Dylan's music has an
eloquently elegiac feel ('gettin' dark, too dark for me to see/I
feel like I'm knockin' on heaven's door'). The song that most
often accompanies Billy has a complex and varied function. It
enlarges the mood of ominous inevitability ('They say that Pat
Garrett's got your number/So sleep with one eye open when you
slumber'); it seems almost an internal monologue giving explicit
expression to the thoughts humming silently inside Billy's head
('shot down by the man who was your friend'); and it is finally
an exposition of what Billy represents ('Billy, they don't like you
to be so free . . . ').

Although the inclusion of Dylan's score might well have been
influenced by the successful integration of Leonard Cohen's songs
into Robert Altman's *McCabe and Mrs Miller* (1971), it is likely that
the real inspiration to use Dylan came from the personality and
success of his 1968 album, *John Wesley Harding*. As several commentators have pointed out, there are a lot of similarities between
Dylan's Harding and Peckinpah's Billy the Kid: both are roman-
ticised outlaws who befriend the poor, 'never known/To hurt an
honest man'. One could even stretch that further and suggest that
there's a certain kinship between Peckinpah's Billy and Dylan
himself.

In his Dylan biography, Anthony Scaduto described him as 'one of those outlaws who instinctively reject a standardised society, whose consciousness has not been frozen in the immediate and confining present . . . ' This could stand as an exact description of Peckinpah's Billy the Kid. Indeed, it is interesting that the people portrayed as the villains in Peckinpah's film – the politicians like Jason Robards's Governor Lew Wallace (who subsequently wrote the novel *Ben-Hur*), the business barons like the unseen John Chisum, the zealots who, like R.G. Armstrong's deranged deputy, believe that God is on their side – are precisely the types whom Dylan named as the enemies of progress in all those Sixties songs. The irony is that in the early 1970s, as in the 1880s of the film, such figures are back in the saddle and riding righteously on the wave of a reactionary backlash.

As the man who articulated so much of the anarchic, rebellious mood of the 1960s, Dylan is an important symbolic presence in this film, a clue to its tone of doomed romanticism and emotional disillusionment. As Alias, Dylan can only stand to one side and mutely watch and mourn the death of youth, individualism and outlawed vitality as the forces of expedience, reaction, vested interest and moral conservatism – in a phrase, Nixon's America – move in. The times they are a-changin', but not for the better.

It should be noted that this article was based on viewings of the 1973 release print of the film. More recently, a longer version of the film, closer to Peckinpah's original intention, has come to light. Most significantly, the new version restores the prologue and epilogue depicting the death of Pat Garrett in 1909, at the hands of the people who had hired him to kill the Kid 28 years earlier. This in turn casts an ironic shadow over the rest of the film, making the narrative an extended flashback from Garrett's recognition, on the point of death, that killing the Kid was an act of self-destruction. As far as Dylan's score is concerned, it is used in a similar way to the original version but less insistently. The most important difference is that 'Knockin' on heaven's door' is now hummed rather than sung over Slim Pickens's death scene, and the scene's length and elegiac feeling are correspondingly reduced – to the film's detriment or advantage, according to taste. Dylan's performance as Alias remains intact; and the argument in the article about the meaning and significance of his contribution applies equally to this fuller version as to the original release, which is, of course, much better known.

FIVE

Winterlude

FRANK KERMODE and
STEPHEN SPENDER

The metaphor at the end of the funnel

Esquire, May 1972

According to Dylan himself, anything he can sing is a song and anything he can't sing is a poem. It's a useful distinction, but here it will have to be flouted, since the subject is precisely the poems Dylan sings. Everybody knows that the words, or for that matter the notes, on the page give a very poor idea of what a Dylan song really sounds like – he is a virtuoso executant, and since he writes the words with virtuoso performance in mind, they can't, on the page, be more than the musical notes are: reminders, hints, or shadows. All the same, there's quite a lot of good poetry which started life in a similar way – Greek tragedy, medieval ballad – and has survived the loss of music and performance. How do Dylan's poems stand up?

In his own kind it goes without saying that he has no close rival; the Beatles' 'Eleanor Rigby' is a more accomplished lyric, probably, than any of Dylan's, but it isn't of the same kind. Some of Dylan's work is avowedly based on traditional models, but he always reinvents them; a poem that starts 'As I went out one morning' soon loses its resemblance to its predecessors, and even in straight imitations of ballads about folk heroes he tends to shed the regularities of rhyme and metre which, in the old days, were an unconscious tribute by the poet to high-class culture.

155

> Jesse went to rest with his hands on
>   his breast;
> He died with a smile on his face.
> He was born one day in the county
>   of Clay,
> And came from a solitary race.

That's closer to Wordsworth than Dylan will ever want to be.

Some folk song acquires obscurities simply by long transmission, or because special meanings are lost. (Who can be sure that 'the foggy dew' is a euphemism for virginity?) Sea shanties are obscure and distorted because they are work songs and the scribes probably had trouble sorting out words from grunts. Art songs can be transformed into poetic obscurity within a few years of their adoption by folk singers. This kind of obscurity interests Dylan; it has what he called in an interview 'mystery' – 'its meaninglessness is holy', he said, and he likes to put that kind of mystery into his own lyrics from the start. He has achieved this in a variety of ways. A recent song, 'If dogs run free', uses the delicious wordless vocal scribble of a Black scat-singer to render mysterious a rather empty lyric. This seems as much in character as those unfocused colour photographs on his record sleeves. Certainly his long-established preference for mystery in the verbal texture has been an important factor in his development.

Dylan's career of a decade or so is already conventionally divided into three periods. The first is Protest. The second is marked not only by the use of electric guitar and so forth, but by a change of tone more easily recognised than described: Protest offered too simple a kind of authenticity, and the songs of 1964–5 have to do with a more complex notion of the truth, with what he called in 'Tombstone blues' 'the geometry of innocence'. There is now no alternative society, no easy way to drop out of the general guilt, no absolute freedom: 'Are birds free from the chains of the skyway?' The recommendation, insofar as there is one, is against 'lifelessness', the sort of self-betrayal against which he warns Ramona, and for some kind of recognition that after you've escaped from the meaninglessness of appearance into unglamorous reality – down the manhole, or into 'Desolation Row' – innocence and authenticity lie only in responding truly to the casual challenges of precisely the kind of mystery represented by the incoherence and irrationality of Dylan's own texts. The third period is what we now have: musical experiment and pastiche or re-exploration of old styles – country, blues, rock-'n'-roll, etc., including reminiscences of his own earlier manners.

Shakespeare and Beethoven are traditionally allowed four periods, so how is Dylan using his up so fast? There are two interrelated reasons, one personal and the other public. Dylan is a great rejecter – he rejects his own role-playing ('I'm really not the right person to tramp around the country saving souls'), his own audience (he says he's not a 'performer' and the songs would exist without an audience), and his own songs. He dislikes anything programmatic, mistrusts the wrong kind of relevance or specificity ('there's nothing, absolutely nothing, to be specific *about*'). If you look at the song that had the greatest political effect – 'Blowin' in the wind' – you'll see that even there the questions are not all about pacifism or liberty or equality, and those that are lack specificity, are very abstractly presented, and answered only by the mysterious ballad refrain. 'With God on our side', though undoubtedly more pointed and ironical, is more complex, notably in the Jesus and Judas reference, than its simple occasion requires. Dylan often speaks of his distrust for 'messages', and even in the relatively straightforward 'Who killed Davey Moore?' the message is partly concealed behind an ancient and practically universal folk motif.

This preference for mystery, opacity, a sort of emptiness in his texts, a passivity about meaning, is no doubt a deep temperamental trait. Some of the best of the early poems are talking blues, and even then he was a master of the obliquely subversive drop-out lines at the ends of the stanzas, as in 'Talkin' World War III blues' ('And I drove down 42nd Street/In my Cadillac/Good car to drive after a war'), or in the celebrated closing lines. The movie *Don't Look Back* has some casual remarks that illustrate a refusal to accept the responsibility of being explicit or suasive. 'I just go out there and sing 'em . . . I got nothing to say about these things I write.' The gushing High Sheriff's Lady of Nottingham is presented with a mouth organ, which constitutes a parable about mystery in personality and in song: Hamlet gave the tiresome and unmusical Guildenstern a recorder for the same reason. 'Why, look you now,' says Hamlet, 'how unworthy a thing you make of me! You would play upon me, you would seem to know my stops, you would pluck out the heart of my mystery . . . 'Sblood, do you think I am easier to be play'd on than a pipe?' The second and third periods, different as they are, have in common bigger and more various musical sound and the rougher, more random

verbal texture that ensures the protection of mystery. The listener
provides the response, brings his own meanings; he is offered no
message, only mystery. Dylan says that audience reaction 'doesn't
matter', but also that he welcomes 'with open arms' people who
analyse his songs.

The necessary public participation is a factor in his rapid
changes of style. For earlier poets, change was a slower process,
issuing from an active dialogue with an audience that was always
ready for a manageable extension of the poet's language. Of course
the whole process speeded up when it became an ambition on
the part of poets to shock by dropping out of public syntax
and crossing commonplace semantic limits – say, after Rimbaud.
Now, however, there is a new factor: instant response from a
public which is not interested in old styles of verbal precision,
doesn't care much if the words are inaudible or obscure, seeks
the gut before the mental response. In this situation there is no
interpretive feedback, no check on sense; liberated from linguistic
responsibility the poet cultivates his own mystery, does his own
thing only.

Dylan can rely on the crispness, accuracy and immediacy
of the musical performance to cover semantic blur. Thus the
brilliant second-period 'Subterranean homesick blues' – modern
Skeltonics delivered with great pace and verve – has as a very
general theme the hostility between drop-out drug users and the
police, with observations on the obscenity of the whole social
and education system; but it is full of allusions to which every
man brings his own key. The most ambitious example of these
procedures is 'Desolation Row'. This strange narrative begins:
'They're selling postcards of the hanging/They're painting the
passports brown.' We're in a surrealist town with a circus, a beauty
parlour for sailors, a restless riot squad. Behind all this stands the
unattractive but apparently stable Desolation Row. From it may
be seen a procession of figures, all behaving uncharacteristically:
Cinderella, Romeo, the Good Samaritan, Ophelia, 'Einstein, disguised as Robin Hood' and, having abandoned the electric violin,
on the bum; a Doctor Filth, the Phantom of the Opera in disguise,
Casanova; finally T.S. Eliot and Ezra Pound in a seascape with
mermaids. All this is a deliberate cultural jumble – history seen
flat, without depth, culture heroes of all kinds known only by
their names, their attributes lost by intergenerational erosion – all
of them so much unreality against the background of Desolation
Row, the flat and dusty truth, the myth before the myth began.

That this is the plot Dylan makes clear in a last verse which rejects a correspondent for trying out culture figures on him: 'I had to rearrange their faces/And give them all another name.' Send me no more such letters, he adds; send no more letters at all, 'Not unless you mail them/From Desolation Row.' Here the general deviance, the lack of stereoscopy in the cultural reference, gives the poem its whole force.

The later work continues to be unpredictable, offering no interpretive handholds. There is even an alteration or extension of the quality of Dylan's own voice. How different from the characteristically rebarbative whine is the baritone assurance of 'Lay, lady, lay'. This song also has a very accomplished lyric: no explanations, but enough suggestiveness (in 'His clothes are dirty, but his hands are clean', for example) to keep it clear of the banality of pop love-song. 'New morning' is a simple sketch which the dependable buffs have filled with enormous symbolisms of rebirth; what's characteristic here is the line 'Automobile comin' into style', which doesn't belong to the pictures in any obvious way and might push the date of the action back a century. This is tough on the allegorists but good for Dylan, who needs organised ambiguity rather than automatic writing to preserve himself best as a poet.

And Dylan remains a poet, as he has remained a virtuoso of the voice – snarling, pushing words and tunes askew, endlessly inventive. His peculiar relationship with his audience – they must teach themselves to do the work of performance and interpretation – has its dangers, which is why he often tells them that it is not his business to solve their problems but simply to get on with his own work. They can be co-creators if they want to, or drop out. So far, despite the occasional outburst of dismay, they have stayed with him, and he has himself probably seen that he can be too inward, too solipsistic. What he offers is mystery, not just opacity, a geometry of innocence which they can flesh out. His poems have to be open, empty, inviting collusion. To write thus is to practise a very modern art, though, as Dylan is well aware, it is an art with a complicated past.

* * *

Bob Dylan's lyrics are popular in a way that such songs haven't been in a long time. For they are ballads and they go back to the songs of the lumberjacks and cowboys pressing the Frontier forward. These in turn go back to Irish and English songs of the places where these pioneers came from.

These old ballads usually told simple stories of love and death. However, they didn't exist in a vacuum. They came out of a lot of people living in a situation of violence or adventure or war which the singer shared with each member of his audience. He was one of them, and he voiced both their longings and their fears.

Bob Dylan's lyrics are different from the jazz or blues of the Twenties or Thirties because they're not for sophisticated upper-class people . . . or the group of connoisseurs mad about the technique of jazz. They are for a public which is more concerned with identifying with the situations which the words are about than with admiring the wit of a song like [Harold Arlen's] 'Let's fall in love' or the brilliance of a jazz band. They are not followed by the kind of middle-class smart audience which went to Coward revues. However, the audiences are not workers either. They are the young.

This kind of singing with the singer accompanying himself on his guitar seems to happen, more or less spontaneously, when there is a strong sense of community and perhaps also of social crisis. It happened as the Frontier advanced westward again during the First World War, with songs whose words were very like those of Bob Dylan, for example:

> I want to go home,
> The coal-box and shrapnel they whistle and roar,
> I don't want to go to the trenches no more.

It happened during the Depression with 'Buddy, can you spare a dime?' and the Thirties had ballads sung by the Red Army, Fascists, Spanish Republicans, etc. There was, a few years ago, a bar in Warsaw where they sang the whole lot.

In the same way there was a revival of the guitar-accompanied lyric in America during the time of the protests against the war in Vietnam. Youth has become a Cause not so much on account of the famous age gap between the old and the young, but because the old are that much nearer death than the young, so they are less worried by things like the H-bomb, pollution, etc., which probably won't happen in their lifetime. On the other hand, the young are the most threatened generation-with-fifty-years-of-life-before-them in the world's history. The young have become a worldwide party shouting at the top of their voice, and to a background of electric guitars and drums, that they want their life.

After this one can understand the phenomenon that is Bob Dylan, though he is also, to my mind, a bit of a disappointment.

What is good is that out of the vastly rich, vastly corrupt world of pop entertainment a few human voices, like those of the Beatles when they were young, have arisen. Bob Dylan is certainly one of these voices. Highly skilled, he is not submerged in his professionalism, he can write and sing with real feeling, his words show real concern about the fate of the world and he seems both his own voice and that of his audience.

It is difficult to judge the lyrics as 'poems' because they don't really have to be poetry. They just have to produce their simple effects of feeling, colour and mild wit, which show in the voice and are not outrhythmed by the guitar. They do all this well, especially as they are compounded by the handsome young singer himself and by the enthusiasm of the kids.

They don't have to be poetry, nor do any ballads, but some, like those in various anthologies, have succeeded in being it. Up to a point they do work as poetry works. For example, Bob Dylan sets up a number of questions, like 'how many deaths will it take till he knows/That too many people have died?' and finds that 'The answer is blowin' in the wind.' This is a poet's answer to an unanswerable question and it has the effect of poetry, which is to open up the sky. In another lyric, 'Lay, lady, lay, lay across my big brass bed', he does something which illustrates, for me, the doubt I feel about the kind of thing he does a lot of the time. He says to her, 'Whatever colours you have in your mind/I'll show them to you and you'll see them shine.' This looks poetic but in me it raises doubts. W.B. Yeats has some lines which express my objection: 'When I was young,/I had not given a penny for a song/Did not the poet sing it with such airs/That one believed he had a sword upstairs.'

It is the peacock poet who should be showing his dazzling plumes, not bringing out the latent colours in his dumb chick's mind.

I prefer the anti-war, anti-society poems like 'With God on our side' and 'Subterranean homesick blues'. The first of these expresses the ironic idea that God's on the side of the big battalions, and makes a very neat and bitter survey of American history in which 'The cavalries charged/The Indians died.' This is a true ballad and every point is clearly made. 'Subterranean homesick blues' expresses the young American's frenetic disillusionment with his society very vividly. Every line hammers in the hysteria: 'Better jump down a manhole/Light yourself a candle/Don't wear sandals.'

There's an extraordinary wildness and freedom of fantasy here and yet the examples of behaviour that will get you into trouble with the authorities are near enough to reality for it to be rather frightening and for 'social criticism' really to be made.

Apart from this last lyric, the others are a bit soft. The trouble is they don't really come out of the front line or the frontier or poverty. They come out of the entertainment industry and immense sums are being made. Bob Dylan may be sincere in every line he sings, but the atmosphere of the industry soaks through an awful lot of this, like incontinent urine through pants. It is very sad to say this because, as with the Beatles, one feels that here there is talent and goodwill on the part of the artists and innocent response from the audience.

But though the independent views expressed in the songs might be unpopular with some cop, there is nothing that would not be immensely approved of by the conventional young rebels who buy the tickets.

CHRISTOPHER RICKS
Clichés and American English *

from *The Force of Poetry*

Geoffrey Hill's poems are not aloof, but they are high. Yet he has his own proper accommodation with our casually down-to-earth clichés. So does an artist of a very different kind. Bob Dylan's art does not traffic in clichés, but it travels far and near by the vehicle of cliché. For what could a popular song be which scorned or snubbed cliché? Those who wish to disparage the art of Dylan ought to make sure, at least, that they go no further than did William James in his affectionate disparagement of William Shakespeare:

> He seems to me to have been a professional *amuser*, in the first instance, with a productivity like that of a Dumas, or a Scribe; but possessing what no other amuser has possessed, a lyric splendour added to his rhetorical fluency, which has made people take him for a more essentially serious human being than he was. Neurotically and erotically, he was hyperaesthetic, with a playful graciousness of character never surpassed. He could be profoundly melancholy; but even then was controlled by his audience's needs . . . Was there ever an author of such emotional importance whose reaction against false conventions of life was such an absolute zero as his?[1]

For Shakespeare, read Dylan? But would it anyway be the best thing for an artist to do with false conventions of life, or of language: to *react against* them?

Dylan has a newly instinctive grasp of the age-old instincts which created a cliché in the first place and this is manifest on all the occasions when he throws new light on an old cliché, or rotates a cliché so that a facet of it catches a new light. At the same time, like the very unlike Geoffrey Hill, he often grounds his wit,

---

* An earlier version appeared as 'Clichés that come to pass' in *The Telegraph*, 15.

humour, and pathos on an intuition as to how a cliché may incite reflection, and not preclude it, by being self-reflexive.

> Well, ask me why I'm drunk alla time,
> It levels my head and eases my mind.
> I just walk along and stroll and sing,
> I see better days and I do better things.
>
>   ('I shall be free')

The phrase 'seen better days' has itself seen better days – that would do as the definition of a cliché. But Dylan brings it from its past into his and our present, by turning it into the present tense, 'I see better days'; and by marrying it to 'and I do better things' he does a far better thing with it than usual. He eases it from a dim past into a bright present. He helps us see it in a better light, so that instead of its ordinary sad backward glance, there is a step forward, the strolling of an unaggressive intoxication which refreshes the flat old phrase. Just an accident? There are too many such happy accidents in Dylan's songs for them not to be felicities. Anyway, Dylan knows perfectly well that the tired phrase 'seen better days' is usually imprisoned within its exhausted meaning – you can hear him sing the glum words in someone else's song on a tape from 1961. His own 'I shall be free' is free from the clichéness of its clichés, without getting proudly trapped in the illusion that you can free yourself from clichés by having no truck with them.

'I see better days' has its appealingly wide-eyed hopefulness. But Dylan can narrow his eyes, suspicious of too easy a sympathy with those who are dangerously wrong. So take the cliché 'see through your eyes'. Ordinarily, casually, it means putting yourself in the other man's place, seeing things through his eyes. Far harder to do than the easy saying of it would suggest. Possibly a very misguided thing to do, too. So Dylan wrests the cliché into the more stringent sense which goes with sharp-eyed suspicion: 'seeing through things' as knowing their cunning and hypocrisy.

> But I see through your eyes
> And I see through your brain
> Like I see through the water
> That runs down my drain.
>   ('Masters of war')

For the first verse had sung 'I just want you to know/I can see through your masks' – the vigilant sense of 'see through' – so that when we hear 'But I see through your eyes' we see that it doesn't mean the usual blandly magnanimous thing ('from your point of view'), but the stubborn opposite: I see what your eyes are trying to hide. The cliché has been alerted, and we are alerted to its clichéness, seeing the words from a new perspective, a different point of view, and seeing penetratingly through them.

A cliché begins as heartfelt, and then its heart sinks. But no song about lovers and their hearts can afford to turn away from those truths which may never get old but whose turns of phrase have got old and grey and full of sleep. The trouble with a cliché like 'take it to heart' is that by now it's almost impossible to take it to heart. Yet genius with words is often a matter, as T.S. Eliot said,[2] of being original with the minimum of alteration, and such is one of the evidences of Dylan's genius.

> So if you find someone that gives you all of her love,
> Take it to your heart, don't let it stray . . .
>
> > ('I threw it all away')

'Take it to heart' becomes 'take it to your heart', just enough to take it into the heartfelt; 'it' stands for 'all of her love', and there is the tiny touching swerve from 'someone' in the previous line – you'd think it was going to be 'So if you find someone that gives you all of her love/Take *her* to your heart', and take her in your arms.

'Make it new,' commanded Ezra Pound from the captain's tower. It goes for clichés too. Not one is irredeemable, thanks especially to the grace of that self-reflexiveness which, so long as it doesn't escalate its claims as if it were the only thing which art were ever preoccupied with, can rightly be valued as a great deal of late twentieth-century criticism has valued it: as a power for wit, humour, true acknowledgement, thought and feeling in the renovation of the state of the language.

The distinctive poignancy of American English within American literature has much to do with its making its own linguistic transience – the unlikelihood that the battery could be charged afresh with energy – an acknowledgement and not just an admission. The sense that some of the most vivid words in today's language are – to take up Eliot's terms of disparagement – 'inherently transitory', 'certain to be superseded', 'certain to pass away' and 'cannot endure': this sense can then itself be constitutive of some of the great effects of distinctively American literature, so that the degradation and deterioration of the language become, though always losses, the source of new gains.

Every user of language, whatever his or her politics, is engaged not only in conversation but in conservation. In any language, 'the conservative interest' predominates. The terms are those of Henry James:

> The question is whether it be not either no language at all, or only a very poor one, if it have not in it to respond, from its core, to the constant appeal of time, perpetually demanding new tricks, new experiments, new amusements of it: so to respond without losing its characteristic balance. The answer to that is, a hundred times, 'Yes' [not 'Yeh-eh' or 'Yeh-ep'], assuredly, so long as the conservative interest, which should always predominate, remains, equally, the constant quantity; remains an embodied, constituted, inexpugnable thing. The conservative interest is really as indispensable for the institution of speech as for the institution of matrimony.[3]

But the *extent* to which the conservative interest within language predominates varies greatly from one society to another. It predominates more in Britain and in British English than in American and American English.

The American poet Ed Dorn has said:

> Our articulation is quite different from other people's; we arrive at understanding and meaning through massive assaults on the language, so no particular word is apt to be final. It's rapidly rerun all the time. And I think that can be healthy usage. On the other hand, there's so much of it that it gets the reputation for being loose. A lot of it in fact is.[4]

Put like that, it might sound blithe. The best American poets convey the poignancy of there being nothing final. Bob Dylan, for instance. 'It's rapidly rerun all the time.' With personal experience and with American technology in his mind's eye, Dylan sings, in 'If you see her, say hello':

> Sundown, yellow moon, I replay the past
> I know every scene by heart, they all went by so fast.

There is no such thing as a video of the heart; replaying the past does depend on knowing every scene by heart; but what makes this heartfelt is the unspoken 'and yet'. 'And yet they all went by so fast'; not 'because they all went by so fast'. You'd have been right to expect that it would have been by their having gone by so slowly that they were known by heart. It isn't that by some audacity 'fast' means 'slow' (Black English sometimes likes 'bad' to mean 'good'); simply that you have to be quick on the uptake as Dylan kisses the joy as it flies, in both senses of 'it flies'. Again, in 'Is your love in vain?', he sings: 'Are you so fast that you cannot see that I must have solitude?' – where 'fast' means slow on the emotional uptake because of being so determinedly ahead of the game. To say of someone, especially of a woman, that she was 'fast' was itself once a fast (indecorous and suggestive) thing to say; but this sense faded. The language, sensitive to these glowings and fadings, is in sympathy with the love-experience which likewise has its glowing and fading.

'No time to think'? That is the title, and the refrain, of a Dylan song. But in terms of the transitory language, it is not that there is no time to think, but rather that one of the things that must be promptly thought about is that there's no time. The refrain in this Dylan song is always 'And there's no time to think' – until the last verse. Then the refrain line both expands and contracts: it expands, in that it takes over the whole of the last verse; it contracts, in that in the final end when it is time for the last refrain, time so presses ('no time to lose') that instead of 'And there's no time to think', the refrain is curtailed to 'And no time to think'.

> No time to choose when the truth must die,
> No time to lose or say goodbye,
> No time to prepare for the victim that's there,
> No time to suffer or blink
> And no time to think.

The point is not that British English is insensitive to time (no language ever can be); rather that, because it gives a less important role than does American English to the ephemeral or transitory or obsolescent, there are certain effects occluded from it – effects which cannot as clearly be seen and shown from the vantage point of this one form of English as against the other. Effects, for example, of rueful admission; of American English itself conceding that much of it not only is not built to last, but is built not to last. Some love affairs are like that, and a poet or singer is likely to create something worth his and our while when his love affair with his medium, language, is intimate with this sense of what a 'while' is (in language and in life) that something should be worth it. Dylan sings, as no English singer quite could,

> You will search, babe,
> At any cost.
> But how long, babe,

> Can you search for what's not lost?
> Ev'rybody will help you,
> Some people are very kind.
> But if I can save you any time,
> Come on, give it to me,
> I'll keep it with mine.
>
> ('I'll keep it with mine')

An English counterpart could have effected the spectral presence there of 'keep . . . time'; but could not have trusted British English so perfectly to compact, as American English here does, the smallest social offer and the largest offer of salvation:

> But if I can save you any time . . .
> But if I can save you   anytime . . .

It is not only the compacting of the two senses within the one line which shows the sheer egalitarian width of American English, but the compacting within the second sense – 'But if I can save you   anytime' – of the most serious magnanimity with the casual largesse of conversational acknowledgement – 'any time' in that sense is pure American in the way in which, socially at ease, it fosters such ease. It can even be printed as one word in American English; when *sung* by Dylan it is not unmistakably two words as it is when he prints his words. Within art (and the daily language too can be used with art), 'any time' gets some of its force, breezily fresh, from the sense that it is not itself a phrase which could have figured in American society and American English '*any* time'.

'No particular word is apt to be final,' said Ed Dorn. But *finally* to be apt, that is a different matter; and the word 'final' or 'finally' stands differently to experience in American English for this very reason: that a consciousness of how little is final in words or out of them pervades the saying. There is a gambling song by Dylan, 'Rambling, gambling Willie', which has the line: 'When the game finally ended up, the whole damn boat was his'. The game didn't just end, it ended up (those verbal phrases which Eliot deprecated); and it didn't just end up, it finally ended up. ('No particular word is apt to be final.') There is a mild surprise at its being possible to say 'finally ended up' without sheer tautology; and yet it makes perfect sense, since a gambling game is always ending and beginning again, until the last hand, when it finally ends up; in this, the gambling game is like the song itself, which is always coming to an end with each verse (ending with the refrain 'Wherever you are a-gamblin' now, nobody really knows'), but does finally end up. Or again, Dylan sings to Ramona: 'You've been fooled into thinking/That the finishin' end is at hand.' Not one of those temporary or tentative ends, but the finishing end. In 'All I really want to do', Dylan sings:

> I ain't lookin' to block you up,
> Shock or knock or lock you up,
> Analyse you, categorise you,
> Finalise you, or advertise you.

– where 'finalise' gets it pouncing power not just from being a word that was American before English (though Australian before American), but also – given the American sense of how finality fleets away, like an advertisement ('Finalise you, or advertise you') – from being such a shrug of a word. And one might (in passing . . .) notice Dylan's dexterity with the phrase which is apocryphally taken as getting the Englishman into trouble, when he asks for an early call in the morning:

> I ain't lookin' to block you up,
> Shock or knock or lock you up.

The sly propriety tactfully, pregnantly, separates 'knock' from 'you up' for a couple of words; after all, the preceding 'shock' would more suggest 'shock you' than 'shock you *up*' (though one of the things that Dylan is doing is giving a shake to the phrase 'shake you up'). Nobody need feel embarrassed; it all goes by so fast.

You can hear the acknowledgement of the transient, the obsolescent, in the imaginative use in American English of such a sturdily old-time phrase as 'come to pass'. In British English, this could be well-used with simple archaic dignity, with the sense of something more grave than any simple happening: under 'come to pass', *Collins Dictionary* (1979) is flatly reduced to '*archaic*. To happen'. But the creative use of the phrase within American English is likely to pick up the poignancy of 'come *to pass*', a poignancy which the English poet may believe has to be spelt out rather than intimated; spelt out, for instance, as Christina Rossetti does when she makes her two-stanza poem 'May' turn upon a change of these words:

> I cannot tell you how it was;
> But this I know: it came to pass –

> Upon a bright and breezy day
> When May was young, ah pleasant May!
> As yet the poppies were not born
> Between the blades of tender corn;
> The last eggs had not hatched as yet,
> Nor any bird forgone its mate.
>
> I cannot tell you what it was;
> But this I know: it did but pass.
> It passed away with sunny May,
> With all sweet things it passed away,
> And left me old, and cold, and grey.

This is altogether more explicit, more explicated even, than the American way with the phrase. There is a poem by John Crowe Ransom, 'Spectral lovers', which has the stanza:

> And gesturing largely to the moon of Easter,
> Mincing his steps and swishing the jubilant grass,
> Beheading some field-flowers that had come to pass,
> He had reduced his tributaries faster
> Had not considerations pinched his heart
> Unfitly for his art.

'Jubilant' swings on into 'Beheading some field-flowers', but does sadden at 'that had come to pass'. Ransom uses the phrase with an Anglophile elegance that is yet tinged with what is now an un-English shivering of the phrase. Dylan, in a song ('I pity the poor immigrant') which has its connections with the 'polyglot' immigrations that perturbed Dr Leavis, ends his vision of this suffering with:

> I pity the poor immigrant . . .
> Whose visions in the final end
> Must shatter like the glass.
> I pity the poor immigrant
> When his gladness comes to pass.

'In the final end' finds some resilience in the fact that this is itself nearing the *last* ending of a verse; furthermore its near-tautology is effectively American. Moreover, those last lines of the song, 'I pity the poor immigrant/When his gladness comes to pass', sharply challenge the British English sense of the phrase. You can of course imagine kinds of gladness for the happening, the arrival of which somebody is to be pitied (sadistic kinds, for instance); but the pressure of the phrase is essentially to make you acknowledge that gladness comes *to pass*. 'We Poets in our youth begin in gladness;/But thereof come in the end despondency and madness.'

'The conservative interest' is present in the old-world phrase 'come to pass', but in the Dylan song it does not predominate. Something has happened since the old days of the phrase; has come to pass. Sometimes, though, Dylan does need to help the conservative interest predominate. Then he will move from a quintessentially American phrase like 'big dreams' to a British English way of speaking.

God don't make no promises that He don't keep.
You've got some big dreams, baby, but in order
    to dream you   gotta still be asleep.
When you gonna wake up, when you gonna wake up,
When you gonna wake up and strengthen the things that remain.
                    ('When you gonna wake up')

For there the language to which he means to awaken his audience is not American English, with its 'big dreams', but the conservative and conserving force of the *Revelation* of the King James Bible: 'Be watchful, and strengthen the things which remain, that are ready to die.'[5] The line is itself one of the things which remain; and it impinges newly within a sense of the language itself as elsewhere so 'ready to die'.

For American English is especially alive with words and phrases that are ready to die; this can be a great resource, provided that the words and phrases admit it – not so much admit that they *have* seen better days as admit that before very long they will have seen better days. In every language there are clichés (phrases which have seen better days), and slang; clichés and slang can be very different, but they are both likely to have a short life-expectancy, if life is vividness and vitality. Then they can become zombies or ghosts; dead but they won't lie down, like that phrase itself. In every language an artist, or an imaginative conversationalist, can unexpectedly show that they are not really dead but sleeping; or not quite dead, and so can be given the kiss of life; or quite dead, but can be resurrected. Yet it is in American English – with its constitutional need to be novel, since how else could it free itself from British English? – that there can most often be created this particular poignancy, of a language acknowledging that much of it is not long for this world, and building an art which lasts out of a medium which admits that many of its characteristic components will not last. 'The order is/Rapidly fadin',' sings Dylan (in 'The times they are a-changin''), with some play of *rapidly* against *fading*. Or, in one of the loveliest lines on *Infidels*: 'Only a matter of time 'til night comes steppin' in.'

TIMOTHY O'GRADY
The Prince

I read *Hamlet* again while recovering from an operation to my spine and was forcibly struck, as I lay there in my bed, by two notions quite irrelevant to the play. I was, at the time, four years into a novel which would occupy me for another six months, and such was the play's magnificent cohesion, its grandeur of passion and intent, its ability to say the unsayable, that I thought, Why bother? Such crises of unnerving are, I think, endemic to the composition of long prose works, and it passed.

The other was the recognition – in passing, and perhaps strange to relate – of the similarity between the character of Hamlet and that of the subject of this book, as I had known him through his utterances and his work. Their myriadness, their wearing of masks to unmask others, their capacities to hurt and be hurt, their venom, wit and tenderness expressed in a poetry so pure as to make all around it seem prosaic, their seductive mysteriousness, their almost incandescent intensity. Such qualities as these.

I had first thought of Bob Dylan's resemblance to Hamlet while reading Act III, scene ii, the scene with Rosencrantz and Guildenstern after the entrance of the Players with their recorders. It is about Hamlet's unknowability, and it has about it the quality of one of Dylan's press conferences. Hamlet knows that his two friends are now effectively agents of Claudius in his attempt to comprehend and neutralise him. He seizes a recorder and thrusts it into Guildenstern's hand, demanding that he play. 'My lord, I cannot,' comes the reply. Hamlet grows intimidatingly insistent, while Guildenstern continues to protest his incompetence.

> GUILDENSTERN: I know no touch of it, my lord.
> HAMLET: It is as easy as lying. Govern these ventages with your finger and thumb, give it breath with your mouth, and it will discourse most eloquent music. Look you, these are the stops.
> GUILDENSTERN: But these cannot I command to any utt'rance of harmony; I have not the skill.
> HAMLET: Why, look you now, how unworthy a thing you make of me! You would play upon me; you would seem to know my stops; you would pluck out the heart of my mystery; you would sound me from my lowest note to the top of my compass; and there is much music, excellent voice in this little organ, yet cannot you make it speak. 'Sblood, do you think I am easier to be played on than a pipe? Call me what instrument you will, though you can fret me, you cannot play upon me.

Lesser figures than he have of course been trying to play upon Bob Dylan ever since he opened his throat to sing. It would seem they have wanted to nail him down, to impose some pattern of development on him, to pluck out the heart of his mystery, and it would seem they want these things because they want what he has. But if there is anything definitive which could be said about his nearly thirty years of writing and performing it is that he has been undefinable. I do not think that he can be met head-on with an instrument as blunt as discursive prose. Like mercury he would evade the grasp. Sam Shepard could only approach him in prose by describing shades of blue. I am reminded of the ridiculous bewilderment of Claudius and his courtiers as they strive to unriddle Hamlet's feigned madness. In writing about him here I do not wish to add to the suffocating pile of exegesis, to track or trace him, to presume to know who he is or what are the definitive meanings of his songs. I could say that in a small way it is a repayment of a debt – for among other things he makes you want to write – but I doubt whether the creditor would wish to collect. Nor is it an analysis of either Dylan or Hamlet. It is simply a discovery of some of the points where they intersect, a metaphor of a kind, each of the other.

For Hamlet, the world as he has known it has been obliterated.

The play begins, like some of Dylan's songs, in darkness and uncertainty, a 'Who's there?' uttered on the midnight battlements, with the Prince having suffered a psychological wound so catastrophic as to reach to the centre of his mind and upend all certainties of family, state and self. The agent of this destruction is a woman. Hamlet is tormented by the death of his father, offended by the state of the Danish court and nauseated by the likes of Polonius, but it is the behaviour of his mother which has poisoned his soul. It is as though his security, his very identity even, lay somehow in her. And while his need for her is extreme and all-encompassing, it is accompanied by a fear that she might withdraw from him at any time, a fear of her capriciousness and the power of her sexuality, so that when she foreshortens the period of mourning for his father and marries Claudius – incestuously in Hamlet's eyes – when, that is, she betrays his vision of her, it is not only Hamlet's sense of his mother which decomposes before him but, by extension, of women everywhere, of practically everything he has seen and known. His mother has to him become a whore and the world in consequence has withered around him – its chief inhabitant, man, once 'infinite in faculties, in form and moving so express' and so on, is now 'this quintessence of dust' and the world itself, which had been 'this goodly frame' to him, has become 'a foul and pestilent congregation of vapours'. Hamlet clearly has it bad. I cannot recall anyone in literature who has been so thoroughly undone by a woman.

I opened a collection of Dylan's lyrics at random and found that of the succeeding fifty songs, thirty-eight seemed to me to be addressed to women. Apart from those which are open declarations of love, what marks them is what marks the character of Hamlet – an awesome sensitivity to pain and betrayal, accompanied by an equivalent capacity to hurt. Hamlet is in a rage precariously governed only by his own articulateness. In a line which is, in its way, like

> I wish that for just one time
> You could stand inside my shoes
> And just for that one moment
> I could be you
> Yes, I wish that for just one time
> You could stand inside my shoes
> You'd know what a drag it is
> To see you

Hamlet tells his mother he will 'set you up a glass/Where you may see the inmost part of you', and then commences a lengthy assault detailing the nature of her crime:

> Such an act
> That blurs the grace and blush of modesty,
> Calls virtue hypocrite, takes off the rose
> From the fair forehead of an innocent love,
> And sets a blister there, makes marriage vows
> As falls as dicers' oaths . . .

the whole of it escalating in fury and growing more sexually graphic,

> Nay, but to live
> In the rank sweat of an enseamèd bed,
> Stewed in corruption, honeying and making love
> Over the nasty sty . . .

In the way that Dylan knows that he 'can find you . . . /In somebody's room', Hamlet is tormented by his mother's fickleness, her sexual treachery, a crime that he cannot stop himself from seeing in every woman's face, even that of Ophelia, his lover, and probably the only character of significance with a plausible claim to innocence. It is Ophelia, far more than Gertrude, who really gets it in the neck. When Ophelia remarks that the prologue of the play-within-the-play is brief, Hamlet immediately responds 'as a woman's love'. Dylan's line, 'You told me that you'd be sincere,/Every day of the year's like playin' Russian roulette' could, in spirit, be contained within the onslaught: 'Get thee to a nunnery. Go, farewell . . . Or if thou wilt needs marry, marry a fool, for wise men know well enough what monsters you make of them. . . . I have heard of your paintings, well enough. God hath given you one face, and you make yourselves another. You jig and amble, and you lisp; you nickname God's creatures, and you make your wantonness your ignorance. . . .'

It is such bitterness as this which drives the caustic brilliance of songs like 'Idiot wind' or 'Like a rolling stone'. Hamlet taunts Ophelia sexually as they watch the play, ridicules her vanity in the manner of the song 'Leopard-skin pill-box hat', plays like a juggler with her emotions, and dismisses her as casually as, 'I ain't sayin' you treated me unkind/You could have done better but I don't mind/You just kinda wasted my precious time/But don't think twice, it's all right.' Finally he kills her father without

conscience, driving her first mad and then to suicide. In all of this
she is not Ophelia, but Woman, the face of Woman as blighted by
the transgressions of his mother. Ophelia he loved, even to the end.
He says as much as he stands over her grave: 'I loved Ophelia. Forty
thousand brothers/Could not with all their quantity of love/Make
up my sum.' And Bob Dylan wrote such songs as 'Love minus
zero/No limit', 'Wedding song', 'Sad-eyed lady of the lowlands'
and 'Tomorrow is a long time'. But love and pain of this degree
are indissoluble. The love expressed in these songs turns to the
naked anguish of being alone and lost in the world, as in the beautifully rendered pain of the songs on *Blood on the Tracks* and *Street
Legal*, a state without time or space or point of reference at all.
And Hamlet's love, gone awry, has atomised all that he has known.

Hamlet arrives at the beginning of the play with the world
in effect a *tabula rasa*. For him the world that he has known
– the secure world of a court and state presided over by a
mother and father whom he loved – has been banished, been
made to disappear, become unreal, an illusion devised by others,
a trick. What remains in its place is the world unravelled in the
play, a world of skeletons and monstrosities who had once been
disguised in the clothing of respectability, a world too of threat
and upheaval, of war-mongering and the stockpiling of arms, of
political assassination and treachery, in which the land is governed
by killers and manipulators and windbags who wear masks of propriety, who 'smile and smile and be a villain', so that to Hamlet 'the
time is out of joint' and Denmark 'a prison', an insane, perverse
and squalid place where the law is a lie and all orders have been
reversed. The person sitting at the summit of this world is the
King, Claudius, the murderer of his father and the seducer of his
mother, and to Hamlet the title 'King' on the person of Claudius
is an obscenity, a kind of gaudy clothing. The life-long royalist
might now declare, like Dylan, 'Steal a little and they throw you
in jail,/Steal a lot and they make you king,' so debased does the
title now seem to him. Hamlet sees Claudius standing naked, like
the President of the United States in Dylan's song, past the pomp
and circumstance and the ceremonial robes to a soul so corrupt
as to infect all who support it – the time-servers, bureaucrats and
courtiers, the Osrics and Poloniuses. The whole of the court, and
more, are engulfed in Hamlet's damning vision.

I came into the 1960s at a different place and somewhat later
than Bob Dylan, but the mythology of that time – to which Dylan,
I would say, was the most original and most relentless contributor

– and the way it felt to me had much in common with Hamlet's Denmark. What is 'wrong in the state of Denmark', that upended world, is the world of 'Highway 61' or '115th Dream', or the view from 'Desolation Row'. Throughout the play Hamlet suffers such over-exposure to political hypocrisy that his despair becomes in part political:

> There's no respect
> That makes calamity of so long a life:
> For who would bear the whips and scorns of time,
> Th'oppressor's wrong, the proud man's contumely,
> the pangs of despised love, the law's delay,
> The insolence of office, and the spurns
> That patient merit of the unworthy takes,
> When he himself might his quietus make
> With a bare bodkin?

Hamlet's hatred of the author of this political hypocrisy, Claudius, is as cold and violent and complete as that expressed in 'Masters of war', and he has too an equivalent social rage, a contempt for convention, for 'society's pliers', as embodied in the person of Polonius. He insults Polonius throughout the play as a matter of course, and in the end kills him with indifference, as though he were no more than a waste of space. His contempt for Polonius – the ingratiator to the powerful, the custodian of the social order, the complaisant purveyor of clichés that enshroud him in dimness and insulate him from reality, full of preening self-regard and an inability to comprehend anything beyond his own narrow parameters – is the contempt displayed to Mr Jones, who has read 'all of F. Scott Fitzgerald's books', but has no idea what is happening. Polonius is an archetype. He could as easily be an alderman in a small Minnesota town in the 1950s as the Willie Whitelaw of Elsinore. His advice to his son Laertes prior to the young man's departure for France is, in its triteness and conservatism, rather like,

> Ah get born, keep warm,
> Short pants, romance, learn to dance
> Get dressed, get blessed,
> Try to be a success
> Please her, please him, buy gifts
> Don't steal, don't lift
> Twenty years of schoolin'
> And they put you on the day shift.

Bob Dylan grew up in Hibbing, Minnesota, during the Truman and Eisenhower years, a time of cold war certainties, deep parochial retrenchment and moral simplicities. Hamlet grew up in the court of Elsinore. His life too was governed by certainties – the wondrously subtle and seemingly everlasting hierarchies of the court, the glory and rightness of kingship. But then, in America, came presidents like Johnson and Nixon, napalm-dropping generals, judges who would go easy on the likes of William Zanzinger, patriots who murdered Medgar Evers. And, in Denmark, a murderer became king. What gives both Dylan and Hamlet their extraordinary vividness is the sense that they have awakened from a long illusion, that the world they had known has become manifestly insane, that they are looking upon it as it has never been looked upon before. What they have awakened to is uncertainty. There is no Garden of Eden of Peace and Love to replace what has been lost, no political or religious orthodoxy with which to stem the chaos. In their way they have nothing, and therefore nothing to lose, they are invisible, and ultimately have no secrets to conceal, they are out on the street with no way back, alone and naked in an impossibly varied universe.

It is an awakening such as this which is depicted in the song 'It's alright, ma (I'm only bleeding)'. In it there is the decaying world of 'fake morals', 'false gods', where 'the masters make the rules' and 'not much/Is really sacred' and 'money doesn't talk, it swears', along with the discovery that 'You lose yourself, you reappear' and 'suddenly find you got nothing to fear', that 'it is not he or she or them or it/That you belong to', that 'life outside goes on/All around you', that 'he not busy being born/Is busy dying' and that, in the end, 'it's life and life only'. There are too in this song the lines,

> For them that think death's honesty
> Won't fall upon them naturally,
> Life sometimes
> Must get lonely.

Death is the only certainty, the final equaliser. When Hamlet is in the graveyard with Horatio he moves among the bones and decaying corpses, speculating rather cheerfully, it seems, on whether they might have been politicians or courtiers, men of law or property, all of them knocked here and there with indifference by the gravedigger's spade, their positions and their property come finally to nothing, and wonders whether even the great Alexander, rotting away to dust, the dust become earth, the earth turned to loam, might now be engaged stopping up a beer barrel. And earlier, in the same vein, he outlines a brief parable of power for Claudius, who is searching in vain for the corpse of Polonius.

KING: Now, Hamlet, where's Polonius?
HAMLET: At supper.
KING: At supper? Where?
HAMLET: Not where he eats, but where he is eaten. A certain convocation of politic worms are e'en at him. Your worm is your only emperor for diet. We fat all creatures else to fat us, and we fat ourselves for maggots. Your fat king and your lean beggar is but variable service – two dishes, but to one table. That's the end.
KING: Alas, alas!
HAMLET: A man may fish with the worm that hath eat of a king, and eat of the fish that hath fed of that worm.
KING: What dost thou mean by this?
HAMLET: Nothing but to show you how a king may go a progress through the guts of a beggar.

I would have thought this could, with some surrealistic emendations, have likewise appeared among the liner notes on one of Dylan's records.

Hamlet does not in the usual way possess an overriding theme. It is not in the main about jealousy or vanity or betrayal or corruption. It is, if anything, about consciousness, about a mind that moves with phenomenal speed and intensity and which takes nothing for granted, which 'knows not "seems"' and has within it that 'which passes show'. Reality hits Hamlet with awesome force because he no longer has any defences against it – no platitudes, philosophies or effortless explanations. For a man who is forever berating himself for his inertia and indecisiveness, who is at times so miserable that he wishes to die, and for whom the world has become 'an unweeded garden that grows to seed', he possesses such mental vigour, breadth and courage that he makes all around him seem mediocre, untruthful and weak. The world is to him wondrous or painful or hilarious or any number of other things, but above all it is inescapable. It comes to him whole, and however intellectually dextrous he may be, or however brilliant his language, he cannot make the grief it gives him disappear with contrived solutions or charm it away with words. He does, in this sense, live outside the law of convention, and he is, in this sense, honest.

When Dylan arrived in Greenwich Village in the early 1960s he was, according to Irish musician Liam Clancy, like 'blotting paper. He soaked everything up. He had this immense curiosity. He was totally blank and ready to soak up everything that came within his range.' Someone else who knew him at that time, Sybil Weinberger, said, 'When we walked down the street he saw things that nobody else saw. He was so aware of his surroundings, in every situation, it was almost . . . frightening. . . . His reactions to things amazed me – to weather, people, cars, buildings, shapes. I always felt his comments had a great deal of objectivity. He would reach for that little spiral notebook and write about animals on the street or a newspaper headline.' He has, it would seem, like Hamlet, an excruciating sensitivity accompanied by an acute mental power, the capacity to see and be pained or exhilarated or convulsed by it, to 'know and feel too much within'.

Hamlet's 'antic disposition', a madness which reflects the world, is a contrivance – 'I am but mad north-northwest' – a cover which he uses while he attempts to discover the truth. It is a dislocation of the senses which makes him incomprehensible to others, opaque to any scrutiny, while allowing him to see what might not otherwise be seen, to speak in riddles that carry an ultimate truth, to discover those 'things in heaven and earth' that cannot be dreamt of in Horatio's philosophy. It does, in a way, bring reality nearer. It makes it more intense.

Dylan's antic disposition, the vexer of his interviewers, biographers and critics, has been a fundamental of his identity. Whether introducing himself as a drifting orphan from the Dust Bowl, creating another face with greasepaint, playing the surrealist clown for interviewers, passing through such diverse incarnations as folk balladeer, visionary scourge and down-home country singer, hiring a fat man with a beard to play 'Bob Dylan' in his film *Renaldo and Clara*, bending reality a little with 'Texas medicine' or whatever else might be brought along by 'Quinn the eskimo', or informing his audience, 'It's Hallowe'en and I've got my Bob Dylan mask on', he has kept himself well hidden while straying beyond the confines of his self. He has strayed quite a long way. He has passed through so many forms of identity that the question of who he is becomes meaningless. It is almost as though he has dispersed himself, disappeared into the world in all its random multiplicity. This is, I suppose, what he means, and maybe what

he feels, when he says, 'There is no Bob Dylan.' In both Hamlet
and Dylan there is a kind of heroism in this, in cutting loose from
the security of self and looking into the variable unknown. It is
only heroism of this kind which can explain the peculiar paradox
of charisma without a singular identity – Hamlet is mad, no one
knows what has become of him, yet he is, as Claudius says, loved
by 'the distracted multitude'. Dylan, I would say, could not do
otherwise except to keep himself hidden, to be many people and
no one, if he wishes to stay close to the source of his work. To
be endlessly reminded of who he is, to accept, for example, the
ossification of stardom, would be to remove himself from all that
has given such powerful immediacy to his writing.

The quality of Hamlet's speech leaves all around him standing
dumbfounded. In its speed and agility, its incisiveness and its
luminous concreteness, it is unique in the play, in Shakespeare, and
probably in all dramatic literature. Hamlet is not a soaring, heavens-
shaking rhetorician, nor is he much given to theory or abstraction.
His language derives from the commonplace, from the things of
the real, visible world and the most fundamental emotions, but he
speaks of them with such uncanny vividness that it seems as though
we are being presented with their very essences. Hazlitt wrote
about the play that in it we are not given 'fine versions and para-
phrases of nature', but rather 'the original text. . . . We read the
thoughts of the heart, we catch the passions as they rise.'

It is this fundamental quality of seeming to look upon the
world in a way that it has never been looked upon before that to
me distinguishes Dylan's writing. At its best, it is as though the
language has arrived whole from the unconscious, complete and
pure. It conveys experience, emotion, thought in themselves, as
they happen, and, in this way, it is indissoluble, unsummarisable,
impervious to analysis.

The story of Hamlet and the story of Dylan are, in part
at least, the story of the unconscious becoming conscious. At
the beginning of the play Hamlet is engulfed in a Freudian
nightmare which through unrelenting honesty he forces into the
light and comes finally to accept. Dylan had to do similarly with
his art. 'Right through the time of *Blonde on Blonde*,' he says, 'I was
writing songs unconsciously. Then one day I was half-stepping,
and the lights went out. And since that point, I more or less
had amnesia. Now, you can take that statement as literally or
metaphorically as you need to, but that's what happened to
me. . . . It happens to everybody. Think about the periods when

people don't do anything, or they lose it and have to regain it, or lose it and gain something else. . . . I was convinced I wasn't going to do anything else, and I had the good fortune to meet a man in New York City who taught me how to see. He put my mind and my hand and my eye together in a way that allowed me to do consciously what I unconsciously felt. . . . So now I'm connected back, and I don't know how long I'll be there. . . . '

Dylan and Hamlet both have the minds of artists, and this essay is really about writing. At their best they face the world without defences and attempt to deliver it whole in words. All great art comes from a profound well of experience – of pain and euphoria and observation – of which only the gleaned essence is presented. Wells of course run dry, and if so the great among us will do anything to fill them again. There is about this an amoral and extraordinarily courageous relentlessness. Whether by design or by some freak operation of the genes they will uproot and demolish themselves, enter exile or wilderness and struggle blindly to remake themselves, perhaps partly in a spiritual or psychological quest but I think finally to create art. Hamlet goes through this in the course of a five-act play and Dylan has done it again and again throughout his life.

I do not know where Dylan is now in terms of these intense and bewildering processes, but may his well always be refilled, may he always get reconnected, and good luck to him and God bless him in all that he does.

Postscript: Bob Dylan once owned a dog called Hamlet.

PAUL HODSON
Bob Dylan's stories about men

In 'Desolation Row' the blind commissioner comes, the good samaritan goes and the riot squad are restless. Ezra Pound and T.S. Eliot fight. The Phantom of the Opera shouts to skinny girls. Meanwhile Cinderella seems so easy, the lovely mermaids flow and Ophelia's sin is her lifelessness. Strong verbs describe men doing things alone and together and to women; weak verbs describe women who are smooth or contained. In this and many of Dylan's other songs, men and women seem to be quite different types of person. This essay is about the stories his songs tell about men.

'I'm still very patriotic to the highway.'⁶

Dylan often tells stories about men alone. They are rarely in houses or cities. They travel, often arduously. These solitary journeys seem to be essential parts of the character of admirable men:

> And when it's over I'd just as soon go on my way
> Up to some paradise
> Where the trout streams flow and the air is nice
> And ride a horse along the trail –
> But then they took him to the jailhouse
> Where they try to turn a man into a mouse
> ('Hurricane')

I woke up on the roadside, daydreamin' 'bout the way things
  sometimes are

> ('Idiot wind')

> How many roads must a man walk down
> Before you call him a man?
> ('Blowin' in the wind')

The blue-eyed son in 'A hard rain's a-gonna fall' journeys repeatedly and attains a kind of heroism by the end of the song:

> I'm a-goin' back out 'fore the rain starts a-fallin'
> I'll walk to the depths of the deepest dark forest ...

And I'll tell it and think it and speak it and breathe it,
And reflect it from the mountains so all souls can see it,
Then I'll stand on the ocean until I start sinkin'
But I'll know my song well before I start singin' . . .

These men often start their journeys by leaving women. Think of 'Don't think twice', 'Going, going, gone', 'We better talk this over', or 'Isis' ('I married Isis on the fifth day of May/But I could not hold on to her very long/So I cut off my hair and I rode straight away/For the wild unknown country where I could not go wrong.'). Sometimes at the end of a journey there is a cabin, nightfall and a woman – as in 'I'll be your baby tonight', 'On a night like this' or, again, 'Isis'. In this way, women set the boundaries of Dylan's men's journeys. But they have no place on the road.

'My friends have been the same as me, people who couldn't make it as the high-school football halfback, junior Chamber of Commerce leader, fraternity leader, truck driver working their way through college. I just had to be with them.'7

Men come in pairs in Dylan's stories as often as they come alone. They are usually doing something together, and while they do it Dylan seems to take sidelong glances at their relationship. Like men alone, men's activity together is often to travel: 'We set out that night for the cold in the north' ('Isis'); 'Rubin Carter and a couple of friends are drivin' around' ('Hurricane'); 'With his faithful slave Pedro behind him he [Gypsy Davey] tramps' ('Tombstone blues').

A second thread in Dylan's stories is men coping with the idea and effects of violence towards each other. In 'Joey', 'When they tried to strangle Larry, Joey nearly hit the roof'; later, 'I heard his best friend Frankie say, "He ain't dead, he's just asleep".' In 'Tombstone blues', 'John the Baptist, after torturing a thief/Looks up at his hero the Commander-in-Chief'. The narrator of 'Isis' responds to his fellow traveller's mysterious death by successively 'hopin' that it wasn't contagious', thinking he'd been had, saying 'a quick prayer' and telling Isis he loves her.

As that last response suggests, a third strand in Dylan's stories about men together is when their relationship pivots on a woman. This is the story in 'Lily, Rosemary and the Jack of Hearts'. Lily's lines are pause lines, cut-aways which draw out the growing tension of the relationship between Big Jim and the Jack of Hearts – 'Lily . . . took her dress off and buried it away.' Rosemary's is the pivotal role. Dylan uses her eyes to punctuate and underline each contact between the two men. When Big Jim and the Jack of Hearts first meet, 'She *fluttered her false eyelashes* and whispered in his ear,/"Sorry, darlin', that I'm late," but he didn't seem to hear/He was starin' into space over at the Jack of Hearts'. Then when 'the house lights did dim', presumably blocking Rosemary's sight, 'in the darkness of the room there was only Jim and him': Rosemary herself was 'tired of playin' the role of Big Jim's wife . . . She was *gazin'* to the future, riding on the Jack of Hearts'. When the story breaks, Rosemary is *'steady in her eyes*/She was with Big Jim but she was leanin' to the Jack of Hearts'. And on the gallows, with Big Jim dead and the Jack of Hearts missing, 'she didn't even *blink*'. It may be that Rosemary killed Big Jim, but it is the relationship between two men that is at the core of the story. Where Rosemary puts her eyes matters more to this story than where she put her penknife.

Dylan tells stories about the many different feelings men have for other men. These include competition – for power (as in 'Joey'), for a woman (many of the songs on *Blonde on Blonde*), for the high ground of morality ('Blowin' in the wind') or hipness (in 'Ballad of a thin man'). A frequent theme is buddies in adversity: 'There was me and Danny Lopez, cold eyes, black night and then there was Ruth' ('Something there is about you'). He also speaks of compassion – '"No reason to get excited," the thief he kindly spoke' ('All along the watchtower'). And 'Isis' is one of several songs shot through with sexuality between men: 'I gave him my blanket, he gave me his word.' The relationships between Dylan's men are complex, developing and rarely summed up. 'No one ever knew for sure where they were really at' ('Joey') is a common sentiment. 'Well, Frankie Lee and Judas Priest,/They were the best of friends' ('The ballad of Frankie Lee and Judas Priest') is a much rarer one, and the song goes on to undermine this flat simplicity.

'I do read Hemingway. He didn't have to use adjectives. He didn't really have to define what he was saying . . . That's what I want to be able to do.'[8]

In Bob Dylan's stories about men alone and together there is a sympathy for difference – for men who are working out their lives and coming to different ways of living. Listen to the many stories about men on *John Wesley Harding*. The lonesome hobo is separate, the wicked messenger silences himself, John Wesley Harding is 'a friend to the poor'. Dylan demands our sympathy for all these ways of coping. *Desire*, too, is full of men's stories, with Dylan asking us to admire a boxer, a gangster, a treasure hunter. These and other songs are about men choosing between evils, finding a way: 'Rubin could take a man out with just one punch/But he never did like to talk about it all that much' ('Hurricane'). The stories accept difference and complexity.

'If I don't get some girl that I like, or if I don't get something like that, I always just figure that if I know where I'm at, then nothing will hurt me.'⁹

Men in Dylan's stories rarely extend this acceptance to women. Instead two roles stand out: men defining women, and men teaching women.

Dylan often sings about women who are mysterious. Their mysteries are powerful, they undermine male genius: 'The geometry of innocence flesh on the bone/Causes Galileo's math book to get thrown/At Delilah . . . ' ('Tombstone blues'). Men do not let women's mysteries rest. Dylan tells many stories about a man's quest to define a woman's mystery. In some of these stories the quest is for the mystery *per se*: 'Love is so simple, to quote a phrase/You've known it all the time, I'm learnin' it these days' ('You're a big girl now').

More often, it is the mysterious woman herself who is the subject to be pinned down, 'Somethin' there is about you that I can't quite put my finger on' ('Something there is about you'); 'So easy to look at, so hard to define' ('Sara'). Sometimes the woman helps the quest along: 'You gimme a map and a key to your door'; other times, it requires a good deal of lonely male effort, 'Stayin' up for days in the Chelsea Hotel/Writin' "Sad-eyed lady of the lowlands" for you' (both lines from 'Sara'). In that story at least, the effort paid off. 'Sad-eyed lady of the lowlands' is an epic of cheap fairground mystery ('your deck of cards missing the Jack and the ace') deconstructed by the persistent narrator. On the way, rivals are defeated – 'your magazine-husband who one day just had to go' – and an unspoken phrase seems to ring out in each chorus: 'The sad-eyed prophet says that no man comes – *but I do!*'

When not skilfully plumbing woman's mysterious depths, Dylan's men often treat women as teachers treat children. In 'Lay, lady, lay', the man teaches self-knowledge: 'Whatever colours you have in your mind/I'll show them to you and you'll see them shine.' In 'Tombstone blues', men teach the hysterical bride to behave sensibly: 'My advice is to not let the boys in' (the doctor); 'Stop all this weeping, swallow your pride/You will not die, it's not poison' (the medicine man). The unpleasant mockery in 'Ugliest girl in the world' sounds like nothing more than teachers' common-room conversation about the lovable buffoon at the back of the class: ' . . . She's got a hook in her nose/Her eyebrows meet, she wears second-hand clothes'. And the narrator of 'Is your love in vain?' sets an examination for his prospective lover: 'Can you cook and sew, make flowers grow,/Do you understand my pain?' While Dylan tells stories which accept and admire men as they are, the male characters in these stories seem to be trying constantly to understand or change the female ones.

(JOSEPH HAAS) Can you explain why you were booed at the Newport Folk Festival last summer?

(BOB DYLAN) . . . I didn't cry . . . I mean, what are they going to shatter, my ego?[10]

Our culture hands privileges to White heterosexual men – the attention of school teachers, the right to walk the streets noisily at night and the power to define the world. These privileges are created by oppressing Black people, women and gay men. By taking advantage of them we contribute to and benefit from other people's oppression. We also constrain our own potential as human beings.

In 1968 Bob Dylan told Hubert Saal, 'There's myself and there's my song, which I hope is everybody's song.'[11] But Dylan's stories do not feel like everybody's song, they feel specifically male. Iain Chambers places Dylan (with Jack Kerouac, James Dean and Jim Morrison) at the head of 'a particular mode of male romanticism . . . a masculine iconography of White rebellious Americana'.[12] Dylan has contested many aspects of the dominant culture, but not its preferred styles of masculinity.

Enjoying White heterosexual man's position does not always feel comfortable, especially at a time when Blacks, women and gays are organising more and more widely to contest their oppression and our privileges. In his recent essay 'Who's that man?'[13] Jeremy Rutherford describes heterosexual masculinity as:

An identity that is in constant struggle to assert its centrality in cultural life, yet . . . attempts to ensure its absence, and to evade becoming the object of discourse. Heterosexual masculinity shifts its problems and anxieties, defining them as belonging to others. . . . It organises its legitimacy by constructing the Other, that which is outside and questionable.

There are noticeable traces of masculinity 'attempting to ensure its absence' in Dylan's idea that he is writing 'everybody's song'. There are traces of 'shifted problems and anxieties' in Dylan's stories of men becoming men by heroic solitary journeys, and in his glancing descriptions of intense relationships between men. These are often ended by violence in a way which resonates with Rutherford's analysis of the film *Stand By Me*: 'Four twelve-year-old boys . . . go off on a hike in search of the dead body of another boy killed in a train accident . . . The message in the film is the transience of . . . love between men, its hovering on the edge of an eroticism that is taboo.' Men are central to most of Dylan's stories. He reproduces men's privileges over women when he places women as bookends to their journeys or pivots for their interesting relationships. In the stories where a woman is central, it is men's task either to understand and define her mystery (her Otherness) or to underline their own superior knowledge.

Bob Dylan has not written 'everybody's song'. He rarely sings of women coming, going, initiating, coping (there is an exception in 'It takes a lot to laugh, it takes a train to cry', and another in 'Black Diamond Bay', though 'She wears a necktie and a panama hat'). He rarely sings of men *not* coping, though the blank narrator of 'Fourth time around' comes close to the edge. He rarely sings of women and men as friends. 'We better talk this over' gets half-way there, then across the story comes the line, 'I guess I'll be leaving tomorrow'. Dylan has only hinted at tenderness between men – imagine 'Knockin' on heaven's door' addressed to a man ('Papa wipe the blood from my face'). And, though stories about what men do and say are constantly in his songs, their masculinity still 'evades becoming the object of discourse'. He has not yet written 'Just like a man'.

Notes

1. To T. S. Perry, 22 May 1910, *The Letters of William James*, ed. Henry James, Boston, Little, Brown, 1920, ii, p. 336.

2. Introductory essay to *London* and *The Vanity of Human Wishes*, by Samuel Johnson, Oxford University Press, 1930.

3. *The Question of Our Speech*, by Henry James, Boston, Houghton Mifflin, 1905, pp. 46–7.

4. Quoted by Donald Davie in *Trying to Explain*, Manchester, Carcanet Press, 1980, p. 15.

5. Dr Eric Griffiths noted this biblical allusion.

6. Dylan quoted in Nat Hentoff's *Playboy* interview (1966), reprinted in *Bob Dylan: A Retrospective*, ed. Craig McGregor, 1972, p. 143.

7. Dylan quoted in 'Well, what have we here?', Jules Siegel (1966), reprinted in McGregor, p. 149.

8. Dylan quoted in 'The crackin', shakin', breakin', sounds', Nat Hentoff (1964), reprinted in McGregor, p. 59.

9. Quoted in *Dylan – In His Own Words*, compiled Barry Miles, London, Omnibus Press, 1978, p. 15 (referenced as 'New York City, August 1961').

10. From 'Bob Dylan talking', Joseph Haas (1965), reprinted in McGregor, p. 110.

11. Dylan quoted in 'Dylan is back', Hubert Saal (1968), reprinted in McGregor, p. 247.

12. Iain Chambers, *Urban Rhythms*, London, Macmillan, 1985, p. 122.

13. Jonathan Rutherford, 'Who's that man?' in *Male Order – Unwrapping Masculinity*, ed. Rowena Chapman and Jonathan Rutherford, London, Lawrence & Wishart, 1988, pp. 21–67.

SIX

On the Road Again

SIMON WINCHESTER
Blowin' in the Windy City

Guardian, 5 January 1974

Suddenly the blue spot streaked out through the drifting smoke and the swaying balloons, and in the vivid blue pool on the stage the man was flooded in colour – smallish, spindly on long, rubbery jeans-covered legs, with old boots and a rough cloth jacket, shortish frizzed hair and the slightest fuzz of a beard, and with a harmonica perched on a strangely cantilevered neckstrap and an old-looking guitar held softly to one side.

The sound that broke with the light was like Chicago tearing in half. A vast mush of swelling, cheering, yelling and stamping from thousands upon thousands of people crammed into every possible hard-backed red wooden seat in this crummy basketball stadium on Chicago's gin-soaked West Side. The sound went on and on until the spindly little man picked up his guitar and turned to his five companions with a nod and the first notes crashed out. Bob Dylan, after eight long years on the cold outside, was back on the road again. His return, by all accounts last night, was a truly welcomed event.

For the man who took us from 'Blowin' in the wind' to 'Desolation Row' in five years, his tour had been promoted with as little publicity as is humanly possible. A single full-page advertisement in one newspaper in each city of the tour, announcing the stark white and black simple fact that 'Bob Dylan and The Band' would arrive there soon and asking for ticket applications was all that ever appeared.

But still millions of people wrote in for the tickets, a response which Dylan's new young manager said yesterday was 'pure crazy'. Only half a million will get to see Dylan perform in person. The rest will just have to go out and buy the records – one to be issued in a fortnight's time, another at the end of the last session if, as the manager said, 'it turns out to be any good'.

The 16,000 people who came to Chicago Stadium last night – men in their late forties, girls in their late teens and tens of thousands of couples in their late twenties, must all have been wondering the same thing as they waited for that spot to switch on. Had Bob Dylan changed? They would all remember *John Wesley Harding*, the first big record after the motorcycle crash, in which they had to accept that the old nasal whining voice that had lent so very much to lines like 'Here's to the hearts and the hands of men / That come with the dust and are gone with the wind' had become fuller and mellower and slicker. They would remember that the Isle of Wight had been an utter disaster.

And as they filed in last night, past the blue and gold Andy Fraim security guards, who last guarded Nixon at the Miami convention but who were as polite and as gentle as airline girls at the Dylan concert – they must have wondered whether the crash and the move from Woodstock and the marriage and the five children and the house in Malibu had altered the old master out of recognition. It seemed too much to hope that they would not be leaving a little disappointed.

But then he came on. First Dylan and then The Band, alternating, playing the songs of *Nashville Skyline* times ... 'Lay, lady, lay' and then, without warning, 'Ballad of a thin man' – copyright, as the note in the book says, 1965, back at the peak of Dylan's career. And he teased us slowly backwards, letting The Band rush noisily through some new songs, taking us back past the accident, past Newport '65 and '64, back into a warm, welcome, exquisite nostalgic trip. Then The Band disappeared. Dylan changed into a white jacket and picked up his old acoustic guitar and came back on stage for forty minutes alone. Just Dylan, his guitar, his wailing harmonica and 'It's alright, ma', 'The lonesome death of Hattie Carroll', and 'Boots of Spanish leather'. Then he turned and walked off without a smile, a shrug or a wave to his fans.

The stadium erupted into a blizzard of howling sound. Thousands cheered, clapped and held out lighted matches and gaslighters until the chamber looked like the inside of a Catholic church on a feast day. Hundreds of lights waved and flickered, the cheers went on and cries for Dylan to return swept down from above. And so he came back and The Band came back and they played for another forty minutes and tried to leave again.

More howling, and he came back once more. In the utter silence before he sang, someone shouted rudely. 'Quiet, you swine,' someone hissed back at him. 'You may frighten him off.' It was a fragile moment. But then Dylan was singing again until half-past eleven, almost three hours after he had first stepped nervously and shyly out of that eight-year vacuum. His last line was 'You go your way, and I'll go mine' – he gave a single bow, a faint fleeting smile touched his lips as he turned and left.

The audience yelled again and again, but we all knew it was no good. He was gone now, and anyone who wanted to see Dylan again had best be in Philadelphia to try to get a ticket from a scalper.

In all there were about thirty songs, at least four of them brand new – love-songs, each one, that will appear on the new recording. To those who had come last night from as far away as the West Coast, Dylan was as masterful as ever.

'Jesus Christ, man,' said one ginger-bearded man in a blue-and-white Yale scarf, 'it was just as though he'd never been away. He walked right out of Johnson's time like he'd never left.'

W. T. LHAMON JR
A cut above

New Republic, 5 April 1975

Despite the blood he finds in his history and ours, despite the undistinguished musicians backing him, Dylan, his imagination and his voice are all in control again as they haven't been so fully since *Blonde on Blonde* in 1966. And we can therefore expect *Blood on the Tracks* to flash the shape of the Seventies as richly as his electric albums of the mid-Sixties voiced their own weird and wired days. If Dylan is right, our current days are less wired and more acoustic, less grandiosely apocalyptic but more personally ominous, less anxious for surprise but more ambitious for nuance than our immediate past has been. Thus, this new Dylan is less the madman at the mainstream's edge than the pied piper at the centre of an established rock culture.

Hence his album's wonderful reflectiveness, the way it calls on, judges and finds amply sustaining all the music that backed and amplified the stress of the last twenty years. Nearly every cut refers to earlier songs by Dylan himself or others. 'Idiot wind' recalls 'Blowin' in the wind', 'You're a big girl now' reappraises 'Just like a woman' and 'She belongs to me'; 'If you see her, say hello' evokes 'Girl from the north country'; 'Buckets of rain' reminds us of 'A hard rain's a-gonna fall'; and so on down the line. Still the titles are just beginning, for rock is now in that most interesting instant when an art turns from innocence to recouped sensibility.

Dylan has been trying to turn the corner ever since his mis-conceived *Self Portrait* (1970), in which his heavy affection fondled old favourites to death. Although 'Blue moon' and 'Copper kettle' couldn't take it, the idea was to reimagine the past for the present. The idea succeeds in *Blood on the Tracks* because he's found a way to make songs like 'Blue moon' weave in and out of various cuts, leaving here a spoor, there a mood – resulting in a mature attitude that readjusts rock's age of innocence and that also refracts our own zealous innocence. Rock speaks to audiences who still remember the form's earliest inklings in the span of their own lives. When a song today alludes to an earlier song, say 'Blowin' in the wind', it not only calls up scrapped phrases, riffs and licks, but also scrapped moments in our lives from the summer of '63. Where were you when you first heard 'how many seas must a white dove sail/ Before she sleeps in the sand?' Remember Elvis's 'Hound dog' in 1956? We've come a long way since then, as Dylan knows with some pride: 'Well, I struggled through barbed wire . . . You know I even outran the hound dogs. /Honey, you know I've earned your love.'

Indeed he's earned our love. He's earned it by the constancy of his protean changes, which sanctioned our own flux. From protest posturing through surreal symbolism to country caricatures, his slippery style has always been hard to define. While his mercurial career has surely frustrated us, it has also been deeply attractive, for we too were trying on and wearing ragged America's many costumes. If he has always come out on top, why, so can we: 'I can change, I swear . . . I can make it through,/You can make it too.' And he's earned our love by his involvement with common language, even in his most uncommon moods. He has saved phrases from our culture's rhetorical slag heaps and centred them so singularly that they lease new life. He shoots juice to banality simply by kicking everything up several notches – best seen in the way these aren't love-songs, not love-songs alone, but songs to his *audience* as lover. That's no new trick for Dylan – he was performing it as early as 'It's all over now, baby blue' (1965) and repeatedly the next year with *Blonde on Blonde*. But he hasn't so consciously built an album around it before this one, which begins and ends talking to the audience as lover, which ends side one with 'You're gonna make me lonesome when you go', and nearly ends side two with the line, 'I'm takin' you with me, honey baby,/When I go.' These are the remarks of a lover, perhaps, but they are more likely the musings of a man engaging his audience at a turning point and at a point that turns on the resources of common speech. For it was Dylan who, more than anyone else, saw how to go beyond copying the pop staples of blues, ballads and country in order to create a newly distinctive idiom.

Dylan's role in the Sixties was to expand the limits of popular song. He stood beyond the pale and called us to an outlaw reality. But now he's returned to deepen rock's cultural centre. Quarrelling with society in personal terms, he simultaneously sings of self and society in a way that profoundly enriches all our anguish about being separate from – yet within – our inevitable institutions. His new songs are about continued anger and acceptance, about continued hatred and love, about 'the howling beast on the borderline' that separates his lover from himself, his audience from his voice, his country from his ideas (or vice versa) and audiences everywhere from performers everywhere. When he kisses that howling beast goodbye, as he says he finally has, the gain is not a solipsistic turn to himself and his lady alone. Rather he turns to a mature knotting with his audience and the sensibility he helped create: a stand-off embrace.

The last verse of the album's last song describes how the performer finds his highest art by attending to himself in order to attend to others: 'Life is sad, life is a bust/All ya can do is do what you must./You do what you must do and ya do it well,/I'll do it for you, honey baby,/Can't you tell?' And that's it right there: that immediate, consistent and thorough involvement with an audience both characterises rock as the primary popular form of our time and determines its promising aesthetic. We can tell he's doing what he sang nine years ago he'd do: 'I'm pledging my time to you,/Hopin' you'll come through, too.' We can tell: Dylan is back on the tracks.

LARRY SLOMAN

Bob Dylan and friends on the bus – like a Rolling Thunder

Rolling Stone, 4 December 1975

New York – It was four o'clock on a brandy-soaked October Thursday morning in Greenwich Village as about twenty friends and assorted hangers-on gathered in the shuttered-to-the-public Other End to hear Bob Dylan and his friends pick a few tunes. They'd been going strong since 2.30 a.m. when David Blue finished his regular set and by now the bulk of the audience had surrounded Dylan at the piano on stage.

An obviously well-fuelled Roger McGuinn kept goading Dylan to sing his new 'Joey Gallo' song by breaking into the 'Joooey' chorus a capella every chance he got. Allen Ginsberg hunched over the piano, staring intensely, hanging on to his every word. Ronee Blakley, the *Nashville* neurotic, sidled close to Dylan, sharing his piano stool, playing the high keys and adding vibrant harmonies. Ramblin' Jack Elliott was rambling around in the back looking for some 'tee-keela', while Bobby Neuwirth acted as ringmaster, directing this folkie circus. Everyone seemed caught up in some kind of high-energy harmonic hysteria and the drinks flowed faster and faster. Everyone was caught up, that is, but Lou Kemp, Dylan's Minnesota boyhood buddy and all-round factotum, who viewed the proceedings from a stageside seat with a wary eye. 'I can't believe this,' he told no one in particular. 'We've been in town just four days, haven't been to sleep before sunrise, I'm totally wasted and we haven't even started this goddamn tour yet.'

This 'goddamn tour' is, of course, the Rolling Thunder Revue, Bob Dylan's travelling band of gypsies, hoboes, lonesome guitar stranglers and spiritual green berets. In just four days the tour buses would roll out from the Gramercy Park Hotel, where the Revue had been holed up, and head up to Plymouth, Massachusetts, for the first stop of a whirlwind blitz of the North-east, running from four to six weeks.

The tour was conceived at the Other End back in the summer, when Dylan was vibing out the Village street scene and co-writing with Jacques Levy positively New York songs. Like the hymn for 'Joey' (Gallo) and the story of the 'Hurricane', a plea for Rubin Carter, the one-time number one contender for the middleweight boxing crown who now languishes in Trenton State Prison, convicted of murder.

The idea behind the tour, Dylan said, was to 'play for the people', the people who never get the choice seats at a Dylan concert because they're occupied by flacks and celebrities.

'Bob decided he wanted to do it,' said Lou Kemp, 'but he didn't have anyone to coordinate it. I came back from Alaska, where I have a salmon processing plant, and he asked me to help with the tour. So I hired Barry Imhoff, who'd already left Bill Graham, to be in charge of the technical aspects of the tour.' Imhoff, while with Graham, helped coordinate Dylan's twenty-one-city, thirty-nine-concert tour early last year. Kemp also accompanied Dylan on numerous stops during that tour.

Both Imhoff and Kemp declined to answer questions about the financial aspects of this tour. While Dylan had mentioned wanting to play mostly 'clubs', the initial stops were at halls ranging from 1,800 to 3,000 in capacity – with ticket prices at a uniform $7.50 – and, in the tour's second week, there were dates at two 12,000-seat auditoriums, in Providence, Rhode Island, and in Springfield, Massachusetts. 'We gotta pay the rent, the expenses,' Dylan explained. But he said there would be only 'one or two' such concerts during the tour.

The Rolling Thunder Revue had also been planned as a spiritual reunion of the early Sixties Kettle of Fish folk crowd, the Dylan/Blue/Neuwirth/Elliott/Ochs axis.

'Bob's just an ordinary fucking guy,' David Blue said, 'a great songwriter who got swept up in this whole fame thing and was smart enough to know how to control it, who rode with it and was shrewd, damn shrewd. And now he's just paying everyone back with this tour. It's like a family scene.'

But the cast mushroomed, especially since Dylan becomes effusive when he's bar hopping and winds up inviting every bouncer, bartender, juggler or otherwise kindred spirit he meets to come along. Joan Baez was the first addition to the basic Dylan/Elliott/Neuwirth show, followed by Ronee Blakley, on the basis of her strong showing at the Other End jam. Allen Ginsberg came next, with his fog, his natural adrenalin and his harmonium. Roger McGuinn, who was concentrating on a bottle so hard that he didn't hear Dylan the first two times he was invited along, has dropped a few bookings, hopping aboard with his twelve-string and banjo. In fact, the only picker who met up with the Thunder crew and didn't get swept up into it was Lou Reed.

Baez's story is typical of the tour additions: 'Bob called up and asked what I was doing for the month of November. I had a tour lined up. Usually I'm not working with a dollar sign in front of my face, but this time I was, so I had to give it considerable thought. But I'm bright enough to know what this tour will mean. I didn't trust a lot of it. I said, look, what if Ramblin' Jack decides he wants to live in a freight train for the month of November instead? I've known these guys for a long time and I love them dearly but everybody *is* slightly unstable. But it's delightful working with Bobby again. He's relatively impossible to follow and that's a challenge, but I need that.'

In Dylan's words, the Revue is playing in places other than large auditoriums because 'the atmosphere in small halls is more conducive to what we do'. Still, it seemed natural that the proceedings should be filmed for later distribution, so Dylan called up his old friend Howard Alk, of *Eat The Document* fame. 'That film was a project we did to rescue a bunch of garbage footage that ABC shot on our 1966 tour,' Dylan explained. 'It was never released because the film didn't have much to do with anybody. The whole thing fell through, but Howard and I, we got together and decided if we ever got the chance again to shoot good footage before we get to the editing room – some things that we can make into a fantastic movie on the screen – we'd do it. There's so much we got here already. We'll probably end up making four or five movies and the public can definitely be into this one.'

So it came as no shock to show up at a surprise birthday party for Mike Porco, the owner of Gerde's Folk City who gave Dylan his first paid gig in 1961, and be greeted by a four-man film crew who explained their presence to Porco with a cover story of 'filming for NET'. Word was out on the streets that Dylan just might show up and before midnight the normally sparse weekday crowd was elbow-to-elbow. Phil Ochs had a head start on everyone and wandered around, drink in hand, lecturing about 'the Jewish Mafia' and the strange case of Sonny Liston. Patti Smith shyly slunk into one corner, while Commander Cody showed up with two limos full of shitkickers. Roger McGuinn sat outside in his Sunshine limo, never one to arrive too early. Then, just past 1.00 a.m., a red Cadillac Eldorado pulled up and Dylan strode briskly in, followed closely by Kemp and Neuwirth. They greeted Mrs Porco, hugged Mike and retreated to a far corner of the club. Then with the inevitable tableside introduction, 'Ladies and gentlemen, the greatest star of all, Bobby Dylan', Dylan found his way up to the stage, grabbing Baez on the way for a duet of 'Happy birthday' and 'One too many mornings' – but the music stopped abruptly when bassist Rob Stoner's bridge snapped right out of its mooring.

Jack Elliott joined in on stage and Dylan seized the opportunity to shout, 'Let's turn the stage over to Ramblin' Jack Elliott,' and headed back to the semi-solitude of his table. Jack did a hauntingly beautiful ballad, 'South coast blues'; Bette Midler fell on stage to duet with Buzzy Linhart; Allen Ginsberg sang some poem/songs backed by female guitarist Denise Mercedes. Then Eric Andersen and Patti Smith harmonised a bit. Finally, Neuwirth, looking like some turn-of-the-century Cuban porno star in a black eye-mask and cowboy hat, grabbed the stage and sang a touching 'Mercedes Benz' for 'someone who couldn't be here with us tonight'.

It seemed over but then Phil Ochs, who's been battling some of his own private phantoms recently, performed a moving medley of folk and country, stuff like 'Jimmy Brown the newsboy,' 'There you go', 'Too many parties' and 'The blue and the grey'. Everyone at Dylan's table was standing, gaping at this poignant moment.

Ochs spotted Dylan heading for the bar. 'Hey, Bobby, come up with me,' he shouted. 'I'm only going to the bar, Phil,' Dylan replied reassuringly. 'Well, here's a song of yours that I've always wanted to do,' Ochs answered, breaking into a dirge-like 'Lay down your weary tune'. But things lightened up when Ochs stumbled off the stage into the waiting arms of David Blue who, with Kemp and Neuwirth, was part of an ambush designed to retrieve the cowboy hat from Ochs that Dylan had worn in *Pat Garrett and Billy the Kid*.

By the next day, Friday, things were really rolling. A session was planned to re-record 'Hurricane' to be released as the tour begins. The idea was born at the Kettle of Fish when Dylan was talking animatedly about Rubin Carter and the need for publicity about his case. He had written 'Hurricane' in the summer, recorded it and performed it at the retirement tribute to Columbia Records' John Hammond, taped for the *Soundstage* PBS-TV show. But that show won't be seen until December. 'We gotta get the song out, we gotta get it right out,' Dylan had said, slamming his fist on the table.

So Tuesday, Dylan, Kemp and his camera crew, after a filmed scuffle with security guards at the CBS building, barged into the offices of CBS Records president Irwin Segelstein and CBS Records Group president Walter Yetnikoff and demanded rush release of the 'Hurricane' single. Late that night Dylan entered Studio E, pre-empting a Janis Ian listening session, with his band – bassist Rob Stoner, drummer Howie Wyeth, violinist Scarlet Rivera, percussionist Luther and back-up singers Steve Soles and Ronee Blakley. Four hours later, producer Don DeVito was left with the task of mixing, mastering and getting the story of the 'Hurricane' out on the streets, in Dylan's words, 'as soon as possible'.

The reason for the recutting of 'Hurricane' was the subject of some speculation, most of it centring on an allegedly libellous line about a person involved in Carter's arrest. Ken Ehrlich, producer of *Soundstage*, said he talked with Dylan's attorney about snipping parts of Dylan's taped performance 'to avoid libel'. The attorney, David Braun, has refused comment. At Columbia Records, Segelstein said only that 'it's a very conventional name confusion, he had to correct a lyric. I do not know the details.' And DeVito, a Columbia executive who produced the session, said Dylan made changes 'just like last year with *Blood on the Tracks*. He's just totally unpredictable.'

After the re-recording session, Dylan reflected on Rubin Carter. 'The first time I saw Rubin, I left knowing one thing: that this man's philosophy and my philosophy were running on the same road and you don't meet too many people like that, that you just kinda know are on the same path as you are, mentally. I never doubted him for a moment. He's just not a killer, not that kind of a man. You're talking about a different type of person. I mean, he's not gonna walk into a bar and start shooting. He's not the guy. I don't know how anybody in their right mind is gonna think he was guilty of something like that.'

'Hurricane' is an eight-minute rocker, a scorching defence of Carter and an attack on a system that allows an allegedly innocent man to rot in a cell for nine years. Carter's is the kind of situation that spurred some of Dylan's greatest protest songs years ago. 'There's an injustice that's been done and you know that Rubin's gonna get out,' Dylan said. 'There's no doubt about that, but the fact is that it can happen to anybody. We have to be confronted with that; people from the top to the bottom, they should be aware that it can happen to anybody, at any time.'

Rubin Carter, for his part, is thrilled with the song. 'I listened to it at first and thought, eh, it was just another song to me,' Carter said in his cell at Trenton State Prison in Trenton, New Jersey. 'I ain't got no time for music in here. This is not a place to be soothed. But the more I sat there and listened to it and really understood what he was saying, I said, "Wow, man." I mean, he took this case, this nine years of whatever, and put it together, wop, like that, and covered every level, every facet of it. I said, "Man, this cat's a genius. He's giving the people the truth." And it was inspiring to me. I told myself, "Rubin, you got to keep pushing, 'cause you must be doing something right, you got all these good people coming to try and help you."'

More rehearsals followed and, on Monday 27 October, three chartered buses pulled out for Cape Cod. There, the troupe settled into the Seacrest Hotel and ran through three additional days of rehearsal in the hotel's indoor tennis court.

The tour opened on 30 October on a cold, damp New England night in Plymouth, advertised only by handbills that included a photo of Dylan and by random radio mentions in Boston. The 1,800-seat Plymouth Memorial Auditorium sold out, though it took almost twenty-four hours to do so. But it was evident in the opening moments of the show that this crazy-quilt tour and its music – 'the new sound is Plymouth rock' was an often heard comment – was working. It seemed that the pre-tour tensions between Neuwirth's gin-soaked, good-timey camaraderie and musical director Rob Stoner's slick professionalism had been resolved into a balanced mixture of sound.

'Welcome to your living room,' Neuwirth announced on stage, and it was true. There was none of the forced ambience of the last Dylan tour with its sofas and Tiffany lamps on stage. All the tour participants – Elliott, Blakley, McGuinn, Neuwirth, Baez, Dylan – got their moment in the spotlight, in front of the basic band of Mick Ronson, T-Bone Burnette, Stoner and Soles. After Elliott's four-song set, Neuwirth introduced 'another old friend' and Dylan ambled on stage in a black leather jacket, jeans and the *Pat Garrett* hat. The audience gave him a warm welcome, but there was little surprise in the air. Dylan and Neuwirth opened with a slow version of 'When I paint my masterpiece', Dylan singing harmony and Neuwirth taking the lead.

They harmonised on 'It ain't me, babe' and 'A hard rain's a-gonna fall', and then Neuwirth left and Dylan brought out violinist Scarlet Rivera to lead the band through 'Romance in Durango'. Then it was Dylan alone to sing 'Isis' – no guitar, no accompaniment, just Dylan at the mike gesturing dramatically as he told the story of the goddess. 'See you in a few minutes,' he said, and went off to a standing ovation.

After a short intermission, the curtain crawled slowly up to the strains of Dylan and Joan Baez singing 'The times they are a-changin''. After 'Never let me go' (an old Johnny Ace tune) and 'I shall be released', Dylan left, patting Baez on the head and leaving her to do a seven-song set. Roger McGuinn took her place for 'Chestnut mare' and then gave the stage back to Dylan for 'Mr Tambourine Man' and, from the next album, 'Oh, sister'.

'This is', said Dylan, 'a song about Rubin Carter,' and behind him a screen slowly whirred to the floor and the band went into 'Hurricane', the single that would be released the next day – 31 October. A huge picture of Carter in boxing gear was projected on to the screen and that was the extent of Dylan's comment on the song. 'One more cup of coffee' was next and then Dylan broke into 'Sara', a bittersweet song to his wife.

He wound it up with 'Just like a woman' and then the entire cast gathered for 'This land is your land', with even Allen Ginsberg joining in. The three-hour show was over, the audience responded with a ten-minute standing ovation. The second Plymouth show, again a sell-out, drew a quieter crowd, one almost polite toward its elders on stage. The show was virtually the same except for the substitution of 'I don't believe you' for 'Mr Tambourine Man' and 'Mama, you been on my mind' instead of 'The lonesome death of Hattie Carroll'.

From Plymouth, the buses and campers rolled on to North Dartmouth, Massachusetts, to Southeastern Massachusetts University. The crowd of 3,000 had been prepped. A week before, an advance party, accompanied by the ever-present camera crew, descended on the dorms at 10 p.m. to pass out Rolling Thunder handbills.

The night before the buses rolled, Dylan had been sitting in the bar of the Gramercy Park Hotel, sipping Remy Martin. He was asked by someone on the tour why it was called Rolling Thunder. Dylan thought for a minute. 'I was just sitting outside my house one day,' he finally replied, 'thinking about a name for this tour, when all of a sudden, I look up into the sky and I hear a boom. Then, boom, boom, boom, boom, rolling from west to east' – Dylan punched at the air, like a prize-fighter – 'then I figured that should be the name.'

Dylan got another drink and the questioner asked him: 'You know what Rolling Thunder means to the Indians?'

'No. What?'

'Speaking truth.'

A pause. Dylan shifted his hat and rocked back. 'Well, I'm glad to hear that. I'm real glad to hear that, man.'

ADAM LIVELY
Adolescence now

I can remember myself at sixteen sitting through empty hours after school had finished, listening to Bob Dylan's *Desire* over and over again. I'd never heard any other Dylan and I forget now what had prompted me to buy the record. Bob Dylan was a name that I vaguely associated with the Sixties, one of those 'hippies' that the suburban punks at school sneered at. Perhaps that was why I got the record, to be different.

I loved *Desire*. I loved Dylan's own sneering anger on the protest song 'Hurricane':

> Now all the criminals in their coats and their ties
> Are free to drink Martinis and watch the sun rise
> While Rubin sits like Buddha in a ten-foot cell
> An innocent man in a living hell

I walked around my bedroom singing that out loud. I loved the bitter, oriental sound of Dylan and Emmylou Harris's voices on 'One more cup of coffee'; and the love-song 'Sara' made me want to cry. But the song that intrigued me most was 'Black Diamond Bay', which Allen Ginsberg described on the sleeve as 'a short novel in verse, old-fashioned Dylan surrealist mind-jump inventions line by line'. The song was about a group of blurred but vaguely glamorous characters – a mysterious woman in a panama hat, a Greek whom she mistakes for the Soviet ambassador – in a hotel in an equally vague tropical location. At the end of each verse, in which Dylan details their surreal manoeuvres in gambling room and bedroom, he describes the gathering storm outside.

> As the rain beats down and the cranes fly away
> From Black Diamond Bay

As the moon fades away, the party continues. When the volcano finally erupts, it's just part of the story. In the gambling room, 'As the island slowly sank/The loser finally broke the bank.' Then the scene suddenly cuts to Dylan himself:

> I was sittin' home alone one night in LA
> Watchin' old Cronkite on the seven o'clock news.

The eruption in Black Diamond Bay is just another one of those hard-luck stories you're gonna hear.

'Black Diamond Bay' had three things that appealed to me enormously at that time: some sexual mystery, in the shape of the woman with the panama hat; a sense of impending catastrophe; and a glimpse of wonderful America, with its anonymous vastness and careless, cruelly ironic affluence. ('And I never did plan to go anyway/To Black Diamond Bay.') I could see – more vividly than any of the drab, school-uniformed figures around me – Dylan get up from the couch, switch off Cronkite and go over to the ice-box for a beer. Outside, the screen door banged shut. Friends were coming round.

I had no curiosity to hear any of Dylan's other records. *Desire*, together with some Simon and Garfunkel, was quite enough to summon forth the America of my imagination, with its wide, sun-baked highways and melting-pot cities. It was a few years till I came to listen to what had gone before *Desire*, the great outpouring of surreal poetry, bizarre humour and sad balladry that Dylan had produced in the Sixties and early Seventies.

To many of my generation – though perhaps not to those of a

newer one – the Sixties will always exist as the time we missed, a mythic object of fascination and resentment. Whereas the young of the 1920s felt relieved guilt that they had missed the carnage of the First World War, we just felt cheated that we had missed out on festivals and a sense of change. The myth was of a time when the future was speeding up behind in the fast lane. ('Your old road is/Rapidly agein'./Please get out of the new one/If you can't lend your hand . . . ') By the time of my adolescence, in the mid to late Seventies, the future was already here and now. And it was nothing to have a be-in about.

Everyone has their own Dylan, which is what makes him a great popular artist. Mine – like many others – was forged in the hot crucible of adolescence. For me, he encapsulated that sense that I loved about the Sixties – that the world had been about to be turned upside down, that strange beauties were going to be born. That those things never happened merely added to the poignant power the period had over me. In Dylan's songs of the Sixties the coming transformation was never something as simple as the Revolution. In more recent songs, it is true, it appears to be something as simple as the Last Judgement ('Gotta serve somebody', for example, on *Slow Train Coming*). But Dylan's conception of the coming crunch in his finest songs is entirely visionary – spiritual in the best sense of the word. It is the *idea* of change, of transfiguration and redemption, that he sings about, rather than any particular manifestation of it. What, or who, is on that ship that approaches the shore, that ship for which 'the chains of the sea/Will have busted in the night' and for which 'the fishes will laugh/As they swim out of the path/And the seagulls they'll be smiling'? It hardly matters. What matters is the vision itself.

Adolescence is less a discrete phase of life, like puberty, than an attitude of mind that can visit people of any age. It can combine appalling egocentricity, self-pity and humourless-ness with a healthy contempt for conventional categories and pre-conceptions. Having its origins at a time when the individual is struggling to assert his/her identity against the enormous pressures of adulthood, its basic idiom is one of difference, estrangement and catastrophic change. For better or worse, my Dylan will always be an adolescent Dylan. When I came to hear music of his other than *Desire*, it was those songs with an exotic flavour and an apocalyptic theme that attracted me most.

'Desolation Row' was my anthem. It combined the details of a Felliniesque festival with a sense of impending and actual chaos in a way that seemed to me to distil the essence of 'Black Diamond Bay'. And in 'Desolation Row', with its romantic, lyrical guitar lines riding the chords, the two elements were woven together – frozen – in a beautiful tapestry.

There is a particular, exotic Dylan landscape that both of these songs inhabit. It is a small place – forgotten, gone to seed – by the sea. (The sea has an important and special place in Dylan's songs.) It is somewhere on the coast of Central or South America – indeed, it could almost be a place out of a novel by Gabriel García Marquez, or the seedy Peruvian port that is the setting of Mario Vargas Llosa's *Who Killed Palomino Molero*? The bars are filled with sailors, gypsies and whores. The sky is filled with stars. There's bad feeling between the raffish waterfront crew and the town's more upright citizens (those who send the agents to 'Come out and round up everyone/That knows more than they do'; those who 'rise/With the sleep still in their eyes . . . /The hour when the ship comes in.') But this picture has its surreal, incongruous elements too. There's a medieval castle, with its princes on the watchtower and fairy-tale crew.

But the most important thing about this place of the imagination is that it's at the end of the world. Not just physically, in that it's across all the oceans we can think of, but in a deeper sense it is, like Desolation Row itself, a repository for all the world's accumulated hopes, fears, nightmares and other dreams. It is the ultimate testing-ground of human experience.

> Don't send me no more letters no
> Not unless you mail them
> From Desolation Row

I wanted to send Dylan letters and I liked to think that, even if just once or twice, I'd been down along Desolation Row.

And beyond this end of the world, beyond this point where all the conventional categories are thrown into the melting pot of chaos, is Dylan's voice itself. It is a unique and instantly recognisable voice – personal in that sense – but at the same time strangely distant, even objective. Prophecy uses precisely this tone. It seems to stand beyond all experience, singing back to those who still struggle through the world. ('Now when all the clowns that you have commissioned/Have died in battle or in vain/And you're sick of all this repetition/Won't you come see me, Queen Jane?') At the same time, with its yelps and its drawls, it's the voice of a holy fool, a clown and a gambler. Yet the clown is one who can turn serious on you, like the thief in 'All along the watchtower':

> There are many here among us who feel that life is but a joke.
> But you and I, we've been through that, and this is not our fate.
> So let us not talk falsely now, the hour is getting late.

'The hour is getting late.' My own adolescence seemed like grey and dismal dawn compared with that. Gone was that sense of endings and beginnings. Where? Why had it *come*? Compare the apocalyptics of the Sixties with a similar, but much smaller, cultural movement of twenty-five years earlier. During the Second World War, a group of British writers coalesced who called themselves the New Apocalyptics. They followed the direction particularly of Dylan Thomas, the poet who was to inspire the young Bob Zimmerman to change his name twenty years later. One of their number could have been describing that later Dylan when he wrote of apocalyptic art that it occurs 'where expression breaks through the structure of social conventions . . . giving birth to images and prophecies of ruin; where in fact absolute norms break down and man stands forth as the ultimate reality to be reckoned with on earth'. The turbulent Sixties find their echo in a time when the old European world seemed, literally, to be collapsing. Thomas Pynchon's *Gravity's Rainbow*, one of the great novels of the Counterculture, is set (if that is the right word for a book of such fluid form) in London during the war. The poetry of the New Apocalyptics recalls the language of the Sixties, even down to the curious obsession with medieval iconography.

So particular historical conjunctures – uncertain times – bring forth visions of the destruction of old orders. They encourage a search for real, sometimes mystic, alternatives. But the basic impulse to celebrate the idea of change, to hold hands and dance with the Other, is always there. My Dylan is still there somewhere in the space outside my sixteen-year-old window. And I still think *Desire* is his most beautiful album.

LESTER BANGS

Bob Dylan's dalliance with Mafia chic

Creem, April 1976

It is automatically assumed that every Bob Dylan album is an event and *Desire* is certainly no exception. It is not, however, the event that it might appear to be. It is not an event because of the inclusion of several drearily rambling Marty Robbins-cum-*Pat Garrett and Billy the Kid* sagas of outlaw's progress from cantina to cantina. This album is a landmark neither because of the back-cover slice of imitation Patti Smith poesy by (presumably) Dylan nor because of the offensively portentous liner puffery provided by a senile Allen Ginsberg, who ironically was one of Dylan's major influences back when Ginsberg was perhaps the premier American poet and Bob on his way to being declared that by people who didn't know any better (like me, for instance).

We can't even assign historic import to *Desire* on the basis of 'Hurricane', the undeniably powerful single which in a con-trolled spasm of good old rabble-rousing, spits an inflammatory account of the railroading of Rubin Carter, one-time contender for the Middle-weight Boxing Championship of the World, on a mid-Sixties murder rap.

If you feel yourself responding cynically when someone relates that 'Dylan's returned to protest songs' as if it is exciting news, it just may be that your instincts are in healthy working order. Look at it this way: every four years Dylan writes a 'new' protest song and it's always about a martyred nigger and he always throws in a dirty word to make it more street-authentic. I don't use the word 'nigger' for effect or to make myself look hip, but rather because just like our fathers before us that is all Jackson and Carter have been to him: another human life to exploit for his own purposes.

Dylan doesn't give a damn about Rubin Carter, and if he spent any more than ten minutes actually working on the composition of 'George Jackson' then Bryan Ferry is a member of The Eagles. Dylan merely used Civil Rights and the rest of the Movement to advance himself in the first place; *The Times they are a-Changin'* and 'Blowin' in the wind' were just as much a pose as *Nashville Skyline*. Which actually was not only kosher but a fair deal, because the exchange amounted to symbiotic exploitation – the Movement got some potent anthems, Dylan got to be a figure-head, and, even if he was using his constituency, art is more important than politics in the long run anyway.

But why, in 1975, should Dylan return to what, in such a year, passes for activism? Because he's having trouble coming up with meaningful subject matter closer to home, that's why; either that or whatever is going on in his personal life is so painful and fucked up he is afraid or unwilling to confront it in his art. And, again, one is not sure that one can honestly blame him. When *Blood on the Tracks* was released, I felt as ambivalent about it as it was about its subject matter and I remained that way. After initially dismissing it on one hearing as a sprawling, absurdly pretentious mess whose key was the ridiculously spiteful 'Idiot wind', I found myself drawn back to it repeatedly by a current that I was not at all convinced was entirely wholesome; I would get drunk and throw it on, finding profound aphorisms alternating with oblique poetry, belching outbursts of muddled enthusiasm: 'Goddamn, he's still got it!' Then I would sober up and it would sound, once again, dull, overlong, energyless, the aphorisms trite and obvious, the poetry a garbled parody of the old Dylan. But I persisted; there was *something* there that mattered to me and I ultimately found out what is was. I discovered that I only really wanted to play this record whenever I had a fight with someone I was falling in love with – we would reach some painful impasse of words or wills, she would go home and I would sit up all night with my misery and this album, playing it over and over, wallowing in Dylan's wretched reflection of my own confusion: 'Women – who can figger 'em?' I imagine it was also a big hit with the recently (or soon-to-be) divorced.

At length, I concluded that any record whose principle utility lay in such an emotional twilight zone was at worst an instrument of self-abuse, at best innocuous as a crying towel and certainly was not going to make me a better person or teach me anything about women, myself or anything else but how painfully confused Bob Dylan seemed to be. Which was simply not enough.

So I looked forward to *Desire*. Maybe Bob had managed to figger the critters out in some flash of revelation, or could at least provide some helpful tips for the rest of us involved in the great

Struggle. Perhaps, at last, he had something honestly uplifting to say about men and women, male bonding, pet training and all the other baffling forms of interpersonal relationships known to this planet. So if it seems like I'm hard on him now, if I seem unduly vitriolic, it's only because (a) everything I say is the truth and (b) I myself was such a sucker I still looked to him to *tell* me something and now must suffer the embarrassment which is *my* just deserts.

Because *Desire* is a sham and a fake-out. Ignoring the 'El Paso' rewrites and ersatz Kristofferson plodders like 'One more cup of coffee' (which is easy), we come at length (and it is reflective of neither generosity nor inspiration that side two of this album is almost thirty minutes long) to 'Sara', wherein Dylan, masks off, naming names, rhapsodises over his wife in mawkish images ('Sweet virgin angel . . . Radiant jewel'), cheap bathos (when in doubt, drag in the kids playing in the sand on the beach), simple grovelling ('You must forgive me my unworthiness'), and, most indicatively of *Desire* as a whole, outright lies. To wit: 'I'd taken the cure and had just gotten through/Stayin' up for days in the Chelsea Hotel/Writin' "Sad-eyed lady of the lowlands" for you.'

Bullshit. I have it on pretty good authority that Dylan wrote 'Sad-eyed lady', as well as about half of the rest of *Blonde on Blonde*, wired out of his skull in the studio, just before the songs were recorded, while the session men sat around waiting on him, smoking cigarettes and drinking beer. It has been suggested to me that there are better things to do with albums than try to figure out what drug the artist was on when he made them, but I think this was one case where the chemical definitely affected the content of the music. Those lyrics were a speed trip, and if he really *did* spend days on end sitting up in the Chelsea sweating over lines like 'your streetcar visions which you place on the grass', then he is stupider than we ever gave him credit for.

Now, I know I stand at this point in possible danger of plunging quill-first into full-scale Webermanism, but I do think that if you are going to assert that a piece of music is the unburdening of your soul down to the personal pronouns, then you should tell the truth. I also think that if he is capable of lying about and exploiting his own marriage to make himself look a bit more pertinent, he is certainly capable of using the newsy victims of his topical toons with even less attention to moral amenities. 'Hurricane', like many Dylan songs of his distant past, purports to be a diatribe expressing abhorrence of racism, but there are many forms of inverted, benevolent prejudice known to the liberal mentality, and I find a song like 'Mozambique' rather curious:

> I like to spend some time in Mozambique . . .
> Among the lovely people living free
> Upon the beach of sunny Mozambique.

Ah, yes, a beautiful, simple people, aren't they, Mr Christian? Unfettered by the corrupting complexities of civilisation, no? So primitively pure and natch'l, just fuckin' and a-dancin' barefoot there on the beach. Maybe that's what enables Rubin Carter to sit 'like Buddha in a ten-foot cell'.

Which brings us to Dylan's demonology, and the biggest lie of all. Now, just as *Blood on the Tracks* was ultimately redolent of little more than mixed-up confusion as regards romantic obsessions, so a line like 'all the criminals in their coats and their ties/Are free to drink Martinis and watch the sun rise' is not exactly going to enlighten us as to the subtleties of social injustice today. Because the processes of oppression, however brutal, *are* subtle, Ralph J. Gleason was *right* when he extrapolated old Dylan lyrics into 'No more us and them', and Dylan himself, in the mid-Seventies, is still playing Cowboys and Indians.

I said earlier that Dylan was merely using Carter and George Jackson as fodder for the propagation of the continuing myth of his own 'relevance'. It's difficult to prove that from 'Hurricane', in part because the performance is so drivingly persuasive, in part because Dylan does seem, at least superficially, to have his facts down: a man was framed for a crime he most likely didn't commit, and the probable reason he was framed was that he preached Black liberation in an atmosphere of White supremacy. Of course, the fact that he was framed doesn't prove that he was *innocent* of the crime either; but for once Dylan's simplistic broadsides seem to have coincided with reality, justice and Rubin Carter being on the side of the angels.

But I have to make a confession: I don't give a damn about Rubin Carter, whether he is guilty or innocent, or about racism in New Jersey. At least for the purposes of the present inquiry, all I care about is Bob Dylan and whether he is being straight with me or not. I don't think he is, anywhere, and I think you can find all the evidence you need in *Desire*'s longest cut, the ponderous, sloppy, numbingly boring eleven-minute ballad 'Joey', about yet another folk hero/loser/martyr, mobster, 'Crazy Joey' Gallo, who was murdered in a gang war in Little Italy in 1972.

New York City readers may not believe this, but it's probable that most of the people, especially young ones, who buy this album across the rest of America do not know who in the hell Joey Gallo was. Since this song is hardly going to help them find out, is in fact one of the most mindlessly amoral pieces of repellently romanticist bullshit ever recorded, let me preface an examination of Dylan's most transparent dishonesty with a brief bit of history.

During the Sixties, there were five Mafia 'families' dividing up the pie of various turfs and rackets in New York City, under the control of one Godfather-like 'boss of bosses'. Although the modern Mafia encourages more of a 'businessman' image and tries to play down the blood-letting, the families are usually fighting among themselves for greater power and influence, and one of the most successful families during the Sixties was the Profaci family, which later became the Colombo family. In intermittent but very bloody opposition to them were the Gallo family, led by the brothers Larry, Joey and Albert 'Kid Blast' Gallo, who were never quite able to attain equivalent power even though they remained the overlords of one small section of Brooklyn. According to a detailed analysis of mob warfare by Fred J. Cook in the 4 June 1972 *New York Times*, 'The severe blood-letting in the Profaci-Colombo family began when the greed of the Gallo brothers set them lusting after (the former's) power. Indeed, it touched them with the kind of madness that drives a shark berserk in a blood-stained sea', and the Gallos tried every lethal ploy they could think of to muscle their way into a bigger piece of the action. In October 1957, Joey Gallo, acting on a Profaci contract, blasted the notorious Albert Anastasia, one-time lord of Murder, Inc., out of his barber's chair in a celebrated rub-out, thus paving the way for Carlo Gambino to become, and remain, boss of bosses through the Sixties and early Seventies. But the Gallos never found any more favour with Gambino than they had with his predecessors, so they embarked on an all-out war with the Profacis that lasted from 1961 to 1963; though there were no real winners, the Gallos were no match either in numbers or tactically for the Profacis, and the war ended in early 1962 when Crazy Joe Gallo was sentenced to seven to fourteen years in prison for extortion and, a few months later, Joseph Profaci died of cancer.

While Joe Gallo was in prison, he read extensively, becoming a sort of jailhouse intellectual, and when he was finally released in 1970 he began to cultivate contacts in the literary and show business worlds, who welcomed him to their parties and obviously considered him an exotic amusement indeed. Jimmy Breslin's book *The Gang That Couldn't Shoot Straight* had been inspired by the legendary ineptitude of the Gallo family in their early-Sixties bids for power and Joey developed close contacts with Jerry Orbach, who played a character corresponding to him in the movie based on the book, and his wife Marta, with whom, in the last months of his life, Joey began collaborating on various autobiographical literary projects. Out of Radical Chic bloomed Mafia Chic; he became something of an above-ground social figure and told columnist Earl Wilson that he was 'going straight'.

Apparently that was a lie, however. While Joey was in prison, his gang languishing and awaiting his return, a new figure had arisen from the Profaci ranks to bring New York mob power to a whole new, all but avant-garde level: Joe Colombo. Colombo founded the Italian-American Civil Rights League, an organisation ostensibly devoted to deploring and 'legitimately' opposing the 'prejudice' which caused most Americans to link mob activities with citizens of Italian descent. Between 150,000 and 250,000 Italian-Americans ultimately joined the League, and the impact on politicians was considerable, which was how Nelson Rockefeller and John Lindsay ended up having their pictures taken with underworld toughs. Joey Gallo returned from prison with his power on his own turf intact, but of course completely cut out of the Colombo empire. On 28 June 1971, Joe Colombo was gunned down by a supposedly lone and uncontracted Black man in front of thousands of his horrified followers at a rally in Columbus Circle. The consensus was that Crazy Joey was behind it, especially since he'd perplexed other mafiosos by hanging out with Black prisoners during his stay in the joint and ostensibly aimed to start a Black mob, under his control, when he got out. According to many inside sources, there was a contract out on Joey Gallo from the day Colombo died, and on 7 April 1972, as he celebrated his forth-third birthday in Umberto's Clam House on Mulberry Street in Little Italy, an anonymous hit-man walked in off the street and shot Crazy Joey to death much as Joey had murdered Albert Anastasia. It was the end of a gang war that had lasted almost a decade and a half – a few more of their henchmen were disposed of and the Gallo family was decimated, their power gone. Mobsters in general breathed a collective sigh of relief – the Gallos had always been hungry troublemakers – and went back to business as usual.

It is out of this fairly typical tale of mob power-jostlings that Dylan has, unaccountably, woven 'Joey', which paints a picture of Joey Gallo as alienated antihero reminiscent of *West Side Story*'s 'Gee, Officer Krupke' lyrics: 'We ain't no delinquents, we're misunderstood.'

> Always on the outside of whatever side there was
> When they asked him why it had to be that way,
> 'Well', he answered – 'just because'

Joey Gallo was a psychopath, as his biographer Donald Goddard confirms, although the analyst who examined him while he was in prison diagnosed Joey's disease as 'pseudo-psychopathic schizophrenia'. Joey's answer: 'Fuck you. Things are not right or wrong any more. Just smart or stupid. You don't judge an act by its nature. You judge it by results. We're all criminals now ... Things exist when I feel they should exist, okay? *Me, I* am the world.' Towards the end of his life, his wife routinely fed him Thorazine, which he docilely took, even though it still didn't stop him from beating the shit out of her.

Dylan then goes on to paint a romantic, sentimental picture of Joey and his brothers in the gang:

> There was talk they killed their rivals, but the truth was
>   far from that
> No one ever knew for sure where they were really at

Well, according to the DA at Joey's early-Sixties extortion trial, 'In the current war taking place between the Gallo gang and established interests, there have been killings, shootings, stranglings, kidnappings and disappearances, all directly involving the Gallos. Interestingly enough, since the defendant's being remanded on 14 November in this case, there have been no known offensive actions taken by the Gallos in this dispute. This would give some credence to the belief that Joe Gallo is, in reality, the spark plug and enforcer of the mob.' But who believes DAs, right? Okay, try his oft-times enormously sympathetic biographer:

'Almost all the charges ever brought against him, even in the beginning, were dismissed. No witnesses. Once people got to know that careless talk was liable to bring Joe Gallo around to remonstrate and maybe make his point with an ice pick, witnesses in Brooklyn became as scarce as woodpeckers. Once the story got around that Joe had gripped a defaulter's forearm by the wrist and elbow and broken it over the edge of a desk to remind him that his account was past due, the Gallos had very few cash-flow problems with their gambling, loan-sharking and protection business.'

Most interestingly of all, his wife tells the story of how she became innocently entangled for a moment with a member of Joey's gang as they drunkenly tried to pull their coats off the racks of a nightclub cloakroom. Later, in bed, Joey accused her of kissing the guy and she responded that that was absurd because, for one thing, he was wildly unappetising. But Joey hounded her about the matter, convinced that her confession would prove that he had seen what he had convinced himself he had seen and was therefore not insane. Finally, to prevent further harassment (to perhaps, in fact, save her own life) and reassure him as to his sanity, she 'confessed'. The next night, as they lay awake together in bed again, he casually remarked. 'Say, listen – you remember that guy at the club? The guy you were fooling around with? He's dead. I forgot to tell you . . . Yeah. Last night. He had a terrible accident on the bridge. His car went out of control . . . That's a terrible thing. He was a nice guy.'

Later in the song Dylan asserts that 'The police department hounded him'. Considering the number of rackets that the Gallos were involved in, nothing could be further from the truth.

Goddard:

'Right from the start, relations between the Pizza Squad [NYC anti-Mafia cop team] and the Gallo gang had been imbued with a grudging professional respect which, in certain cases, shaded into something close to affection. They played the game by the rules.'

Adds a cop:

'They're a peculiar mob . . . They knew what we had to do and they weren't going to question it. They treated us like gentlemen. That don't make them good guys, but they had a little more savvy [than the Colombos]. It was like "Why stir the pot? If you're going to be down here, let's make it pleasant for both of us." It's a game. If you get caught, you get caught.'

Perhaps most curiously of all, Dylan says that 'They got him on conspiracy, they were never sure who with'. Funny, because everybody from Goddard to the courts and cops agree that Joey's downfall came when, early in May 1961, he tried to muscle in on a loan shark named Teddy Moss. Moss resisted and, in the presence of undercover cops, Joey said, 'Well, if he needs some time to think it over, we'll put him in the hospital for four or five months, and that'll give him time.'

But how can Dylan have a martyred Mafioso without an evil judge:

'What time is it?' said the judge to Joey when they met
'Five to ten,' said Joey, The judge says, 'That's exactly what
    you get.'

This is what, for want of a better phrase, must be termed poetic
licence. The truth is that Joey's lawyer was as lame as his gang and
never made it up from Florida for his trial and Joe refused to have
anything to do with the two other lawyers appointed to represent
him, choosing to stand mute while the DA delivered a steady
stream of evidence that was pretty solid in the first place and never
disputed. That Joey allowed this to happen suggests, not that he
was railroaded, but merely that he was incredibly stupid.
    Goddard:
    'Readily concurring that Joey was "a menace to the commu-
nity", Judge Sarafite chalked up the first victory in the Attorney
General's [Robert Kennedy, who once branded Joey Public Enemy
No. 1] assault on organised crime by handing down the maximum
sentence of seven and one-quarter to fourteen and one-half years'
imprisonment.'
    Dylan: 'he did ten years in Attica, reading Nietzsche and
Wilhelm Reich.' He also read Freud, Plato, Spinoza, Hume, Kant,
Schopenhauer, John Dewey, Bergson, Santayana, Herbert Spencer, William James, Voltaire, Diderot, Pascal, Locke, Spengler,
Wilde, Keats, Shakespeare, Goethe, Will Durant, Oliver Cromwell,
Napoleon, Adenauer, de Gaulle, Lenin, Mao Tse-tung, Clarence
Darrow and Louis Nizer, as well as taking part in a homosexual
gang rape about which he bragged at a cocktail party after his
release.
    'He described how, with several other convicts, he had spotted
a pretty young boy among a new batch of prisoners and laid in
wait for him. Dragging him into the Jewish chapel, they ripped
his pants off and were struggling to hold him down when one
of them heard the rabbi talking in the next room. A knife was
immediately put at their victim's throat with a whispered warning
not to cry out and the rape proceeded in an orderly fashion, each
man taking his turn in order of seniority. They wanted this kid,
Joey said, while his asshole was still tight.'
    This was most likely not, however, the reason that (according
to Dylan) 'his closest friends were Black men'. It was ''Cause they
seemed to understand/What it's like to be in society/With a
shackle on your hand.' And also, as previously stated, because Joey
for a while entertained dreams of launching a Black Mafia when he

got out. The psychoanalyst who interviewed Joey in prison voices agreement with Dylan in more clinical terms, but adds 'Joey was a terrifically prejudiced guy . . . on a strictly, and deeply, personal level, he was a knee-jerk nigger-hater,' and also allows that it was 'entirely possible' that 'I was conned by one of the greatest con artists of all times.'

After Joey is finally sprung, Dylan has him blessing both the beasts and children: 'It was true that in his later years he would not carry a gun.' Of course not; no Mafia chieftain ever has, unless in unusually dire fear for his life. The cops would like nothing better than to send one of these guys up on a carrying concealed weapons rap and anyway that's what the wall of protective muscle that accompanies them everywhere is for.

'"I'm around too many children," he'd say, "they should never know of one."' Again true – mob leaders have always been scrupulous about keeping their wives and children universes removed from the everyday brutality of their work. Anybody who saw *The Godfather* knows that. But as for Joey's magical touch with children, let his daughter, Joie, speak: 'He would come home and say, "Make me some coffee." And I would say, "Daddy, I have homework. Can I do it later?" "No. Now." It was like I was refusing him and nobody ever did that. He was the king, and I couldn't stand it . . . He used to abuse Mommy terribly, and I resented him coming between us. He broke her ribs once . . . I used to complain to Mommy about him and beg her to leave him. "What a man you picked," I'd say. "Who'd want to live with that maniac? You've got to be crazy to put up with this." So then I'd divorce him as my father. I'd take a piece of paper and draw a very fancy certificate that said, "I, Joie Gallo, hereby divorce Joey Gallo as my father."'

But who but a biographer would let a goddamn kid mouth off like that anyway? A good slap in the puss and they hie to their place. Which is where they belong when the fast bullets fly, as Dylan's vocal lurches to the denouement of his most mythic of sagas:

> Yet he walked right into the clubhouse of his lifelong
>   deadly foe
> Emptied out the register, said, 'Tell 'em it was Crazy Joe'
>
> One day they blew him down in a clam bar in New York
> He could see it comin' through the door as he lifted
>   up his fork . . .

And someday if God's in heaven overlookin' His preserve
I know the men that shot him down will get what they deserve

And then, for the last time, the chorus that drones through this whole long, boring song:

Joey, Joey.
What made them want to come and blow you away?

There are several theories in answer to that question. The most prevalent was that, since most people took it for granted that Joey was behind the shooting of Joe Colombo almost a year before, there was an open contract out on Gallo by the Colombo family, meaning that Joey had effectively committed suicide in having Colombo rubbed out. Two other theories advanced by investigators extremely close to the case have Gallo once again trying to muscle in on territory occupied by other, more powerful mob factions. In one case, he could have told two thugs to crack a safe for $55,000 in Ferrara's Pastry Shop in Little Italy, a landmark frequented by Vinnie Aloi, at that time a very powerful capo in the New York Mafia. This would certainly have been the straw that broke the camel's back in regard to the mob bosses' patience with Gallo's hustles, as would another incident reported in the 4 June 1972 *New York Times*:

'Three weeks prior to Gallo's getting killed, he, Frank (Punchy) Illiano and John (Mooney) Cutrone went out to the San Susan night-club in Mineola, LI, in which John Franzese [another powerful capo in the Colombo family] is reported to have a hidden interest. Joey is reported to have grabbed the manager and said, "This joint is mine. Get out." In other words, he was cutting himself in. This was the first sign we had that Crazy Joe was acting up again.'

In any case, any of these courses of action (and Gallo may well have undertaken all three) amounted to signing his own death warrant. An interesting side-light is that at this time Joey was broke, practically reduced to the shame of living off his bride of three weeks; his mother had already mortgaged her house and hocked her furniture to pay for bail bonds. Meanwhile, of course, he had begun to hang out with what Goddard calls 'the show-biz, table-hopping cheek-peckers' club': Jerry and Marta Orbach, the Ben Gazzaras, the Bruce J. Friedmans, Neil Simon, David Steinberg, Joan Hackett and her husband – people that, as his bride Sina warned him, 'might be exploiting him for the thrill of having a real live gangster empty their ashtrays and talk about life and art'.

Marta Orbach told him Viking Press was interested in publishing whatever literary collaboration he could cook up with her, so they began making daily tape recordings of his reminiscences at her house. At first it was supposed to be a black comedy about prison life, but then there was talk of an outright autobiography and even a meeting with an MGM representative to discuss selling it to the movies – so there is also the remaining possibility, as a final theory, that just about anybody in the underworld, getting wind of this, might be nervous enough about possible indiscretions to want him snuffed.

The two key points here are that (a) by this time he was totally pathetic (Goddard: 'He had outgrown the old life. To allow himself to be forced back into it was unthinkable – a submission to circumstance, a confession of failure. As for his new life, the prospect was hardly less humiliating. It entailed another kind of surrender – to show-biz society and public opinion. His self-esteem would depend, not on his power and sovereign will, but on how long an ex-gangster could stay in fashion. Like an ex-prizefighter, he might even be reduced someday to making yoghurt commercials'), and (b) Dylan got even the very last second of Gallo's life wrong: 'He could see it comin' through the door as he lifted up his fork.' Gallo was shot from behind.

So all that remains now is the question to Bob Dylan: Why? And since that is one I doubt he is going to answer (his new collaborator, Jacques Levy, already put in a defence to the effect that Dylan wrote about Billy the Kid, so why not Joey Gallo), the only thing remaining is to suggest antihero fodder for future Dylan compositional produce: Elmer Wayne Henley, William Calley, Arthur Bremer, and that kid who tried to rob a bank at 13th Street and Sixth Avenue, and ended up drunkenly requesting replays of the Grateful Dead on the radio. Certainly they all qualify as alienated victims of our sick society, every bit as much on the outside as Joey Gallo.

One does wonder, however, what Gallo would have made of Dylan's tribute to him; and one receives a possible answer in Goddard's book, where Gallo's ex-wife describes borrowing a hundred bucks from Joey's father to buy records so that the Prince of Brooklyn, always a fan of contemporary music, could catch up on what had been happening in Soundsville during the decade he'd been away reading Reich in the slams: 'He got especially mad over a Byrds album called *Chestnut Mare* that I wanted him to hear. "Listen to the lyrics," I said. "They're so pretty, and so well done." "I don't want to hear any fags singing about any fucking horse," he says – and he's really venomous. "It's not about a fucking horse," I said. "If you'll listen, it's about life." But he doesn't want to hear about life either . . . Next thing I know, he jumps out of the bathtub, snatches the record off the machine, stomps out in the hall stark naked and pitches it down the incinerator.'

A. MANAKOV
Bob Dylan's trajectory

Literaturnaya gazeta, 7 September 1977

In contrast to the recently deceased 'King of rock-'n'-roll', Elvis Presley, another singer who is no less popular in America – Bob Dylan – is not as imposing. The first time I saw him, I was struck by the unprepossessing appearance of this thin, slightly awkward, modestly dressed young man. He gave the impression of an amateur appearing on stage during the intermission between performances by 'stars'. But as I listened to the lyrics of his songs and the sound of his guitar and got accustomed to him, I understood why Bob Dylan does not want for fame and renown in America.

American young people quickly claimed Dylan's songs for their own, as distinguished from commercial hits. Bob boldly revealed the flaws of the 'Great Society'. On stage, he won over his listeners not so much by how he sang as by what he sang. He praised love, damned war and ridiculed the money-grabbers and pseudo-intellectuals. He sang about how oppressive, exhausting labour kills people and he said that in America patriotism is understood merely as defence of the ruling elite's interests.

This is just what students and young workers wanted to hear in the 1960s. High school pupils demanded that their teachers include Dylan's songs in their English courses and university students called him their 'favourite poet'.

The poets Lawrence Ferlinghetti and Allen Ginsberg noted that the chief merit of his poetry was that it went out into the streets and gripped young people. Dylan found the surest road to young hearts – through song and truth. And isn't this the dream of all poets?

He demolished many canons as he sought for poetry in living, conversational speech. People heard him and quickly caught his meaning. 'For me,' Bob said, 'everything is very plain and clear. I know myself and the people around me. I've never written about things that I haven't really seen. I sing about living people and I put into words only what I know.'

In the world of his songs – 'a chain of images that explode and then die out' – there is almost no sun or colour. They are more like a carnival of grotesque figures in which alienation, hypocrisy and sanctimoniousness reign. In this world one can see Napoleon in rags, Einstein in Robin Hood's clothes, Don Quixote on Rocinante making his way through neon jungles. Dylan openly mocked lawmakers, clergymen and militarists.

The tenderest chords of young people's hearts responded to his words. 'I try to bring my words into harmony with the chirping of a lone sparrow. A song flows by itself and doesn't need anybody's help,' he said. 'Poetry is like a naked man and songs should be honest to the point of madness.'

But all this is in the past – it was left behind in the 'stormy Sixties'. Today it's hard to recognise the old Bob Dylan. The fate of this popular singer has become intertwined with rock-'n'-roll. The founders of this musical genre called it a 'revolutionary art form', but with time it has become clear that powerful 'pop culture' has turned it into just one of its commercial enterprises. Rock-'n'-roll quickly became a form of business.

Rock songs, many young Americans still feel today, challenged their 'fathers' culture'. But what happened? The fathers had experience and business acumen on their side. 'Get mad, but only on the playing field,' they said to themselves. 'Don't go beyond that, or we'll punish you.'

The 'apostles' of rock-'n'-roll signed contracts with the same people they had ridiculed in their songs. Called upon to be 'liberating heroes', they fell one after another into a cleverly laid trap in which the 'rock revolution' served as bait.

The first time that Dylan appeared at a music festival performing not protest songs but ordinary ones with rather obscure lyrics, he was greeted with unconcealed disappointment. When he came on stage for the first time with a rock-'n'-roll band and began to sing songs in fashionable rhythms to the band's accompaniment, the audience hooted. His fans were puzzled and confused. 'Has Bob sold out?' they asked. A major record company answered for him: 'Bob has already made a million.'

Intoxicating popularity, which covers an enterprising spirit like a shroud, has extinguished more than one 'star' in the firmament of American art. Bob Dylan could not escape this fate. Many of the old protest songs that brought him fame have gradually left his repertoire.

'I'd like to write like I used to,' he says, as if justifying himself, 'but I can't any more. I don't know why. In the old days, I knew what I wanted to say before I began to write. Today I just compose a song that will make it, but I don't know what it's about.'

PAULINE KAEL
The Calvary gig

New Yorker, 13 February 1978

Suppose some people in their late teens or early twenties, imagining in their plain innocence that Bob Dylan is a famous composer-singer, no more, no less, go to see his film *Renaldo and Clara* – what can they make of it? During the opening titles, Dylan is heard singing 'When I paint my masterpiece' and then we see a small man on stage performing; he wears a hat straight across his forehead, like Billy Jack, and a clear plastic mask with a twisted big mouth and a stretched-out nose. Eventually, he pulls off the disguise and we see Dylan's scowling, impassive face, but during the three hours and fifty-two minutes of the movie Dylan puts on other masks, or paints his cheeks and nose white and then shows us the sweat pouring through the paint. The film was shot mostly in the course of a Bicentennial (1975–6) tour (the show was called the Rolling Thunder Revue) and the performance footage, with the singers and musicians lighted in strong, bright, near-psychedelic colour against black or deep-blue backgrounds, is handsomely photographed and has good sound quality. But we never get the build-up of excitement that one can feel at a live performance (and sometimes at a performance film, too), because *Renaldo and Clara* keeps cutting away from the stage to *cinéma-vérité* fantasies of Dylan's life, which occupy more than two-thirds of the movie. In this material, Dylan tries some role-playing, camouflage, going incognito, and he's joined by Joan Baez, Sara Dylan, Ronee Blakley, Allen Ginsberg, Arlo Guthrie, Sam Shepard; Ramblin' Jack Elliott, Harry Dean Stanton and a large cast of other friends and musicians, who half-heartedly assume make-believe identities. Everything circles around Dylan who, despite his many guises, is always the same surly, mystic tease.

Although the film was made by Bob Dylan, he didn't direct it (nobody did). The cameramen are following a floating crap game – panning, zooming, frantically trying to catch whatever looks promising. And he didn't write it: the participants seem to be saying whatever comes into their heads. (Only David Blue, working a pinball machine and telling us how he first met Bob Dylan, shows an instinctive feeling for the camera and some wit.) But Dylan must certainly have been in control of the editing. He has given himself more tight close-ups than any actor can have had in the whole history of movies. They are so close you don't see the whole face – only from under the brims of his hats down to midway across the chin. His eyes are heavily lined in black, for a haunting, androgynous effect, and you get the skin blemishes, the face hair, the sweat and bad capillaries, and, when he sings, the upper lip pulling back in a snarl and the yellow teeth like a crumbling mountain range. He is overpoweringly present, yet he is never in direct contact with us – not even when he performs. We are invited to stare at the permutations of his masked and unmasked face in close-up to perceive the mystery of his elusiveness – his distance.

This is a shocking miscalculation, because, of course, Bob Dylan is no longer the oracle, perhaps not even to his entourage and his troupe of associates. In the Sixties, his songs were said to have defined a generation, but what he does on the screen here is painfully out of key with the times. Where is the audience that will see him as he sees himself? He and Allen Ginsberg visit a Catholic grotto in Lowell, Massachusetts, and as they examine the glassed-in sculptures, Ginsberg, in the role of The Father, explains the Stations of the Cross to him. Dylan's songs include his own 'What will you do when Jesus comes?' and 'Knockin' on heaven's door'. A street philosopher holding forth in a diner says, 'The people still love Dylan and they'll still follow Dylan.' And wherever Dylan goes – visiting Kerouac's grave and observing, 'I want to be in an unmarked grave', or tramping in the Vermont snow in his Hasidic-pathfinder costume – there is an aura about him. The camera keeps saying: this is no ordinary man who walks among you. In one sequence, he pays a visit to the Tuscarora Indians and receives homage with a humility unrivalled by Jeffrey Hunter in *King of Kings*. It's not just people previously unexposed to Dylan who are likely to be repelled by his arrogant passivity; even those who idolised him in the Sixties may gag a little.

The Bob Dylan they responded to was a put-on artist. He was derisive, and even sneering, but in the Sixties that was felt to be a way of freaking out those who weren't worthy of being talked to straight. Implicit in the put-on was the idea that the Establishment was so fundamentally dishonest that dialogue with any of its representatives (roughly, anyone who wore a tie) was debased from the start. And Dylan was a Counterculture hero partly because of the speed and humour of his repartee. (*Playboy*: 'Did you ever have the standard boyhood dream of growing up to be President?' Dylan: 'No. When I was a boy, Harry Truman was President. Who'd want to be Harry Truman?') In *Renaldo and Clara* his mocking spirit is just bad news: he's a sour messiah. After you've watched him for a few hours, in his medicine-man paint, his superannuated hippie clothes and the big hats that sprout feathers and flowers and plumes, you may begin to wonder if his visionary double-talk isn't just another form of the usual showbiz patter of people who keep looking back. The chief duty of David Blue's monologues at the pinball machine is to give us the legend of how things used to be, in the Sixties – to place Dylan in history for those who never knew or have forgotten. When Blue explains how Dylan came to write 'Blowin' in the wind', it's not very different from Comden and Green on stage reminiscing about *their* great days, the Fifties.

In recent years, in Hollywood, industry executives have been dumbfounded to discover that awesomely rich singers and TV stars will take a financial loss for a shot at the movies. Even for people whose faces and voices are known to many more millions than ever went out to the pictures, working in the movies still represents the real glamour and the real challenge. And artists whose reputations might suggest that they are above such dreams may also want to be movie stars. At the extreme, for Bob Dylan as for Norman Mailer, stardom isn't enough. Though these artists don't – can't – give to movie-making the struggle to find their way which went into their primary art, they take on the burden of the film-maker as well as of the star. Except for a streak of messianism, Mailer's writing and Dylan's songs could hardly be more different, but when these men turn to film the results are startlingly similar. For all Mailer's theoretical bullslinging about how movies should be made and for all Dylan's forlorn holiness, they both set themselves in the centre of a group of friends, admirers, old flames and flunkies, and, while *cinéma-vérité* camera crews keep shooting, they play-act identity games. It's what Louis and Marie Antoinette might have done at Versailles if only they'd had the cameras.

Like Mailer, Dylan is an artist who intended to do something in advance of conventional movies – more poetic, more 'true' – yet *Renaldo and Clara*, like Mailer's *Wild 90*, *Beyond the Law* and *Maidstone*, is marked by an *absence* of artistic intelligence. The picture hasn't been thought out in terms of movement or a visual plan. Dylan merely gives his actor friends some clues as to what he'd like them to do and they improvise, without reference to what has gone before or what will follow. Thousands upon thousands of feet of film are exposed and then editors, with 'the film-maker' supervising, try to cut it all into some sort of shape. It's a lazy, profligate way to make a movie; the technicians are forced to try to compensate for the fact that nobody has done the thinking. There were four camera crews working simultaneously on *Renaldo and Clara* and, with the compositions left to the cameramen, there's no overall clarity of style.

Dylan has been involved with movies at least since the mid-Sixties; *Don't Look Back*, in which he starred (and which his manager helped produce) was about his 1965 tour of Britain and showed him as a sensitive artist harassed by people who didn't understand his art. He put them on mercilessly and squelched them with satisfaction. *Renaldo and Clara* has the same ridicule of outsiders (in one sequence, the elderly women at a poetry reading are rattled by a hipster's deadpan remarks introducing

Allen Ginsberg); the same self-protective way of tossing out thoughts (one can never be sure whether Dylan means what he says); and the same sweet-Jesus liberalism (in *Don't Look Back*, the footage of the British tour was interrupted by a sequence of Dylan playing for Mississippi sharecroppers, while in *Renaldo and Clara* the footage of the Rolling Thunder tour is interrupted by man-on-the-street interviews with Black people about the Rubin Carter case, which seem included to show us that Bob Dylan cares more about Black people than they do themselves). *Renaldo and Clara* is a continuation of *Don't Look Back*; it hasn't solved any of that film's problems, it just extends them over almost three times the length. In movies, you can force connections in the cutting room and think you're using associational editing, but the result may still affect viewers as random footage spliced together. The variable colour values in *Renaldo and Clara* and the frequent returns to situations that one thought were finished (for example, to the philosopher and the other men in the diner talking about God's work and what truth is and how 'if you follow Bob long enough, maybe you can translate these things,' or to scenes with several of the women dressed up as hooker señoritas and talking over life's problems) add to the feeling of randomness. *Renaldo and Clara* doesn't take form in the mind, like a movie, even though one can discern the thematic links. They're not hard to spot, so many of them are biblical.

No matter how skilfully the footage is cut, there's still a basic discrepancy in using hand-held or shoulder-mounted lightweight *cinéma-vérité* equipment on acted scenes and this is particularly apparent when they take place in small rooms. The falseness of the amateur-theatricals acting here is compounded by the fact that the cameramen are bouncing around as if they were shooting a news event. In most Hollywood films, the danger is of set-ups so patterned that the film is static; the danger in this kind of film is that, with the camera necessarily active, the movement will be jumpy. In a backstage scene in which Ronee Blakley and Steve Soles act out a quarrel, the camera is a jack-rabbit leaping from wall to wall, chasing the action. This sequence is so glaringly bad both as improvisation and in terms of film technique that one wonders why Dylan put it in. But it's followed by Ronee Blakley on stage singing her own song 'Need a new sun rising' and then one can guess why. Singing in a rougher, more passionately all-out style than in *Nashville*, she gives the film a fresh, reckless energy that makes the other performers and Dylan himself seem jaded, familiar. Was the quarrel scene, in which she comes across as a completely undesirable woman, stuck in just ahead of her number to sabotage it? The other women in the movie keep their place; the saintly film-maker may be putting Ronee Blakley in hers.

Sara Dylan has a flirtation scene with Sam Shepard that is like a *cinéma-vérité* nightmare. She goes through womanly-wisdom routines while he plays the juvenile and you feel it will never end. Slender and smiling, Joan Baez is pleasantly relaxed (except when she does an arch parody of a gypsy accent). She never takes what's going on seriously enough to be embarrassing; playing something called The Woman in White, she just seems to be humouring Dylan. But her slightly blank, ironic off-handedness makes the viewer feel a fool for watching and she does more necking than singing. Part of Dylan's psychodrama here involves a triangle – hot revelations about his past life with Sara Dylan and Joan Baez. With the improvisational techniques he's using, what is revealed amounts to this: Baez has a soliloquy on the soundtrack about wanting somebody. (The women in this movie are very hard up.) Then she sings a song about her relationship with Dylan, and asks him, 'What do you think it would have been like if we'd gotten married?' This is capped by her switching drinks with him; they're playing Hollywood lovers for us. Somewhere toward the fourth hour, Dylan and Sara Dylan are referred to as Renaldo and Clara, and a little later we sit watching while Sara Dylan gives Dylan a little soft pawing and Baez plays the rejected other woman. And, in one howling moment, he stands between the two women and the camera moves down his torso, as if he were the oak tree of life. This triangle is the big number (Mailer having already played a love scene on screen with *his wife*). Dylan tries an artistic-film-maker device by having Sara Dylan ride in a carriage and then step out and enter a building to be replaced by Joan Baez, inside the building, wearing Sara's clothes. Only Dylan could imagine that either of the characters they're playing has enough identity to transfer. (And in visual terms, he picked the wrong woman for this transfer scene: in long shot, Joan Baez and Ronee Blakley look enough alike to confuse viewers.)

The pretence that Dylan is playing someone named Renaldo collapses when we see how he is received by the Tuscarora Indians. They're delighted and honoured that Bob Dylan, the star, has come to visit them. And this star, who in his lyrics identifies himself with the 'poet who died in the gutter' and the 'clown who cried in the alley', reacts as if he were blessing them by his presence. (He wants to be buried in an unmarked grave. Of course. That's why he's made a four-hour movie about himself and his pilgrimage.) Is Dylan still so impressed by adulation? Doesn't he know that even fourth-rate actors in a TV series who rent themselves out to open a supermarket are received as if they were saviours?

SEVEN

I Threw It All Away

RON ROSENBAUM
Born-again Bob: four theories

New York Magazine, 24 September 1979

A couple of years ago I was sitting in a luncheonette in Burbank, California, asking Bob Dylan about God. Like many in my generation, I grew up thinking Bob Dylan generally had The Answers so, given the opportunity, I thought I'd ask Dylan what he thought about The Big Guy.

'I don't particularly think that God wants me thinking about Him all the time.' Dylan deadpanned. 'I think that would be a tremendous burden on Him, you know. He's got enough people asking Him to pull strings' [*Playboy*, March 1978].

At the time I thought this was an eminently sensible approach – believing but not pestering. But now look what's happened. Dylan, the son of Abraham Zimmerman, the Jewish appliance-store owner, has become a born-again Christian who worships at a Fundamentalist church in Tarzana, California. Not only that, he's released a new album filled with evangelical pieties urging everyone to think about God and ask Him to pull strings.

Now, there are two terrific songs on the new album ('Precious angel' and 'Slow train') that would be classic Dylan songs even if they were about the Dalai Lama. However, many of the other songs contain a high quotient of preaching and *pestering* without the brilliant musical signatures that redeem the other two.

But the controversy about this album must necessarily go beyond the music. A recent analysis of the Italian terrorist Red Brigades in the *New York Review of Books* claimed that the kidnap,

233

kneecap and ski-mask guerrillas have 'embraced Dylan rather than Marx'. While this formulation may have little to do with the Dylan of the past decade – unless one wishes to conjure up ridiculous images of terrorists sitting around singing 'Peggy Day' and other ditties from Dylan's country-pie period to a hapless Aldo Moro – it does illustrate how 'Dylan' has become an accepted shorthand for a kind of anarchic, absurdist anti-ideology – black humour as opposed to the red flag.

Up until now, with all his changes, the actual Dylan has still preserved some element of that symbolic 'Dylan'; up until now he was one of the last formative figures of the Sixties to survive the Seventies without succumbing to some conversion experience. Why did he have to do it now, with just a few months left in this depressing decade? And why, of all things, did he have to convert to Christianity, at precisely that moment when the self-consciousness of Jews is even more acute? Wasn't it enough he changed his name? Because of these questions and the larger meaning of 'Dylan' to a whole generation, the conversion is a cultural as well as musical phenomenon.

Let's examine some explanations that have been offered for his conversion, beginning with **Theory Number One: Cherchez la femme**. Friends of Dylan's report that when he was last in New York he appeared in Gerde's Folk City accompanied by a tall Black woman said to be the person most responsible for encouraging him to undergo the conversion. Dylan's life before he met her – and Him – certainly was the kind of mess that leaves one vulnerable to conversion experiences. His wife of twelve years had left him, claiming half his assets, a piece of his heart and all four of his kids. The bitter trauma of the divorce and the fractious custody fight still haunt his post-conversion songs. In 'Precious angel', a song about the woman who brought him to Christ, there is one particularly uncharitable reference to a wife who was constantly feeding her husband spiritual advice: 'You were telling him about Buddha, you were telling him about Mohammed in the same breath/You never mentioned one time the Man who came and died a criminal's death.' It does seem un-Christian of him to blame his wife for not turning him into a Jesus freak, but it indicates the bitterness of the split.

In addition to losing his wife he's lost much of his artistic reputation in the last few years, as packs of savage critics in a veritable feeding frenzy tore apart his most recent albums and crucified the four-and-a-half-hour movie he had hoped might open up a new career for him. When I saw him in Burbank, his copper-domed Malibu palace was sliding into the sea, he was living alone in Marina Del Rey, of all places, and hanging out with the Nicholson/Beatty New Hollywood crowd. It's enough to drive anyone to that old-time religion. But why Christianity?

Here we must entertain **Theory Number Two**: Dylan is **trying to erase once and for all his Jewish identity**. In some ways I blame it all on a certain interviewer from *Rolling Stone*. Now, this guy is a brilliant writer and thinker, but a couple of years ago he did a long interview with Dylan in which he bombarded the poor folk singer with voluminous quotations from Hasidic masters, Talmudic tales, and rabbinic sages. Not long before, Dylan had complained about how he was constantly besieged by queries from Jewish quarterlies and freelance cabbalists doing elaborate analyses of the Old Testament imagery in his songs. At a certain point I wonder if Dylan didn't OD on it all and say to himself, 'The only way I'm going to avoid hearing these interminable Hasidic tales for ever is to become a Christian.'

Needless to say, this is over-simplification, but Abraham Zimmerman's son was never comfortable with either his father's religion or his father's name. (Remember the line from *Highway 61 Revisited*: 'God said to Abraham, "Kill me a son"/Abe says, "Man, you must be puttin' me on."')

Before he came to New York City back in 1961, he calculated that the name Bob Zimmerman would not harmonise well with the ramblin' hillbilly persona he had fabricated for himself. When, a decade later, in the early Seventies, he began to 'go Jewish', it wasn't in the comfortable assimilationist style of his father but with a fanaticism peculiar to the son. He was photographed wearing a yarmulke on a pilgrimage to the Wailing Wall in Jerusalem. Under the tutelage of an enthusiastic Zionist named 'One-Legged Terry', he was reported to be in close contact and sympathy with Rabbi Meir Kahane and his Jewish Defense League. But when cabbalistically inclined fans and fanatics began to bug him he backed away with a vengeance. By 1977 he was telling me, 'I've never felt Jewish . . . I don't have much of a Jewish background.' By 1978 he was going even further and telling an Australian interviewer that his blue eyes meant that he wasn't genetically Jewish. 'I have different blood in me. Cossack blood.' A man who would go so far as to boast implicitly that his great-grandmother was raped by Cossacks to prove he wasn't really 100 per cent Jewish would certainly not think twice about getting born again to put an end to the subject.

Having safely put his Jewishness behind him, Dylan seems on his new album for the first time to feel comfortable enough with himself to treat his original surname playfully in one of the songs: 'You may call me Bobby, you may call me Zimmy . . . ' And almost, one imagines, out of guilt at abandoning his heritage, as a sop to his former Zionist buddies, he throws in a gratuitous, almost racist attack on Arab sheikhs in 'Slow train'.

When I heard the born-again Bob album, I felt a sense of loss as a Jew. But on the other hand it could have been worse – he could have become a Krishna, a Moonie, an EST-oid [a follower of Erhard Seminar Training], a heroin addict. I, for one, would counsel tolerance for this conversion, because throughout his career Dylan has had a habit of undergoing conversions and according to **Theory Number Three: He hasn't really changed at all.** Remember how outraged all the folkies were when Dylan made that 'drastic' conversion from folk guitar to electrified rock-'n'-roll? Remember how all the rock-'n'-rollers were enraged when he converted from electric to Nashville country? And hasn't he always taken the stance of a biblical prophet using the word and fables of both Testaments to convey his outrage? Aren't the new songs in some ways the second coming of the critical social conscience his original disciples have been praying for? Hasn't he always been arrogant and self-righteous in his jeremiads? Even when he made fun of those who thought they had 'God on their side', you had the sense it was because, deep down, he knew *he* had God on *his* side. Perhaps we're lucky he's only claimed he's *found* Jesus; it wouldn't be totally surprising if he claimed he *was* Jesus.

Still, in the past – and here's where the nothing-has-changed theory breaks down – there was always a sense of humour. In the autobiographical song 'My back pages', he recognised 'I'd become my enemy/In the instant that I preach.' The disturbing thing about the new album is not that it's Christian but that it's so humourlessly preachy. Which brings us to my own theory – **Theory Number Four: The trouble is not the Christianity but the Californian in the conversion.** One tell-tale sign that California is the culprit is the logo of Dylan's Vineyard church in Tarzana. There's a picture of Jesus in that logo which makes Him look like a Marin County coke dealer, a late-Seventies smoothie, a quintessentially Californian Christ.

One could argue that any sensitive human being who lived in Malibu and Marina Del Rey for more than a year would be driven to seek a transcendent saviour from those modern Babylons. Nevertheless, Dylan's conversion has some disturbing hints of cult brainwashings – get a guy whose personal life makes him vulnerable and turn him into a solemn soul-saver. I'm not saying it's time to call on Ted Patrick to kidnap and deprogramme Dylan. I think the best solution is tolerance and some selective consumer response. Buy the album because of the two great songs but pass by the simple-minded single they've decided to release, 'Gotta serve somebody'. Perhaps this conversion too shall pass.

After all, Dylan once wrote, 'he not busy being born/Is busy dying'. So it's not enough to be born again. One has to be born again and again.

As for me, Bob, I don't necessarily want you to leave Christ and come back to your roots. But I do think you ought to leave California and come back to New York.

GREIL MARCUS
Amazing chutzpah

New West, 24 September 1979

Listening to the new Bob Dylan album is something like being accosted in an airport. 'Hello,' a voice seems to say as Dylan twists his voice around the gospel chords of 'When He returns'. 'Can I talk with you for a moment? Are you new in town? You know, a few months ago I accepted Jesus into my life – ' 'Uh, sorry, got a plane to catch!' ' – and if *you don't* you'll rot in hell!'

Slow Train Coming is the first testament to Bob Dylan's recent embrace of a certain version – Southern California suburban – of fundamentalist Christianity. Produced by rhythm-and-blues legend Jerry Wexler, with Dire Straits's Mark Knopfler and

Pick Withers on guitar and drums, it's an initially commanding but ultimately slick piece of music: 'a professional record', as Dylan has said, which mostly means you've heard its pumped-up Muscle Shoals sound before. The record offers surprises – Dylan celebrates his belief in Christ with blues, which is nicely heretical; his singing is often bravely out of control – but they're irrelevant to the burden he's seeking to pass on to whoever will listen. What we're faced with here is really very ugly.

It's not that *Slow Train* is drenched in religious imagery, or that a Jew has decided that the New Testament truly completes the Old. Throughout his career, Dylan has taken Biblical allegory as a second language; themes of spiritual exile and homecoming and of personal and national salvation have been central to his work. In 'All along the watchtower', Dylan defined a crisis of faith – faith in life; the song remains as profoundly religious as any in pop music. What is new is Dylan's use of religious imagery, not to discover and shape a vision of what's at stake in the world, but to sell a prepackaged doctrine he's received from someone else. Despite an occasional sign of life ('She can do the Georgia crawl/She can walk in the spirit of the Lord,' Dylan sings, and who knows what the Georgia crawl is, or wouldn't like to know?), the songs on *Slow Train* are monolithic; Jesus is the answer and if you don't believe it, you're fucked.

Religious revival courses through our history as a response to collapsing social structures and the need for values that make sense of struggle. Dylan is pre-eminently an American artist, and conversion, after one has spent years as a quester and a solitary, is a pre-eminently American way of continuing that quest – not within the vast open spaces that once filled the country and still fill the American mind, but within the warmer confines of solidarity, of fellowship, of a church. But conversion is also a way of ending a quest, of falsely settling all questions. With *Slow Train*, we don't touch the liberated piety of the Reverend Thomas A. Dorsey, who abandoned a career as 'Georgia Tom', master of the dirty blues, to write 'Peace in the valley'; we don't sense the awful tension of Hank Williams and Elvis Presley, who could sing about the light without ever finding a way to live in it. Dylan's new songs have nothing of the sanctified quest in them: they're arrogant, intolerant (listen to the racist, America-first attack on Arabs in 'Slow train', otherwise a pretty good tune; listen to what's said about anyone who thinks answers are not the question) and smug. Much of the writing is insultingly shoddy – some songs are no more than glorified lists.

This is not the music of a man who's thinking something through, but of a man who's plugging in.

'Ya either got faith or ya got unbelief and there ain't *no* neutral ground,' Dylan chants; in case you might imagine he's using 'faith' as some kind of spiritual metaphor, he quickly adds: 'Sister, lemme tell you about a vision I saw/ . . . you were telling him about Buddha, you were telling him about Mohammed in the same breath/You never mentioned one time the Man who came and died a criminal's death . . . ' And on and on, screed upon screed.

The best religious music makes me wish I could put aside my emotional and intellectual life and accept what the singer has accepted; though I cannot or will not, I can at least recognise the absence of the singer's joy, clarity and commitment in my own life. Dylan's received truths never threaten the unbeliever, they only chill the soul, and that is because he is offering a peculiarly eviscerated and degraded version of American fundamentalism. In 'Do right to me, baby', *Slow Train*'s Golden Rule number, the beautiful, devastating entreaties of Matthew 5:44 are corrupted. 'But I say unto you, Love your enemies, bless them that curse you, do good to them that hate you' turns into you-scratch-my-back-I'll-scratch-yours. Dylan is promoting a very modern kind of gospel: safe, self-satisfied and utilitarian. There's no sense of his own sin on *Slow Train*, no humility, and it's less God than Dylan's own choice that's celebrated. Thus there are no moments of perfect sight, of deliverance, as there are on Van Morrison's astonishingly rich new album, *Into the Music*. Where Morrison's language is inspired – 'Like a full-force gale/I was lifted up again,' he sings, 'I was lifted up again/By the Lord' – Dylan's is ranting, full of promises that are false because they have been made banal. 'There's a Man on the cross and He's been crucified for you,' Dylan affirms. 'Believe in His power, that's about all you gotta do!' [sung version].

That's not all you gotta do if you want what Dylan claims to have. What Dylan does not understand – what most New Fundamentalists have neatly side-stepped – are the hard spiritual facts that have always formed the bedrock of traditional American faith. What he does not understand is that, by accepting Christ, one does not achieve grace, but instead accepts a terrible, life-long struggle to be worthy of grace, a struggle to live in a way that contradicts one's natural impulses, one's innately depraved soul. Sin does not vanish, it remains constant; but now one cannot hide from it and one must accept the suffering recognition brings. Though one is renewed by moments of incredible peace and justification, nothing is finally settled except the fact of one's quest. What sustains that quest is not self-righteousness but the paradox God has made of life on earth, the tension between what men and women know they could be and what, in most moments, men and women know they are. 'And I'll be changed,' Elvis sang in 'Peace in the valley', 'Changed from this creature/That I am.'

One never rests. One never claims, as Dylan does throughout *Slow Train*, that redemption is a simple affair. Against Dylan's blithe declaration of allegiance to God, gospel music sets a hymn like 'I would be true'. The distance implied by the conditional, the implication that without God's help one cannot 'do' anything, is very great.

American piety is a deep mine and, in the past, without following any maps, Dylan has gone into it and returned with real treasures: *John Wesley Harding* is the best example, but there are many others. *Slow Train Coming* strips the earth and what it leaves behind is wreckage.

NOEL PAUL STOOKEY
Bob Dylan finds his source

Christianity Today, 4 January 1980

There is little need to recount Scripture or to specify chapter and verse to substantiate the proposition that *Slow Train Coming* is a Christian album. And while there may be inquiries about the surety of his commitment, *Slow Train* is more than a testimony to Bob Dylan's completion into the Christian faith: it is a call into the bars, into the streets, into the world, to repentance, to 'a Man on the cross . . . crucified for you. Believe in His power, that's about all you gotta do!'[sung version]. Bob, Jerry Wexler and Barry Beckett have taken outreach and made it happen in the raw musical vernacular of the roadhouse.

Bob Dylan's credentials are impeccable. Who continually encouraged us to find the truth for ourselves, not to follow leaders (not even himself, in 'It ain't me, babe')? Who suspected the status quo, the cool, the compromising ('don't know which one is worse,/Doing your own thing or just being cool')? Who warned the complacent that 'the times they are a-changin'' or cried for the realisation of a mutual hope 'blowin' in the wind'? Who painfully re-examined his talents and asked, 'For whom does this prosper?' so that we might be strengthened in our own hope for righteousness?

Not only as edification for the body, 'Gotta serve somebody' must touch any listener just because it identifies so many of us: our jobs, our traits, our likes, our dislikes. How clearly in this context do we begin to see the single choice available at the bottom line: you cannot serve two masters.

As the blind lead the blind, the political activist has misread the reference to sheikhs controlling America's power in 'Slow Train' as a conservative political posture; it is, in fact, an accurate portrayal of the larger picture of world greed and man's subsequent dependence upon its luxuries and niceties as though they were life itself. Remember the line: 'We have met the enemy and he is us'? This is the ultimate war – the extension of our own battle for control in a situation that has been given to us. A man named Adam and a woman named Eve ate of the Tree of the Knowledge of Good and Evil and at once became 'self-conscious', and hid from God. That seed of discontent and guilt has been passed down through the centuries and extruded through into defensive postures that bear no relation to turning the other cheek.

Juxtaposing seemingly unrelated characters and situations, Bob historically has spoken to us of a larger pursuit – a game bigger than local politics or the one-night stand. His *John Wesley Harding* album marked an adventurous step into the spiritual realm. And most Dylan *aficionados* are agreed that 'My back pages' was the most revealing track from *Another Side of Bob Dylan*. It prophesied his dissatisfaction with himself and with goals that suddenly seemed too obvious and short-sighted. His search wound its way through his albums with occasional discoveries – like love, as revealed in a personal relationship.

Scriptural references were commonplace in Dylan songs, mostly Old Testament images. The allusions were rather strong and there was no denying the power and authority of lines like 'the first one now/Will later be last' in 'The times they are a-changin''.

Our Father is leading this musician into areas that are unreachable by the pastel-suited, bouffant-haired, highly stylised 'gospel singer'. No one can fully recognise the diversity of gifts or talents within the body of Christ. Bob's new album is a special success: not only for him personally, as God will contrive to work through him as a person; but also musically, as it reaches for the shadows. It beseeches a decision from the hardest-hearted, the one who is hardest to find, the outlaw – that one who never committed himself for fear of being hurt. It is an inspiration to all brothers and sisters. Remain in your station.

FRAN LANDESMAN
Sorry Bobby

from *New Departures*, 12 (1980)

I'm sorry for you Bobby
And I know that it's been hard
But my eyes can't see the glory
Of your bloody-minded God

I think that Jesus Christ must have been an OK guy
I just don't have any time for his Daddy
I think Jesus Christ must have been real cool and high
But I think that God the Father was a baddy.

I love the baby Jesus underneath the Christmas tree
But his heavy-handed Father is the One that worries me

When He gave to the world His only gotten Son
To be truly crucified for all us sinners
Does it say anywhere He consulted holy Mum
He was hers as well as His, just for beginners –

And I'm sorry for you Bobby and I know what you've been
    through
As a rock star and a legend and a lover and a Jew

But don't preach to me that God is love and joy
And tell me I should try to do His bidding
'Cause He told Abraham to kill his little boy
And then He said, 'No, I was only kidding'.

I hear you singing Bobby of this God you gotta serve
And the record's really selling but I think you've lost your nerve

I'm sorry for you Bobby and I know that it's been hard
But my eyes can't see the glory of your bloody minded God.

KURT LODER
God and man at Columbia

Rolling Stone, 18 September 1980

Of all Bob Dylan's public personae over the past nineteen
years, none has more confounded his long-time admirers than his
latest incarnation as a born-again Christian. Unveiling his new and
obviously heartfelt beliefs on last year's *Slow Train Coming*, Dylan
was a perfect caricature of a Bible-thumping convert, zealously
proclaiming that 'Ya either got faith or ya got unbelief and there
ain't no neutral ground' and prophesying a day of judgement –
coming soon, of course – 'When men will beg God to kill them
and they won't be able to die.'
    Though producers Jerry Wexler and Barry Beckett gave Dylan
one of the cleanest sounds of his career – and Dire Straits' Mark
Knopfler contributed the most lyrical electric guitar lines ever to
grace a Dylan album – the result seemed curiously embalmed:
a record bereft of the rhythmic exuberance that has always
characterised this artist's best work. The songs themselves were
graceless and chilly in their self-righteous certitude. Bob Dylan,

whose search for modern moral connections once summed up an entire generation, had found the Answer: 'Repent, for the end is near.'

This ancient wheeze long ago failed the simple test of time and the clunky fervour with which Dylan advanced it only made him sound ridiculous. Abandoning the greatest of human religious quests – the intellectual pilgrimage toward personal transcendence – Dylan settled for mere religion. His art, which arose out of human complexity and moral ambiguities, was drastically diminished. With a single leap of faith, he plummeted to the level of a spiritual pamphleteer. What made the Gospel According to Bob especially tough to take was his hook-line-and-sinker acceptance of the familiar fundamentalist litany, and his smugness in propounding it. Dylan hadn't simply *found* Jesus but seemed to imply that he had His home phone number as well.

Saved is a much more aesthetically gratifying LP than its predecessor, particularly because of the hope (mostly musical, I admit) it offers that Dylan may eventually rise above the arid confines of biblical literalism. Maybe he'll evolve, maybe he'll just walk away. Whichever the case, stagnation has never been his style, and after *Saved* there seems precious little left to say about salvation through dogma.

Lyrics aside, Dylan's band is sharper and more spirited than I thought possible after its sluggish playing on *Saturday Night Live* last year. Dire Straits drummer Pick Withers, who performed a mostly metronomic function on *Slow Train Coming*, has been replaced by rock-'n'-roll veteran Jim Keltner, whose controlled yet emphatic cooking covers every base without calling undue attention to itself. As a lead guitarist, Fred Tackett still seems severely limited (either by God or the arrangements), but he's amiably efficient and probably preferable to the departed Knopfler, whose rampant tastiness was ultimately more a distraction than an asset. Spooner Oldham's and Terry Young's keyboards interweave easily throughout most of *Saved*'s nine tunes. With Keltner and bassist Tim Drummond irreverently goosing things along, the group actually approaches flat-out rock-'n'-roll on two cuts: the careening gospel rave-up 'Saved' and the unabashedly syncopated 'Solid rock', which boasts a sinuous bar-room riff that the Allman Brothers would feel right down-home with.

Perhaps the most likeable aspect of Bob Dylan's genius has always been his ability to evoke the phantom strains of traditional American music, from country blues to gospel to good old rock-'n'-roll. At his most spectacularly effective (with The Band on *The Basement Tapes*, on the best parts of the *Pat Garrett and Billy the Kid* soundtrack) he seemed to conjure up the nation's historical heart with the strum of a few guitar chords. This gift – utterly absent from *Slow Train Coming*, which affected a faceless R&B ambience – is again in evidence on *Saved*, particularly in the bravely eccentric, almost disembodied reading that Dylan gives the folk classic, 'Satisfied mind'. He lays out the song's stately melody like a winding pilgrim's path through the wailing, tent-show melismatics of his three back-up singers, Clydie King, Regina Havis and Mona Lisa Young.

Subtly gathering harmonic power behind Dylan's rough but finely felt vocal, 'Saving grace' is so persuasive on its own terms that one can disregard the lyrical lapses ('There's only one road and it leads to Calvary') and accept the track as a genuinely moving paean to some non-specific Providence. In a similar manner, the serenely stoic 'Pressing on' (in part, a melodic descendant of The Band's 'The weight') utilises a gentle gospel piano and some inspired lead and back-up singing to make a simple statement of spiritual commitment, with Dylan acknowledging both his past and present in the lines: 'Shake the dust off of your feet, don't look back/Nothing can hold you down, nothing that you lack.' Such a generous observation may bode well for the future.

'Covenant woman' could have been one of Bob Dylan's most engaging love-songs. A gospel-tinged ballad written in Dylan's mid-Sixties chordal style, it posits a God who 'must have loved me so much to send me someone as fine as you'. There's an American Gothic earnestness to such a sentiment that's rather winning. Yet the song is sunk when Dylan explains that among his reasons for loving this woman is the fact that she's 'got a contract with the Lord/Way up yonder, great will be her reward'. He sounds like the kind of guy who counts the spiritual spoons behind her back, and it's more than a little irritating.

'What can I do for you?' suffers from its flat-footed form of address (he's propositioning God, of course), but 'In the garden', which is also explicitly biblical, is blessed with a lovely, billowing arrangement, and Dylan sings with stirring conviction. If non-believers could be converted by music alone, 'In the garden' would be the tune to do it.

'Are you ready?' is as close as Dylan comes to R&B on this record. His harmonica-playing harks back to Little Walter, and the slightly claustrophobic production recalls that of Ray Charles's 'Lonely avenue' (thanks, no doubt, to Jerry Wexler, who produced Charles in his heyday). 'Are you ready to meet Jesus?' the singer asks. 'Are you where you ought to be?/Will He know you when He sees you?/Or will He say, "Depart from me"?/ . . . Am I ready?' Interestingly, Dylan leaves that last question unanswered.

The only miracle worth talking about here is Bob Dylan's artistic triumph – qualified though it may be – over his dogmatic theme. Musically, *Saved* may be Dylan's most encouraging album since *Desire*, yet it's nowhere near as good as it might have been were its star not hobbled by the received wisdom of his gospel-propagating cronies. Dylan doesn't stand much chance of becoming the White Andraé Crouch (or even the next Roy Acuff, who was no slouch with a gospel number either), not just because he lacks the vocal equipment but because he's too inventive, too big for the genre. Because he's Dylan.

As born-again gospel LPs go, *Saved* is a work of some distinction. Now that Bob Dylan's had his shots at that old-time religion, perhaps his secular fans may be forgiven for hoping that this, too, shall pass.

WILFRID MELLERS

God, mode and meaning in some recent songs of Bob Dylan★

Popular Music, 1 (1981)

There is an apocryphal legend that when Louis Armstrong was asked whether he considered his music to be folk music he replied: 'Wal, yeah, I guess so: leastways, I never heard of no horse making it.' If and when we talk of Bob Dylan as a folk singer, we do so partly of course in this fundamental sense: his music is of, about and for people. But we also mean – as Satchmo's interviewer must have done – that Dylan calls on resources and techniques that pertain to oral cultures rather than ostensibly to our own. Unlike 'real' folk song, Dylan's words and music are written down; yet what is notated is no more than an approximation of the sounds heard, which are created empirically for each performance, from verbal inflection and from the body's gestures. Dylan is a 'folk' artist in that his sources are absorbed at a more or less pre-conscious level: from the monody and banjo-picking of 'poor White' Americans and the traditions of White British folk music behind them; from the Black blues and the African heritage it stemmed from; and from some more sophisticated, or at least literate, sources such as White hymn, march and parlour ballad.

To these musical roots there are literary parallels: Dylan's verses have been deeply influenced by rural folk ballads, by the poetry of the blues, by the Bible, by Bunyan's *Pilgrim's Progress* (scarcely less pervasive in the Bible belts than the Good Book itself), by *Hymns Ancient and Modern*, by children's rhymes and by runic verse of all kinds, including Blake's *Songs of Innocence and Experience*, which are close to the core of Dylan's experience and which, although literary, were sung by the poet himself to improvised, presumably folk-like, tunes. In his early days Dylan operated with his voice – untrained, 'natural', veering between speech and song – and his

---

★ An earlier version appeared in *Conclusions on the Wall*, ed. Elizabeth Thomson (1980).

acoustic guitar. The gradual sophistication of his resources in a sense represents a growth towards 'conscious' awareness; in another sense, however, electric presentation, with Dylan as with other pop artists, implies a merging of individual awareness into a communal consciousness (for how does one assess the relationship between 'composer', arranger(s) and technicians?). A singer such as Dylan becomes a shaman in relation to the Global Village's tribe: his songs are ritual as well as art. I want to explore this idea with reference to the albums *Street Legal*, *Slow Train Coming* and *Saved*. . . .

When we consider Bob Dylan's music in relation to White and Black folk monody, White march and hymn and Black blues, we understand why he is a figure of archetypal significance. He began of course as a creator of protest songs; what has become evident through the years is that this protest is not to be construed in narrowly political terms but is rather an intuitive reassessment of philosophical as well as social values. Sometimes, in his early days, his use of a primitive technique – for instance, the drone-accompanied pentatonic monody of 'The ballad of Hollis Brown' – induces only acceptance of and habituation to a state of spiritual as well as material deprivation, with political action perhaps feasible *after* the musical event, since 'protest' is not evident in the music nor even in the fact-recounting words. Sometimes – as in 'Mr Tambourine Man' – folk-derived lyricism offers, within the psyche, a release musically as well as narcotically provoked. Sometimes – in 'When the ship comes in', for example – the euphoria of the White American march is itself invested with the power creatively to hit back. But always Dylan's 'criticism of life' involved the possibility of a 'religious' interpretation. It was not specifically Christian and did not need to be; given his Midwestern background, however, it is hardly surprising that, in *Slow Train Coming*, it should have taken a Christian revivalist form. The music, despite a more explicit reference to White and Black gospel musics (which themselves evolved from an amalgam of folk monody, White hymn and Black blues), is basically unchanged, though not undeveloping. Certainly there are no musical modes in *Slow Train Coming* that had not been explored in the previous disc, *Street Legal*.

If we consider the songs in *Street Legal* in relation to our basic categories of monodic folk incantation, Black blues and White march-and-hymn, we can trace a pattern evolving from rejection to affirmation; what is interesting, and a new development, is that the 'primitive' elements are now a step towards a *regeneration* of the more sophisticated techniques. The simplest song, 'New pony', is a mean-old, low-down, twelve-bar blues riddled with false-related blue notes and with an opening phrase as primitive as an African tumbling strain. [Tumbling strains: descending melodic shapes common in many 'primitive' musics.] Dylan's vocal production too is at its rawest and most raucous; his bleat and blue notes sear the senses. This gives a twinge of venom to the words, which are a love-song in that the ponies, new and old, turn out to be girls. Yet although the sexual vigour of the song is a kind of affirmation, Dylan's plain words and abrasive vocal line have the toughness of the genuine Black blues and, like them, discount personal involvement. This is the more pointed because the solo vocal line is answered antiphonally by choric refrains. Sexual energy is not exactly dismissed in becoming thus communal, but it is 'placed' especially in the context of the other songs. One might almost say that it blows itself up, by internal combustion! As the solo part grows more frenzied, the words referring to voodoo magic, so the instrumental parts become more savage, culminating in a brilliant fuzz-buzz solo – an effect similar to many in the wilder types of African tribal music.

One could not call this number a gospel song, for its sexual energy is too potent for its erotically dismissive message to count for much. None the less it is interesting that antiphony between solo voice and chorus is basic to it, as to most of the other songs; if, in 'New pony', the antiphony is that between shaman and tribe, in 'Señor (Tales of Yankee power)' it is on the way to becoming that between gospel music's preacher and congregation. This magnificent song complements 'New pony'; the latter is an apparent affirmation that implies rejection, whereas 'Señor' is a rejection that turns out to be affirmation. What is rejected is an American Dream, a Texan way of life in threatened ruin; a hazardous personal relationship seems to be involved too, though that is destroyed by a world's desuetude rather than by its own failure. One of Dylan's mythic figures – 'a gypsy with a broken flag and a flashing ring' – plays the part of avenging angel; we are left to 'disconnect these cables,/Overturn these tables', because 'This place don't make sense to me no more'. Musically, the technique is at once starkly primitive and highly sophisticated: primitive because the melody is a chastely pentatonic folk incantation, this time destitute of blue notes, with an instrumental bass rigidly in the aeolian mode; sophisticated because the instrumental sonorities, with chittering mandolin and whining guitar, are precisely evocative of time and place, yet generate a cumulative, 'universalised' power. Dylan's voice, beginning with the 'speaking' minor third that addresses the anonymous 'señor', grows from intimacy to deep resonance in the lower register, to an almost hymnic majesty as, in the last stanza, on the words 'This place don't make sense', he descends from the song's highest note to the tonic. Throughout, the austere modal harmonisation never compromises with chromatic alteration and it is that, rather than the music's steadily increasing dynamics, which convinces us that some kind of religious affirmation may be the only answer to society's distress.

Rural folk hymnody, rather than the hymns of urban chapel and parlour, is evoked at the end of this number. In 'No time to think', Dylan calls explicitly on the manner of the urban White hymn and parlour ballad, and gives us a song of rejection without compensatory affirmation. This, I suspect, is intentional, for this long number is a message-song, as were the talking blues of Dylan's early days. In nine nine-line stanzas, metrically intricate with internal rhymes, the poem deals with the disparity between the cinematic mutability of modern life and the abstractions we think we live by. The 'no time' Dylan encompasses in a fatuous 6/8 tune that gyrates around itself in step-wise movement, breaking into choric ululations on long notes for each pair of 'abstractions' in the refrains. The sonority whirs and wheezes, like a cross between a chapel organ and a fairground steam-organ; the footling tune – entirely diatonic and non-modal though with a curious partiality for subdominants and a reluctance to embrace the traditional dominant–tonic relationship – chugs mindlessly around. Driven, always in strict time, as though on a merry-go-round, it has no time for thought, and precious little for feeling; and that is the point. Though this song debunks our mundane deceits and this time offers no spiritual alternative to them in the music, it includes in the text a few covert Christian references: we have no time to think because we are 'Betrayed by a kiss on a cool night of bliss/In the valley of the missing link'.

If 'No time to think' is deliberately heartless, 'Baby, stop crying' is passionately heartfelt, maturely balanced between desperation and hope. It seems at first to be a straight secular love-song, the girl's sobs being broken, drooping in syncopations and appoggiaturas. Dylan's approach to her begins conversationally ('You been down to the bottom with a bad man, babe'), acquiring lyrical, almost tender, nuance as the line floats through pentatonic seconds, droops through a sixth, lifts through a sixth when he tells us that he can provide no easy answers to the pain that makes her (and us) tempestuously cry, since 'I can't tell right from wrong.' Yet throughout the antiphony of the chorus a private love-song grows into a public hymn; in the refrain the 'crying' seems to involve us all, reflecting on the human condition; and is safeguarded from hysteria by the fact that the music reiterates an ostinato of I–III–IV–V–I triads, purely diatonic, but not modal, and without blue notes. Though Dylan says in the last stanza that he 'don't have to be no doctor, babe', that, in effect, is precisely what he has been, for he has here renewed life from the acceptance of pain. His art is therapeutic, like the blues; in old-fashioned terminology one could call this therapy religious consolation, and perhaps it is not fortuitous that he invites his honey to 'go down to the river', and even promises to 'pay your fare'.

In one song, 'Is your love in vain?', Dylan totally regenerates the White American hymn into spiritual grandeur. The verses sound a bit self-regarding, asking whether he can take his girl's protestations of love as true, whether she will allow him to be himself as well as her lover, and decides to 'take a chance' and fall in love with her. But though a queasy note remains ('Can you cook and sew, make flowers grow,/Do you understand my pain?'), the music demonstrates that he is asking fundamental questions that concern them both, and us all. It differs from 'No time to think', the only other number in which tonality is unambiguously diatonic major and rhythms squarely metrical, in that it is non-satirical. Though aware of human fallibility (consider the quivery little arabesque on the words 'in and out of happiness'), the tune, over a stable bass falling in dotted rhythm, is grave in its alternation of level repeated notes with scale-wise declining fourths, while the texture, often proceeding in sonorous parallel tenths, is both rich and solid. The instrumentation, resonantly organ-like, dominated by Steve Madaio's trumpet, is germane to this nobility, which ends in the kind of apotheosis White hymns aspired to in the days when they were validated by experience. Dylan has won the right to see sexual love as heroic triumph, at least *in potentia*, in this religious sense as well as, or rather than, in an erotic sense.

Dylan's hymnic vein in *Street Legal* is not usually as unequivocal as this. More typical is 'True love tends to forget', which opens with 'hollering' falling thirds, at first minor (from fifth to third), then major (from third to tonic). Yet the music is not simply euphoric, for the five-bar phrases are oddly truncated, and the middle eight, as he lies in the reeds without oxygen, abruptly lurches to the triad of the flat seventh, and modulates to the *minor* of the subdominant before re-establishing the tonic. After this hint of 'reality' the falling thirds recur, exuberantly decorated and sung with harsher vocal timbre; as climax they are expanded into (god-like?) fifths, backed by more animated percussion. The number is somewhat paradoxical, since its affirmation is for real, yet is humanly imperfect – unlike the love of God, which presumably does not forget. This kind of paradox is more overt in 'We better talk this over', in which jazzy elements further compromise hymnic solemnity. It might be a song of loss in that its ambiguous thirds are very blue and its rhythms both broken and irregular, the four pulse alternating with uneasy fives. Yet although Dylan says he is 'displaced, I got a low-down feeling', because his woman has been double-dealing, and although he says he will have to leave tomorrow because there is nothing left of their love except 'the sound of one hand clappin'', the song's *general* statement is far from being a negation. 'Somewheres in this universe there *is* a place that you can call home', and the final couplet advises her not to 'fantasise on what we never had', but to 'Be grateful for what we've shared together and *be glad*' [author's italics]. Despite the rhythmic jitteriness of the 'tangled rope' that enchains them, it is 'time for a new transition': which is manifest in the winging freedom of the melody's peroration, as it is in Dylan's relatively open, songful rather than bleating, vocal production. There is another rejection here; but since it is a rejection of fantasy it may also be an acceptance of truth and a beginning of faith – such as we have heard reflected in the 'grandeur' of 'Is your love in vain?' and 'Señor'. This receives a more overtly religious metamorphosis in the first and last songs of the cycle.

The poems are both very fine, in Dylan's psychedelic or partially surrealist manner. 'Where are you tonight? (Journey through dark heat)' evokes a lover who seems to be (like that sad-eyed lady of the lowlands) both an eternal beloved and a devil of destruction. We move through a hallucinatory landscape wherein whirl the 'dark girl' and her Cherokee father, a 'golden-haired stripper', a lion and a demon: until it appears that the separation is of self from self as well as of lover from beloved. In that case the longing for the undivided whole may count as religious experience in a fundamental sense, and the ecclesiastical flavour of the music is validated. The vocal line, at first primitively in speech rhythms, oscillates between major and minor thirds, unable to define a tune, while the harmony alternates between tonic and subdominant, the former often garnering a flat seventh to hint at, but not to consummate, a real modulation flatwards. The flat sevenths, though indeterminate in pitch, are sufficient to forestall any assertiveness of the dominant; not until the last clause, after three eight-bar phrases, is there a dominant triad and a change from the pendulum of tonic–subdominant in the bass, which now swings down the scale. In the middle section, the melody's vacillating thirds turn into blue false relations, again indefinite in pitch, though flat enough to hint at the subdominant of the subdominant. The words here refer explicitly to the divided self ('I fought with my twin, that enemy within, 'til both of us fell by the way'), and add that 'If you don't believe there's a price for this sweet paradise, remind me to show you the scars'. Because Dylan has come through, the reprise of the original music can grow grander as well as louder, until the splendour of the coda sounds like authentic religious experience in an age of unfaith. There is no deception, no retreat into Zen quietism, let alone into narcotic delusion. There are courage and strength, which may be related to Dylan's confrontation of a crisis in his own life – the failure of the marriage that, on the evidence of the previous discs, would seem to have promised so much. But while personal crisis may have nurtured the further maturation of experience in *Street Legal*, the songs are not 'about' that crisis. Dylan has used his own pain to investigate experience relevant to us all; and it is no accident that the remaining song, 'Changing of the guards', relates neurotic distress, expressed in mythological rather than personal terms, to the possibility of religious and overtly Christian conversion.

The opening of the visionary poem refers to the sixteen years of Dylan's musically creative life. We are *all* divided selves, riding past 'destruction in the ditches/With the stitches still mending 'neath a heart-shaped tattoo'. Yet through endless roads, empty rooms and 'the wailing of chimes', 'the sun is breaking/Near broken chains'; and that 'good shepherd', addressing us as 'gentlemen', tells us he does not need *our* organisation. Dylan had issued similar appeals in his early youth, in a social rather than religious context. The evolution has been both natural and inevitable; and although the purely pentatonic melody has a lyrical grace, even innocence, recalling songs of Dylan's first years, and is unsullied by even a tentative modulation, the build-up of its lilting phrases within the beat's momentum gives it an apocalyptic fervour. Perhaps the final stanza suggests that we are not yet ready for peace, tranquillity and 'splendour on the wheels of fire'; but the choric responses to Dylan's resonant lyricism have at least involved us in a foretaste of gospel-glory, while the brassy sonorities exuberantly sublimate Salvation Army sanctity. The apocalyptic flavour of this song is thus, in a near-theological as well as musical sense, an annunciation for the next album, *Slow Train Coming*, the aesthetic significance of which is, in the context of Dylan's work as a whole, independent of one's acceptance or non-acceptance of its Christianity.

In this cycle the simplest songs are those closest to gospel tradition, White and Black. The opening number, 'Gotta serve somebody', has an almost pre-pentatonic melody over an ostinato bass undulating between pentatonic major seconds and minor thirds, with the synthesiser twittering in pentatonic parallel fourths. This remains unchanged throughout the first eight bars and merely moves down a fourth when thoughts of the world and the devil momentarily hot up the harmony with a dominant seventh. When this is sequentially repeated a tone higher, the bass fleetingly acquires a chromatic note, but this is soon dispersed in the repeat for the second verse, so the modal folk incantation and the driving beat are not seriously undermined. The seven stanzas trenchantly and wittily put down the manifold deceits of the world we live in, and Dylan enunciates with an insidious intimacy that is half seductive, half wry: consider his weird stresses in phrases like 'high *degree* thief', 'live in a *dome*' or 'with a *long* string of pearls'. When the verses merge into the chorus, however, Dylan's voice is reverberantly confident, becoming a clarion call echoed by the choric voices. The refrain is powerfully memorable, as a gospel song needs to be, but the forcefulness of the song remains if one discounts the specifically Christian message, for it is an appeal to all sorts and conditions of men, including preachers, city councilmen, barbers, construction workers, bankers and what-else, that they should respect something beyond self-will; and no one could quarrel with that.

The title song, 'Slow train', works in a similar way but is more complex musically and more particularised poetically. The sundry naughtinesses and hypocrisies of modern industrial civili-sation are again castigated with a vigour recalling that of Dylan's protest years; but though the pentatonic–modal incantation of the vocal line is comparable with that of 'Gotta serve somebody' and is likewise reinforced by stabbing parallel fourths from the synthesiser, it is more jazzily fragmented. In particular, Dylan's tumbling-strain-like ululations are emotionally fraught, with blue notes on the fifth rather than the third: the top notes are always sung flat, though not as flat as a whole semitone. This ambiguity of pitch makes the more telling the flat submediant major triad which announces the coming of the slow train. Again the burden of the song is an appeal for human rather than supernatural sanctions: 'I don't care about economy, I don't care about astronomy,/But it sure do bother me to see my loved ones turning into puppets'; the slow train, melodically and rhythmically, can reinstate our humanity.

'When you gonna wake up' again teeters between social protest and religious affirmation, is again centred on a pentatonic–aeolian A and again chunters in parallel fourths on synthesiser. Although there is a hint of a modulation to the dominant of the relative (G major), there is virtually no harmonic evolution in the song; many of the I, III, IV and (occasionally) V chords have no third, emphasising their primitivism. On the other hand, the melodic line is here more sustained, and its forward thrust is reinforced by the cross-rhythmed (3 plus 2 plus 3) ritornelli and by the surging triplets that exhort us to 'strengthen the things that remain', despite the malpractice of 'Adulterers in churches and pornography in the schools/ . . . gangsters in power and lawbreakers making rules'. Nor is the point ethically loaded against evil-doers who would be damned by any church; 'Karl Marx has got ya by the throat, Henry Kissinger's got you tied up into knots' applies to thousands of folk who are not criminals, and one recognises that Dylan is telling us – his voice is here strongly resilient – that another and more fundamental truth is feasible. He does not seem to be defining it, nor even claiming that he has possessed it, since it is not public or private property in senses that Marx and Kissinger would appreciate.

The hymnic qualities of these songs link up with some of the numbers from Street Legal, though their pentatonic–modal folk vein shows little trace of the White hymn, except those 'White spirituals' that are closely related to and almost indistinguishable from Black gospel music. 'Gonna change my way of thinking' is also very Black, and formally a twelve-bar blues. Both tune and bass are purely pentatonic, the voice ejaculating brokenly like a tumbling strain; again primitivism is a means towards regeneration for 'There's a kingdom called Heaven, 'A place where there is *no pain of birth*'. One has to go 'beyond' or beneath consciousness in order to be reborn: an Edenic quality would seem to be implicit, despite the nervous rhythm, in the music's total absence of chromatic alteration, in its consistent pentatonicism and in the synthesiser's unremittent parallel fourths. Dylan has a point when he tells us that he 'don't know which one is worse,/Doing your own thing or just being cool': again he is making an appeal for human responsibility, as he has done throughout his song-making career, and his vocal inflections – for instance the wail on the phrase 'Blood and water flowing through the land' – spring with directly committed spontaneity. There may be 'only one authority,/And that's the authority on high', but he has an intermediary in that 'God-fearing woman' who can 'do the Georgia crawl' as well as 'walk in the spirit of the Lord'. Dylan says he can 'easily afford' her: which he presumably does not mean in a material sense, since materially he could afford the Queen of Sheba!

This God-fearing woman must be also the 'Precious angel' who 'show[ed] me I was blinded . . . /How weak was the foundation I was standing upon'. The harmony evades dominants in favour of plagal subdominants and shows an odd partiality for first inversions of the tonic, but the song is too jazzily nervous and fragmented to be hymnic, at least in the early stanzas. The choric refrains, however, shine light on his blindness with cumulating fervour each time they are repeated, ending in gospel-style corybantic ecstasy. The weighty part played by the choric voices here is pertinent to the theme because the point of the song is that 'I just couldn't make it by myself.' The young woman is not only a gateway to God but also to communion with other people.

Throughout the songs human beings, especially the 'God-fearing woman', are apt to merge into Christ. A very touching number, 'I believe in you', is a love-song addressed at once to a woman and to Jesus. It is the first song from this cycle to be in a diatonic major key, with a tune that begins with a scalic descent through a fourth, answered by a scalic *rise* through a fourth, resolving the sharp seventh leading note on to the tonic. If this suggests White hymnody it is counteracted by a metrical truncation of the phrase at the cadence and by a substitution, in what starts like a repeat, of a chord of the flat seventh for the tonic. This momentary shiver reflects society's distrust of the singer in relation to God or to the God-fearing woman or to both, yet at the same time makes his belief seem the more real, because the more humanly precarious. Subtly, the 'shock' chord of the flat seventh, originally prompted by alienation, becomes at the climax identified with the fact of belief – 'I believe in you even through the tears and the laughter.' Having heard it as a positive liberation, our response is modified when, in the last stanza, it is associated once more with 'pain' and the 'driving rain'. After the wild upward ululation at the end of the phrase 'even that couldn't make me go back', the song closes in gentle vulnerability. The final amen (IV–I) cadence seems the less assertive because it has been approached by way of the subdominant of the subdominant, that insidious flat-seventh triad verbally associated with being 'A thousand miles from home'.

The only number to exploit directly the manner of the White hymn and parlour song is 'When He returns', in which Dylan for the most part accompanies himself on a domestic piano. The lurching 12/8 rhythm is as remorseless as the 6/8 lilt of *Street Legal*'s 'No time to think', but there is no hint of irony in this metrical rigour and unmodulating diatonicism. The number has passion in its wide-arpeggiated phrases and powerfully employs repeated notes in cross-rhythms to express God's inexorability. In so far as He is inexorable He will, however, seem to some of us rather nasty: so that we welcome the more readily the two songs wherein belief is, musically as well as verbally, tempered by wit. 'Do right to me, baby (Do unto others)' incorporates a Christian message into its refrain but is basically a delightful appeal for compassion:

> Don't wanna judge nobody, don't wanna be judged . . .
> Don't wanna wink at nobody, don't wanna be winked at.

It's ethical rather than religious, though we have noted that in Dylan's songs human imperfection is a foil to divine perfection, since 'God' may be construed as a yardstick beyond our fallible egos. The song is notated in a very sharp B major, though the sevenths are consistently flattened. Moreover they are treated harmonically, in dominant seventh sequences veering between A and B, the harmonic point being marked by a rhythmic elision of half a bar. This gives an infectious jauntiness to the musical line yet also makes a poetic point, since it comically stresses the verb in the capping phrases: 'Don't wanna *be* judged', 'Don't wanna be *winked* at', and so on. If the tune is sophisticated in being thus rhythmically displaced and harmonised in these flickering sequential sevenths, it remains innocent in being a miniature tumbling strain. The chorus ('If you do right to me, baby,/I'll do right to you, too') piquantly introduces a major triad on the upper mediant and therefore in false relation, preparing the way for what looks as though it is going to be the song's only real modulation: but is not, since the bass substitutes E for the expected G, and leads into a *da capo*. This entrancing song does indeed revive flagging spirits, without being revivalist.

The engaging 'Man gave names to all the animals' is not revivalist either, though the choric voices here function in traditional gospel fashion. Its manner is childlike, since it is about the growth from pre-consciousness to consciousness and, in theological terms, about the Fall. Naming ceremonies are important for all primitive peoples, including children; *infans* means 'unable to speak', and to evolve beyond the infant's inchoate cry is to learn to speak the identifying Name. Dylan whimsically allows man in Eden to name God's creatures in a snatch of tune that undulates between three consecutive notes of a pentatonic scale, appending the remaining two notes only at the tune's conclusion. The accompaniment is in the mixolydian mode on E, percussion being light and lilting; the cadential leading notes are sometimes sharpened, however, and this deliciously points the 'namings', especially since the 'Ah, think I'll call it' phrase has been preceded by a risible false relation on the subdominant. The song ends with the relinquishment of Eden; after naming bear, cow, bull, pig and sheep, man sees 'an animal as smooth as glass/Slithering his way through the grass'. The snake disappears by a tree, and the song abruptly ceases, rather than ends, on a dominant triad that, being unresolved, goes nowhere and dominates nothing. In this song Dylan's vocal production is open, warm, tender, yet faintly amused; the snake and the Fall obliterate Eden as consciousness learns to speak the identifying names. So this unpretentious little song proves to be central to the cycle's theme. We have regressed to 'pre-consciousness' – to Eden, to childhood, to the savage state – in order to be reborn; we grow to consciousness and utter the Names; then, having fallen with the snake, we must make the 'eternal return', and the tale must be told again and again, as it was in the beginning, 'long time ago'. This is why the song must end *on*, but not in, the dominant.

It is refreshing that two of the best songs in *Slow Train Coming* should be funny but not frivolous. Only occasionally is there in the words a hint of self-righteous tub-thumping; for the most part the words re-emphasise Dylan's habitual concern with human responsibility and compassion. In any case, even in the overt gospel numbers the musical message is what it always was. The most recent disc, however, with the trenchantly direct title of *Saved*, seems to lack the ironic overtones in *Slow Train* and sounds at first like straight gospel music in which the words are destitute of Dylanesque ambiguities and are, in any case, minimal. The music modifies this impression somewhat, both in its intrinsic nature and also in its vocal and instrumental presentation. The first two numbers are interlinked. 'A satisfied mind', which is not by Dylan, is sung-spoken by him in primitive pentatonics that emulate real gospel music, both White and Black, and lead into the continuous beat and sharp clear textures of 'Saved', which grows cumulatively more excited. There is an element of frenzy, of course, in genuine gospel music; Dylan's, coming from a man who may be saved, but is not and never was innocent even in the sense that poor White and alienated Black might be said to be innocent, has an uneasier edge, more nervously strained – and this is echoed in the weird choric refrains, which bleat raucously, like the whines of grown-up babies. There is a comparable flavour in 'Solid rock', which is a technical description of the music but also a pun; God's Rock needs to be *very* solid if it is to be any use as a bulwark against the savage tempest raging in the beating music. Sometimes the hint of dubiety is inherent in the tunes themselves: 'Covenant woman', for instance, begins with a gentle tumbling strain but then meanders in an oddly directionless line, over simple triadic harmonies which are painfully distorted by the synthesiser. Still weirder is 'What can I do for You?', the 'You' being God who has given me life and breath. Here the displaced rhythm inculcates a kind of bemused bewilderment, echoed again in the whining choric refrains, sounding like lost children. The instrumental postlude reinforces the song's strangeness, for over corny organ hymnody the synthesiser plays very Black and blue arabesques, leaving the title's question unanswered.

So perhaps Dylanesque ambiguities are latent in the cycle after all; if they were not, I doubt if the finest song in the collection could be so impressive. This song, 'In the garden', deals with Christ as miracle-worker, and musically it indeed works a miracle. Its entirely diatonic tune is conceived on a large scale, and its unfolding paragraphs carry the music through continual modulation, usually to keys a tone apart. There is no easy certitude, but a musical annealing through growth, whereby the song generates both power and *wonder*. Even if we cannot swallow some of the verbal implications, we can accept that in this gospel number Dylan's musical message is what it always was, and is perhaps so on a grander scale. This song seems to me as honest as it is affirmative: a summons to hope that remains aware of hazard.

DAVID GRIFFITHS

Talking about licence to kill

Along with John Lennon and Henry Mancini, Bob Dylan was once voted one of the three best-known composers in a poll held among American college students. Anticipating that his audience of musicians would wish merely to substitute three other names, Milton Babbitt, who tells the story, says, 'That is not what concerns me. Rather, it's the different cultural attitude. It's a different connotation of simply the word *composer*. They didn't mean *songwriter*; they meant *composer*. This is a confusion.'[1]

One imagines that the students would in turn be surprised at the criticism of their choice for two reasons: one, they may not have heard, or heard of, Glass, Reich and Adams, let alone Babbitt, Carter and Perle; two, songs clearly *do* involve music, if not composition as such – 'Blowin' in the wind', 'Imagine' and 'Moon river' spring to mind as three ordinary but good tunes, hummed on many a bus. Quirky juke-box selection it may be, but the mechanics are understandable.

The story is a salutary reminder that pop songs involve, beneath their cheery clarity, a series of confusions, be that a con-fusion or the derivation neatly captured by Bob Dylan's phrase 'Mixed up confusion'. 'Song or performance?' asked Dylan, reducing to a dichotomy an increasing and increasingly bewildering series of extensions: song or performance, or live recreation, or cover version, or video, or sampling . . . ? A second confusion. Songs are always about something outside the song, to twist an opinion of Christopher Ricks: 'In the best of songs there is something which is partly about what it is to write a song, without in any way doing away with the fact that it is about things other than the song.'[2] Commenting on this observation, Simon Frith puts it this way: 'songs are about themselves, about language'.[3] This is only and exactly half a story since, finally, songs involve the fundamental confusion of words and music. 'They didn't mean *songwriter*, they meant *composer*': Milton Babbitt here furnishes a fine epigram for writing on the songs of Schumann, Wolf and Webern, where song, being a setting of poetry, is considered to be a musical matter. With Bob Dylan, for composer read poet: when one encounters the literature around these songs it is understood that they don't mean *songwriter*, they mean *poet*. This ought to involve a confusion.

Having defended the innocence of those college kids, what then is wrong with regarding the songs of Bob Dylan as poetry, writing or lyric? Among several dull arguments the canniest is that, were it not for his pop milieu, Bob Dylan might be just another obscure poet, a tiny footnote in American literary history (which anthologies of American literature seem to think he is anyway). But merely by positing a tussle in this way the false dichotomy is created and entertained. Imagine a literary version of our opening story, recast in terms of those who are able only to rattle off the lengthy narrative of Don McLean's 'American pie' or the weird collage of David Bowie's 'All the young dudes', or to rap along with Public Enemy. So be it. Where poetry and musical composition end is defined the space of cultural difference which pop music inhabits, and it is that definition – or the power to define – which invites argument. It's the different cultural attitude.

Here are two particular ways in which a Bob Dylan song differs from written prose or verse. On paper, the line 'You been down to the bottom with a bad man, babe' can either be read aloud, actor-like, in a variety of ways, with different emphases, or be read to oneself, critic-like, with attention to the verbal action along it: both may well avoid doing much with the last word. But it is to the end that a tonal melodic line gravitates, towards the cadence where, because music works in time, one's left without that left–right appearance of a page. That line sings as a series of babbled 'ber-dums' – 'ber-dum berdum', as the Buzzcocks sang – 'been down', 'boddum', 'bad man', ending with a plunged and very present 'babe'. Cadence then rolls in with rhyme and, moving from song to its performance, is often further emphasised in a kind of caricature Dylan trademark, where the phrasing takes a sudden lift at the last, requiring italics, as in 'How does it *feel?*'

A second area in which song differs from printed text emanates from the first, as the accompaniment, specifically the chords, take on a structure of their own. This is inevitable since the harmonic range of a pop song is very limited – not necessarily a bad thing when the words are then taken into account – as Milton Babbitt writes:

A popular song is only very partially determined, since it would appear to retain its germane characteristics under considerable alteration of register, rhythmic texture, dynamics, harmonic structure, timbre, and other qualities.[4]

So if a song is in a major key, the presence of a minor chord can become a big event, to the extent that the different chords form themselves into a signifying group. The big vertical signifier in a Bob Dylan song is nearly always a harmonica break, which sometimes plays on the subliminal expectation of finality. The pop song lends itself readily to a structurally heard, aurally discernible music semiotic.[5]

In the case of 'Licence to kill' one has to imagine the structures sketched in the accompanying example superimposed on to the text, giving the effect of one transparency superimposed on another in overhead projection. The voice appears to place a particular emphasis on the c-cell (see example), with these lines: 'man has invented his doom', 'they bury him with stars', 'all he believes are his eyes', and 'man is opposed to fair play'. This links them cell-wise to the middle eight, the make-or-break line and the one to do with acting a plot. The four verse c-cells are united in a kind of heightened rhetoric, but that is nothing really exceptional in this song. The middle eight's c-cell differs from that of the verse in its chordal support, a relative minor which works as an anathema to the anthem-like major key harmony of the verses. Except, that is, for the repetitions at y, which support the ritornello of the woman on the block. This in turn suggests that it is the relative-minor woman who speaks the middle eight. Because of the strophic nature of the song, it is *she* who has the last word, always trumping the verse material, and ending with the characteristic melodic descent marked bq for 'Licence to kill'. This phrase closes the verse and both halves of the middle eight: the second of these halves, 'error you clearly learn', involves forcing the final note of bq on to a dissonant harmony, pre-empting the note which begins the last verse. In the words too the 'n' of 'learn' is picked up in the 'n' of 'now'.

Having said that, I would prefer the last paragraph to be read as a necessary preliminary to song analysis. Such description prepares the ground for a fuller understanding: one's reading then knowingly builds upon it. Analysis of music always depends upon its language, and thus returns to words, but knowingly, in the manner of the phrase *reculer pour mieux sauter*. Music analysis is itself a performance, a cover version with every sense of engagement and argument, a sense of audience and of theatre, and the sense of working to an ideology, to an aesthetic.

'Licence to kill' is quite unlike a pop song, however much it

Licence to Kill

* i.e. 1½ tones − 1 tone *down* becomes 1½ tones − 1 tone *up*

may sound like one. As with 'Jokerman' on the same record, its concerns lie far outside traditional pop terrain. If 'Jokerman' is a lyric of sorts, 'Licence to kill' is a sermon; and where the former invokes the books of Leviticus and Deuteronomy, it is the prophets Isaiah and Jeremiah who inform the latter.

In the songs of Bob Dylan there is often a creative collision, or collusion, between an elevated or formal language – rhyme will furnish several examples – and one more colloquial or demotic.

There is a sense that Bob Dylan's work, as pop song and as song, *period*, does what a lot of contemporary cultural artefacts can only attempt to do. One can envisage a song like 'Hurricane' divided into two colours, one for the precise minutiae ('Pistol shots ring out in the barroom night', 'brave and gettin' braver'), one for the heady patois ('no idea what kinda shit was about to go down'), with some bits turquoise, a bit of both: 'We want to put his ass in stir,/We want to pin this triple murder on him/He ain't no Gentleman Jim.'

In 'Licence to kill', the formal side is clearly bound up with the biblical imagery – 'rules the earth', 'worships at an altar', 'hell-bent for destruction', 'fulfilled'. And in a notably turquoise patch, the list which opens the middle eight – 'noisemaker, spirit maker,/Heartbreaker, backbreaker' – takes biblical words and chimes them with the modernity of its being a make-or-break situation.

These images of contemporary life which flash across the surface are what prevents the song from turning into a 'telly-pulpit' sermon. At the start is that damning, curious critique of Apollo XI, inventing doom by touching the moon. The lunar and astral imagery here – from the 'first step' on the moon to being buried with stars – picks up from the preceding song on the record. Of the 'Neighbourhood bully' Dylan asks, 'Does he pollute the moon and stars?', while earlier still that very 'licence to kill' is 'given out to every maniac'. I shall return to this latter idea, but for the moment the insistence upon the Cowboy freedom to possess a gun and the notion of messing around with space come together as Star Wars, and point in my imagination to that particular 'actor in a plot' during whose presidency *Infidels* appeared. More evident is that where the plight of the 'Neighbourhood bully' is projected through this one man, 'just one man', 'Licence to kill' counterposes him, his desires, his attitudes, his life, with this one woman, rock solid.

The direct polarity of 'man' and 'a woman' is unusual for Bob Dylan, who is more often heard directly addressing 'his' women, albeit in public: from 'my own true love' in 'Boots of Spanish leather' through 'babe' of 'Baby, stop crying' to 'girl' of 'Don't fall apart on me tonight'. This development takes place against a background in which the rights of women, and of the women's movement, are increasingly asserted – to the extent that the male voice, and the issues of difference and alliance it engenders, is itself problematic.

While Dylan has occasionally wandered close to the edge in this respect – all the 'ache' rhymes in 'Just like a woman', 'Can you cook and sew, make flowers grow?' in 'Is your love in vain?', telling the 'Sweetheart like you' that 'a woman like you should be at home,/ That's where you belong' – the songs rarely feel as misogynistic as they may read out of context: 'Sweetheart like you' sounds far more generous and understanding than it looks there.

Returning to the solitary woman of 'Licence to kill', we come to one of Dylan's striking images. In the third verse man is 'hell-bent for destruction, he's afraid and confused,/And his brain has been mismanaged with great skill'.

In Frederick Seidel's profound meditation on memory and loss, 'The blue-eyed doe', the contemplation of a mother's hospitalisation brings this gloss on the sequence 'brain . . . managed . . . great skill':

> Warm sun, blue sky; blonde hair, blue eyes; of course
> They'll shave her head for the lobotomy,
> They'll cut her hair, they'll kill her at the source.
> When she's wheeled out, blue eyes are all I see.[6]

This is not to suggest an Oedipal source for 'Licence to kill': it is rather the relation of being 'afraid and confused' to 'thinking' the verb 'to kill'. There is death, through age and illness, and there is the licence to kill.

Dylan devotes most of his song to an examination of all this and, in a telling extension of the second verse, he pierces the tough guy's inflated ego. In the studio recording he sings, dutifully:

> Now, they take him and they teach him and they
>   groom him for life
> And they set him on a path where he's bound to get ill.

In the live recording, the slightest alteration shifts the sense, as the thought of being 'set' on a path runs into the clichéd 'set-up' with its manipulations and mendacity. So he sings, in phrasing which seethes with rage:

Well they take him, and they teach him, and they
   groom him for life,
And they set him up on a path where he's bound to get ill.

For this is where the song stands – and a political criticism
starts by choosing this song, and making clear one's agreement
with its central stance: with the notion that, although people are
'bound to get ill' at some point, the freedom to possess guns is
not, as some would have it, the freedom to defend but is rather
a licence to kill. In Britain, the crazed massacre at Hungerford
and the charged killings which linked Gibraltar and Belfast bear
witness to that fact and to a problem all too literally masculine.

Notes

1. *Milton Babbitt: Words about Music*, ed. Stephen Dembski and
   Joseph N. Straus, New York, University of Wisconsin Press,
   1987, p. 181.

2. Christopher Ricks, 'Can this really be the end?', in *Conclusions on
   the Wall*, ed. Elizabeth Thomson, Manchester, Thin Man, 1980,
   p. 48.

3. Simon Frith, 'Why do songs have words?', in *Lost in Music:
   Culture, Style and the Musical Event* [*Sociological Review Monograph
   34*], London, Routledge, 1987, p. 99; reprinted in his *Music for
   Pleasure*, Cambridge, Polity Press, 1988, p. 121.

4. Milton Babbitt, 'Who cares if you listen?', *High Fidelity*, 8, ii
   (1958), pp. 38–40; reprinted in *The American Composer Speaks*,
   ed. Gilbert Chase, Baton Rouge, Louisiana State University
   Press, 1966, and in *Contemporary Composers on Contemporary
   Music*, ed. Elliott Schwartz and Barney Childs, New York, Holt,
   Rinehart and Winston, 1967.

5. See Jonathan Dunsby, 'A hitch-hiker's guide to semiotic music
   analysis', *Music Analysis*, 1, iii (1982), pp. 235–42; Jonathan Dunsby
   and Arnold Whittall, 'From means to meaning: analysis and the
   theory of signs', in *Music Analysis in Theory and Practice*, London,
   Faber, 1988, pp. 211–31, and *On Signs*, ed. Marshall Blonsky,
   Oxford, Blackwell, 1985.

6. Frederick Seidel, 'The blue-eyed doe', in *Men and Woman*, London,
   Chatto and Windus, 1984, pp. 67–70.

EIGHT

Too Much of Nothing

JOAN BAEZ
Renaldo and who?

from *And a Voice to Sing With*

In spite of everything, the Rolling Thunder tours had been a success, at least musically. I suppose it was because of them that years later I thought Europe 1984 would work out. Bob and I had talked occasionally over the years about touring Europe, and I figured he would like to tour if it were totally convenient and he could make piles of money. At our European promoter's urging, I proposed a short tour with him, but he'd said no, no way. He was goin' t' Latin America with Santana cuz it was easy and cuz people down there didn't know nuthin' 'bout nuthin' anyways, meaning, I guess, that he was less pressured to do music they demanded and freer to do as he pleased.

My promoter, Fritz Rau, and his associate, José Klein, both of whom I loved and with whom I'd worked for years, had a fifteen-year-old dream of organising the great Dylan/Baez reunion in Europe. So when, a month after Bob's and my conversation about Latin America, they called me and said, '*He'll do it! He wants to do it!*' I assumed they had come up with a good enough offer to make the reunion attractive to Bob. I was suspicious because the tour was already being planned as a Dylan/Santana tour.

I insisted on approval of everything from size and order of the names on posters and ads to order of the show and length of sets. Mainly, I insisted that Bob and I have equal billing and perform together somewhere in the show, and that Santana open the show.

Much was promised.

Nothing was in writing.

Everything was insinuated, assumed, or simply wished for.

For weeks before the tour, I tried to reach Bob, but he was never available. I pinned José down.

'I need some reassurance that Bob intends to sing with me.'

'Bill Graham's speaking to him about that today.'

'What's the story on the order of the show?'

'Everything's set for Frankfurt and I think the others are coming together.' A personal manager would have pulled me out of the show at that point. I had not had a personal manager since parting with Manny [Greenhill] in 1978.

At the request of Fritz and José, I did a press conference, a TV rock show and special interviews to promote the great Dylan/Baez event. Like Fritz and José, I was heading into the reunion blind, and with growing excitement. I didn't reach Bob until two days before the first show. Trying to reach my blood brother by phone went like this:

'Hello, this is Joan. I'd like to speak to Bob.'

'Oh, hi, Joan. Gee, I don't know, he was around here earlier. I'll have him call you back.'

'No, I'd like to talk to him now. I can wait.'

'Gosh, ummm. I just saw him somewheres, ummm . . . '

New voice.

'Hi, Joan. This is Stanley. What can I do for you?'

'Probably nothing, Stanley, because I don't know you. Unless you can produce Bob . . . ' Much clicking and covering of the receiver. Bob, realising he can't get me off his back, finally deigns to speak.

He sounds awful, but I jolly him along and tell him I heard he'd had a great opening concert in Venice. He is only grunting today. I suggest that we rehearse a couple of songs for the show. He has a terrible reaction and I realise that he is allergic to the word 'rehearse'. He finally says we can 'go over some stuff'.

I flew into Hamburg to meet him and 'go over some stuff', only to discover that he was not at the same hotel and would not be in town until the next day. In fact, he would arrive in his private plane just in time to go on stage for his own set.

So started Fritz and José's balancing act between Bill Graham's organisation and their own *schmetterling* (Fritz's affectionate nickname for me, meaning 'butterfly'). And so started one of the most demoralising series of events I've ever lived through. It compared only to Ring Around Congress under Hurricane Agnes [an anti-war demonstration of June 1972 blighted by the elements and a clash of personalities].

Somehow the first concert stuck to a crumbling semblance of all the things I had been promised. Carlos Santana, bless his heart, threw his ego out the window and opened the show. My set was very successful, even in a half-sold stadium in the rain. I went up to Bob during a break in his set. He had been unapproachable before, surrounded by bodyguards. Now he was standing by himself, picking his nose.

'Hello, Robert,' I began.

'We supposed to do sumpin together?' he said.

'Yeah, I think it would be appropriate to do sumpin together. I think they kind of expect it.'

'Shit. My fuckin' back is killin' me.' He stopped digging in his nose and began to rub the base of his spine. He hobbled off grimacing. I assumed that I was giving Bob a terrible pain in the back, but, still thinking that we were having a reunion, I told him I'd walk on stage and join him and Santana on 'Blowin' in the wind', as Bill Graham had desperately suggested.

'Sure, if you feel like it,' said poor Bob.

The results were ragged at best. My tour manager, Big Red, began a campaign to separate me from him. Soon I lost the battle to appear after Santana, who is also Bill Graham's property, and I became the opening act. I was not in a financial position to walk out on eight well-paid concerts, but each new demotion overwhelmed me.

One evening in Berlin, Fritz and José tried to get me to start my set fifteen minutes before showtime. There was a problem with a curfew, they said. The local act was on and off, and by half an hour to showtime, 17,000 soggy Germans were standing in the rain, blaming me for their discomfort. I went on ten minutes after showtime and the audience was soaked, miserable, drunk and nasty. Later, when the night had fallen and the rain had stopped, I went to watch Bob's show. The stars were out and twinkling, and bright coloured lights danced on the stage. I'd long since stopped bugging him about singing together. The curfew didn't affect him, of course: he did his usual straight two hours. That night I lay in bed hurting from head to toe, mainly in the throat, behind the eyes, and in the stomach. At three in the morning I got up, went out and walked the streets of Berlin until six.

My suite had a picture window looking out on a huge maple

tree. I lined up the couch pillows on the floor so that I could lie down and look directly into the leaves which were flipping gently like the pages of an abandoned book, their two sides of slightly different hues, and I entered those lovely branches and rested there in the kindly arms of that tree for four hours, dozing lightly, healing slowly.

At noon I got up and decided to concentrate on salvaging the French concerts. I called José and made him promise to personally investigate the posters and advertising for our three French shows. I demanded fair billing or I wouldn't appear. He promised. He probably tried. He failed. In a sauna in Vienna, over the bony white knees of some distinguished Austrian, I saw an ad in an issue of *Libération*, a Paris daily newspaper: in print barely large enough to read, Joan Baez was once again billed as a guest star.

I called Bill and told him I wouldn't be going to Paris. He thought I wanted more money. I didn't. Did I want to sing with Bob again? No, I said, it's too late; I would probably never want to sing with Bob again. I hung up as Bill began to raise his voice. I felt as if I'd had a steam bath, an ice dunk, a facial, a manicure, and then been to Quaker Meeting. I was at peace for the first time in nearly four weeks. A storm of phone calls, telegrams and threats followed. I sent off a telex to the French press giving some diplomatic excuse for the unfortunate cancellation of my appearance in Paris. The Paris promoter called his own press conference and said that Madame Baez would *indeed* be appearing, and any rumours to the contrary were false.

Happily, for once, our own sloppiness worked to my advantage. We had no binding contract with Bill Graham. When it was clear that I was not making idle threats, the Paris promoter announced that if Ms Baez didn't appear it was because she was impetuous and felt like snubbing the Parisians and that she'd never play Paris again.

He was winning the public relations battle; I was losing sleep but staying clean. I went to Italy. Bill flew in from Spain to try to talk me into changing my mind. I was flattered. The way I had been treated I didn't think anyone would notice if I left the tour. Bill tried everything, between pleas and lures setting me up for possible legal proceedings saying things like 'I wish you thought you were *capable* of walking out on that stage', and 'Of course, there was never a *guarantee* that you were going to sing with Bob, it was just a *hope*.' When he finally gave up, I ordered him a big bowl of ice cream, four flavours, because he was not used to losing battles and needed some sort of compensation. In the end, I paid him a monetary forfeit, which I had expected to do. But paying money was nothing compared to the battering my ego and spirit had taken for over a month.

The last time I saw Dylan was backstage, in Copenhagen. That night I'd had a wonderful set and I was listening to a little of Santana before catching the plane to Italy, where I had my own extremely successful tour in process. Bill came up and said he'd heard I was leaving.

Bob's heavies began materialising.

'If you're *really* leaving, Bob wants to talk to you.'

I laughed. 'Not if I'm just pretend leaving?'

When 'Bob wants to talk to you', it means that you go to where he is. He never comes to you.

'Here I am,' I said cheerfully.

'He's in his room, over past the stairway –'

'If I happen to pass his room on my way out, grab me. I'll be leaving in about ten minutes, but I'll be in a hurry.'

Guards were stationed between me and the sacred room and, as I passed, they converged upon me.

'He's in here,' they pointed, and I was ushered through his door in a reverent hush, as though I were entering a cathedral.

Bob was lying on a sofa with his head toward the door, dressed in what looked like a formal suit. His eyes were shut and his feet were up on the arm of the sofa. He had jumped when I walked in, so I knew he was awake.

'Don't get up,' I joked. He didn't move, except to look up as I approached.

'Oh, yeah, hey, wow, I'm tired, real tired.'

'Yeah, well, you don't look so hot. Have you been taking care of yourself?'

I leaned over and kissed his sweaty forehead. It was covered in white-face. He looked, as the British say, as if he'd been dragged through a hedge backwards.

He peered sleepily around the room.

'I think I dreamed I seen you on TV. At least I think it was a dream. Hard to tell the difference any more. You was wearin' this blue scarf. That was some scarf!'

'It wasn't a dream, Bob. That was a broadcast from Vienna.'

'Shit, you're kidding. I must be more tired'n I thought.' Bob started running his hand up under my skirt, around the back of my knee and partway up my thigh.

'Wow, you got great legs. Where'd you get them muscles?'

'From rehearsing,' I said. 'I stand up and rehearse a lot.' I took his hand out from under my skirt and placed it on his chest.

'So,' he said, stretching his arms out straight with a cat shiver. 'You leavin' already?'

'Yeah, I gotta go.'

'How come?'

'I have to catch a plane. It's the kind of plane you have to go and get. It doesn't come and pick you up.'

'You don't wanna hang around and maybe do sumpin together later?'

'You mean sing?'

'Yeah, do sumpin together.'

'Naw, I don't think so, Bob. Not that way. I wanted to do it right, you know, but it didn't work out. Maybe some other time. I gotta go.'

'That's too bad. You bin enjoyin' yourself?'

'Yeah, Bob. It's been my favourite tour in the world.' And I kissed him again and left.

Goodbye, Bob. You looked happy on Farm Aid. I thought maybe I shouldn't write all this stuff about you, but as it turns out, it's really about me anyway, isn't it? It won't affect you. The death of Elvis affected you. I didn't relate to that, either.

JAMES WOLCOTT
Bob Dylan beyond Thunderdome

Vanity Fair, October 1985

Watching Mick Jagger flash his titties on the Live Aid broadcast, I thought, well, the teen titans of the Sixties and Seventies have held up pretty well, considering. True, the Beach Boys threaten to pop a valve every time they crank up for one last falsetto (when they sing 'Help me, Rhonda', it sounds as if they're calling for a nurse), and Stephen Stills and David Crosby, flattening notes in their sleep, resemble papa bears who have spooned too much porridge. But Jagger has kept his girlish figure, David Bowie has a hickory-switch swish and snap, Pete Townshend can still execute power chords without throwing his arm out of whack and Robert Plant has stored enough lung power to touch off avalanches and reroute birds in flight. Most amazing of all is Tina Turner, the unrefrigerated Lena Horne of soul rock. Their appearances at Live Aid were a tribute to talent, perseverance and sensible eating.

Then at the end of the evening Jack Nicholson, cool as lemonade, appeared on the screen to introduce the show's final biggie. 'Some artists' work speaks for itself; some artists' work speaks for a generation,' he said. So welcome 'one of the great voices of freedom . . . the transcendent Bob Dylan!'

Flanked by Keith Richards and Ron Wood of the Rolling Stones, Bob Dylan did not appear transcendent. Cigarettes stuck in their yaps, Keith and Woody themselves looked weedy and self-incinerating, but the goofy grins creasing their faces as strings broke and guitar picks fell placed them in the land of the living. Dylan – Dylan was his own golem, a phantom of wax, burning mission, and words of resurrection. His complexion was dead of colour and his beard clung sickly to his skin. Gleaming perspiration coated his face so thickly that it was as if the clear plastic mask he had worn in *Renaldo and Clara* had melted.

Reviewing *Renaldo and Clara*, Dylan's 1978 hippie-messiah home movie, Pauline Kael observed, 'He is overpoweringly present, yet he is never in direct contact with us – not even when he performs' [see p. 225]. And that was true of Dylan at Live Aid. Intense close-ups bounced off his deflector shields. It was impossible to take a reading on his eyes, impossible to know who was at home in his head. Bob Dylan rigs every performance, no matter how direct, with decoys and trip wires. His welcome mat is set above a trapdoor.

Dylan's mini-set at Live Aid was anticlimactic but not a fiasco. First he dusted off an old prairie howl from his folkie protest days called 'The ballad of Hollis Brown', a doomy lament about how poverty leads to family slaughter on a South Dakota farm. It was a message number that Dylan amplified by remarking how nice it would be if some of the proceeds from Live Aid were skimmed to pay off the mortgages of American farmers. His next song – 'When the ship comes in', with its stress on the lyric 'the whole wide world is watchin'' – was also apropos. But Dylan's delivery was rushed and spitting, Keith and Woody kept fishing in their pockets for their car keys, and 'Blowin' in the wind', the closing anthem, was given such rickety treatment that floodwaters rushed between the slats. This was a hootenanny that had lost its hoot. A supporting belief was missing.

When Jack Nicholson called Dylan the voice of a generation, he couldn't have meant the White kids cheering the video monitors at Live Aid. They're too young to have Dylan's lyrics tattooed on their memories. Bruce Springsteen is the hammer striking their hearts, the electronic scoreboard by which they check America's standing. To them, Bob Dylan is a rasp of static encoded with esoteric prophecies already come to pass. He's history, babe.

Not that Dylan hasn't tried to bridge the gap. His most recent album, *Empire Burlesque*, is a throwback to the blue-eyed-gospel revivalism of *Street Legal* (1978), but with more accessible love lyrics and social commentary and fewer myths on horseback. The album even has a video shot by Paul 'Mishima' Schrader in Tokyo, which features a blue wig falling in slow motion down a flight of stairs and Dylan, pudgy, debauched, gesturing with his big thumbs. (This, too, echoes *Street Legal*, whose back cover showed Dylan in white clown make-up and a Las Vegas entertainer's horror outfit, complete with vest and puffed sleeves. Like Elvis at the end, Dylan appeared incarcerated in his own soft flesh.) *Empire Burlesque* has been hailed as a comeback for Dylan (which isn't saying much – he's had more comebacks than the *Saturday Review*), and it opened well on the charts. But it doesn't have a song as mobilised and image-packed as *Street Legal*'s 'Changing of the guards', and his legendary phrasing has become rote and insincere. When Dylan professes love on *Empire Burlesque*, he's as full of plaster as a pissing cupid. 'I could be learning, you could be yearning . . . ' – yech. And something has queered Dylan's voice. Except on *Nashville Skyline*, where his tonsils were drenched in peach syrup, Dylan's voice has always been nasal, and over the years it hasn't mellowed or developed nicks of character (as, say, Willie Nelson's has). It's simply climbed higher in his sinuses. Vocally, soul resides in the throat and chest and diaphragm. So when Dylan croons and woos on *Empire Burlesque*, he sounds not romantically expansive but pinched and whiny. He's locked his soul in a small upper vault.

The Sixties were Bob Dylan's Thunderdome. The girlish taper of his pale fingers on the cover of *Highway 61 Revisited*, his angry-genius glare, the cloudburst of words accompanied by lightning, the Tiny Tim hat and trailing scarf, the congested perceptions of *Blonde on Blonde*, and the eerie clean-swept calms of *John Wesley Harding* – it was a great movie, this blaze of vision, and no wonder everyone wanted to be in it. (A desire exploited by Dylan in *Renaldo and Clara*, where he turned even Joan Baez and Sam Shepard into camp followers.) It's tempting to explain the failure of Dylan's later career by saying that he went off like Mad Max into the desert and found God, and God looked like Bob Dylan. Dylan certainly behaved as if he were the messiah he had been searching for in *Renaldo and Clara*, and his born-again-Christian stance proved to be the most damaging conversion since the Jewish cabalistic messiah Sabbatai Zevi bowed to the blade and embraced Islam in 1666.

Dylan's born-again trilogy – *Slow Train Coming, Saved, Shot of Love* – did a dismal swan dive, and Dylan is said to have retreated somewhat into Judaism. But as the explanation for Dylan's decline, religion won't do. From the beginning he has played the role of mystic bard, and accusatory songs such as 'Like a rolling stone' and 'Ballad of a thin man' indicate that he has always been a man of the Old Testament, quick to judge, quick to scourge. All born-again Christianity did was enable Dylan to make his religious bombast more shrill and programmatic. He could now break stone tablets over our heathen heads.

The reason for Dylan's artistic fade may be closer to home and bed. Bob Dylan may be one of the last visionary rhymers to require the services of a muse. Since Dylan went electric, a gallery of raven-haired women wearing smoke rings for halos have haunted the foreground of his love-songs and provided a dreamy, broody depth. (Joan Baez, of course, was the folkie Madonna for Dylan's acoustic phase.) Supreme among these inscrutable divinities was Dylan's wife, Sara, who blew in like a sultry breeze in *Renaldo and Clara* and tried to wilt Bob's curly locks. Dylan openly declared his debt and devotion to Sara on *Desire*, and that declaration – 'Sara', in which he confides that he wrote 'Sad-eyed lady of the lowlands' for her in the Chelsea Hotel – is one of Dylan's most dubious and emotionally forced numbers. Even the critic Wilfrid Mellers, whose recent book, *A Darker Shade of Pale*, tries to insert Shelley's heart into Dylan's chest cavity, catches a whiff of falsity in 'Sara': 'The effect of both words and music is discomforting. Perhaps it is only with hindsight that one feels that Dylan may be trying too hard to assert the truth of his marriage.'

By 'hindsight', Mellers is referring to the fact that Dylan's marriage later broke up, acrimoniously. The divorce cost Dylan plenty, but Mellers shies away from speculating on the psychic cost. 'Biography is not our concern and is ultimately irrelevant to an artist's work.' Dat so? Well, to indulge in crass speculation: *Empire Burlesque*, which features a dark-haired Bianca Jaggerish young woman on the back cover, can be seen as an attempt to conjure a new Sara figure and seek reconciliation with his flown muse. 'Come baby, find me, come baby, remind me of where I once begun,' he petitions on 'Emotionally yours'. The problem, as in 'Sara', is that he loads on so much sweet talk that you don't believe a word he moos.

Perhaps Dylan, stocky and removed, and Jagger, scrawny and in your face, aren't so far apart after all. In the absence of inspiration, professionalism and old habits seize the reins, and Dylan and Jagger are both determined to be inexhaustible. 'You want each new record to be your best, but you know you're going to write more songs and make another album anyway,' Dylan told *Rolling Stone* in 1978. In that sense *Empire Burlesque* is impressive, even inspiring. On it Dylan sounds vigorous, disciplined, refreshed; he hasn't allowed rust to slow his wheels. My God, he sounds as if he could go on grinding out this crap *for ever*.

GEOFF DYER
Figured I'd lost you anyway*

I am a second-generation Dylan bore. I was eight years old and living in downtown Cheltenham when he released *Blonde on Blonde*; the first album I listened to and bought was *Desire* and from there I went back through his work in reverse chronological order. Within two years I was a chronic Dylan casualty, meeting strangers through the pages of the *NME* and exchanging badly recorded bootlegs of little-known concerts. Every nuance of a relationship I was involved in could be articulated by lines from Dylan songs: 'I wish there was somethin' you could do or say/To try and make me change my mind and stay/We never did too much talkin' anyway' – what a joke: we did nothing *but* talk. I can even remember saying to someone: 'No one knows more about women than Dylan.' Well, he certainly knew more than I did. Just as during my (later) Real Ale phase I organised holidays around *The Good Beer Guide* so, during the Dylan years, I plotted possible holidays around places mentioned in his songs (El Paso, Delacroix, San Pedro, Tangier, Savanna-la-Mar, Lily Pond Lane – where on earth was *that*?).

In recent years my interest has lain dormant but secure. I haven't bought the recent albums and rarely play the ones that I do have, but everything up to *Slow Train Coming* is perfectly preserved in my affective memory. It came as a surprise, then, flicking through the cumbersome edition of *Lyrics 1962–1985* and listening to *Biograph*, the five-record retrospective, to find that these words, these songs, had lost their magic for me. Exhumed from the recent past, they crumbled in the daylight of the present. As thoroughly as they had held me in their thrall, they had, as completely, emptied themselves of all but archaeological meaning. Rather than convert this anaesthesia of response into critical judgement, we can use it as a way of articulating more precisely the particular character of Dylan's genius. Some things still seem to me to be indisputable.

First, the printed words are the mere ghosts of songs; like

---

* A shorter and slightly different version appeared in the *Listener*, 28 May 1987.

prose translations of poems, they suffer from having to state what the songs can suggest.

Second, in every piece the greatest lines and the most banal coexist in such astonishing proximity that, as we listen, the latter actually take on some of the qualities of the former – but not vice versa. In memory the songs radiate from their best moments, but in the cold light of the printed page the pieces look so patchy that there seems something felicitous about the best lines – 'I can't help it if I'm *lucky*' – as if they are better than they have any right to be, as if the critical instinct lags way behind the creative. No sooner have we formulated this idea, however, than we have to revise it, for Dylan's continual tampering with old songs usually improves them. The great national rhyme,

> Idiot wind, blowing like a circle around my skull,
> From the Grand Coulee Dam to the Capitol.

made its first rather feeble appearance as:

> Idiot wind, blowing every time you move your jaw,
> From the Grand Coulee Dam to the Mardi Gras.

Difficult, though, to argue consistently about a talent so consistently *in*consistent: other adjustments to the same song substantiate exactly the opposite view of such revisions. One of his best ever rhymes –

> Figured I'd lost you anyway, why go on, what's the use?
> In order to get in a word with you
> I'd've had to come up with some excuse

– only appears in the rejected version of 'Idiot wind'.

Third, there is his massive and hard-won technical skill. Rhyme he mastered early on, but it is not until *Blood on the Tracks* and *Desire* that he is able to use compacted quatrains and stanzas of Donne-like complexity for long novelistic narratives.

Fourth, Dylan no longer has anything to say. By this I don't mean to dig up the notion of Relevance, that notorious Sixties irrelevance. The protest songs and anthems – like the interminable 'Blowin' in the wind' – on which his reputation was built are, with a few exceptions, among the least interesting things he produced. What I *do* mean is that, aside from the fact that they're littered with the debris of phrases from previous songs, there is nothing in the last five albums to suggest that they are from the same person who could hold together the intricate detail of 'Hurricane'.

That this kind of atrophy set in is not surprising (the surprising thing is that his last great creative surge, from *Blood on the Tracks* to Blackbushe, came as late as it did) since by his mid-twenties he had everything an artist could wish for: not simply wealth and fame but critical acclaim and the freedom to produce more or less as he pleased. Where could he go from there? For Picasso and Miles Davis (both of whom Dylan resembles in many ways) a similar situation was less problematic because the potential for exploration in paint and jazz is greater than is the case with what is loosely known as pop music. At a time when the expressive potential of pop music was still considerable, a number of complex possibilities converged on Dylan's immense and extraordinarily volatile combination of talents. These talents remain unique but, whereas initially they could follow the general drift of pop, soon, in order to continue to flourish, they had to defy the essential trajectory of the medium in which he was working. His masterpiece, *Blood on the Tracks*, with its sparse acoustic arrangements, was the triumph of this denial, but in the Eighties his lyric gift has been unable to resist the plodding rock arrangements to which he has succumbed. It is a tribute to his powers of vocal phrasing that, on record, even lines as silly as 'Don't fall apart on me tonight/I just don't think that I could handle it' *sound* quite effective – but in the context of the Dylan opus we are here talking minor with a very small 'm'. For a while I was content to argue that Dylan had been through arid patches before but not only has the expiry date for such a claim passed but, this time, any kind of progress depends on a denial of what his *own* work has become.

Within the world of his work, Dylan's achievement has never really been as a spokesman for a generation (whatever that means) but as the private artist 'Stayin' up for days in the Chelsea Hotel/Writin' "Sad-eyed lady of the lowlands" for you'. Even as a writer of love-songs, however, Dylan's talents have deserted him – or rather he has deserted his talents. Since about 1978 – and coinciding with the consolations of his religious phase – Dylan has made no demands on himself; like an athlete who has outclassed everyone in his event, he has grown tired of breaking his own records (though he has, regrettably, persisted in making new ones) and has gone to flab.

I often find myself wondering what Dylan *does* in a day and the only answer that ever suggests itself is the Dylanesque: pretty much what everyone else does. It is as if he has succeeded so thoroughly in his motivating ambition – to have 'nothing in common with anyone' – that, paradoxically, it no longer conveys any sense of distinction: he has simply got used to the idea of being himself.

That phrase is from a description of an anonymous singer in Peter Handke's novel *The Long Way Around* and it gets closer than anything actually written about Dylan to expressing what it is about his work that gives it its unique capacity to tantalise and, for a while at least, *hold* us:

> What his voice produced was not song but rather the sounds made by someone who, after long intolerable brooding, suddenly lets loose . . . He was able, with a voice which he took from outside and drove deep into himself, to tell about the people he had inside him – what he wanted most of all was to have nothing in common with anyone. He didn't sing with feeling but searched frantically for a feeling which was as puzzling to him as to anyone else.

STANLEY MIESES
The Dead and Dylan★

New Yorker, 27 July 1987

At five o'clock on a sweltering afternoon, the phone rang and we recognised the voice of our friend the Music Maven.

'I've got an extra ticket to see the Dead,' he said, sounding uncharacteristically animated, and when we didn't respond immediately he added, 'The Grateful Dead – with Bob Dylan!' He went on to tell us that the veteran psychedelic rock band from the San Francisco Bay Area was teaming up with Bob Dylan for a limited-engagement tour and would be appearing within the hour at Giants Stadium, in the Meadowlands.

★ Originally appeared unsigned.

We said that in such weather the prospect of sitting in an open-air stadium with over 70,000 Dead Heads, as fans of the group are known, while they exulted in their inimitable fashion for hours (the length of the Dead's shows is legendary) sounded to us like a living hell.

'But no one else I know will go with me,' he whined.

We gave in, and when we arrived at Giants Stadium we realised that the Music Maven hadn't been deceiving us. We saw thousands upon thousands of people – filling the parking lots, spilling out of double-length caterpillar buses – and few of them looked like people the Music Maven might know. We saw more young people with wild hair and wearing tie-dyed shirts with ripped jeans and, in many cases, going without shoes, than we'd seen since the Central Park Be-In over twenty years ago. The parking lots had become home for a community of Dead Heads, who seemed to have been there for days, living in vans and campers – vehicles that had apparently been modified to sleep at least six and looked as if they needed an on-board mechanic. The occupants of many of these vehicles had arrived at the show without tickets and, it seemed, without any pressing desire to seek tickets; they had pitched a whole row of tents on a narrow grassy strip and were just hanging out – talking, reading and visiting among themselves, like neighbours. The ground around them was carpeted with little grey canisters that looked like tiny scuba tanks and contained nitrous oxide – laughing gas. For these people, we gathered, non-attendance at the concert testified to a higher allegiance to the Dead, whose much-chronicled 'alternative life-style' has been as essential to their long-lasting popularity as their music.

The Music Maven pulled us toward the stadium, where the entrances were clogged by ticket holders and the trash they had dumped there – so much trash that if you stood in one spot too long your shoes stuck to the ground (if you were wearing shoes). Inside, the ushers had retreated, and we and the Music Maven had to hunt for our seats on our own. When we found them they were occupied by four people, two in each, who politely withdrew to a single unoccupied seat in a row behind us. By this time, our shirts had become one with our skin, and we were miserable, and yet when the concert started there was such unbounded joy pouring out of the audience in response to every note played by Jerry Garcia, the group's lead guitarist – grey-bearded and pot-bellied and wearing red-tinted shades not unlike the ones he wore during the 1967

Summer of Love, when the Grateful Dead first drew national attention – that we began to feel ungenerous. The Music Maven, who is a little younger than Garcia but somewhat older than the new wave of flower children in Giants Stadium, folded his hands neatly in his lap and, with a gleam in his eye, acknowledged that we might be the only two people there who really hoped to see Bob Dylan.

We bided our time, three hours, watching whole sections of the audience get hosed down by the stage crew, looking at surreal images of the band on giant video monitors that had been set up on freight containers at the sides of the stage and listening to the Grateful Dead churn out their characteristic, well-worn boogie music. They ended their set with a rendition of 'Not fade away', and the chants of the audience – 'Love so real will not fade away' – followed the band off stage. The sun finally went down, and there was just a hint of a breeze. Then the Dead returned, with a man carrying an acoustic guitar . . . and, in darkness, he struck up the first chords of a song. When the spotlight hit the stage, it revealed Bob Dylan to the crowd and he began to sing one of his newer songs, 'Slow Train,' with serious menace in his voice.

'He's wearing a beret!' the Music Maven shouted. 'The international symbol of revolution!'

Dylan next sang 'Stuck inside of Mobile (with the Memphis blues again)' and then 'Tomorrow is a long time', 'It's all over now, baby blue', 'Ballad of a thin man' – just about every song we've ever wanted to hear Bob Dylan perform and rarely have, certainly not all at once – and we very quickly felt connected to the free-floating joy that had been whipped up by the Dead Heads. Dylan's vocal style, which has grown more preachy over the years, was harmoniously balanced by Jerry Garcia's ringing, melodic guitar, and songs like 'The wicked messenger', 'All along the watchtower', and 'Chimes of freedom' – songs that represent Bob Dylan's writing at its most pointed – seemed to be just as fresh to the Dead Heads as they were to us twenty years ago. When Dylan closed with 'The times they are a-changin'', we had every reason to believe that that was true – again.

JOHN PEEL
Dylan at Wembley

Observer, 18 October 1987

Nancy Bowling of Bryan Adams High School, Dallas, introduced me to the work of Bob Dylan and many was the night we heavy petted to *Freewheelin'*. I wonder what Nancy would have made of Dylan's recent performances in Britain.

But first, 'Ladies and Gentlemen, the founder of the Byrds, Roger McGuinn.' Twenty-one years ago the Byrds headlined a concert in San Bernardino, a concert in which they were supported by the Buffalo Springfield and introduced by me. As we waited backstage I introduced myself to McGuinn and he totally ignored me.

On Thursday I was delighted to have the opportunity to ignore him and, as he launched into a song about a 'fine lady' and urged everyone to clap along, I went for a beer. I discovered in the process that Wembley sells a particularly fine chocolate chip cookie. I returned to my seat as the former Byrd, now joined by Tom Petty and his Heartbreakers, demonstrated that he still has difficulty with the introduction to 'Eight miles high'.

Eventually Petty and his *équipe* took over in their own right and set toes tapping to songs in which men sing 'no' when they mean 'any'. As in 'there ain't no point to this sort of piffle no more'.

During the interval I spoke with a passer-by who had attended three Dylan concerts in the Midlands. 'He didn't speak to us once,' he said enthusiastically, as though this failure to communicate was a mark of excellence. 'I don't think', he said uncertainly, 'that he is being contemptuous of us, as the papers have said.' When I suggested that the money he had placed in Bob's pocket entitled him to a friendly word or two, my new-found friend nodded.

Warming to the theme, I posited that being an enigma at twenty is fun, being an enigma at thirty shows a lack of imagination and being an enigma at Dylan's age is just plain daft.

Why is it that no rock star who has continued rocking into middle age has done so without becoming sentimental, repetitious, embarrassing or, in Dylan's case, impertinent? From the moment that the living legend took to the stage it was evident that here was business he wanted accomplished with the minimum of effort. Sounding like one of those talent competition impersonators who have to tell you who they are 'doing' – 'that was Mister Tommy Cooper, bless him, and now do you remember Mister Bobby Dylan?' – it appeared to be as much as Dylan could bear to grumble out his lyrics at all. By the time he reached 'The lonesome death of Hattie Carroll', he was gasping each word as though playing a dying man trying to communicate the name of his murderer in an amateur production of a thriller.

The audience and Tom Petty and his exceptionally well–drilled Heartbreakers followed all this foolishness uncomplainingly. Nearing apoplexy in seat 99, I thought to myself that somewhere out there Freddie and the Dreamers are probably still playing their old hits – and with greater dignity and thought for the paying customer than this. To quiet my pounding heart I went for another chocolate chip cookie, and, finding the booth closed, kept going.

BRUCE SPRINGSTEEN

Speech delivered at the annual Rock-and-Roll Hall of Fame induction dinner held in New York City, 20 January 1988

The first time I heard Bob Dylan, I was in the car with my mother listening to WMCA and on came that snare shot that sounded like somebody'd kicked open the door to your mind: 'Like a rolling stone'. My mother – she was no stiff with rock-'n'-roll, she liked the music – sat there for a minute, then looked at me and said, 'That guy can't sing.' But I knew she was wrong. I sat there and I didn't say nothing but I knew that I was listening to the toughest voice that I had ever heard. It was lean and it sounded somehow simultaneously young and adult.

I ran out and bought the single and ran home and played

it, but they must have made a mistake in the factory because a Lenny Welch song came on. The label was wrong. So I ran back to the store, got the Dylan, and came back and played it. Then I went out and got *Highway 61 Revisited*. That was all I played for weeks, looking at the cover with Bob in that satin blue jacket and the Triumph motorcycle shirt.

When I was a kid, Bob's voice somehow thrilled and scared me, it made me feel kind of irresponsibly innocent – it still does – when it reached down and touched what little worldliness a fifteen-year-old high-school kid in New Jersey had in him at the time. Dylan was a revolutionary. Bob freed your mind the way Elvis freed your body. He showed us that just because the music was innately physical did not mean that it was anti-intellectual. He had the vision and the talent to make a pop song that contained the whole world. He invented a new way a pop singer could sound, broke through the limitations of what a recording artist could achieve and changed the face of rock-'n'-roll for ever.

Without Bob, the Beatles wouldn't have made *Sgt. Pepper*, the Beach Boys wouldn't have made *Pet Sounds*, the Sex Pistols wouldn't have made 'God save the Queen', U2 wouldn't have done 'Pride in the name of love', Marvin Gaye wouldn't have done *What's Goin' On?*, the Count Five would not have done 'Psychotic reaction', Grandmaster Flash might not have done 'the message', and there never would have been a group named the Electric Prunes. To this day, wherever great rock music is being made, there is the shadow of Bob Dylan. Bob's own modern work has gone unjustly under-appreciated because it's had to stand in that shadow. If there was a young guy out there writing the *Empire Burlesque* album, writing 'Every grain of sand', they'd be calling him the new Bob Dylan.

About three months ago, I was watching *The Rolling Stones Special* on TV. Bob came on and he was in a real cranky mood. He was kind of bitching and moaning about how his fans come up to him on the street and treat him like a long lost brother or something, even though they don't know him. Now, speaking as a fan, when I was fifteen and I heard 'Like a rolling stone', I heard a guy who had the guts to take on the whole world and who made me feel like I had to too. Maybe some people misunderstood that voice as saying that somehow Bob was going to do the job for them, but, as we grow older, we learn that there isn't anybody out there who can do that job for anybody else. So I'm just here tonight to say thanks, to say that I wouldn't be here without you, to say that there isn't a soul in this room who does not owe you his thanks, and to steal a line from one of your songs – whether you like it or not – 'You was the brother that I never had.'

RICHARD WILLIAMS
The calm after the storm

The Times, 23 September 1989

Ease your favourite Bob Dylan fan into an armchair, drop the needle almost anywhere on the surface of *Oh Mercy*, and the next sound you'll hear is bound to be a sigh of relief. Stick around for the follow-up. 'It's his best since *Blood on the Tracks*, of course' is likely to become the most over-familiar critical assessment of the year.

Well, is it his best since 1975? In many ways, yes. For that we have to thank his producer, Daniel Lanois. The inventive mind, broad musical knowledge and exquisite taste that brought distinction to U2's *The Joshua Tree*, Robbie Robertson's solo album and the Neville Brothers' *Yellow Moon* ensures that *Oh Mercy* is pretty close to the album that you or I would make if Bob Dylan called us for production advice. Let's face it, there could hardly be a higher compliment than that.

For a start, Lanois makes Bob Dylan sound like Bob Dylan. You can always tell a bad Dylan record by the sound of his voice: it gets strained, distorted, ugly. He sounds uncomfortable in his own skin. You suspect that he'd rather be off on location in somewhere like Durango, shooting the follow-up to *Renaldo and Clara*. Throughout *Oh Mercy*, by contrast, his delivery is relaxed and confident. He never makes you feel that you don't know whether you're supposed to be laughing or not. He's serious, straight-faced, in places quite serene. He sounds like a Bob Dylan you could talk to.

How did Lanois pull it off? At a guess, by enfolding the notoriously nervy Dylan in a sympathetic working environment. In a recent interview he described how he set up a temporary studio in New Orleans, using portable equipment in a converted building to escape the prefabricated studio-as-factory atmosphere. Nothing new about that, of course: it was how Dylan and The Band recorded the seminal *Basement Tapes* and *Music from Big Pink* in a Woodstock mansion twenty-two years ago. Lanois seems to have rediscovered and refined a sensible technique at just the right time, providing a necessary challenge to the increasing homogenisation of record production.

Lanois is an unusual producer. Rather than obviously supervising a construction process, he seems to spend his time stripping tracks down to their bare essentials. Sometimes the rhythm arrangements seem to consist entirely of echoes; the effect, as the critic Andy Gill wrote recently in a wonderfully perceptive remark, is 'as if within the song [is] contained the song's shadow'. *Oh Mercy* is full of such shadows, flickering around the tired, plaintive sound of Dylan's voice.

There are some fine songs here. No admirer of 'Knockin' on heaven's door' is likely to be disappointed by 'Man in the long black coat', another last-days-of-the-West ballad sung with strange staccato phrasing against strummed guitars and the chirrup of cicadas. 'Disease of conceit' is a bit of a sermon, but those uncomfortable with its message can concentrate on the extraordinarily subtle piano and bass accompaniment, and on the bell-like slow-motion guitar solo which closes the piece. 'Ring them bells' and 'Shooting star' both take hackneyed ideas and refresh them, the former via a hymn-like harmonic progression and the latter through a lyric that goes deeper just when you think it is settling for platitudes.

The lyric is also the point of 'Most of the time', a study in irony taking its cue from 10cc's 'I'm not in love' ('I can smile in the face of mankind/I don't even remember what her lips felt like on mine/Most of the time . . . '), where fuzzy rhythm guitars rub up against a liquid lead in a way reminiscent of Lou Reed's Velvet Underground ballads. Lanois's ability to create an unusually deep aural focus is evident in 'What was it you wanted?', where he positions a variety of guitars all the way from the foreground to a distant horizon, without any sense of crowding the frame.

A song called 'Everything is broken', though, is the one that stops the traffic. A neat, compact, and very basic boogie-shuffle built on a solid rimshot backbeat and shivering reverb guitars that could have been played by Pop Staples and Lonnie Mack, it serves as a setting for one of Dylan's litanies of the apocalypse: 'Broken bodies/Broken bones/Broken voices/On broken phones/Take a deep breath/Feels like you're chokin'/Everything is broken.' It's a sort of 'Subterranean homesick blues' for fortysomethings.

If *Oh Mercy* is indeed his best since *Blood on the Tracks*, it must be said that it does not remotely resemble that masterpiece. What's missing here is the person-to-person voice, the direct communication of experience, the redefinition of emotions, the interplay of conflicting feelings he gave us in 'You're gonna make me lonesome when you go', 'Tangled up in blue' and 'You're a big girl now' (not to mention such earlier explorations of the world of interiors as 'Don't think twice' or 'She belongs to me').

If this is not a record that tells you anything new about yourself, neither does it tell you anything you didn't already know about Bob Dylan. In its craftsmanlike impersonality, its respectful appropriation of traditional styles and its conservative attitude to Dylan's own various modes of expression, *Oh Mercy* seems much more akin to *John Wesley Harding*. In terms of his post-Sixties work, it plays very safe. Nothing rages out of control like 'Hurricane', achieves the wrecked majesty of the *Dylan and the Dead* version of 'Queen Jane approximately', or spins rich imagery like 'Changing of the guards'.

How typical that he should make this new album, so full of quiet, reflective, adult songs, and then go out and flatly contradict it with the snarling, spitting, death's-head-grinning maximum rock-'n'-roll shows we saw in the summer. You can forgive him a lot for that kind of barefaced perversity. For once in his recent history, though, *Oh Mercy* allows us to listen to a new Bob Dylan album without needing to forgive him anything. It may very well be the Bob Dylan album we want; whether it is the one we need is another matter.

ROBERT SHELTON
Trust yourself

Trying to convert non-believers is a waste of time. Trying to lead others towards the beauty in that craggy voice is quite hopeless. And attempting to persuade the prejudiced about the poetry in, and between, his lines is sailing a boat towards the waters of oblivion. Bob Dylan discovered himself and all new devotees of his can only discover him for themselves.

I sat in that Radio 4 studio a while ago as the host of *Bookshelf*, who is something of a minor poet himself, told me that it was absurd to regard Dylan as any kind of a poet. 'Give me just one line from Dylan we can regard as poetry,' he jeered. 'Not even Christopher Ricks calls him a poet,' the radio host added, showing at a stroke how little he understood Ricks, as well. And the reviewer of the *Times Literary Supplement*, also something of a minor poet, wrote of Dylan: 'He's no writer.'

Those sort of idiot winds have been blowing around Dylan's head for twenty-nine years and, for most of that time, I've tried to sit in his corner. As an intermittent friend, more often observer, chronicler and biographer, it's been rather blustery. That young woman at the London *Hearts of Fire* première put it well when she said to me: 'If an author tries to defend Dylan, all you're going to do is attract to you the anger people really want to direct at him.'

What about my own anger with him? It gets intense, sometimes, because he can be selfish, mean, petty, ungrateful, self-obsessed, heedless. But actually what right do I, or anyone, have to make demands on him? Because he's affected us deeply on any level, does that give us the right to tell our gifted brother to shape up, regain control, sing this or that, write like he used to, and just go on thrilling us 'down the road to ecstasy', year after year?

Aren't five hundred songs, twenty-nine years and all those stacks of albums enough? No, we expect the impossible. We want to freeze time and be back with those feelings we once experienced. We want him not to follow Orson Welles and Marlon Brando and turn his career upside down, early triumphs slipping into parody or sherry commercials. That's as much our problem as his.

Being a Dylanite is akin to being a religious zealot or a wounded lover. And the Dylan-bashers won't stop bashing him. No matter what he does today or tomorrow, they'll still ask about the mistakes he made last year. This shy, sensitive and often frightened artist is misunderstood mostly because of his elaborate defence system. They don't appreciate how you have to turn crusty and arrogant to survive in the jungle he has chosen as his workplace. It's not the only way, but it's his way, and it's too late to change that.

Tough Dylan tells us that those clean-cut kids in the music business and media world are killers, so watch out. The audience is omnivorous, the critics want you to stand on your head, he says. Defend yourself or they will take everything you've got. Philosophically, he'll say: 'It's the price of fame.' More often, he'll say: 'What do they know?' Oh, those sweet times in Greenwich Village, 1962, when the White Horse Tavern closed and Bobby and Suze and Gil Turner and Mike Harrington and I staggered over to McGowan's saloon, 'down on Montague Street', where we could swill our wine and talk until 4 a.m. Yes, there was music in the café and some sort of revolution in the air.

We turned nights into days and swapped dreams, only Bobby dreamed bigger than any of us. He was so funny then, so filled with life. Later, Suze said he was also so filled with death, she had to split. But for that moment in time, he *was* bursting at the seams with life and his direction *was* straight up.

So, I thought I'd freeze those times and write a book about those Greenwich Village days. Bob said fine, man, and arranged for me to meet him on tour. He didn't want me to talk to his mum or Sara, but I did anyway.

Years later, an American editor, who knew of my tacit agreement with Dylan to keep his 'madonna-like Sara' in the background, glimpsed my manuscripts and said: 'We need more about the marriage.' I said: 'I want another editor.' And long before that, another American editor, known widely for her personal secretiveness, had told me to 'tell more'. I asked her why. 'It'll sell more copies.' She didn't say it was to help us understand his erratic genius.

But I told her it was all there, all the sex and drugs and rock-'n'-roll, if she could only understand Dylan's subtlety, and mine. And through an associate in London, she said: 'You'd earn a lot more money if you said Dylan was a homosexual.' Sarcastically, I parried: 'And more still if I said he was a murderer?'

Years later, after switching to another publisher in New York,

I was told to 'tell less'. He offered me 70 per cent more money if I would cut my manuscript almost in half. I said: 'No deal. I won't scrap all that work for your market conditions.' That same publisher later gave Albert Goldman sixteen times more money than I received for his interminable fiction about John Lennon. Showbiz biography is a debased form in America, and the rot is spreading. These publishers are abandoning ordinary concerns to give us the dirt, the warts, on Leonard Bernstein, Jackie Kennedy and *Rock Stars in Their Underpants*. The Kitty Kelleys and Albert Goldmans are distorting the original intent of biography, their publishers cheering them on with promises of greater financial rewards. The more this type of publisher salivated for a hatchet job on Dylan, the more I was driven towards sympathy and analysis.

On so many scores, Dylan is a maddening fellow, so cool and holding so tight to his 'secrets', until he blurts it all out in song. Opaque, on the surface, but transparent, if you can read his code. Bob's got his mother's contradictions, his late father's cunning. What a combination! And because they had carved that canyon in his home town to rob the earth of its ore, he had to turn creative to mine his own verbal-musical ore, then to refine it and build a mountain of his own.

In a period of great personal loss, guilt and confusion, Bob reached toward Jesus for solace, but lost fans. After too much of nothing, he found relief and direction and renewal with the Jesus myth. Even then, we wouldn't let him call paradise his abode, and so, once again, it was no direction home for Bob Dylan.

They say real biographers, not hacks, assume the personality of their subject. Victoria Glendinning says she thought she was Virginia Woolf while she drew her portrait. And the scholar Theodore Besterman actually moved into Voltaire's house to get the feel of his subject there. They say the real biographer, not the hack, develops such an empathy with his subject, he can defend even his worst behaviour. After forty years grappling with Thomas Jefferson, Dumas Malone could even understand Jefferson's quirky attitude towards slavery. Knowing the worst about Bob Dylan, I could still admire him for his best traits. Underneath his crust was a decent guy, I know.

Oh, those great old days, when Bob got an instant crush on gospel singer Mavis Staples, and even though Pop Staples chided him, he went after Mavis anyway. Or that night in the crowded Limelight, when I was so low about Linda and Bob came back to me from the door to pat me on the shoulder, because he knew how I was feeling. I should have called my book *How Does It Feel*? Would those who think he's a manipulative, arrogant little snot have understood *that* title?

Oh, those great days, even in 1978, when he was knocking out audiences and himself with the music he made at Earls Court and Blackbushe. Backstage one night, after I had tried to talk to actor Jack Nicholson but got only those rolling, stoned eyes replying, Bob came in. He kissed my lady, Gabrielle, and told me 'how emotional a thing' it was to see me again. His old Woodstock pal, Happy Traum, was there. Did he see his children, Traum asked him. 'Not enough,' Bob replied. Bob said he had his band and his shows together, 'and that's the only thing in my life I do have together'.

Already, by then, in his 'Journey through dark heat' on *Street Legal* he was hearing his slow train coming. The three religious albums contain some of his best music-making of all, whatever we thought of his lyrics. Sure, his religious imagery was even stronger before he became a Jesus follower, but just listen again to that music. Poets and kings have turned to religion for solace and inspiration, but not our Bob, we all said. Not Dylan!

What about his warts? He's got thousands. The money it cost me to quote lyrics, to fix the discography in type, to settle scores on that myth about a child. Warts? Those crazy, hazy times when he seemed to be going up in a cloud of smoke, bad habits, little food. Precious talent there, so why does he so hurt himself? Life-style and death-style curled around each other, like yin and yang, in symmetry. There's a symmetry to all the forty-nine years, if you know how and where to look. But also, there's too much surly regression to stay close to him. Baudelaire and Poe and Rimbaud would understand the regression, but who else?

A ruthless man, or possessor of a ruthless artist's psyche? Jung spelled it all out generations ago, the ruthless part of the creator's psyche that carves out time and energy. So, friends and family and the healthy elements of a personality have to get out of the way when the Ruthless Express leaves blood on the tracks.

If we didn't demand so much of Dylan, we'd probably get more from him or his work. He could have died in 1966, or after, and still have changed the face of popular music, and its metabolism. Even as recently as 1981 there was the old sting we missed. Listen to 'The groom's still waiting at the altar', on *Biograph*. What a cutting edge! Rhyming 'temperature' and 'furniture', 'January' and 'Buenos Aires'! Singing about his own misunderstood, slandered and humiliated shyness. A curtain's rising on the new age, he sang, and maybe we must now go and find it.

If you had been me, what would you have said to that Radio 4 fool, talking about Dylan's 'so-called poetry'? What would you have said to those wart-collecting publishers? *No Direction Home* was no best-seller, but there are 200,000 copies out in twelve editions in six languages. I have a mountain of debt, but I also have my self-respect.

Ultimately, I've learned so much from Dylan that I can't complain. He never short-changed me and he won't short-change you. He's given you fair warning about not following leaders and about trusting yourself. The keys to Dylan are on stage and in the microgrooves of a recording, in Hibbing and Greenwich Village more than in Woodstock or Malibu. Let's appreciate him while he's around, not wait till after he's gone. He is, after all, whether you believe me or not, a very human being.

And, like a few other larger-than-life twentieth-century artists – Picasso, Chaplin, Welles and Brando – let him have his flaws and blind spots. What gives you pleasure most, these artists' best or worst? If you are going to be as perfectionist as they are with themselves, you might end up being, like them, exiles, 'refugees on the unarmed road of flight'.

Notes

1. From the trilogy *Slow Homecoming*, London, Methuen, 1985, pp. 81–2.

Selective Bibliography

A plus sign following a page number indicates that the article continues on unspecified pages later in the volume or issue. Items marked with an asterisk are represented in this book.

Adams, Val, 'Satire on Birch Society barred from Ed Sullivan's TV show', *New York Times* (14 May 1963); reprinted in *Bob Dylan: A Retrospective*, ed. Craig McGregor, London, Picador, 1975, p. 28

Agel, Jerome, 'Music, that's where it's at', *Books* (26 December 1965), pp. 1, 12

Allen, Gary, 'That music: there's more to it than meets the ear', *American Opinion*, 12 (February 1969), pp. 49–62; reprinted in *The Age of Rock 2*, ed. Jonathan Eisen, New York, Random House, 1970, pp. 193–213

Allsop, Kenneth, 'Folk – the fine and the fake', *Nova* (May 1965), pp. 144, 146

*——, 'Beat and ballad', *Nova* (November 1965), pp. 38, 40

——, 'Ballad and beat', *Nova* (December 1965), pp. 26, 28

Anderson, Denis, *The Hollow Horn*, Munich, Hobo Press, 1981

Aronowitz, Al, 'Enter the king, Bob Dylan', *Saturday Evening Post* (2 November 1968), pp. 34–5

——, 'Dylan: he's only just begun', *Melody Maker* (1 December 1973), p. 13

*Baez, Joan, *And a Voice to Sing With*, London, Century Hutchinson, 1988

Baker, Kathryn, 'Bob Dylan on Bob Dylan', *Stars and Stripes* (7 September 1988), p. 17

*Balfour, Victoria, *Rock Wives*, New York, Beech Tree/William Morrow, 1986

Ballantine, Christopher, 'Say it straight', *New Society* (4 June 1970), pp. 967–8

*Bangs, Lester, 'Bob Dylan's dalliance with Mafia chic', *Creem* (April 1976), pp. 48–51, 63–5

——, 'Bob Dylan's vs. Don Kirshner', *Creem* (December 1976), pp. 51–2

Barnes, Clive, 'Dylan's civilized moan is no more', *New York Times* (2 September 1969), p. 38

Bauldie, John, 'Bob Dylan & Desire', *Wanted Man Study Series*, 2, Bury, Wanted Man, 1984

Biermann, Wolf, 'Kennen sie Dylan?', *Konkret*, 7 (29 June 1978), pp. 42–4

Bizot, Jean-Francois, 'Les pop heureux ont une histoire', *Musique en Jeu*, 2 (March 1971), pp. 74–8

Bloom, Fred, 'Seeing Dylan seeing', *Yale Review*, 71 (Winter 1982), pp. 304–20

Bohlen, Celestine, 'Blowin' into Russia', *Washington Post* (27 July 1985), pp. D1, D6

Bowden, Elizabeth Anne (Betsy), 'Performed literature: words and music by Bob Dylan', University of California dissertation, 1978

Bowden, Betsy, *Performed Literature*, Bloomington, Indiana University Press, 1982

Bratfisch, Rainer, 'Friedenskonzert mit Bob Dylan', *Musik und Gesellschaft*, 37 (November 1987), pp. 612–13

Braun, Jonathan, 'Is Bob Zimmerman really Jewish?', *Flame*; reprinted in *Rolling Stone* (8 July 1971), p. 12

Brock, George, 'Mr Tambourine Man blows in', *Observer* (18 June 1978), p. 4

Brown, Mick, 'Dylan at forty', *Guardian* (26 June 1981), p. 11

——, 'Stone turned', *Guardian* (27 June 1981)

——, 'Dylan', *Sunday Times* (1 July 1984)

Brummell, O. B., 'Bob Dylan – a far cry from Aristotle', *High Fidelity*, 16 (October 1966), p. 125

Bussey, Charles J., 'Bob Dylan: driven home', *Christianity Today* (26 June 1981), pp. 47–8

Cable, Paul, *Bob Dylan: His Unreleased Recordings*, London, Scorpion Publications/Dark Star, 1978

Campbell, Duncan, 'One step forward, two steps back', *International Times*, 157 (28 June 1973[?]), p. 10

Campbell, Gregg M., 'Bob Dylan and the pastoral apocalypse', *Journal of Popular Culture*, 8, 4 (September 1975), pp. 696–707

*Campbell, Robert D., 'Dylan's new morning', *Christian Century* (25 August 1971), p. 1009

Cannon, Geoffrey, 'Dylan in the big country', *Guardian* (22 April 1969)

——, 'Bob Zimmerman', *Village Voice* (1969); reprinted in Eisen, *The Age of Rock 2*, pp. 77–82

——, 'The gospel according to Dylan', *Guardian* (2 September 1969)

——, 'Bob Dylan's public domain', *Guardian* (26 June 1970)

——, 'The day they booed Dylan', *Guardian* (12 June 1971)

Cantor, Louis, 'Bob Dylan: a bibliographical essay', University of Indiana-Purdue at Fort Wayne, unpublished essay

*Capel, Maurice, 'The blessing of the damned', *Jazz Monthly* (December 1965), pp. 13–16

*——, 'The man in the middle', *Jazz Monthly* (January 1966), pp. 21, 23

Cartwright, Bert, 'The Bible in the lyrics of Bob Dylan', *Wanted Man Study Series*, Bury, Wanted Man, 1985

Cawelti, John G., 'Reply to Poague' (see below), *Journal of Popular Culture*, 8 (Summer 1974), pp. 57–8

Christgau, Robert, 'Rock lyrics are poetry (maybe)', *Cheetah* (December 1967); reprinted in *The Age of Rock*, ed. Jonathan Eisen, New York, Vintage, 1969, pp. 230–43

——, 'Secular music', *Esquire* (May 1968), pp. 18–28

——, 'Obvious believers', *Village Voice* (May 1969); reprinted in *Any Old Way You Choose It*, Baltimore, Penguin, 1973, pp. 198–204

——, 'Consumer guide: Self Portrait', *Village Voice* (30 July 1970); reprinted ibid.

——, *'Tarantula', *New York Times Book Review* (27 June 1971), pp. 3, 30; reprinted ibid., pp. 205–9

——, 'I am Dylan', *Village Voice* (December 1971); reprinted ibid., pp. 209–11

[*Christianity Today*], 'Has born-again Bob Dylan returned to Judaism?', *Christianity Today* (13 January 1984), pp. 46, 48

Clark, Sue C., 'Dylan at Guthrie memorial', *Rolling Stone* (24 February 1968); reprinted in *The Rolling Stone Rock-'n'-Roll Reader*, ed. Ben Fong-Torres, New York, Bantam, 1974, pp. 232–3

Cleave, Maureen, 'If Bob can't sing it, it must be a poem or a novel or something', *Evening Standard* (16 May 1964), p. 7

——, 'So very, very bored . . . the curious Mr Dylan', *Evening Standard* (27 April 1965), p. 15

Cocks, Jay, 'Freaky fresco of Hell', *Time* (24 May 1971), p. 74

——, 'Dylan and Young on the road', *Time* (6 November 1978), p. 89

——, 'Here's what's happening, Mr Jones', *Time* (10 June 1985), p. 45

——, 'Hellhound on the loose', *Time* (25 November 1985), p. 52

Cohen, John and Traum, Happy, 'Conversations with Bob Dylan', *Sing Out!* (October–November 1968), pp. 6–23, 67

Cohen, Scott, 'Don't ask me nothin' about nothin' I might just tell you the truth', *Spin*, 1, 8 (December 1985), pp. 26+

Cohn, Nik, 'Dylan in England: trauma or triumph?', *New York Times* (7 September 1969), II, p. 24; reprinted in McGregor, *Bob Dylan: A Retrospective*, pp. 198–200

——, 'Bob Dylan' in *Awopbopalooboplopbamboom*, London, Paladin, 1970, pp. 168–74

Collins, Judy, *Trust Your Heart*, Boston, Houghton Mifflin, 1987

Collis, John, 'His back pages', *Time Out* (19–26 November 1986), p. 22

Connelly, Christopher, 'Dylan makes another stunning comeback', *Rolling Stone* (24 November 1983), pp. 65–6

Connolly, Ray, 'Dylan's ticket to Ryde', *Evening Standard* (16 August 1969), p. 7

Cott, Jonathan, 'Back inside the rain', *Rolling Stone* (13 March 1975), pp. 31–2

——, 'Standing naked', *Rolling Stone* (26 January 1978), pp. 38–45

——, 'The Rolling Stone interview', *Rolling Stone* (16 November 1978), pp. 55–62

——, *Dylan*, London, Vermilion, 1984

Cusimano, Jim, 'Dylan comes back to the wars', *Crawdaddy* (April 1975), pp. 67–8

Cutler, Chris, *File Under Popular*, London, November Books, 1985

Dallas, Karl, Denselow, Robin, Laing, Dave and Shelton, Robert, *The Electric Muse*, London, Methuen, 1975

Davey, Frank, 'Leonard Cohen and Bob Dylan: poetry and the popular song', *Alphabet*, 17 (December 1969), pp. 12–29; revised and reprinted in *Leonard Cohen: The Artist and His Critics*, ed. Michael Gnarowski, Toronto, McGraw-Hill, 1976, pp. 111–24

Davies, Russell, 'Return of a superstar', *Sunday Times* (18 June 1978)

——, 'Mr Tambourine Man', *Observer* (18 November 1984)

——, 'Knockin' on Dylan's door', *Observer* (19 October 1986)

Day, Aidan, 'Bob Dylan: "Escaping on the run"', *Wanted Man Study Series*, 3, Bury, Wanted Man, 1984

——, *Jokerman*, Oxford, Basil Blackwell, 1988

Deeley, Peter, 'Dylan changes with the times', *Observer* (28 June 1981)

Denisoff, R. Serge, 'Dylan: hero or villain?', *Broadside*, 58 (15 May 1965), p. 15

——, 'Folk-rock: folk music, protest, or commercialism?', *Journal of Popular Culture*, 3, 2 (1969), pp. 214–30

——, *Great Day Coming: Folk Music and the American Left*, Urbana-Chicago, University of Illinois Press, 1971

——, *Solid Gold*, New Brunswick, New Jersey, Transaction Books, 1975

——, 'Massification and popular music: a review', *Journal of Popular Culture*, 9, 4 (1976), pp. 886–94

——, *Tarnished Gold*, New Brunswick, New Jersey, Transaction Books, 1986

—— and Fandray, David, 'Hey, hey, Woody Guthrie, I wrote you a song: the political side of Bob Dylan', *Popular Music and Society*, 5, 5 (1977), pp. 31–42

Dennis, Felix, 'The Great White Wonder', *Oz*, 25 (1969)

Denselow, Robin, 'The most embarrassing piece of plastic ever produced in the name of a great artist', *Guardian* (3 January 1974)

——, 'Bob Dylan', *Guardian* (21 January 1974)

——, 'Bob Dylan', *Guardian* (25 June 1974)

——, 'Bob Dylan', *Guardian* (8 February 1975)

——, 'Bob Dylan', *Guardian* (16 June 1978)

——, 'Times still a'changing', *Guardian* (3 January 1986)

——, *When the Music's Over*, London, Faber, 1989

De Somogyi, Nick, 'Jokermen and thieves: Bob Dylan and the ballad tradition', *Wanted Man Study Series*, 5, Bury, Wanted Man, 1986

De Turk, David A. and Poulin, A., 'I will show you fear in a handful of songs' in *The American Folk Scene*, New York, Dell, 1967, pp. 270–9

De Voss, David, 'Dylan: once again, it's alright, ma', *Time* (21 January 1974), pp. 54+

Dickstein, Morris, 'The age of rock revisited' in *Gates of Eden: American Culture in the Sixties*, New York, Basic Books, 1977, pp. 183–201

Dowley, Tim and Dunnage, Barry, *Bob Dylan: From a Hard Rain to a Slow Train*, Tunbridge Wells, Midas, 1982

Dudek, Louis, 'Poetry as a way of life', *English Quarterly* 1, 1 (June 1968), pp. 7–17

Dunaway, David King, *How Can I Keep from Singing: Pete Seeger*, London, Harrap, 1985

Durbin, Karen, *et al.*, 'He speaks good English and he invites you up into his room', *Village Voice* (30 January 1978), pp. 25–6

*Dyer, Geoff, 'Figured I'd lost you anyway', *Listener* (28 May 1987), p. 25

Dylan, Bob, *Tarantula*, London, MacGibbon and Kee, 1971

——, *Writings and Drawings*, London, Jonathan Cape, 1973

——, *Lyrics 1962–1985*, London, Jonathan Cape, 1986

Ephron, Nora and Edmiston, Susan, 'Bob Dylan interview'; reprinted in Eisen, *The Age of Rock 2*, pp. 63–71 and Mc Gregor, *Bob Dylan: A Retrospective*, pp. 61–8

Evearitt, Daniel J., 'Bob Dylan: still blowin' in the wind', *Christianity Today* (3 December 1976), pp. 29, 31

Fager, Charles E., 'Cryptic simplicity', *Christian Century* (19 June 1968), p. 821

——, 'Up from the Basement', *Christian Century* (11 March 1970), pp. 301–2

*Fariña, Richard, 'Baez and Dylan: a generation singing out', *Mademoiselle*, 59, 4 (August 1964), pp. 242, 338–9, 342; reprinted in Eisen, *The Age of Rock*, and De Turk and Poulin, *The American Folk Scene*, pp. 250–8

Feather, Leonard, 'Bob Dylan: rolling stone gathers moss', *Cavalier* (December 1967), p. 9

Fields, Sidney, 'Only human', *New York Mirror* (12 September 1963)

Fong-Torres, Ben, 'Bob Dylan: knockin' on Dylan's door', *Rolling Stone* (February 1974); reprinted in *What's That Sound?*, ed. Ben Fong-Torres, New York, Anchor, 1976, pp. 148–68

Foster, John Wilson, 'John Greenway on folksong – a reply', *Australian Literary Studies*, 3, 1 (June 1967), pp. 63–5

Franks, Alan, 'With Bob on His side', *The Times Higher Education Supplement* (3 July 1981), p. 8

——, 'Bringing it all back home', *The Times* (14 June 1984), p. 10

Frith, Simon, 'Try to dig what we all say', *Listener* (26 June 1980), pp. 822–3

*Gaboriau, Linda, 'Ken Kesey: summing up the '60s, sizing up the '70s', *Crawdaddy* (19 December 1972), pp. 31–9

Gahr, David and Shelton, Robert, *The Face of Folk Music*, New York, Citadel Press, 1968

Gannon, Frank, 'Bob Dylan: forever young', *Saturday Evening Post*, 246 (June/July 1974), pp. 48–9, 128, 132

Gelly, Dave, 'Bob Dylan and the message', *Observer* (5 July 1981)

——, 'Dylan's return', *Observer* (15 July 1984)

Gelmis, Joseph, 'Show sold out; but did Dylan?', *Newsday* (30 August 1965); reprinted in McGregor, *Bob Dylan: A Retrospective*, pp. 59–60

Gill, Andy, 'Dylanology', *Q*, 9 (June 1987), p. 94

——, 'Hearts of Fire', *Q*, 15 (December 1987)

Gilmore, Mikal, 'Positively Dylan', *Rolling Stone* (17–31 July 1986), pp. 31–4, 135 +

*Ginsberg, Allen, *First Blues: Rags, Ballads and Harmonium Songs, 1971–74*, New York, Full Court Press, 1975

——, 'Rolling Thunder Stones', *Rolling Stone* (15 January 1976), p. 39

Gleason, Ralph J., 'The children's crusade', *Ramparts*, 4, 11 (March 1966), pp. 27–34

——, 'Like a rolling stone', *American Scholar*, 36, 4 (Autumn 1967), pp. 555–63; reprinted in Eisen, *The Age of Rock*, pp. 61–76

——, 'The many faces of Bob Dylan', *Jazz & Pop* (October 1967), pp. 17–18

——, 'Bob Dylan '65: meeting the press', *Rolling Stone* (14 December

1967 and 20 January 1968); reprinted in Fong-Torres, *The Rolling Stone Rock-'n'-Roll Reader*, pp. 214–30

——, 'Bob Dylan: poet to a generation', *Jazz & Pop* (December 1968), pp. 36–7

——, 'The blood of a poet', *Rolling Stone* (13 March 1975), p. 39

Goddard, J. R., 'Dylan meets the press', *Village Voice* (25 March 1965), p. 24

Goldberg, Steven, 'Bob Dylan and the poetry of salvation', *Saturday Review* (30 May 1970), pp. 43–6, 57; reprinted in McGregor, *Bob Dylan: A Retrospective*, pp. 242–57

Goldman, Albert, 'That angry kid has gone all over romantic', *Life*, 66, 18 (23 May 1969), pp. 16–18; reprinted in *Freakshow*, New York, Atheneum, 1971, pp. 133–5

——, 'The paradox of Bobby Dylan', *Life* [US] (17 March 1972), p. 23

——, 'Writings and Drawings', *New York Times Book Review* (30 September 1973), pp. 42–3

Goldman, Lawrence, 'Bobby Dylan – folk-rock hero', *Studies on the Left*, 6, 5 (September/October 1966), pp. 85–90; reprinted in Eisen, *The Age of Rock*, pp. 208–13

Goldstein, Richard, 'Don't look back', *New York Times* (22 October 1967); reprinted in McGregor, *Bob Dylan: A Retrospective*, pp. 123–7

——, 'Bob Dylan, the recluse of rock', *Vogue* [US] (15 March 1968), p. 42

Gollan, Antoni E., 'The evolution of Bob Dylan', *National Review* (28 June 1966), pp. 638–40

*Gonczy, Daniel J., 'The folk music of the 1960s: its rise and fall', *Popular Music and Society*, 10, 1 (1985), pp. 15–31

Gonzales, Laurence, 'Personna Bob: seer and fool', *Costerus*, 3 (1972), pp. 33–53

Gonzalez, Alberto and Makay, John J., 'Rhetorical ascription and the gospel according to Dylan', *Quarterly Journal of Speech*, 69, 1 (February 1983), pp. 1–14

Gordon, John, 'Dylan: a few year's older than Israel', *Fusion* (25 June 1971); reprinted in McGregor, *Bob Dylan: A Retrospective*, pp. 114–16

Gott, Richard, 'The airport where nobody is going anywhere any more', *Guardian* (17 July 1978)

Gray, Michael, 'What's so good about Bob Dylan?', *Oz* (October 1967), pp. 5–9, 27

——, 'Dylan starts first concert tour for eight years', *Guardian* (3 January 1974)

——, 'Blowing in the winds of change', *Guardian* (29 May 1976), p. 9

——, *Song and Dance Man*, London, Abacus, 1973; revised edition, London, Hamlyn, 1981

——, 'Unlike a Rolling Stone', *Independent* (21 October 1988), p. 15

——, and Bauldie, John, *All Across the Telegraph*, London, Sidgwick and Jackson, 1987

Greenway, John, 'Folksong – a protest', *Australian Literary Studies*, 2, 3 (June 1966), pp. 179–92

Griffiths, David, 'Three tributaries of The River', *Popular Music* 7, 1 (1987–8), pp. 27–34

Gross, Michael, *Dylan: An Illustrated History*, London, Elm Tree, 1978

Grossman, Edward, 'Dylan's Odyssey', *Dissent*, 20, 4 (Fall 1973), pp. 491–3

Haas, Joseph, 'Bob Dylan talking', *Chicago Daily News* (27 November 1965); reprinted in McGregor, *Bob Dylan: A Retrospective*, pp. 78–83

Hamilton, Ian, 'Dylan – a bard but not a poet', *Observer Magazine* (11 June 1978), p. 28

Hammond, John [with Irving Townsend], *John Hammond on Record: An Autobiography*, Harmondsworth, Penguin, 1981

Hampton, (Charles) Wayne, 'Working class heroes: counter-cultural politics and the singing hero in twentieth-century America', University of Tennessee dissertation, 1983

——, *Guerrilla Minstrels: John Lennon, Joe Hill, Woody Guthrie, Bob Dylan*, Knoxville, University of Tennessee Press, 1986

Hattenhauer, Darryl, 'Bob Dylan as clown and guru', *Journal of American Culture*, 2, 2 (Summer 1979), pp. 176–85

——, 'Bob Dylan as hero: rhetoric, history, structuralism, and psychoanalysis in folklore as a communicative process', *Southern Folklore Quarterly*, 45 (1981), pp. 69–88

Haver, Fritz Werner, 'Bob Dylans surrealistische Songpoesie', University of Marburg dissertation, 1987

Hentoff, Nat, 'Hootenanny on TV – McCarthy style', *Village Voice* (14 March 1963); reprinted in *Sing Out!* (April/May 1963), pp. 32–3

——, 'The crackin', shakin', breakin' sounds', *New Yorker* (24 October 1964), pp. 64–6+; reprinted in McGregor, *Bob Dylan: A Retrospective*, pp. 30 – 49

——, The Playboy interview: Bob Dylan', *Playboy* (March 1966), pp. 41–4, 138–42; reprinted in McGregor, *Bob Dylan: A Retrospective*, pp. 88–111

——, 'Something's happening and you don't know what it is, do you, Mr Jones?', *Evergreen Review* (1966); reprinted in Eisen, *The Age of Rock*, pp. 3–8

——, 'The pilgrims have landed on Kerouac's grave', *Rolling Stone*

(15 January 1976), pp. 32–8; reprinted in Fong-Torres, *What's That Sound?*, pp. 169–88

Hepworth, David, 'Bob Dylan down in the groove', Q (July 1988), p. 80

Herdman, John, *Voice Without Restraint*, Edinburgh, Paul Harris Publishing, 1982

Herman, Gary, 'Highway 61 re-routed', *New Society* (18 September 1980), pp. 570–1

Hersch, Charles Benjamin, 'Liberating forms: politics and the arts from the New York intellectuals to the Counterculture', University of California dissertation, 1987

Hewson, Paul (as Bono) with Morrison, Van, 'Bob Dylan in conversation', *Hot Press*, 8, 16 (24 August 1984), pp. 17–18 +

Heylin, Clinton, *Bob Dylan – Stolen Moments*, Romford, Essex, Wanted Man, 1988

Hill, Derek, 'Fresh and welcome', *Listener* (17 January 1963), p. 139

Hinchey, John, 'Bob Dylan's Slow Train', *Wanted Man Study Series*, 1, Bury, Wanted Man, 1983

Hobbs, Stephen James, 'Male mentor relationships: a study of psychosocial development in early adulthood', University of California dissertation, 1982

Hobsbawm, E.J. (as Francis Newton), 'Bob Dylan', *New Statesman* (22 May 1964), p. 819

Hodgson, Clive, 'The concert for Bangla Desh', *Oz*, 44 (September 1972), p. 50

Hoffmann, Raoul, 'Dreimal in Sachen Beat', *Neue Musikzeitung*, 18 (June/July 1969), p. 10

——, 'Dylan: Erstgeborener der Pop-Generation', *Neue Musikzeitung*, 21 (December/January 1972–3), p. 10

——, 'Bob Dylan: Pop-Poet oder Moral-Apostel', *Neue Musikzeitung*, 25 (June/July 1976), p. 9

Hoggard, Stuart and Sheilds, Jim, *Bob Dylan: An Illustrated Discography*, London, Transmedia, 1977

Holmes, Tim, 'Dylan: a life in music', *Rolling Stone* (16 January 1986)

Hoskyns, Barney, 'As Arthur Rimbaud once said', *New Statesman* (30 November 1984), p. 36

Iachetta, Michael, 'Scarred Bob Dylan is comin' back', *New York Daily News* (8 May 1967); reprinted in McGregor, *Bob Dylan: A Retrospective*, pp. 118–23

Jahn, Mike, 'Self-portrait of the artist as an older man', *Saturday Review* (11 May 1968), pp. 63–4

James, Clive, 'Troubadour of protest', *Observer* (23 April 1972), p. 33

——, 'Don't think twice', *Guardian* (26 July 1973)

——, 'Bringing some of it all back home', *Creem*; reprinted in *New Musical Express* (20 April 1974), pp. 10–12

Johnson, Thomas S., 'Desolation Row revisited: Bob Dylan's rock poetry', *Southwest Review*, 62 (Spring 1977), pp. 135–47

Johnston, Sheila, 'Rupert on the barricades', *Independent* (16 October 1987), p. 28

Jones, Alan, 'The lost Dylan album', *Melody Maker* (12 March 1988), p. 18

Jones, Max, 'If you want to do it – then do it!', *Melody Maker* (23 May 1964), p. 12

*Kael, Pauline, 'The Calvary gig', *New Yorker* (13 February 1978), pp. 107–11

Kaiser, Charles, 'Encountering Dylan', *Boston Review* (April 1986), pp. 9–10

Katz, Elia, 'Dylan's unpublished novel', *Carolina Quarterly*, 21 (Fall 1969), pp. 34–7

Keller, Martin, 'Religion today bondage tomorrow', *New Musical Express* (6 August 1983), p. 23

*Kermode, Frank and Spender, Stephen, 'Bob Dylan: the metaphor at the end of the funnel', *Esquire* (May 1972), pp. 110, 118, 188

Kidel, Mark, 'Blood on the Tracks', *New Statesman* (23 June 1978), pp. 856–7

——, 'I'm alive', *New Statesman* (25 July 1980)

——, 'One-way flow', *New Statesman* (July 1981), p. 24

Kneif, Tibor, 'Zartheit und zornige Rhetorik', *Musik und Bildung*, 7 (November 1975), p. 597

Knight, A., 'Cinéma vérité and film truth', *Saturday Review* (9 September 1967)

Kooper, Al, *Backstage Passes*, New York, Stein and Day, 1977

Kramer, Daniel, *Bob Dylan*, New Jersey, Castle Books, 1967

Krogsgaard, Michael, *Twenty Years of Recording*, Scandinavian Institute for Rock Research, 1981

Kuwahara, Yasue, 'The promised land: images of America in rock music', Bowling Green State University dissertation, 1987

Landau, Jon, 'John Wesley Harding', *Crawdaddy*, 15 (May 1968), pp. 11–17; reprinted in Eisen, *The Age of Rock*, pp. 214–29 and McGregor, *Bob Dylan: A Retrospective*, p. 160–78

——, 'After the flood', *Rolling Stone* (13 March 1975), pp. 31, 33–4

Leary, Timothy, 'How our paranoias are hyped for fame and profit', *National Review*, 28 (16 April 1976), pp. 382–90 +

Levin, Bernard, *The Pendulum Years: Britain and the Sixties*, London, Jonathan Cape, 1970

Lewis, George H., 'The pop artist and his product: mixed-up confusion', *Journal of Popular Culture*, 4 (1970), pp. 327–38

*Lhamon, Jr, W. T., 'A cut above', *New Republic*, 172 (5 April 1975), pp. 22–4

——, 'Bicentennial Dylan', *New Republic*, 174 (14 February 1976), pp. 23–4

——, 'Poplore and Bob Dylan', *Bennington Review* (December 1978), pp. 22–29

Lindstrom, Naomi, 'Dylan: song returns to poetry', *Texas Quarterly*, 19 (Winter 1976), pp. 131–6

Lingeman, Richard R., 'Bob Dylan, I'm writing to you', *New York Times* (25 June 1971), p. 32

Lock, Graham, 'Bringing it all back wrong', *New Musical Express* (29 October 1983), p. 33

★Loder, Kurt, 'God and man at Columbia', *Rolling Stone* (18 September 1980), p. 48

——, 'Bob Dylan', *Rolling Stone* (21 June 1984), pp. 14, 17–18, 23–24, 78

——, 'Bob Dylan', *Rolling Stone* (5 November–10 December 1987), pp. 301–3

★Logue, Christopher, 'A feir feld ful of folk', *The Times* (13 September 1969)

London, Herbert, 'American Romantics; old and new', *Colorado Quarterly*, 18, 1 (1969), pp. 5–20

Lupoff, Dick, 'George Jackson: Greatest Hits Vol. II', *Ramparts*, 10, 8 (February 1972), pp. 54–5

McCann, Peter J., 'Bob Dylan: a pre-obituary', *National Review*, 23 (9 February 1971), pp. 156–7

MacColl, Ewan, 'A symposium', *Sing Out!* (September 1965), pp. 9–18; excerpted in De Turk & Poulin, *The American Folk Scene*, pp. 156–8; condensed version in McGregor, *Bob Dylan: A Retrospective*, pp. 69–70

McDonald, James R., 'Bob Dylan: Biograph – a journey into life', *Popular Music and Society*, 10, 3 (1986), pp. 91–4

——, 'Dylan's back – again', *Popular Music and Society*, 11, 2 (1987), pp. 95–7

McEwen, Rory, 'Bard of the folk song boom', *New Society* (20 May 1965), p. 26

McGregor, Craig, 'Bob Dylan's anti-interview', *Sydney Morning Herald* (13 April 1966), p. 1

——, (ed.), *Bob Dylan: A Retrospective*, New York, William Morrow, 1972; condensed edition London, Picador, 1975; revised edition, Sydney, Angus and Robertson, 1980

MacKenzie Jnr, Donald M., 'The conversion of Bob Dylan', *Theology Today*, 37 (October 1980), pp. 357–9

MacKinnon, Lachlan, 'The lives of Alias', *Times Literary Supplement* (31 October 1986), p. 1228

MacRae, Suzanne, 'Bob Dylan is the weatherman', in *Conclusions on the Wall*, ed. Elizabeth Thomson, Manchester, Thin Man, 1980, pp. 20–8

Mamis, Toby, 'To Bob Dylan: with love from an unlikely fan', *Senior Scholastic*, 104 (28 February 1974), p. 30

*Manakov, A., 'Bob Dylan's trajectory', *Literaturnaya Gazeta* (7 September 1977), p. 15

March, Michael, 'The "I wanna be with you if you wanna be with me" fiction interview', *Fusion* (31 October 1969); reprinted in Eisen, *The Age of Rock 2*, pp. 247–50, and McGregor, *Bob Dylan: A Retrospective*, pp. 189–92

Marcus, Greil, 'Self Portrait No. 25', *Rolling Stone* (23 July 1970), pp. 16–19

——, 'Heavy breathing', *Creem* (May 1974), pp. 37–9, 73–4

——, 'Never so utterly fake', *Rolling Stone* (24 August 1978), pp. 51–3

*——, 'Amazing chutzpah', *New West* (24 September 1979), p. 95 +

——, 'Comeback time again', *Village Voice* (13 August 1985), p. 63

——, 'Speaker to speaker', *Artforum*, 24, 8 (April 1986), p. 11

Marriott, John, 'Dylan's disaster', *Observer* (28 February 1988), p. 25

Marsh, Dave, 'Desire under fire: mythic images of women and outlaws', *Rolling Stone* (11 March 1976)

——, 'Hard rain, hard rock, hard sell', *Rolling Stone* (21 October 1976), p. 39

——, 'Ballad in plain dull', *Rolling Stone* (9 March 1978), p. 31

——, 'Knockin' on heaven's door', *Rolling Stone* (10 August 1978), p. 30

——, 'Rockers on the road to salvation', *Rolling Stone* (18 October 1979), p. 43

Medcalf, Lawrence Donald, 'The rhetoric of Bob Dylan 1963–1966', University of Indiana dissertation, 1979

Meehan, Thomas, 'Public writer no. 1?', *New York Times Magazine* (12 December 1965), pp. 44–5, 130–6; reprinted as 'Bob Dylan – is he heir to Faulkner and Hemingway?', *New York Times* (18 December 1965)

Mehnert, Klaus, *Twilight of the Young: The Radical Movements of the 1960s and Their Legacy*, London, Secker and Warburg, 1978

Mellers, Wilfrid, 'Sixties', *New Statesman* (24 February 1967), pp. 268–70

——, *Caliban Reborn*, London, Gollancz, 1968

——, 'Freedom and responsibility' in McGregor, *Bob Dylan: A Retrospective*, pp. 270–81

*——, 'God, mode and meaning in some recent songs of Bob Dylan', in Thomson, *Conclusions on the Wall*, pp. 29–39; revised version in *Popular Music*, 1 (1981), pp. 143–57

——, 'The sacred and profane music machine', *Times Literary Supplement* (date unknown), p. 6

——, *A Darker Shade of Pale*, London, Faber, 1984

Middleton, Richard, 'A darker shade of pale' [review], *Music and Letters*, 67, 1 (January 1986), pp. 90–3

*Mieses, Stanley (uncredited), 'The Dead and Dylan', *New Yorker* (27 July 1987), pp. 24–5

Miles, Barry, *Ginsberg: a biography*, London, Viking, 1990

Miller, Edwin, 'While Bob Dylan sings in Washington Square', *Seventeen*, 21 (September 1962), p. 117

*Miller, Jim, 'Bob Dylan', *Witness*, 2, 2–3 (Summer–Fall 1988), pp. 52–68

Monaghan, David, 'Taking Bob Dylan seriously: the Waste Land tradition', *English Quarterly*, 6, 2 (Summer 1973), pp. 165–70

Monteiro, George, 'Dylan in the Sixties', *South Atlantic Quarterly* (1974), pp. 160–72

Mortimer, Margaret, 'The "thought" of Bob Dylan', *Arena*, 11 (Summer 1966), pp. 20–6

Nelson, Paul, 'Newport folk festival 1965', *Sing Out!* (November 1965), pp. 4–8; reprinted in McGregor, *Bob Dylan: A Retrospective*, pp. 53–6

——, 'Another view', *Sing Out!* (February 1966), pp. 69, 71; reprinted in De Turk & Poulin, *The American Folk Scene*, pp. 266–9, and McGregor, *Bob Dylan: A Retrospective*, pp. 74–7

——, 'Don't look back', *Sing Out!*, 17, 6 (December 1967/January 1968), pp. 22–5

Neve, Michael, 'Queen Mary', *London Review of Books* (20 December–24 January 1985), p. 23

Newfield, Jack, 'Brecht of the juke box, poet of the electric guitar', *Village Voice* (26 January 1967), pp. 1, 12

Norman, Philip, 'Bob Dylan woos a generation out of retirement', *Sunday Times* (18 June 1978)

——, 'Dylan and the angels', *Sunday Times* (28 June 1981)

Ochs, Phil, 'The art of Bob Dylan's Hattie Carroll', *Broadside*, 48 (20 July 1964), p. 3

——, 'An open letter from Phil Ochs to Irwin Silber, Paul Wolfe, and Joseph E. Levine', *Broadside*, 54 (20 January 1965)

O'Connor, Rory, 'Blowin' in the ear', *Vogue* [US] (July 1987), p. 54

O'Hara, J. D., 'Talking through their heads', *New Republic* (20 May 1972), pp. 26–31

Palmer, Tony, 'Pop', *London Magazine*, 8, 3 (June 1968), pp. 102–4

——, 'The Dylan invention', *Observer* (24 August 1969), p. 23

*Pankake, Jon and Nelson, Paul, 'Bob Dylan', *Little Sandy Review*, 22 (1962?), pp. 12–16; reprinted in De Turk & Poulin, *The American Folk Scene*, pp. 259–62

Pattison, Robert, *The Triumph of Vulgarity*, New York, Oxford University Press, 1987

Paxton, Tom, 'Folk rot', *Sing Out!* (January 1966), pp. 103–4

*Peel, John, 'More music: Dylan at Wembley', *Observer* (18 October 1987)

Perlman, Sandy, 'Roto-rooter', *Fusion*; reprinted in Eisen, *The Age of Rock 2*, pp. 328–35

Pichaske, David R., 'Perspectives on the self: the art of Dylan's middle period', University of Bradley, Peoria, Illinois, unpublished essay

——, *The Poetry of Rock*, Peoria, Illinois, Ellis Press, 1981

Pickering, Stephen, *Bob Dylan Approximately*, New York, David McKay, 1975

Platt, Alan, 'Boy wonder', *Guardian* (10 March 1978)

Poague, Leland A., 'Dylan as auteur: theoretical notes, and an analysis of "Love minus zero/no limit"', *Journal of Popular Culture*, 8 (Summer 1974), pp. 53–8

Price, Dan, 'Bibliography of Bob Dylan', *Popular Music and Society*, 3, 3 (1974), pp. 227–41

Radcliffe, Charles, 'In defence of Bob Dylan', *Jazz Monthly*, (11 August 1965), pp. 17–18

Ragan, James, 'Lyrics, 1962–1984', *Los Angeles Times Book Review* (15 June 1986), p. 6

Rawlins, Adrian, 'Bob Dylan and the now mind situation', *Arena*, 10 (Winter 1966), pp. 24–8

Reading, Joseph Donald, 'Tears of rage: a history, theory and criticism of rock song and social conflict rhetoric, 1965–1970', University of Oregon dissertation, 1980

Real, Jere, 'Folk music and Red tubthumpers', *American Opinion*, 7 (December 1964), pp. 19–24

Reeth, Michel van, 'Bob Dylan, profetisch spiegelbeeld van de evoluerende pop-generatie', *Adem*, 9, 4 (1973), pp. 163–7

——, 'Bob Dylan, universaliteit en aktualiteit van het lied', *Adem*, 9, 5 (1973), pp. 222–9

Reitman, David, 'Desolation dribble', *Oz*, 35 (1971), pp. 28–9

Ribakove, Sy and Barbara, *Folk-Rock: The Bob Dylan Story*, New York, Dell, 1966

*Ricks, Christopher, *The Force of Poetry*, Oxford, Clarendon, 1984

Rinzler, Alan, *Bob Dylan: The Illustrated Record*, New York, Harmony Books, 1978

Rioux, Lucien, 'Le roi des coffee houses', *Nouvelle Observateur* (18 August 1965)

Rockwell, John, 'Pop music: Dylan myth', *New York Times* (5 January 1974), p. 32

——, 'Tour's roaring ovations leave Dylan quietly pleased', *New York Times* (8 January 1974), p. 35

——, 'The Basement tapes: Dylan's classic disks', *New York Times* (4 July 1975)

——, 'Bob Dylan tour lands on Plymouth Rock first', *New York Times* (1 November 1975), pp. 31–2

——, 'Dylan returns to Garden with Rolling Thunder Revue in benefit for Carter', *New York Times* (9 December 1975)

——, 'Are the times a-changin' too much for Dylan?', *New York Times* (25 January 1976), D: pp. 1, 17

——, 'Dylan: my film is truer than reality', *New York Times* (8 January 1978), II: pp. 1, 22

——, 'Bob Dylan sums up a life in music', *New York Times* (24 November 1985), II: pp. 1, 28

——, 'Old timers out for a spin cut a couple of disks', *New York Times* (13 November 1988)

Rodnitzky, Jerome L., 'The mythology of Woody Guthrie', *Popular Music and Society*, 2, 3 (1973), pp. 227–43

——, *Minstrels of the Dawn: The Folk–Protest Singer as a Cultural Hero*, Chicago, Nelson-Hall, 1976

*[Rolling Stone], 'Dylan at Old Nassau', *Rolling Stone* (9 July 1970), p. 12; reprinted in Fong-Torres, *The Rolling Stone Rock-'n'-Roll Reader*, pp. 244–6

Roos, Michael, 'Fixin' to die: the death theme in the music of Bob Dylan', *Popular Music and Society*, 8, 3–4 (1982), pp. 103–16

——, and O'Meara, Don, 'Is your love in vain – dialectical dilemmas in Bob Dylan's recent love songs', *Popular Music*, 7, 1 (1987), pp. 36–49

Roques, Dominique, *The Great White Answers*, Salindres, Southern Live Oak Productions, 1979

Rose, Stephen C., 'Bob Dylan as theologian', *Renewal* (October/November 1965); reprinted in *Sounds*, 1, 10 (22 November 1965), pp. 4–9

——, 'Bob Dylan meets Jesus', *Christianity and Crisis*, 39 (12 November 1979), pp. 274, 286–8

Rosenbaum, Maurice, 'Bob Dylan: the man and the myths', *Daily Telegraph* (19 June 1978)

——, 'The Dylan experience', *Daily Telegraph* (22 October 1979)

——, 'In search of a definitive Dylan', *Daily Telegraph* (11 November 1980)

——, 'Bob Dylan', *Daily Telegraph* (29 June 1981)

Rosenbaum, Ron, 'The Playboy interview', *Playboy* (March 1978); reprinted in *Folk News* (May 1978), pp. 12–17

*——, 'Born-again Bob: four theories', *New York Magazine* (24 September 1979), pp. 76, 78, 80

Rosenstone, Robert A., 'The times they are a-changin': the music of protest', *Annals of the American Academy of Political and Social Sciences*, 382 (March 1969), pp. 131–44

Rotundo, E. Anthony, 'Jews and rock and roll: a study in cultural contrast', *American Jewish History*, 72 (September 1982), pp. 82–107

Roxon, Lillian, 'The Guthrie concert', *Sydney Morning Herald* (January 1968); reprinted in McGregor, *Bob Dylan: A Retrospective*, pp. 128–32

Rundall, Jeremy, 'Homer in blue jeans', *Guardian* (6 April 1965)

Saal, Hubert, 'Dylan is back', *Newsweek* (26 February 1968); reprinted in McGregor, *Bob Dylan: A Retrospective*, pp. 156–60

——, 'Dylan's country pie', *Newsweek* (4 April 1969); reprinted in McGregor, *Bob Dylan: A Retrospective*, pp. 179–81

*Sarris, Andrew, 'Don't look back', *Village Voice* (21 September 1967); reprinted in *Confessions of a Cultist*, New York, Simon & Schuster, 1970, pp. 309–14

Scaduto, Anthony, *Bob Dylan*, London, Abacus, 1972

[*Scene*], 'Tomorrow's top twenty?', *Scene*, 17 (26 January 1963), pp. 12–13

Schmidt, Eric von and Rooney, Jim, *Baby Let Me Follow You Down*, New York, Anchor, 1979

Schmidt, Mathias R., 'Bob Dylans message songs der sechziger Jahre und die anglo-amerikanische Tradition des sozialkritischen Liedes', University of Marburg dissertation, 1982

Scholes, Robert, 'Tarantula', *Saturday Review* (3 July 1971), p. 29

Shapiro, Karl, 'The poetry of Bob Dylan', *New Republic* (2 June 1973), p. 28

Shelton, Robert, 'Bob Dylan: a distinctive folk-song stylist', *New York Times* (29 September 1961), p. 31; reprinted in McGregor, *Bob Dylan: A Retrospective*, pp. 25–6

——, 'Bob Dylan sings his compositions', *New York Times* (13 April 1963)

——, 'Joan Baez and Bob Dylan: the voice meets the poet', *Hootenanny*, 1, 2 (March 1964), pp. 10–11, 69–70

——, 'Bob Dylan: the charisma kid', *Cavalier* (July 1965)

——, 'Pop singers and song writers racing down Dylan's road', *New York Times* (27 August 1965); reprinted in McGregor, *Bob Dylan: A Retrospective*, pp. 57–9

——, 'Dylan conquers unruly audience: folk-singer offers works in new mood at Forest Hills', *New York Times* (30 August 1965)

——, 'Dylan sings of lovers, losers', *New York Times* (14 January 1968)

—— (as Stacey Williams), 'Dylan: recluse enslaved by his past', *New Musical Express* (4 March 1972), pp. 16, 29

——, 'The man in the Bob Dylan hat', *Time Out* (16–22 June 1978), pp. 10–11, 13, 15–17

——, 'How does it feel to be on your own?', *Melody Maker* (29 July 1978), pp. 27–30

——, 'Bridgework', *Listener* (4 October 1979), pp. 460–1

——, 'Dylan's Godspell', *Melody Maker* (21 June 1980)

——, *No Direction Home*, London, New English Library, 1986

Shepard, Sam, *Rolling Thunder Logbook*, Harmondsworth, Penguin, 1978

——, 'True Dylan', *Esquire* (July 1987), pp. 59–68

Siegel, Jules, 'Well, what have we here?', *Saturday Evening Post* (30 July 1966), pp. 32–6, 39

Silber, Irwin, 'Bob Dylan', *Sing Out!* (February/March 1964), p. 53

——, 'An open letter to Bob Dylan', *Sing Out!* (November 1964), pp. 22–3

——, 'Newport folk festival 1965', *Sing Out!* (November 1965), pp. 4–8; condensed version in McGregor, *Bob Dylan: A Retrospective*, p. 52

——, 'Highway 61 revisited', *Sing Out!* (February/March 1966); reprinted in De Turk and Poulin, *The American Folk Scene*, pp. 264–5

Singer, David, 'Not buying into the subculture', *Christianity Today* (4 January 1980), p. 33

*Sloman, Larry, 'Bob Dylan and friends on the bus: like a Rolling Thunder', *Rolling Stone* (4 December 1975), pp. 9, 18, 20

——, *On the Road with Bob Dylan*, New York, Bantam, 1978

Smucker, Tom, 'Bob Dylan meets the Revolution', *Fusion* (31 October 1969); reprinted in McGregor, *Bob Dylan: A Retrospective*, pp. 181–8

Sneerson, Grigory, *Amerikanskie Pesni*, Moscow, Sovetsky kompozitor, 1976

Snow, Craig Robert, 'Folksinger and beat poet: the prophetic vision of Bob Dylan', Purdue University dissertation, 1987

Sonenfield, Irwin, 'The mystical rite of youth culture: search and celebration in popular music', *Music Educator's Journal*, 59 (February 1973), pp. 26–31

Spencer, Neil, 'The diamond voice within', *New Musical Express* (15 August 1981), pp. 29–31

Spitz, Bob, *Dylan: A Biography*, London, Michael Joseph, 1989

Springsteen, Bruce, 'Tangled up in Bob', *Harper's* (April 1988), pp. 28–9, 32

*Stookey, Noel Paul, 'Bob Dylan finds his source', *Christianity Today* (4 January 1980), p. 32

Strouse, Jean, 'Bob Dylan's gentle anarchy', *Commonweal* (21 June 1968), pp. 406–7, 410

Street, John, *Rebel Rock*, Oxford, Basil Blackwell, 1986

Sumner, Carolyn, 'The ballad of Dylan and Bob', *Southwest Review*, 66 (Winter 1981), pp. 41–54

Sweeting, Adam, 'Kings of the hill again', *Guardian* (12 October 1987), p. 12

Tang, Jesper, 'Den aestetiske Dylan', *Dansk Musiktidsskrift*, 45, 1 (1970), pp. 16–18

——, ' . . . Og derfor er vidnesbyrd om disse aktiviteter indlysende undervisningsmateriale', *Dansk Musiktidsskrift*, 46, 11 (1971), pp. 266–8

Taylor, Derek, *It Was Twenty Years Ago Today*, London, Bantam, 1987

Taylor, Frances, 'Dylan disowns his protest songs', *Long Island Press* (17 October 1965); reprinted in McGregor, *Bob Dylan: A Retrospective*, pp. 71–3

Taylor, Rogan, *The Death and Resurrection Show*, London, Anthony Blond, 1985

Terkel, Studs, 'The gap', *Sing Out!* (February 1966), p. 79; reprinted in McGregor, *Bob Dylan: A Retrospective*, pp. 86–7

Thomas, Patrick, 'Dylan on the Johnny Cash show: "I was scared to death"', *Rolling Stone* (31 May 1969); reprinted in Fong-Torres, *The Rolling Stone Rock-'n'-Roll Reader*, pp. 233–7

Thompson, Toby, *Positively Main Street: An Unorthodox View of Bob Dylan*, London, New English Library, 1971

Thomson, Elizabeth (ed.), *Conclusions on the Wall*, Manchester, Thin Man, 1980

——, 'Dylan's landscape', *Listener* (10 November 1983)

Tierce, Mike and Crafton, John Michael, 'Connie's tambourine man: a new reading of Arnold Friend', *Studies in Short Fiction*, 22 (Spring 1985), pp. 219–24

*Toynbee, Polly, 'Pop festival blast-off', *Observer* (31 August 1969), p. 1

Trow, George W. S., 'Q & A', *New Yorker* (20 November 1978), pp. 42–45

*Turner, Gil, 'Bob Dylan – a new voice singing new songs', *Sing Out!* (October/November 1962), pp. 5–10

Turner, Steve, 'Times a-changin' for a prophet who just wants to play', *Sunday Times* (17 August 1986), p. 29

Vassal, Jacques, *Electric Children*, New York, Taplinger, 1976

Vulliamy, Edward, 'The Zimmerman enigma', *Guardian* (11 October 1986), p. 15

*——, 'Highway 61 revisited', *Guardian* (10 September 1988), p. 19

Wall, Alan, 'The passage of Bob Dylan', *New Blackfriars*, 54 (1973), pp. 557–64

Wapshott, Nicholas, 'No heights of comedy from this Heaven', *The Times* (8 September 1978)

Wasserman, John L., 'Bob Dylan through a lens darkly', *Life* [US] (11 August 1967), p. 10

Watt, Douglas, 'Something is happening here', *New Yorker* (19 March 1966), pp. 200–2, 205

Watts, Michael, 'Don't looks back', *Melody Maker* (17 June 1972), pp. 23, 44

——, 'The man called Alias', *Melody Maker* (3 February 1973), pp. 28, 29 +

——, 'Dylan: the film's a loser', *Melody Maker* (2 June 1973), pp. 32–3

Weberman, A.J., 'Dylan meets Weberman', *East Village Other* (19 January 1971); reprinted in McGregor, *Bob Dylan: A Retrospective*, pp. 258–70

——, 'The only living Dylanologist', *Oz*, 19, pp. 42, 44, 47

——, 'Great moments in rock', *Oz*, 46 (January/February 1973), pp. 47–8

Wells, Chris, 'The angry young folk singer', *Life* [US] (10 April 1964), pp. 109–10 +

Wells, John, 'Bent out of shape from society's pliers: a sociological study of the grotesque in the songs of Bob Dylan', *Popular Music and Society*, 6, 1 (1978), pp. 39–44

Wenner, Jan, 'Nashville Skyline songs: "I can't remember where they come from"', *Rolling Stone* (15 March 1969); reprinted in Fong-Torres, *The Rolling Stone Rock-'n'-Roll Reader*, pp. 237–9

——, 'The Rolling Stone interview', *Rolling Stone* (29 November 1969) pp. 22–33; reprinted in McGregor, *Bob Dylan: A Retrospective*, pp. 201–42

——, 'The slow train is coming', *Rolling Stone* (20 September 1979), pp. 94–5

Wiener, Jon, 'A soft rain', *The Nation* (3 November 1984), pp. 458–9

Williams, Paul, *Dylan – What Happened?*, Glen Ellen, California, Entwhistle Books, 1979

Williams, Richard, 'Applause for the singer not the song', *The Times Preview* (26 June 1981)

——, 'On common ground', *The Times* (23 June 1984)

——, 'Leaden, but shot with gold', *The Times* (4 February 1989)

★——, 'The calm after the storm', *The Times* (23 September 1989), p. 44

Willis, Ellen, 'The sound of Bob Dylan', *Commentary*, 44 (November 1967), pp. 71–8

——, 'Dylan', *Cheetah* (1967/8); reprinted in McGregor, *Bob Dylan: A Retrospective*, pp. 133–55, and *Beginning to See the Light*, New Work, Knopf, 1981, pp. 3–25

——, 'Dylan and fans: looking back, going on', *New Yorker* (18 February 1974), pp. 108–10

——, 'After the flood', *New Yorker* (7 April 1975), pp. 130, 133–4

——, 'Notes on cant', *Rolling Stone* (23 March 1978), p. 36

*Winchester, Simon, 'Blowin' in the Windy City', *Guardian* (5 January 1974)

*Wolcott, James, 'Bob Dylan beyond Thunderdome', *Vanity Fair*, 48 (October 1985), pp. 22, 25

Wolfe, Paul, 'The new Dylan', *Broadside*, 53 (December 1964), pp. 10–13

Woliver, Robbie, *Bringing It All Back Home*, New York, Pantheon, 1986

Wood, Michael, 'Bob Dylan: wicked messenger', *New Society* (29 February 1968), pp. 314–15

Wooding, Dan, 'Dylan – by his pastor', *Buzz* (November 1980), pp. 4–5

Woods, William C., 'Bob Dylan and the Great White Wonder', *Washington Post* (14 December 1969); reprinted in McGregor, *Bob Dylan: A Retrospective*, pp. 192–5

Worrel, Denise, 'It's all right in front', *Time* (25 November 1985), p. 53

Yenne, Bill, *One Foot on the Highway*, San Francisco, Klonh Books, 1974

Young, Israel, 'Bob Dylan', *East Village Other* (October 1965)

——, 'Frets and frails', *Sing Out!* (November 1965); reprinted in McGregor, *Bob Dylan: A Retrospective*, pp. 70–1

Discography

This discography is selective. It does not attempt to detail every extant recording bearing Dylan's name. We have sought instead to list those recordings – singles, original LPs, compilations – which are useful in building a comprehensive library of Dylan as singer-songwriter.

Thus, we have included only those Dylan singles which contain original compositions unrepresented on US- or UK-originated albums; alternative versions are not itemised. Nor have we documented Dylan's instrumental contributions to recordings by other performers and his songwriting credits for such artists as Joan Baez, George Harrison and Tom Petty. Where Dylan has contributed *original* material to albums of a more 'general' nature – for example, the *Hearts of Fire* soundtrack and the *Traveling Wilburys* album – these are included. For wider coverage of official Dylan recordings in this area – the various Newport collections, *The Concert for Bangladesh et al.* – see Roger Ford's discography in Robert Shelton's *No Direction Home*. Illegally released and circulated recordings are beyond our scope and collectors of these should refer to the excellent volumes by Paul Cable and Michael Krogsgaard.

Discs are cited in the following order: original US release(s) and currently available equivalent(s), followed by current UK issues only.

1962

Bob Dylan

You're no good/ Talkin' New York/ In my time of dyin'/ Man of constant sorrow/ Fixin' to die/ Pretty Peggy-O/ Highway 51/ Gospel plow/ Baby, let me follow you down/ House of the risin' sun/ Freight train blues/ Song to Woody/ See that my grave is kept clean

Columbia	CL 1779
	CS 8579
	CK 8579(CD)
CBS	32001
	CD 32001(CD)

316

1963

The Freewheelin' Bob Dylan

Blowin' in the wind/ Girl from the north country/ Masters of war/ Down the highway/ Bob Dylan's blues/ A hard rain's a-gonna fall/ Don't think twice, it's all right/ Bob Dylan's dream/ Oxford Town/ Talkin' World War III blues/ Corrina, Corrina/ Honey, just allow me one more chance/ I shall be free

Columbia CL 1986
CS 8786
CK 8786(CD)
CBS 32390
CD 32390(CD)

1964

The Times They Are a-Changin'

The times they are a-changin'/ Ballad of Hollis Brown/ With God on our side/ One too many mornings/ North country blues/ Only a pawn in their game/ Boots of Spanish leather/ When the ship comes in/ The lonesome death of Hattie Carroll/ Restless farewell

Columbia CL 2105
CS 8905
CK 8905(CD)
CBS 32021
CD 32021(CD)

Another Side of Bob Dylan

All I really want to do/ Black crow blues/ Spanish Harlem incident/ Chimes of freedom/ I shall be free No. 10/ To Ramona/

Motorpsycho nitemare/ My back pages/ I don't believe you/ Ballad in plain D/ It ain't me, babe

Columbia CL 2193
CS 8993
CK 8993(CD)
CBS 32034
CD 32034(CD)

1965

Bringing It All Back Home

Subterranean homesick blues/ She belongs to me/ Maggie's farm/ Love minus zero/no limit/ Outlaw blues/ On the road again/ Bob Dylan's 115th dream/ Mr Tambourine Man/ Gates of Eden/ It's alright, ma (I'm only bleeding)/ It's all over now, baby blue

Columbia CL 2328
CS 9128
CK 9128(CD)
CBS 32344
CD 32344(CD)

Highway 61 Revisited

Like a rolling stone/ Tombstone blues/ It takes a lot to laugh, it takes a train to cry/ From a Buick 6/ Ballad of a thin man/ Queen Jane approximately/ Highway 61 revisited/ Just like Tom Thumb's blues/ Desolation Row

Columbia CL 2389
CS 9189

CK 9189(CD)

CBS   62572
CD 62572(CD)

1966

Blonde on Blonde

Rainy day women #12 & 35/ Pledging my time/ Visions of Johanna/ One of us must know/ I want you/ Stuck inside of Mobile with the Memphis blues again/ Leopard-skin pill-box hat/ Just like a woman/ Most likely you go your way (and I'll go mine)/ Temporary like Achilles/ Absolutely sweet Marie/ Fourth Time Around/ Obviously Five believers/ Sad-eyed lady of the lowlands

Columbia C2L 41
C2S 841
CGK 841 (CD)
CBS   22130
CD 22130(CD)

1967

Bob Dylan's Greatest Hits

Rainy day women #12 & 35/ Blowin' in the wind/ The times they are a-changin'/ It ain't me, babe/ Like a rolling stone/ Mr Tambourine Man/ Subterranean homesick blues/ I want you/ Positively 4th Street/ Just like a woman

Columbia KCL 2663
KCS 9463
CK 9463 (CD)
CBS   450882 2 (CD)

Bob Dylan's Greatest Hits [UK version]

Blowin' in the wind/ It ain't me, babe/ The times they are a-changin'/ Mr Tambourine Man/ She belongs to me/ It's all over now, baby blue/ Subterranean homesick blues/ One of us must know/ Like a rolling stone/ Just like a woman/ Rainy day women #12 & 35/ I want you

CBS 460907 1

'If you gotta go, go now'/ 'To Ramona' [single]*

CBS 2921

*Benelux countries only

1968

John Wesley Harding

John Wesley Harding/ As I went out one morning/ I dreamed I saw St Augustine/ All along the watchtower/ The ballad of Frankie Lee and Judas Priest/ Drifter's escape/ Dear landlord/ I am a lonesome hobo/ I pity the poor immigrant/ The wicked messenger/ Down along the cove/ I'll be your baby tonight

Columbia CL 2804
CS 9604
CK 9604 (CD)
CBS   63252
CD 63252 (CD)

1969

Nashville Skyline

Girl from the north country (*with Johnny Cash*)/ Nashville skyline rag/ To be alone with you/ I threw it all away/ Peggy Day/

Lay, lady, lay/ One more night/ Tell me that it isn't true/ Country pie/ Tonight I'll be staying here with you

Columbia KCS 9825
CK 9825 (CD)
CBS 32675
CD 63601 (CD)

1970

Self Portrait

All the tired horses/ Alberta #1/ I forgot more than you'll ever know/ Days of 49/ Early morning rain/ In search of little Sadie/ Let it be me/ Little Sadie/ Woogie boogie/ Belle Isle/ Living the blues/ Like a rolling stone/ Copper kettle/ Gotta travel on/ Blue moon/ The boxer/ The mighty Quinn (Quinn the eskimo)/ Take me as I am/ Take a message to Mary/ It hurts me too/ Minstrel boy/ She belongs to me/ Wigwam/ Alberta #2

Columbia C2X 30050
C6K 30050 (CD)
CBS 460112 1

New Morning

If not for you/ Day of the locusts/ Time passes slowly/ Went to see the gypsy/ Winterlude/ If dogs run free/ New morning/ Sign on the window/ One more weekend/ The man in me/ Three angels/ Father of night

Columbia CK 30290
CK 30290 (CD)
CBS 32267

1971

'George Jackson' (band version)*/ 'George Jackson' (acoustic) [single]

Columbia 4 45516
CBS 7688

*also on *Masterpieces*: CBS/ Sony 57 AP – 875/6/7 (Japan), CBS 53 BP – 220502 (Australia/ New Zealand), CBS 462448 2 (CD)

Bob Dylan's Greatest Hits Volume Two

Watching the river flow/ Don't think twice, it's all right/ Lay, lady, lay/ Stuck inside of Mobile with the Memphis blues again/ I'll be your baby tonight/ All I really want to do/ My back pages/ Maggie's farm/ Tonight I'll be staying here with you/ She belongs to me*/ All along the watchtower/ The mighty Quinn (Quinn the eskimo)/ Just like Tom Thumb's blues/ A hard rain's a-gonna fall/ If not for you/ It's all over now, baby blue*/ Tomorrow is a long time/ When I paint my masterpiece/ I shall be released/ You ain't goin' nowhere/ Down in the flood.

*These tracks are replaced on the UK version, *More Bob Dylan's Greatest Hits*, by 'Positively 4th Street' and 'New morning' respectively.

Columbia KG 31120
          C2K 31120 (CD)
CBS   67239
          CD 67239 (CD)

1973

Pat Garrett and Billy the Kid

Main title theme (Billy)/ Cantina
theme (Workin' for the law)/
Billy 1/ Bunkhouse theme/ River
theme/ Turkey chase/ Knockin'
on heaven's door/ Final theme/
Billy 4/ Billy 7

Columbia KC 32460
          CK 32460(CD)
CBS   32098

Dylan

Lily of the west/ Can't help falling
in love/ Sarah Jane/ The ballad of
Ira Hayes/ Mr Bojangles/ Mary
Ann/ Big yellow taxi/ A fool such
as I/ Spanish is the loving tongue

Columbia PC 32747
CBS   32286

1974

Planet Waves

On a night like this/ Going going
gone/ Tough mama/ Hazel/
Something there is about you/
Forever young/ Forever young/
Dirge/ You angel you/ Never say
goodbye/ Wedding song

Asylum   7E 1003
Columbia PC 37637
          CK 37637 (CD)
CBS   32154
          CD 32154 (CD)

Before the Flood

Most likely you go your way
(and I'll go mine)/ Lay, lady,
lay/ Rainy day women #12 &
35/ Knockin' on heaven's door/
It ain't me, babe/ Ballad of
a thin man/ Up on cripple
creek*/ I shall be released*/
Endless highways/ The night they
drove old Dixie down*/ Stage
fright*/ Don't think twice, it's
all right/ Just like a woman/ It's
alright, ma (I'm only bleeding)/
The shape I'm in*/ When you
awake*/ The weight*/ All along
the watchtower/
Highway 61 revisited/ Like a
rolling stone/ Blowin' in the
wind
(*performed by The Band)

Asylum   AB 201
Columbia CK 377661
          C2K 377661 (CD)
CBS   22137
          CD 22137(CD)

1975

Blood on the Tracks

Tangled up in blue/ Simple
twist of fate/ You're a big girl
now/ Idiot wind/ You're gonna
make me lonesome when you go/
Meet me in the morning/ Lily,
Rosemary and the Jack of Hearts/
If you see her, say hello/ Shelter
from the storm/ Buckets of rain

Columbia PC 33235
          CK 33235 (CD)
CBS   69097
          CD 69097 (CD)

The Basement Tapes

Odds and ends/ Orange juice blues (Blues for breakfast)*/ Million dollar bash/ Yazoo Street scandal*/ Goin' to Acapulco/ Katie's been gone*/ Lo and behold/ Bessie Smith*/ Clothes line saga/ Apple suckling tree/ Please Mrs Henry/ Tears of rage/ Too much of nothing/ Yea! Heavy and a bottle of bread/ Ain't no more cane*/ Crash on the levee (Down in the flood)/ Ruben Remus*/ Tiny Montgomery/ You ain't goin' nowhere/ Don't ya tell Henry*/ Nothing was delivered/ Open the door, Homer/ Long distance operator*/ This wheel's on fire
(*performed by The Band*)

Columbia C2 33682
C2K 33682 (CD)
CBS 88147
CD 466137 2 (CD)

1976

Desire

Hurricane/ Isis/ Mozambique/ One more cup of coffee/ Oh, sister/ Joey/ Romance in Durango/ Black Diamond Bay/ Sara

Columbia PC 33893
CK 33893 (CD)
CBS 32570
CD 32570 (CD)

Hard Rain

Maggie's farm/ One too many mornings/ Stuck inside of Mobile (with the Memphis blues again)/

Oh, sister/ Lay, lady, lay/ Shelter from the storm/ You're a big girl now/ I threw it all away/ Idiot wind

Columbia PC 34349
CK 34349 (CD)
CBS 32308

'Rita May'/ 'Stuck inside of Mobile' [single]

Columbia 3 10454
CBS 4859

*also on *Masterpieces*: CBS/Sony 57 AP 875/6/7 (Japan),
CBS 53 BP - 22502 (Australia/ New Zealand),
CBS 462448 2 (CD)

1978

Street Legal

Changing of the guard/ New pony/ No time to think/ Baby stop crying/ Is your love in vain?/ Señor (Tales of Yankee power)/ True love tends to forget/ We better talk this over/ Where are you tonight? (Journey through dark heat)

Columbia JC 35453
CK 35453 (CD)
CBS 86067
CD 86067 (CD)

1979

Bob Dylan at Budokan

Mr Tambourine Man/ Shelter from the storm/ Love minus zero/ no limit/ Ballad of a thin man/ Don't think twice, it's all right/ Maggie's farm/ One more cup of coffee/ Like a rolling stone/

I shall be released/ Is your love in vain?/ Going, going, gone/ Blowin' in the wind/ Just like a woman/ Oh, sister/ Simple twist of fate/ All along the watchtower/ I want you/ All I really want to do/ Knockin' on heaven's door/ It's alright, ma (I'm only bleeding)/ Forever young/ The times they are a-changin'

Columbia PC2 36067
          C2K 36067 (CD)
CBS   96004
          CD 96004 (CD)

'Gotta serve somebody'/ 'Trouble in mind' [single]

Columbia 1 11072

'Precious Angel'/ 'Trouble in mind' [single]

CBS 7828

Slow Train Coming

Gotta serve somebody/ Precious angel/ I believe in you/ Slow train/ Gonna change my way of thinking/ Do right to me baby (Do unto others)/ When you gonna wake up?/ Man gave names to all the animals/ When He returns

Columbia FC 36120
          CK 36120 (CD)
CBS   32524
          CD 86095 (CD)

1980

Saved

A satisfied mind/ Saved/ Covenant woman/ What can I do for you?/ Solid rock/ Pressing on/ In the garden/ Saving grace/ Are you ready?

Columbia PC 36553
CBS   86113

1981

Shot of Love

Shot of love/ Heart of mine/ Property of Jesus/ Lenny Bruce/ Watered-down love/ Dead man, dead man/ In the summertime/ Trouble/ Every grain of sand

Columbia TC 37496
CBS   85178

1983

Infidels

Jokerman/ Sweetheart like you/ Neighbourhood bully/ License to kill/ Man of peace/ Union sundown/ I and I/ Don't fall apart on me tonight

Columbia QC 38819
          CK 38819 (CD)
CBS   25539
          CD 25539 (CD)

1984

Real Live

Highway 61 revisited/ Maggie's farm/ I and I/ License to kill/ It ain't me, babe/ Tangled up in blue/ Masters of war/ Ballad of a thin man/ Girl from the north country/ Tombstone blues

Columbia FC 39944
CK39944 (CD)
CBS 26334
CD 26334 (CD)

1985

Empire Burlesque

Tight connection to my heart
(Has anybody seen my love?)/
Seeing the real you at last/ I'll
remember you/ Clean cut kid/
Never gonna be the same again/
Trust yourself/ Emotionally
yours/ When the night comes
falling from the sky/ Something's
burning, baby/ Dark eyes

Columbia FC 40110
CK 40110 (CD)
CBS 86313
CD 86313 (CD)

Biograph

Lay, lady, lay/ Baby, let me
follow you down/ If not for
you/ I'll be your baby tonight/
I'll keep it with mine (*first release*)/
The times they are a-changin'/
Blowin' in the wind/ Masters
of war/ The lonesome death of
Hattie Carroll/ Percy's song (*first
release*)/ Mixed-up confusion/
Tombstone blues/ The groom's
still waiting at the altar/ Most
likely you go your way/ Like
a rolling stone/ Jet pilot (*first
release*)/ Lay down your weary
tune (*first release*)/ Subterranean
homesick blues/ I don't believe
you/ Visions of Johanna/ Every
grain of sand/ Quinn the Eskimo/
Mr Tambourine Man/ Dear
landlord/ It ain't me, babe/ You
angel you/ Million dollar bash/

To Ramona/ You're a big girl
now/ Abandoned love (*first
release*)/ Tangled up in blue/
It's all over now, baby blue/
Can you please crawl out your
window?/ Positively 4th Street/
Isis/ Caribbean wind (*first release*)/
Up to me (*first release*)/ Baby, I'm
in the mood for you (*first release*)/ I
wanna be your lover (*first release*)/
I want you/ Heart of mine/ On
a night like this/ Just like a
woman/ Romance in Durango/
Señor (Tales of Yankee power)/
Gotta serve somebody/ I believe
in you/ Time passes slowly/ I
shall be released/ Knockin' on
heaven's door/ All along the
watchtower/ Solid rock/ Forever
young

Columbia C5X 38830
C3K 38830 (CD)
CBS 66509
CD 66509 (CD)

1986

'Band of the hand' [single: B
side not by Dylan]

MCA MCA 52811
MCA 1076

Knocked Out Loaded

You wanna ramble/ They killed
him/ Driftin' too far from the
shore/ Precious memories/
Maybe someday/ Brownsville
girl/ Got my mind made up/
Under your spell

Columbia DC 40439
CK 40439 (CD)
CBS 86326
CD 86326 (CD)

1987

Hearts of Fire

includes: The usual/ Night after night/ Had a dream about you, baby

Columbia SC 40870
         CK 40870 (CD)
CBS   460001 1
         460001 2(CD)

1988

Down in the Groove

Let's stick together/ When did you leave heaven?/ Sally Sue Brown/ Death is not the end/ Had a dream about you, baby/ Ugliest girl in the world/ Silvio/ Ninety miles an hour (Down a dead end street)/ Shenandoah/ Rank strangers to me

Columbia OC 40957
         CK 40957 (CD)
CBS   460267 1
         460267 2 (CD)

Traveling Wilburys

includes: Dirty world/ Congratulations/ Tweeter and the monkey man

Wilbury 25796 1
         25796 2 (CD)
Wilbury WX 224/925796 1
         925796 2 (CD)

1989

Dylan and the Dead

Slow train/ I want you/ Gotta serve somebody/ Queen Jane approximately/ Joey/ All along the watchtower/ Knockin' on heaven's door

Columbia OC 45056
         CK 45056 (CD)
CBS   463381 1
         463381 2 (CD)

Oh Mercy

Political world/ Where teardrops fall/ Everything is broken/ Ring them bells/ Man in the long black coat/ Most of the time/ What good am I?/ Disease of conceit/ What was it you wanted?/ Shooting star

Columbia OC 45281
         CK 45281 (CD)
CBS   465800 1
         465800 2 (CD)

Index